Another Finitude

Political Theologies

Edited by Ward Blanton (University of Kent), Arthur Bradley (Lancaster University),
Michael Dillon (Lancaster University) and Yvonne Sherwood (University of Kent)

This series explores the past, present and future of political theology. Taking its cue
from the ground-breaking work of such figures as Derrida, Agamben, Badiou and
Zizek, it seeks to provide a forum for new research on the theologico-political nexus
including cutting edge monographs, edited collections and translations of classic
works. By privileging creative, interdisciplinary and experimental work that resists
easy categorization, this series not only re-assets the timeliness of political theology in
our epoch but seeks to extend political theological reflection into new territory: law,
economics, finance, technology, media, film and art. In *Bloomsbury Political Theologies*,
we seek to re-invent the ancient problem of political theology for the 21st century.

International Advisory Board

Agata Bielik-Robson (University of Nottingham)
Howard Caygill (Kingston University)
Simon Critchley (New School of Social Research)
Roberto Esposito (Scuola Normale Superiore)
Elettra Stimilli (University of Rome La Sapienza)
Miguel Vatter (University of New South Wales)

Titles in the series:
The Withholding Power: An Essay on Political Theology, Massimo Cacciari
The Weakness of Belief, Michel de Certeau
Unnatural Theology, Charlie Gere
Modernity and the Political Fix, Andrew Gibson
Debt and Guilt, Elettra Stimilli
Apocalyptic Political Theology, Thomas Lynch

Another Finitude

Messianic Vitalism and Philosophy

Agata Bielik-Robson

BLOOMSBURY ACADEMIC
LONDON • NEW YORK • OXFORD • NEW DELHI • SYDNEY

BLOOMSBURY ACADEMIC
Bloomsbury Publishing Plc
50 Bedford Square, London, WC1B 3DP, UK
1385 Broadway, New York, NY 10018, USA

BLOOMSBURY, BLOOMSBURY ACADEMIC and the Diana logo are trademarks of
Bloomsbury Publishing Plc

First published in Great Britain 2019
This paperback edition published in 2021

Cover image: *Vision of the Sermon (Jacob Wrestling with the Angel)* 1888
(oil on canvas), Gauguin, Paul (1848–1903) / National Galleries of Scotland,
Edinburgh / Bridgeman Images.

A catalogue record for this book is available from the British Library.

A catalog record for this book is available from the Library of Congress.

ISBN: HB: 978-1-3500-9407-9
          PB: 978-1-3502-2517-6
          ePDF: 978-1-3500-9408-6
          eBook: 978-1-3500-9409-3

Series: Political Theologies

Typeset by RefineCatch Limited, Bungay, Suffolk

To find out more about our authors and books visit www.bloomsbury.com
and sign up for our newsletters.

For my two best life companions:
Czarek, the husband, and Funio, the cat.

The accent of deviation in the living thing
That is its life preserved, the effort to be born
Surviving to be born, the event of life.

Wallace Stevens, *A Discovery of Thought*

If you want to step into infinitude, just go in all directions into the finite.

J.W. Goethe

Contents

Preface

Finitum Capax Infiniti

The main theme of this book is *finite life*. There is nothing original thus far in this choice: the finite life constitutes a staple subject of the post-Heideggerian philosophy, which routinely concentrates on the notion of finitude [*Endlichkeit*] and opposes it to the ontotheological concept of infinity, represented by a being that cannot stop existing: perennial, eternal, immortal, immutable and, because of that, immune to contingent fate. Although critical of Heidegger, whose thought stands in this book as the synecdoche of the late-modern philosophical take on the issue of finitude, I am not going to oppose this development and revert to the ontological idea of infinity secured in the sacred image of the immortal life. But I also do not want to give up on infinity altogether: rather – and this is my claim to originality – I would like to see the infinite transposed, so it can become a necessary moment of the finite life. *Finitum capax infiniti*.

At first glance, this seems like a paradox, but then one soon realizes that the best modern philosophy has to offer has been circling precisely around this problematics: Hegel, Kierkegaard, Rosenzweig, Freud, Arendt, Adorno, Benjamin, Lévinas and Derrida – to name just a few thinkers who will often appear in this book – all try to think about the finitude in a way that does not automatically exclude infinity. This paradox becomes particularly poignant in the secular modern age which, in Hannah Arendt's words, 'meant nothing more or less than that men once more had become mortals'.[1] It is precisely this re/discovery of finitude that makes the contrasting claim to infinity particularly aporetic, up to the point of the Kierkegaardian 'sickness' and 'despair'. In *The Sickness Unto Death* Kierkegaard famously defines the human being in terms of an impossible conjunction of the finite and the infinite: 'For the self is a synthesis in which the finitude is the limiting factor, and the infinite is the expanding factor. Infinitude's despair is therefore the *fantastical*, the limitless'.[2]

Kierkegaard's formulation demonstrates very clearly the asymmetry that hides within the aporia: while the limiting factor appears as irresistibly real, the opposite factor of infinitude melts into air – as a mere phantasy, something vague, intangible and ephemeral – until it evaporates completely, leaving the late-modern man solely on the finite side of things. The paradox, therefore, seems to have a dynamic tendency to exhaust itself and let the flat concept of the biological finitude take the upper hand. While in the aporetic stage, humans are still, as Ernest Becker puts it succinctly, 'gods with anuses' – in the post-aporetic naturalist stage, they prefer to identify with what they seem to know and master better, i.e. their physiological life process of the human species, which starts with birth and issues into inevitable death, according to the ancient Heraclitean rule that 'whatever's born is destined to die'. In this book, I will firmly side with the modern aporia against the late-modern nirvanic principle that aims to dissolve it as no longer problematic: although it is a 'maddening' procedure to maintain oneself in the paradox, as Kierkegaard well knew, it is nonetheless worth the effort, which here amounts to the same as the effort to stay alive – and to be able to take joy in the act of living.

The current climate, therefore, which attempts to think finitude to the end, does not take well the 'human paradox' and treats it merely as a transitory form that needs to be resolved, before the ultimate consummation of disenchantment which will have finally done away with all the 'fantastical'. But there was never a good time to dwell on the 'human paradox' and its aporetic tension between finitude and infinity, real limitation and fantastical limitlessness. Before modernity, the paradox as such could not even come fully to the fore; juxtaposed with the Christian prospect of immortal life, the temporary finite condition could only appear as a form of nothingness, or, in Augustine's formulation, *vita mortalis*, a life destined for death. Now, in late modernity, the resolution presses in the opposite direction and takes two different forms: a naturalist reduction to the life of the human species, which seems so obvious that it goes practically without saying, on the one hand – and a philosophical reflection on finitude focusing only on death, on the other. And while the biological finitude asserts itself without much articulation, the philosophical finitude proceeds under the auspices of the Heideggerian *Todesdenken*, which merely – though one-sidedly – continues the Augustinian strain: the former's *Sein-zum-Tode* appears merely as a late variation of the latter's famous dictum from *City of God* that 'our whole life is nothing but a race toward death'.

Just as Nietzsche prophesied in *The Gay Science*, while warning us about the belatedness of the effect of the death of God, the divine shadow still hovers over the landscape of late-modern humanities, long after the event of the divine demise and, with it, a disappearance of the promise of personal immortality. The Heideggerian treatment of human finitude, in which mortality becomes the defining feature, well testifies to this rule of the prolonged and aporetic Christian influence that persists despite its officially declared end. It keeps on holding to the *negativity* of all things finite – limitation, determination, perishability, precariousness, anxiety and death – still perceived in pejorative contrast to the infinite, even if the latter, reduced to a phantasm, seems to have melted into air a long time ago. The never-questioned premise that 'finitude is privation'[6] attaches itself, as if naturally, first to Kant's finite closure of the human mind, and then to all post-Kantian metaphysical interpretations on human finitude, which culminate in Heidegger for whom the finite life is still nothing but a series of 'imperfections'.[7] Thus, despite all the efforts of the post-Nietzschean and post-Heideggerian line, which tries to bestow finite life with a new glory, the result is oddly reverse: the life that ends sticks to its end as the life destined to die, spent under the dark entropic sun of Thanatos. Instead of celebrating the regained autonomy of the finite world, released from the diminishing and oppressive juxtaposition with the Absolute, we, late moderns, still tarry with the negative. Plato has not blushed, the pandemonium of earthly spirits has not broken, Zarathustra has not entered the stage: after the night of the longest error seemingly gone, none of the Nietzschean affirmative prophesies has been fulfilled: 'The true world is gone: which world is left? The illusory one, perhaps? . . . But no! *we got rid of the illusory world along with the true one!* (Noon, moment of shortest shadow, end of longest error, high point of humanity; INCIPT ZARATHUSTRA).'[8]

The demise of the overwhelming Infinite has not brought the expected fruits of the immanentist joy: the shadow still looms. It is not joy but anxiety, care and concern that constantly remind the finite Dasein about its irremovable precarity in the most traditional mode of *memento mori*: ' "Anxiety" thus understood, i.e., according to fundamental ontology, prohibits us from interpreting "concern" as having the harmlessness of a categorical structure. It gives concern the incisiveness necessary to a fundamental existential and thus determines the finitude in Dasein not as a given property but as the constant, although generally veiled, precariousness [*Erzittern*] which pervades all existence.'[9]

In this book I will call this position an *acephalic Neoplatonism*: the once most meaningful system of Western metaphysics, now devoid of its head – the apex in the form of ontological infinity. Yet, despite its impairment, the Neoplatonic ontological hierarchy remains stubbornly operative in the lower realms of existence which it continues to give an intensely negative colouring. For some – as, for instance, Søren Kierkegaard, with his borderline version of Augustinian Neoplatonism – the persistence of those remnants, now emerging in paradoxical and aporetic forms, testifies to the undying validity of the theological paradigm; once the erring secular man comes back to his senses and, weary of the futile 'tarrying with the negative', recognizes his need for transcendence, it still may be recalled and reconstructed *ad integrum*. For Kierkegaard, therefore, the return of the religious would be like the 'repetition forward': it will bring back the lost primacy of the infinite by the power of the paradox itself, that is, it will mend the broken vessel of the Neoplatonic whole, by working through the aporia of human condition, impossibly torn between *vita mortalis* and the longing for eternity. The more, therefore, the 'human paradox' becomes unbearable, the more there grows the chance of salvation too. The persistence of the negative characteristic of the finite life serves to guard a possibility of a radical reversal, due to which the human soul, ultimately tormented by the meaninglessness of finitude, will bring about the last acrobatic effort and regain the sense of transcendence out of the deepest fall. Later the same intuition will emerge in Walter Benjamin's *Origin of the German Tragic Drama*, where the melancholic modern subject is also expected to turn and, by 'the returning act of resurrection', restore the fullness out of ruins and reconstruct the outline of the divine face out of the terrifying vision of the *skull* – the Calvary of creatureliness, its pointless suffering and ordeal.[9]

If, therefore, the 'horror of finitude' as the sole truth of the mundane condition persists, it is because of the still not fully abandoned hope in the restitution of the Neoplatonic order of being: of crowning it once again with the divine 'head' which is to appear in place of the horrifying 'skull'. Kierkegaard's methodical deepening of the 'despair' bound with the human paradox, Benjamin's deliberate plunge into the Fall and mourning over the loss of meaning, and Scholem's equally resolute exacerbation of the modern sense of nihilism[11] – are all strategies which stake on the radical reversal which, by the power of the Hölderlinian rule,[12] will wrench 'salvation' out of the 'danger', i.e. procure the transcendence out of the most fallen and self-imploding immanence. The worse finitude is portrayed – the more existential 'danger' it contains – the more there appears a chance for 'salvation' as the self-evident answer for the impossibility of being *just* that: the finite being destined to suffer, live in fear and finally die. Creatureliness emerges as a 'living contradiction' so unthinkable – or so unthinkably wrong – that is simply has to snap from within. When things really fall apart and the centre cannot hold – which is probably the best poetic description of the modern acephalic Neoplatonism – then *surely* some Second Coming must be at hand.

The continuing *denigration of finitude* has thus a hidden agenda: it is not just an error of reasoning, which sticks to the categories that lost its integral systematic meaning. If it stubbornly persists, it is because of the hope for the return of the theological paradigm, seemingly lost in secular modernity (in what follows I will also challenge this premise). A good illustration of this obstinate persistence in the late-modern intellectual climate, which goes beyond the sophisticated games of philosophy, is the work of Ernst Becker, the psychoanalyst of the Rankian school, which describes the neurotic modern man as the one who 'knows' the terrible reality of life and simultaneously cannot 'bear' it, a mortified 'dying animal':

> He has no doubts; there is nothing you can say to sway him, to give him hope or trust. He is a miserable animal whose body decays, who will die, who will past into dust and oblivion, disappear forever not only in this world but in all possible dimensions of the universe, whose life serves no conceivable purpose, who may as well not have been born, and so on and so forth. He knows Truth and Reality, the motives of the entire universe.[13]

Needless to say, what Becker has to propose in the end is the 'theological turn' fashioned in the Kierkegaardian manner: a surrender to the 'higher infinite powers' (ibid.) which solely can solve the human paradox and offer the justification for the unbearable terrors of the finite existence.

In this book, I will also be in favour of the theological approach to the issue of finitude, but effected quite differently: not as the triumphant return of theology, once again centring the decentred headless post-Neoplatonic disarray of creaturely condition, but as a religiously motivated challenge to the seemingly self-evident 'horror of existence'. I will indeed insist that it is, in fact, nothing but an error of reasoning, inherent to the acephalic Neoplatonism as the unreflected and obsolete default metaphysics of modernity, which still vainly hopes for the *restitutio ad integrum* of the divine ideal of the Highest Pure Life which knows no harm and death – unlike *this* life, 'here below', *vita mortalis* marked with transience and decay.[14] According to the Neoplatonic prejudice, life can only be life if it is 'life itself', 'pure life', 'nothing but life', which only then deserves to be called 'true life', *vita vera*: any other kind of life is only a lower, vicarious and non-true form of living, which must strive towards the purity of the ideal. Again, it is Augustine who formulates this paradigm with utter clarity in his *Confessions*: 'So great is the force of life in a human being whose life is mortal. What then ought I to do, my God? You are my true life [*tu vera mea vita*].'[15] There is thus a chance that, once this erroneous shadow is removed, thinking will be able to pave the way to another metaphysics of finitude, no longer tinged with the inherited sense of absolute negativity. Very critical of any contemporary attempt to restore the Augustinian–Neoplatonic hierarchy of being, based on the firm opposition of the infinite and the finite, but also reluctant to follow Nietzsche in his attempt to naturalize humanity, I will look for an alternative theological vision, capable of accommodating something seemingly so improbable as the *religion of the finite life*.

My stake, therefore, is to think about our finitude differently, not under the horrific auspices of death: the end, the final destiny, the ultimate verdict, the only reality of the 'lower beings', the desperate veri-dictive 'truth that kills'. I will try to think finitude *positively*, that is, in the manner faithful to what the Jewish messianic tradition calls a *maximalization of existence* and, despite the finite condition, attempt to wrench 'more life' from life seemingly reduced only to its lethal destiny. This juxtaposition immediately explains the title – *another finitude* – as well as the subtitle: *messianic vitalism*, where the new conception of the finite life has been developing, *and philosophy*, the discipline that still remains in the shadow of the Neoplatonic dogma. It will be my aim to prove that the best alternative to the late-modern death-bound concept of *Endlichkeit* – which this book associates firmly with the name of the thanatic 'master from Germany' – lies precisely in what Jacques Derrida, apropos Benjamin, called the 'awakening of the Judaic tradition' (AR, 289). Its radically different notion of finitude presents creaturely life as inescapably finite, yet no longer opposed to any supposedly higher and infinite mode of being which would dwarf it in comparison. At the same time, this 'awakening' is not a move against modern Enlightenment; quite the contrary, in the Adornian vein, it wants to defend Enlightenment against its own destructive tendencies – most of all radical disenchantment waging war on anything 'fantastical' – and rehabilitate the very notion of *belief*. In order to *live*, i.e. not be immediately reduced to the principle of death, life must believe in itself; it can survive only insofar it maintains itself in the state of self-belief.

All the thinkers who, in this book, will come under the heading of *messianic vitalists*, subscribe to this *torat hayim*, the 'Jewish principle of life', deeply mistrustful toward the purely philosophical – *death-bound* – concept of finitude. As Levinas puts it in his critique of Heidegger's 'being-unto-death' that founded this thanatic association: the *torat hayim* takes nothing away from the ineluctable character of death, but it does not leave it the privilege of being the source of all meaning' (GDT, 104). The awakening of the Judaic tradition', therefore, indicates *another finitude* in which death loses the signifying monopoly. 'Life is not eternal life; it flows from birth towards death', as Franz Rosenzweig soberly asserts (USH, 101), but it still does not have to be *determined* by its end; it does not have to be contained within the natural cycle of *genesis kai phthora*, just 'becoming and perishing'. Life, despite its biological finitude, does not have to take its

'measure' from the naturalist norm of *kata phusein* or 'living according to nature':
it can still dialectically hide dimensions that refuse to be flattened into the
monotone rhythm of growth and decay. Thus, when conceived in terms of
messianic vitalism, the finite life derives its meaning and inner rule *neither from
death nor from nature* – that is, neither from the sovereign power of mortality
which dictates its inexorable law of finitude, nor from the naturalist norm of
kata phusein, which regulates life according to the biological 'measure' of the
cycle. Deliberately in/de/finite, elastically maintaining itself in the paradox, life
tests and expands its finitude from within and creates its own element: *the
middle*. For, as Goethe says: 'if you want to step into infinitude, just go in all
directions into the finite . . .'

Philosophically speaking, the image of the finite life as a 'living contradiction' –
torn between the desire for infinity, which pertains to Life in general, and the
verdict of death, which befalls every singular living being – appears for the first
time in Hegel.[18] For Hegel, the 'living contradiction' cannot be endured as such: life,
deeply aporetic in itself, inaugurates dialectical process, the goal of which is to solve
the original contradiction or, in Hegel's own words, the reconciliation of the infinite
and the finite. This reconciliation, however, cannot be achieved in life itself; in order
to properly embrace the infinite, life must be sublated into the higher element of
the spirit which, unlike life, is capable of looking the negativity of death straight in
the eye. Hence, as long as life is an existing and abiding, not yet reconciled,
contradiction, its dominant manifestation is *pain*:

> Pain is the *prerogative* of living natures; because they are the existent Notion,
> they are an *actuality of infinite power*, such that they are within themselves the
> negativity of themselves, that this their negativity is for them, and that they
> maintain themselves in their otherness. It is said that contradiction is unthinkable;
> but in fact, in the pain of a living being it is even an actual existence.[19]

But if, in case of life, contradiction is not only thinkable, but also actual, then
perhaps it would also be possible to suspend the teleology of reconciliation – the
solution to the human paradox – and maintain oneself in it? After all, Hegel
himself says that pain is a *prerogative*: not just a drawback or 'imperfection' to be
removed by higher stages of thought, but a positive moment – the moment of
the birth of dialectics. Thus, even if, in the Hegelian system, the living 'sensuous
soul' [*die fühlende Seele*] is only a middle stage of the dialectical process, it is
nonetheless the site where the dialectic truly takes off and accelerates. A concrete
living being, *das Lebendige*, is a contradictory clash of the infinite power of life
and its finite manifestation; although an instance of Life eternal, invincible and

unscathed – *das unverletzte Leben* – it takes the form marked by the very otherness of unscathedness: a form that is defined by the negativity of its inevitable demise. Life, therefore, is the bedrock of the dialectical method and the proof of its validity as well: *pace* the common sense belief that contradiction is unthinkable, every living thing 'as such' demonstrates its painful, seemingly impossible actuality.[29]

I will return to this Hegelian dialectical image of life very often: it is indeed the crucial moment of the modern reasoning, which gives rise to all possible variants of philosophy of life, from Schelling and Schopenhauer to Bergson and Deleuze – as well as to all possible variants of thinking which will endeavour to rise above the pained clamour of life, from Heidegger and Kojève to Lacan and Žižek. The Hegelian 'life-in-pain' constitutes the *punctum crucis*, but also – theologically speaking – a *cross* on which life's infinite power simultaneously incarnates itself, suffers and dies. Yet, unlike Hegel – after all a Christian thinker of resurrection, even if in most heterodox forms – I will try to endure in what he sees as an unbearable condition of a 'disappearing moment' which, for him, precisely by its painful unbearability, triggers the dialectical process: a process that, at least in Hegel's version, can indeed be defined as an ultimate salvific *escape from life*. In my interpretation, however, the prerogative of pain should not be too easily superseded because it carries an equally crucial message: that every finite life suffers because of its unfulfilled wish of 'more life'. This is precisely the dialectical position adopted by those I will call here messianic vitalists, which employs a careful analysis of all the aporetic symptoms of life, yet remains determined not to escape or venture beyond life itself, but to be rigorously conducted – in the words of Derrida – always 'in life and for life' (AR, 289). The aporetic condition of life cannot be *solved* – one cannot 'learn to live finally' (see LLF) – but it can nonetheless be *accepted*, and even quite lovingly so.

This book enlists four major allies whom it wants to unite under the heading of messianic vitalism, despite all the obvious differences between them: Franz Rosenzweig's New Thinking, Sigmund Freud's psychoanalytic early theory of the drives, Hannah Arendt's natality and last, but certainly not least, Derrida's modernized version of *torat hayim* as the doctrine of life's self-preference or, as I will call it here, self-belief. All four offer analyses of the problem of the *aporetic life*, which can be gathered together under the Wittgensteinian category of family resemblance, because they all resort to a similar manoeuvre in the face of mortality: they summon the counteractive forces of love.

Franz Rosenzweig will figure here very strongly: as the virtual adversary (sic) of Martin Heidegger and the whole thanatic strain of late-modern thought, which he anticipated before its actual blooming and attempted to counteract when it was still in bud. For Rosenzweig, the Jewish formula *love-strong-as-death*, which I see as the family resemblance uniting my four protagonists, is inseparable and defines love precisely as a corrective force that can be revealed *only* after the dark knowledge of death. In his variation/deviation on and from the Hegelian theme, Rosenzweig claims that it is not the death-bound Spirit but the life-loving Soul that can solely abide in the 'living contradiction'. Yet, the gentle touch or small voice, *bat kol*, of love means nothing to those who did not experience the disintegrating power of death: it can only come as the 'second birth' of the Selfhood after it became deadened in the traumatic process of separation. This is why, for Rosenzweig, the deadly stage of the tragic hero, in which Man severs his communal relations and 'dies for the world', is indispensable in the process of revelation – just as the nihilistic stage of modern disenchantment, in which Man withdraws his living participation from the deadened cosmic nature, is necessary to hear the 'small voice' of Judaism as *religion of the finite life*: the more modest post-atheistic kind of faith which does not promise immortality, but only (only!) *singularity*. In *The Star of Redemption*, the eternal relevance of Judaism lies precisely in that: once the 'great voice' of the Neoplatonic Christianity begins to wane due to the process of modern disenchantment, Judaism offers itself as a religious solution to the (re)discovery of human finitude – proposing its own moderate re-enchantment of faith, hope and love, but not staking them on the promise of spiritual immortality. *The Star*, therefore, contains a positive alternative to the negative and death-orientated philosophical accounts of finitude, which stem from the 'headlessly' Neoplatonic, Kojèvian-Heideggerian, thanatic strain: here the 'awakening of the Judaic tradition' means also awakening to a new sense of life after the slumber of the virtual death caused by the sudden demise of the immortal hopes. While the thanatic philosophical account of finitude can, in Rosenzweig's words, 'only recommend suicide', his New Thinking aims to reflect the primordial wish of every living being 'to stay, to remain' (SR, 4). Hence, just as the Rosenzweigian tragic hero, who became intimately acquainted with death, can solely acknowledge the principle of *love-strong-as-death*, so are we, late-modern humankind, thoroughly immersed in the thanatic disenchantment of the twentieth-century philosophies of finitude, ready to appreciate the 'small-voiced' proposition of a way out of the nihilistic clinch. We are not asked to discard our knowledge of negativity altogether. Quite to the contrary, *another finitude* is based on the trauma of negativity and merely offers its *Durcharbeiten*: a working-through in which finitude gradually loses its traumatic aspect.

This quasi-psychoanalytic approach is justified by the fact that has not escaped Rosenzweig: that the epochal re/discovery of finitude very much resembles the event of the death of God as described by Nietzsche in *The Gay Science*. Although the news begin to spread, its acceptance is belated and not yet worked through, still overshadowed by the trauma. More than that, this belatedness is also prolonged by the intervention of defence mechanisms which resemble the Freudian 'reaction formation': prima facie they appear to accept the verdict of finitude and even revel in its 'nihilistic' consequences, yet surreptitiously work against it. One of the main theses of this book is that the most of the late-modern thought practises a *secret denial of the finite life* within the officially accepted condition of *Endlichkeit* – starting with Heidegger himself. If the finite life does not bring the expected fruits of joy, it is mostly because it is not yet truly acknowledged and recognized. As Freud states in his reflections on war and death, 'in the unconscious every one of us is convinced of his own immortality' (SE 14, 291), which also means that every one of us is a more or less a secret finitude denier.

The defensive ruses of our collective philosophical unconscious are indeed multiple and resourceful. Heidegger, to begin with, does not deny either death or finitude, which he overtly turns into the main tenet of his *Todesdenken*, yet he also simultaneously represses the very idea of life, finite life included. What we get in consequence is, as Derrida has put it with some degree of surprise, a strange kind of *mortality without life*: a death-bound and death-defined *existence* of Dasein which is strongly differentiated from all living beings, particularly animals. Similarly at first, the Hegelian line, taken up by Kojève and his French followers, accepts the verdict of death and, by investing in the negativity of the spirit, eliminates the living process too. Yet the result is different. The pure abiding of *der Geist* raises the thinking subject above the level of life where finitude stops being a pressing existential issue: adopted as a subjective mode of being it begins to offer *immortality without life*.

However, a symmetrical ruse is applied by those who make life an explicit theme of their philosophical reflection, which then, *nolens volens*, gravitates back towards the classical solutions of *Lebensphilosophie*, already anticipated in the fragment from Hegel's *Logic*, where the singular living is described as a contradiction between its finite form and the infinity of Life in which it participates. Once contradiction is solved to the advantage of the Infinite Life, the limits set by finitude dissolve, turning both birth and death into merely relative events. In Deleuze, Agamben or Esposito, therefore, the repression of finitude takes the form of, simultaneously, the denial of birth and the denial of death: when limits appear only on the epiphenomenal level, life once again asserts itself as *zoon aionios*, the eternal and infinite life that knows no beginning and no end. The enthusiasm that they officially show for the finite life is thus, in fact, only apparent; deep down it is always '*a Life*', infinite and undifferentiated, which they celebrate.[21]

This way or another, the result is highly confusing. Despite the overt declarations of taking on the re/discovery of finitude – after Kant's having set the 'problem of finitude' and Heidegger having endorsed it as defining for the late-modern thought – almost the whole of the twentieth century's reflection manages to *elude the problem of the finite life*: either by the surreptitious elimination of life, or by the back-door elimination of finitude itself. Accepted officially by the disenchanted mind, the idea of the finite life is constantly rejected by our philosophical unconscious, which stubbornly wants to fantasize in the absolute categories of the infinite, eternal, *unverletzt*, 'unscathed' – and applies them either to death or to life. The great achievement of late Derrida, whose last seminars are devoted to the deconstruction of the 'phantasms of the unscathed', was precisely to spot this aporia. I want to continue this deconstructive task in order to clear the intellectual field of all the *wrong* phantasmatic *miasmata* which obstruct our thinking of finitude – yet not in order to disenchant the 'fantastical' altogether. My aim will be to reclaim a right for the kind of the 'fantastical' that forms an integral part of life's belief in itself, as long as it truly is a 'religion of the finite life' and nothing more.

Yet, in order to start this process of *Durcharbeiten* and gradually discard the defence mechanisms that guard against it, one also has to ease the trauma. The deconstruction of the phantasmatic denial of the finite life can succeed only if we manage to flatten out the knot, the 'double bind', of the shock and the defensive reaction: the typically modern syndrome all of whose complex manifestations I gather here under one name, precursory to the Heideggerian focus on death – 'Arthur Schopenhauer'. The last hero of this book, Sigmund Freud, will emerge here as wrestling with his mighty precursor and thus read against the grain, i.e. in spite of his own philosophical predilection towards the traumatic disenchantment and its bad news, which paints the re/discovery of finitude in gloomy Schopenhauerian colours of irredeemable doom and misery. By pushing Freud into the vicinity of Rosenzweig and Derrida, I wish to emphasize the difference between his middle and late writings: today, a rather unfashionable move, especially when regarded from the perspective of the Lacanian thanatic party which has annexed Freud as the inventor of the death drive. Against this annexation, I will endorse Freud's first hypothesis concerning libidinal economy, formulated in the 1905 *Three Essays on the Theory of Sexuality*, which postulates a conflict between sexual energy and vital order of self-preservation – and reject the second hypothesis, laid down in *Beyond the Pleasure Principle*, where the earlier dualism becomes replaced by the antagonism of Eros and Thanatos: the arrangement of drives Freud himself called a 'sombre mythology' and that indeed regresses into the darkest morasses of the German, Schopenhauer-inspired, *Lebensphilosophie*.[22] By reading Freud through Rosenzweigian-Derridean lenses, I attempt to show how this early dualism of sexuality and *Lebensordnung* anticipates what Derrida calls the 'auto/immunological syndrome of life', with its inner dialectics of self-destructiveness and reactive overprotection, and as such, it constitutes one of the most convincing portraits of the process of the psychic life as a 'living contradiction'. All this – without any need for the hypothesis of the death drive.

But if I find Freud's early theory more promising than the later model based on the apparent dualism of Life and Death (which, in fact, gives such privilege to the latter that it inevitably slides into thanatic monism), it is also because it offers a unique vision of *infinity transformed*: the original libido, with which every newborn psyche is endowed, is not infinite quantitatively (the amount of energy is finite), but *infinite qualitatively*, i.e. *indefinite* when it comes to its future goals and objects, capable of nothing and everything at the same time (TETS, 34). This vision not only allows us to think of life as a 'living contradiction' without thinking away its aporetic nature, but also to complicate, and eventually abolish, the stiff opposition between finitude and infinity: the consciously accepted fact of the finite life, on the one hand – and the unconscious projection of the 'unscathed', which locates itself always beyond this life, on the other. The vision of human life that emerges from Freud's *Three Essays* is still aporetic and problematic, but it is also dialectical, and as such it delivers the best late-modern version of the 'finite capable of the infinite' or *finitum capax infiniti*.

In the move analogical to my analysis of Rosenzweig's New Thinking, I propose to call this transformation *in/de/finity*. The role of this neologism is to capture the unique character which, from the very beginning, appears to set human beings apart from other natural creatures that – according to the founder of philosophical anthropology, Johann Gottfried Herder – spring into being far better determined and thus equipped to survive than the fragile human 'deficient being', *Mangelwesen*. The *anthropological difference*, therefore, which I am going to defend here (although in a deconstructive and non-hierarchical manner), expresses itself already on the energetic level of drives. The Herderian anthropology sees a human being as human from the very moment of birth: a natural 'monstrosity' or an 'error', initially unable to live and survive, which needs to climb to a different level of existence, shaped by symbolic language and culture, in order to escape the precarity of its problematic life. The whole thrust of this book, however, is to prompt a radical *reversal* of perspectives, in which this Herderian 'original lack' will no longer present itself in terms of deprivation, deficiency or – to use the tragic idiom – a 'curse'. The constellation of *torat hayim*, which I will gather here under the heading of 'messianic vitalism', perceives the human error in a much more optimistic perspective: as a potential of *in/de/finity* opening in the enclosure of nature, which lets in, in Scholem's words, an 'apocalyptic breeze', both disturbing and invigorating, subversive and creative, and which Hannah Arendt associates with the chances of human natality. What the whole philosophical tradition 'from Ionia to Jena' (and beyond) stubbornly portrays as nothing but *lack* – the essential negativity of human life, which makes it particularly precarious – this other, timely 'awakened', tradition sees as a mark of potential *excess* where the libidinal in/de/finity, far from constuting a life-threatening deficiency, leads to a new mode of living: finite, yet not ultimately determined by its death, but rather by the other end of the finitude, which is constituted by birth. As Wittgenstein once said: what is an error in one game does not have to be an error in another. That's precisely what I want to achieve here: change the rules of the game in which philosophy has approached the aporecity of human life, so far unable to see it as a *chance*. As Nietzsche announced: life may have indeed become a *problem*, 'yet one should not jump to the conclusion that this necessarily makes one gloomy. Even love of life is still possible, only one loves differently . . . We know a new happiness'.[23]

I will call this libidinal excessive in/de/finity of human drive with yet another neologism – *Erros* – because of its erroneous, errant and erratic quality which, in the psychotheological idiom I am going to adopt here, characterizes the 'drive in the desert'. If there is a common part that unites all those thinkers listed here under the auspices of messianic vitalism, it is precisely the apology of *Erros* – and *not* Eros – as the true life drive capable to oppose the powerful attraction of Thanatos.[24]

Abbreviations

AI	Harold Bloom, *The Anxiety of Influence: A Theory of Poetry (With a New Preface on Shakespeare)*, New Haven, CT: Yale University Press, 1997.
AR	Jacques Derrida, *Acts of Religion*, ed. Gil Anidjar, New York: Routledge, 2002.
ATTIA	Jacques Derrida, *The Animal That Therefore I Am*, trans. David Wills, New York: Fordham University Press, 2008.
B	Roberto Esposito, *Bios: Biopolitics and Philosophy*, trans. Timothy Campbell, Minneapolis: Minnesota University Press, 2008.
BS1	Jacques Derrida, *The Beast and the Sovereign*, vol. 1, trans. Geoffrey Bennington, Chicago: University of Chicago Press, 2009.
BS2	Jacques Derrida, *The Beast and the Sovereign*, vol. 2, trans. Geoffrey Bennington, Chicago: University of Chicago Press, 2011.
BT	Martin Heidegger, *Being and Time*, trans. John Macquarrie and Edward Robinson, Oxford: Blackwell, 1962.
DE	Max Horkheimer and Theodor W. Adorno, *Dialectic of Enlightenment: Philosophical Fragments*, trans. Edmund Jephcott, ed. G. Schmid Noerr, Stanford, CA: Stanford University Press, 2002.
DP1	Jacques Derrida, *The Death Penalty*, vol. I, trans. Peggy Kamuf, Chicago: University of Chicago Press, 2014.
DP2	Jacques Derrida, *The Death Penalty*, vol. II, trans. Elizabeth Rottenberg, Chicago: University of Chicago Press, 2016.
E	Jacques Lacan, *Écrits: A Selection*, trans. Alan Sheridan, London: Routledge, 1989.
FR	*The Freud Reader*, ed. Peter Gay, New York: W.W. Norton, 1989.
FT	Jean-Luc Nancy, *A Finite Thinking*, ed. Simon Sparks, Stanford, CA: Stanford University Press 2003.
GA 96	Martin Heidegger, *Überlegungen XII–XV (Schwarze Hefte 1939–1941)*, ed. Peter Trawny, Frankfurt am Main: Vittorio Klostermann, 2015 (*Martin Heidegger Gesamtausgabe*, vol. 96).

GA 97   Martin Heidegger, *Anmerkungen I–V (Schwarze Hefte 1942–1948)*,
           ed. Peter Trawny, Frankfurt am Main: Vittorio Klostermann, 2015
           (*Martin Heidegger Gesamtausgabe*, vol. 97).

GDT   Emmanuel Lévinas, *God, Death, and Time*, trans. Bettina Bergo,
           Stanford, CA: Stanford University Press, 2001.

HC   Hannah Arendt, *The Human Condition*, Chicago: University of
           Chicago Press, 1998.

HCL   Jacques Derrida, *H.C. for Life, That Is to Say . . .*, trans. Laurent
           Milesi and Stefan Herbrechter, Stanford, CA: Stanford University
           Press, 2006.

HDRL   Jonathan Lear, *Happiness, Death, and the Remainder of Life*,
           Cambridge, MA: Harvard University Press, 2000.

IM   Martin Heidegger, *Introduction to Metaphysics*, trans. Gregory
           Fried and Richard Polt, New Haven, CT: Yale University Press,
           2000.

KL   Georges Canguilhem, *Knowledge of Life*, trans. Stefanos
           Geroulanos and Daniela Ginsburg, New York: Fordham University
           Press, 2008.

L   Jonathan Lear, *Love and Its Place in Nature: A Philosophical
           Interpretation of Freudian Psychoanalysis*, New Haven, CT: Yale
           University Press, 1998.

LA   Hannah Arendt, *Love and Saint Augustine*, ed. Joanna Vecchiarelli
           Scott and Judith Chelius Stark, Chicago: University of Chicago
           Press, 1996.

LLF   Jacques Derrida, *Learning to Live Finally: The Last Interview*, trans.
           Pascal-Anne Brault, New York: Melville House, 2011.

MBH   Otto Rank, *The Myth of the Birth of the Hero and Other Writings*,
           ed. Philip Freund, New York: Vintage, 1959.

MCP   Theodor Adorno, *Metaphysics: Concepts and Problems*, trans.
           Edmund Jephcott, London: Polity Press, 2001.

MM   Theodor W. Adorno, *Minima Moralia: Reflections on a Damaged
           Life*, trans. E.F.N. Jephcott, London: Verso, 2005.

ND   Theodor W. Adorno, *Negative Dialectics*, trans. E.B. Ashton,
           London: Routledge, 2004.

PEL   Eric L. Santner, *On Psychotheology of Everyday Life: Reflections on
           Rosenzweig and Freud*, Chicago: University of Chicago Press, 2001.

PR   Donald Woods Winnicott, *Playing and Reality*, London: Routledge,
           1971.

PS   G.W.F. Hegel, *Phenomenology of Spirit*, trans. A.V. Miller, Oxford:
            Oxford University Press, 1977.

R   Jacques Derrida, *Rogues: Two Essays on Reason*, trans. Pascale-
            Anne Brault, Stanford, CA: Stanford University Press, 2005.

SE1–SE24   Sigmund Freud, *The Standard Edition of the Complete
            Psychological Works of Sigmund Freud*, trans. James Strachey,
            London: The Hogarth Press and the Institute of Psychoanalysis,
            1957.

SM   Jacques Derrida, *Specters of Marx: The State of Debt, the Work of
            Mourning, and the New International*, trans. Peggy Kamuf, New
            York: Routledge, 1994.

SOTW   Jean-Luc Nancy, *The Sense of the World*, trans. Jeffrey S. Librett,
            Minneapolis: University of Minnesota Press, 1997.

SR   Franz Rosenzweig, *The Star of Redemption*, trans. William W.
            Hallo, Notre Dame, IN: University of Notre Dame Press, 1985.

SR-G   Franz Rosenzweig, *The Star of Redemption*, trans. Barbara Galli,
            Madison: University of Wisconsin Press, 2005.

SW1–SW4   Walter Benjamin, *Selected Writings*, vols 1–4, ed. Howard Eiland
            and Michael W. Jennings, Cambridge, MA: Harvard University
            Press, 1996–2006.

TB   Otto Rank, *The Trauma of Birth*, Eastford, CT: Martino Fine
            Books, 2010.

TETS   Sigmund Freud, *Three Essays on the Theory of Sexuality*, trans.
            James Strachey, Mansfield Centre, CT: Martino Publishing, 2011.

USH   Franz Rosenzweig, *Understanding the Sick and the Healthy: A View
            of World, Man, and God*, trans. Nahum Glatzer, Cambridge, MA:
            Harvard University Press, 1999.

Acknowledgments

There are many people without whom this book could not have appeared, but at least few of them deserve full mention. I would like to thank: Adam Lipszyc for his friendly and helpful comments; Arthur Bradley, Mick Dillon, and Yvonne Sherwood, who supported my project from the beginning and encouraged me to pursue it; my husband, Czarek Michalski, with whom I discussed my book in details; as well as Liza Thompson, Frankie Mace, Sue Littleford, Merv Honeywood, Lucy Russell, and the whole Bloomsbury Academic team for a very well organised and swift publication process.

A shorter version of the part of the Chapter 1 appeared earlier as: 'Love Strong as Death: Jews against Heidegger (On the Issue of Finitude),' chapter 7 of *Heidegger's Black Notebooks and the Future of Theology*, eds. Jayne Svengunson and Mattias Björk, London: Palgrave, 2017, pp. 159–90; a small part of the Chapter 3 was published as 'Religion of the Finite Life? Messianicity and the Right to Live in Derrida's Death Penalty Seminar,' Political Theology, vol. 19 (2/2018), pp. 79–94; and the first part of the Chapter 4 appeared in the abridged form as 'Between Therapy and Redemption: Notes Towards the Messianic Psychoanalysis,' in *Judaism in Contemporary Thought: Traces and Influence*, eds. Agata Bielik-Robson and Adam Lipszyc, London: Routledge, 2014, pp. 86–99.

Introduction

Life Before Death, an Outline

To focus on *in/de/finity* and *Erros* as the two characteristics of human finite life is to insist on its radical *denaturalization*: on taking life out of nature. This approach goes completely against the grain of the semi-obvious late-modern tendency to naturalize human beings, which was best summarized by Roberto Esposito in his affirmative embrace of biopolitics in *Bios*: 'From the moment that man appears bound by an unbreakable system of biological determinism, he can be reclaimed by his animal matrix from which he wrongly believes to have been emancipated' (B, 100). In my book, I will often challenge this apparent self-evidence of unbreakable biological bonds, seemingly rediscovered after the demise of the emancipatory illusion. This challenge, however, must begin with the polemics against the main philosophical thesis implied by Esposito's diagnosis – that to be reclaimed by the animal matrix means also to reclaim the ancient rule, once discarded by the Judaeo-Christian theological paradigm, and now returning with the reductionist vengeance: *kata phusein*, living-according-to-nature.

What is the meaning of this norm – *kata phusein*? In the series of lectures devoted to the 'birth of biopolitics', delivered at the Collège de France between 1978 and 1979, Michel Foucault defines biopolitics as a new system of 'governing the living': no longer concerned with the immortality of individual souls, it now concentrates solely on the natural well-being of citizens forming modern nation-states. He describes this transformation as a transition from power interested in the infinite afterlife of its subjects to the power investing in the finite life of citizens, spent within the natural cycle of birth and death. Before, the governing consisted in taking care of the proper Christian existence and legitimized itself as the regime of truth and penitence, allowing the subject to arrive safely at the gate of heaven – now, in modernity, the governing consists merely in administering the living functions of the body of people and catering for their natural needs. Modern biopolitics, therefore, is no longer Christian; the modern paradigm shift announces a new vision of life that does not sustain belief in immortality. It is a finite life: confined within the limits of the natural cycle and governed by the most fundamental law of nature, which was formulated already by the pre-Socratic Greeks in their reflections on the system of *phusis* – the law of *genesis kai phthora*, growth and decay, becoming and perishing.[2] Thus, long before Nietzsche proclaimed the death of God and the end of the great promise of personal infinity, modern Enlightenment politics already proceeds on the basis of the newly recovered concept of natural life spun between cradle and grave.[3]

Modernity, therefore, only rediscovered the 'naturalness' of natural life, as old as philosophy itself. According to the classical definition of Aristotle, *phusis* is a system of all beings that fall under the inexorable rule of cyclical alternation between *genesis* and *phthora*, generation and corruption; the rule that knows no exception. And while the conception of nature and natural laws will be changing during the intellectual history of the West, one general criterion defining the natural mode of existence will always remain: the idea of 'natural necessity' that links birth and death in an insoluble knot. Whether as pre-Socratic *phusis*, scholastic *natura pura*, or Darwin's 'natural selection', nature is always defined in the light of this mysterious ambivalence: 'What causes birth tends to cause death too.'[4]

This transcendental concept of *phusis* designates a paradigmatic point of reference for the whole Western philosophical tradition. But it is also a paradigmatic point of reference for the Jewish *critique* of this tradition, which rightly perceives the idea of *kata phusein* – 'living according to nature' – as the very gist of *Hokmah Yevanit*, 'the wisdom of the Greeks'. The fateful infatuation of philosophy with nature and natural law becomes a frequent target of many polemical interventions coming from the side of modern Jewish thinkers who tend to perceive nature as a homeostatic isolated system operating with the ecomonic minimum of energy, where all powers keep themselves in mutual check. For Scholem, Taubes, Benjamin and Adorno, nature is simply *tautological* and thus boring: it is the dullest and least inventive form of minimal existence which merely 'piles life upon life' and, as Georges Canguilhem put it, is 'poor on monsters' (KL, 136), allowing no true creativity which becomes stifled in advance by the principle of balance and compensation. Just as in Hegel's description of Life / Nature / World Soul, it is a system that may be dynamic on the level of its parts – the particular *Lebendige* – but, when conceived as a whole, remains *at rest*.[5]

But those Jewish thinkers do not criticize nature from the position of 'enemies of life' or 'priestly vengeful spirits', as Nietzsche, Heidegger or Deleuze would like to label them unfairly and, by this simple manoeuvre, dismiss their objections.

Quite to the contrary, they criticize nature and praise anti-natural revelation *not against, but for the sake of life*. For them, revelation constitutes a welcome denaturalizing shock that breaks the homeostatic balance of the closed immanent system and sets living beings on the move – making thus a much more dynamic and free use of life. They all depart from the passage from Deuteronomy where God, deceptively simply, says: *I have set before you life and death: choose life* (Deut. 30:19). *Choosing life* means here something else than just taking the side of life in its opposition to death: Eros against Thanatos. It rather means taking life out of the whole context where life and death lie bound with each other in the circuit of *phusis*; it means – taking life out of nature and the limitation by natural necessities. It does not necessarily imply, therefore, pitching life infinite against mortality: it merely means that human life with its inherent possibilities must be *enhanced* within the conditions of finitude.

It was precisely against this Nietzschean double association – of life with nature and denaturalization with life-negating ascesis – that Jewish thinkers made their greatest critical contribution to the late-modern thought. Absolutely pioneering in this respect is the work of Walter Benjamin, who openly criticized German followers of Nietzsche, coming under the heading of *Lebensphilosophie*, for their grave misconception of life and its creative powers. Benjamin's indirect critique of Dilthey, constituting one of the leading motifs of *The Origins of German Tragic Drama*, as well as of his early essay, 'Critique of Violence' (SW 1), reproaches him for depicting 'the creative force of history' (*die schaffende Kraft der Geschichte*) as nothing else than the generative force of nature. In championing a different, less naturalistic concept of life and history, Benjamin introduces a notion alternative to that of nature, namely 'creatureliness' *Kreatürlichkeit*) – as a category denoting a special condition of a created, not just generated, living being. Contrary to the Greek understanding of *phusis* as the self-regulating totality of becoming and perishing – Life in general – creatureliness is a category which focuses on a singular creature (*Kreatur*) and allows us to rethink the position of a denaturalized human being, conceived no longer as an 'outcast of nature, a life-denying being diminished in natural vitality, but rather as, in Benjamin's words, *ein Fürsprech der Kreatur*, a 'spokesman of creation', representing for the whole of the living a possibility of another – better, freer, more innovative – life.' A life according not to the principle of natural generation, but a life according to the principle of creation: the double bind of the creaturely existence, destined not just to *be created*, but also *to create*.

I will often go back to the concept of creatureliness, but probably the best description of this alternative *torat hayim*, which struggles against the confines of mere physicality and tries to emancipate life from naturalistic biologism and its seemingly self-evident 'unbreakable bonds', is offered by Jacques Derrida's comment on Benjamin. In 'Force of Law: The Mystical Foundation of Authority', apropos Benjamin's vehement rejection of German *Lebensphilosophie*, which today could also be read as a critique of *all* forms of biopolitics, nihilistic and affirmative alike, Derrida says:

> This critique of vitalism or biologism ... here proceeds like the awakening of a Judaic tradition. And it does so in the name of life, of the most living of life, of the value of life that is worth more than life (pure and simple, if such exist and that one could call natural and biological), but that is worth more than life because it is life itself, insofar as life prefers itself. *It is life beyond life, life against life, but always in life and for life.*
>
> AR, 289; my emphasis

This paragraph contains my book in a nutshell, for it criticizes all naturalistic and immanentist types of modern biologism and vitalism alike, yet does so 'always in life and for life' and, because of that proceeds like *torat hayim*, 'the awakening of a Judaic tradition'. Even if our existence is to be spent on earth with no prospect of spiritual afterlife, it does not yet indicate that it is to be ruled by the 'system of nature'. Finitude is not indelibly fused with living *kata phusein*. Finitude and denaturalization can still go hand in hand.

Another vitalism

Some, however, may immediately object that 'this critique of vitalism or biologism' is nothing but an escapist and nostalgic attempt to recreate the sense of subjective freedom, the last post-Christian ditch of the former belief in the immortal soul, which is no longer accessible after, to quote Esposito again, 'man appears bound by an unbreakable system of biological determinism' (B, 100). But the *torat hayim* intuition, which intimates 'more life' in the 'mere life', should not be easily dismissed as yet another lingering idealist illusion: it is confirmed by leading theoretical biologists themselves. In *Knowledge of Life*, the collection of essays on philosophical biology, Georges Canguilhem, by following Bergson, sees *élan vital* as a transgressive force investing in more and more freedom of responses of a 'living subjectivity' to the surrounding world. Canguilhem defines the vitalist position in deliberately phenomenological terms as 'the expression of the *confidence the living being has in life*, of the self-identity of life within the living human being conscious of living' (KL, 62; my emphasis). Never a value-free *Weltanschauung*, 'vitalism translates a permanent exigency of life in the living' (ibid.), i.e. life's self-confidence or, in our terms, self-belief. Even stronger, vitalism, pregnant with strong valuations, may indeed be 'an *exigency* rather than a method and a *morality* rather than a theory' (KL, 63; my emphasis). It has a distinct *ethos* in which life itself gains assertion and articulation. The eponymous *knowledge of life* [*connaissance de la vie*] must thus be understood in both meanings of the genitive – objective and subjective: it is knowledge *about* life, acquired by a biologist, but also knowledge *of* life as life's self-expression and self-recognition. Of life and about life, in life and for life, elaborated within life's self-reflective dialectical process – but never *over* life, proceeding from some abstract, life-less and value-free, 'view from nowhere'.

Having established vitalism's 'independence from the annexationist ambitions of the sciences of matter' (KL, 60), Canguilhem distinguishes roughly two types of the vitalist thought: (1) the earlier holistic organicism that focuses mostly on the self-sameness of the totality of life (German *Lebensphilosophie*) and (2) the later interactive vitalism, linked to the discoveries of Jakob von Uexküll and Kurt Goldstein, which focuses on the crucial relation of mutual exchange between the living centre and its milieu. It is only the latter that gets Canguilhem's attention; while mistrustful towards the vague notion of *la vie*, 'life in general', characteristic of the nineteenth-century 'philosophy of life', he chooses the *nominalistic variant of vitalism* which is always and only concerned with the concrete 'living', *le vivant*. This concreteness, however, is not just a matter of external attribution: in the case of *le vivant*, it is a matter of an internal process of individuation, which takes place in the space between the living, conceived as a centre, and its milieu, *die Umwelt*. It is the vitalism of the living being as a self-centred singular. Thus, while 'the ideal of the objectivity of knowledge demands a decentring of the vision of things' (KL, 118), vitalism, to the contrary, insists on keeping the idea of the centre:

> Physics is a science of fields, of milieus. But it has been discovered that, in order for there to be an environment, there must be a center. It is a position of a living being, its relation to the experience it lives in as a totality, that gives the milieu meaning as conditions of existence. Only a living being, infra-human, can coordinate a milieu.
>
> KL, 70

Pace 'the claim of science to dissolve living beings, which are centers of organization, adaptation, and invention, into the anonymity of the mechanical, physical, and chemical' (KL, 119), Canguilhem stubbornly sticks to the *vitalist recentring*, which resists the dissolution into the indifferent 'field' of being. And it does not matter whether this resistance is offered by plant, animal or human being, which – all being instances of *le vivant* – merely differ in their self-differentiating strategies of confrontation with the environment. Seen from this perspective, human subjectivity would be nothing but 'the irreducible center of resistance' (KL, 110), and because of this an *individuum*: not a simple atom of life, but a complex dynamic strategy of constant self-recentring pointing to the no longer 'divisible' kernel. Even if such description involves a tinge of tautology – a self-recentring pointing to the centre which coordinates recentring – there's nothing wrong with it: *c'est la vie*, this is life. There is no centre *as such*; there is only an autoteleological process of *centring*.

This tautology or autoteleology comes across even stronger in the work of Canguilhem's follower, Gilbert Simondon, who, in 'The Genesis of the Individual', defines the process of living as a continuous recentring/individuation that elaborates on the pre-individual material givens. The living individual here is never a *datum*, it is always a vital effort of an individuating organism, which, because of that, should rather be called with the Latin form of futuristic gerund – *inidividuandum* (to-be-individuated) – than with the noun stating the fact: *individuum*. Life, therefore, is a perpetual individuation and self-differentiation:

> The living being conserves in itself an activity of permanent individuation. It is not only the result of individuation, like the crystal or the molecule, but it is a veritable *theater of individuation*. Moreover, the entire activity of the living being is not, like that of the physical individual, concentrated at its boundary with the outside world. There exists within the being a more complete regime of *internal resonance* requiring permanent communication and maintaining a metastability that is the precondition of life ... The living individual is a system of individuation, an individuating system and also a system that individuates itself ... the physical individual – perpetually excentric, perpetually peripheral in relation to itself, active at the limit of its own terrain – cannot be said to possess any genuine interiority. But the living individual does possess a *genuine interiority*, because individuation does indeed take place within it.[8]

This 'genuine interiority', defined as the centre of the internal resonance, individuates further into a *psyche*, capable of grasping the 'problematic' aspects of life, and then, into subjectivity understood as the centre of agency:

> Both the psyche and the collectivity are constituted by a process of individuation *supervening* on the individuation that was productive of life. The psyche represents the continuing *effort of individuation* in a being that has to resolve its

own problematic through its own involvement as an element of the problem by taking action as a *subject*. The subject can be thought of as the unity of the being when it is thought of as a living individual, and as a being that represents its activity to itself both as an element and a dimension of the world. Problems that concern living beings are not just confined to their own sphere: only by means of an unending series of successful individuations, which ensure that *ever-more preindividual reality is brought into play* and incorporated into the relation with the milieu, can we endow living beings with an open-ended axiomatic

ibid., 306–7; my emphasis

Although formulated in the idiom close to biological sciences, this diagnosis brings in all the familiar notions: what Simondon sees as a 'meta-stable unit', thriving on and constantly producing 'tensions' and 'problems' that increase its inner differentiation and individuation, is precisely the Hegelian 'living contradiction' which, instead of dis/solving, maintains itself in this perpetual strain, struggling against entropy and all sorts of nirvanic releases that for it could indicate only death. The life of the singular living, spun between the 'preindividual' (inorganic matter) and the 'transindividual' (social collective), consists in the semi-tautological process of 'the individuation of the individuating', where the exigency of life translates into creation of the *maximum of difference*. But the highest – *supervenient* – state of this vital art is represented by human subjectivity which brings ever more preindividual reality *into play* – in fact, the whole world, refracted through language as the system of universal reference capable of incorporating anything and everything into the relation with the milieu – and maximizes the difference by turning life into a truly 'open-ended' process, precisely the way Hegel envisaged the perfectly individuated human life as the 'open work of art'. We shall come back to this salient analogy.

But what is the nature of this *supervenience*? Canguilhem and Simondon lead us to believe that subjectivity is but the simple continuation of the self-individuating, self-differentiating and self-centring strategy of the living that already possesses a ready structure of 'inner reflexivity' and 'genuine interiority'. Yet, subjectivity is not just a straightforward *dénouement* of the vital story. The main aporia involved in the process of subjectivization is well reflected by the bifurcation of the two types of vitalism, as described by Canguilhem, that represent the two not wholly convergent aspects of life: *life as self-preservation*, which tends defensively to close off the self-same living unit, on the one hand, and *life as creation*, which lowers the guards and opens itself to the interplay with the milieu, ready to incorporate any 'preindividual' material and contaminate itself with anything alien, on the other. Since it is the inner dialectics of *life-against-life*, in which these two aspects depend on one another, we cannot simply call them opposite – but their coexistence is certainly aporetic, as indeed in the Hegelian 'living contradiction'. And if subjectivity often comes across as alien or even hostile to the natural 'vital order', it is precisely because it represents this other, non-preservatory aspect of *life taken to its extreme*.

Practically all philosophies of nature – from the first Greek conceptualization of *phusis*, through Freud's *Three Essays* and Bergson's *Creative Evolution*, up to Hans Jonas's 'philosophical biology' and Deleuze's *Difference and Repetition* – mention these two antagonistic aspects of life: *dike* versus *hubris*, measure versus excess, inertia versus innovation, vital order versus sexuality, repetition versus creativity, law versus exception, *fixus* versus *fluxus*. Natural life is always divided, two-faced, at once establishing self-reproducing regularities and breaking out of them into the realm of the 'monstrous' and 'pathological'. Canguilhem says:

> An organism has greater latitude of action than a machine. *It has less purpose and more potentialities* ... Life is experience, that is to say, improvisation, the utilization of occurrences; *it is an attempt in all directions*. From this follows a massive and often neglected fact: *life tolerates monstrosities*. There is no machine monster. There is no mechanical pathology ... The distinction between the normal and the pathological holds for living beings alone.
>
> KL, 90; my emphasis[10]

The word *toleration* seems particularly well chosen: natural life does not love or encourage monstrosities, it merely suffers them, but usually not for long – as Nietzsche would have said, 'only for a minute'.[11] Although mildly 'tolerant' towards transgressions 'attempting in all directions' (exactly as in Goethe!), it also mobilizes its punitive aspect of normativization, in which life, structured as the system of nature, *la vie*, strikes against the experimenting singular *le vivant*. Every monster, therefore, is highly precarious and if it is to be offered a stronger chance of survival, it must be *given time* and *taken out of nature* – into a realm of virtual freedom that will protect its anomalous character and *defer* its confrontation with the punishing norm. This, in a nutshell, is a sphere of subjectivity in which the natural pendulum swings decidedly towards the experimental 'monstrosity'.

Seen from the vitalist perspective, therefore, the human subject would be a site of an enduring monstrosity and a permanent crisis, virtually taken out of or exempted from the natural 'punitive' constraints: the Hegelian 'living contradiction', consisting in the constant 'negation of the living by the non-viable' (KL, 136), the amorphous infinity breaking out of the finitude of any given form. While we cannot live at the heights of this infinite 'non-viable' – what the whole post-*lebensphilosophisch* line of thinkers, starting with Simmel, Lukacs, Freud, Bataille and culminating in Deleuze, extols as the *unliveable pure life* – we have to tarry with it nonetheless, by living *with* it, in the plastic form of contradiction, plastic enough to embrace and dialecticize its inner tensions. The pathological 'unviable', encapsulated and protected within the subjective sphere, indeed often transforms into a lethal threat of the 'unliveable' which then, to paraphrase Canguilhem, 'negates the living by the non-living'. But what is crucial is to remember that the monstrous 'non-viability', as the derivative of the experimental aspect of life, always comes first, while its thanatic/lethal form, in which it strikes against life, appears only as secondary. The subject, to use Kojève's phrase, is *not* a 'walking talking death'; it is *still* life, yet so distilled and intensified in its innovative aspect that it becomes deadly antagonistic towards life conceived mostly as the order of self-preservation. The subject, therefore, is the theatre of the vital agon: life-against-life, indeed a 'living contradiction'.

Humankind, therefore – this *almost* 'non-viable monstrosity' in the universe of nature – is the most daring experiment of life in which life becomes truly 'excentric': no longer ruled by the centralized system of *kata phusein*, but venturing out into uncharted territories where it can feel 'more alive'. For Canguilhem, just as for William Blake, this unbounded free realm of life's liberated experimentation is 'Man, the Imagination': the subjective world of infinitely creative fantasy:

> But as soon as consciousness has been led to suspect the eccentricity of life ... what would prevent it from supposing life to be even more alive – that is to say, capable of the greatest freedom of exercise, from supposing life capable not only of provoked exceptions but also of spontaneous transgressions of its own habits? ... *To judge life to be timid or frugal is to sense in oneself a movement to go even further that it will* ... Does this movement come from life's inscription within the arc of a poetic elan made conscious by the imagination and revealed by it to be infinite? Or is it rather that the little follies of life incite imitation in human fantasy, which returns to life what life had lent to it? There is, however, so great a difference between loan and restitution here that it may seem unreasonable to accept such a virtuously rationalist explanation. *Life is poor in monsters. The fantastic is a world.*
>
> KL, 136; my emphasis

'To judge life to be timid or frugal is to sense in oneself a movement to go even further that it will': it is precisely this mysterious *movement* in which messianic vitalism is so vitally interested – a movement encrypted in the symbolism of Exodus, which dialectically pitches life-against-life but always in life and for the sake of life: life shedding its natural form in order to go further, life denaturalizing itself and breaking out of the bondage of Egypt, 'the land of narrowing', not because it perceives nature as evil, but only as too timid, frugal, lacking the 'fantastical', or simply 'poor in monsters'.

The spectre of renaturalization

For Foucault, however, the opposite is true: finitude is, by necessity, strictly correlated with the process of man's *renaturalization*. The moment humankind loses its footing in the religious transcendence and becomes as finite as everything else, it immediately and automatically returns to the 'system of nature', from which it merely 'wrongly thought to have emancipated himself' (B, 100). For Foucault, therefore, *kata phusein* is a simple tautology, as it was for Nietzsche: '*Living according to Nature* means actually the same as *living according to Life* – how could you do differently?'[12]

Foucault's paradigmatic answer to modern biopolitics, therefore, is to accept its basic premise – that life is finite and because of that reduced to the natural law of birth and death – and then only slightly correct the naive physiocratic trust in the 'naturalness' of human existence, by appropriating and internalizing the disciplining practices that, as he convincingly shows, lie at the bottom of the overt dogma of laissez-faire-ism. The naivete, therefore, appears to be only a hypocritical decoy. While liberal ideology claims to be 'physiocratic', i.e. smoothly and minimally administering the life processes of the population living *kata phusein*, it nonetheless submits the life of the citizens to powerful regimes of regulation: it supervises them constantly, treating human beings as always somehow deficient and never sufficiently successful from the purely naturalist point of view. Hence, claims Foucault, the only possible way of resistance to the biopolitical regime is to take over the disciplining macropractices of liberal politics and internalize them as the micropractices of the self: the Stoic 'conversion to self' (*epistrophe eis heauton*) is to serve as a foil for building a system of defence against the biopolitical technologies of the state.[13]

This is the reason why, in the third volume of the *History of Sexuality*, called *Le souci de soi* [*Care of the Self*], Foucault famously advocates a return to the ancient techniques of self-discipline exercised within life finite and mortal, in this manner inaugurating the last – Neostoic – turn in his thinking career, epitomizing the minimalist late-modern ambition to 'take care' of life as it is, without either imposing on it excessive demands or luring it with false promises. Despite being hailed, mostly by Foucault himself, as the last ditch of resistance, the Neostoic option is, in fact, anything but subversive. After all, on both planes – of macro- and microstrategies which reflect one another – there is a basic agreement as to the general rule of *kata phusein*. Nature, regulating the flow of life from birth to death, appears as the ultimate lawgiver offering a model simultaneously for civil discipline *and* inner self-control: self-growth and self-preservation within the pre-established confines which only allow to 'perfect our nature'. And since, within these confines, the finite time is pressing, one needs to 'hasten' to deliver the cure/care (*cura, souci*): 'Find out what is in accord with your nature and hasten to that … Hasten then to the end, discard vain hopes, and if you care for yourself at all, rescue yourself while you still may.'[14]

The whole stake of Foucault's project, therefore, is not so much to break with the biopolitical tendency to renaturalize human beings, which, literally, seems to go without saying – as to supply it with a reflexive discourse drawing from the ancient norm of *kata phusein*: living 'according to nature'. But Foucault also knows well that the 'Greek wisdom', from which his Neostoic technologies of the self derive, is predominantly *tragic*: it presents every singular life as an error and every individuation as the deviation from the norm, which needs to be corrected or 'rescued' by the return to the system. In the tragic vision, life – and most of all human life, the least orderly of all living beings and most prone to 'linger in being' (see Anaximander again) – is the source of the destructive *hubris*: the excessive will of every singular living thing to escape the equalizing verdicts of nature, fate and death. *Phusis*, therefore, is the system of all things, in which *hubris* undergoes necessary correction – which is best exemplified by the lethal punishment of the most hubristic of all individuals: the tragic hero. In that sense, nature is not so much a burgeoning life as the very opposite of it: *phusis* is the reality principle of *zoe* which has to limit itself, contract a *peras* [limitation] and live according to the fateful rule of the totality of all beings, obeying the alternation between growth and decay. This is precisely why Foucault will choose the history of sexuality, starting from the 'Greek tragedy of incest', as the most exemplary domain of the disciplining practices; for it is precisely in the human sexuality where 'the *hubris* is most fundamental'.[15]

Already the very term *cura/souci*, which underlies Foucault's late project of self-governmentality, says it all: it is an elementary care of oneself and others in the form of a *cure*, as if human life were indeed nothing but an affliction to be partly cured and partly endured, or a 'deficiency' to be corrected by the technics of self-help.[16] There is no sense of lucky chance, hope or promise here; as Foucault tells us in his essay on life, life – and especially human life – is an aberrant process that only the conscious correction of the self can mitigate. The only answer to the original hubristic anarchy of human drives is the discipline of self-control, offering a necessary legalistic correction to their deficient 'naturalness'. By alluding to Georges Canguilhem's theory of life as rooted in the process of erring, Foucault says: 'Should not the theory of the subject be radically reformulated, so, instead of basing itself on the consciousness that itself to the truth of the world, it rather finds its roots in the "errors" of life?'[17]

This radical reformulation mirrors the nature of the change that in modernity occurs on the plane of politics, steering away from the sovereign rationality of the law into the immanence of life. Foucault's late project of the care/cure of the self departs from phenomenology, with its unflinching reliance on *cogito* (ibid.) – and moves from the idea of the rational exercise of the *maîtrise de soi* [mastery of oneself], expressing the triumphant external domination of reason over instincts, towards the necessary correction of inner control and discipline in response to the 'erroneous' and anarchic, biological *datum* of human existence. In this alternative approach, *souci* indeed acquires the medicinal character of the remedy to the original, 'hereditary' affliction (ibid., 1593).[18]

But, as we have already seen, such 'tragic' reading of Canguilhem, which fosters Foucault's minimalist Neostoic programme of the 'care of the self', is not the only possible: in the former's *Knowledge of Life*, the 'error' is a much more positive notion, pointing to a *drive of deviation* – here we will call it *Erros* – which the singular livings (*les vivantes*) employ in order to take themselves out of the restrictive system of life/nature (*la vie*). On Foucault's account, where the Christian idea of personal immortality serves as the *only* model for a non-natural human life, the loss of the Christian belief must necessarily entail the biopolitical reduction of the finite life to the basic law / necessity / limitation of nature. Yet, does finitude and denaturalizing Exodus truly exclude one another? Is the Christian model of denaturalization really the only one?

Contrary to what Foucault, and then Esposito, approaches as the non-questionable self-evidence of biological determinism, I claim that there is still hope for *another finitude* that refrains from the renaturalization of human existence. The key move to arrest this process of sliding back into the matrix of *kata phusein* is to understand that it is not so much passively accepted, as actively willed and chosen: what is presented to us as necessary and inescapable – the 'unbreakable biological bonds' – is, in fact, still a matter of choice.

The choice lurking behind the biopolitical *kata phusein* results from what we may call the *nomotropic desire*: the tendency in human psyche to orient itself 'according to the law'. It is precisely the nomotropism, deeply entrenched in the psychic defence mechanisms representing the 'timid and frugal' aspect of life, which is responsible for humankind's active seeking of a 'limit', its wish to 'contract *peras*' and acquire a 'right measure' that would put its vital *hubris* back into order. Though the idea of nomotropism originally applied only to the domain of the Jewish legal system, I want to expand its use and show that the human psyche is predominantly nomotropic in response to its initial anarchy of drives, which it perceives as the primary danger: it seeks law, order, and disciplining structures in order to counteract the terrifying condition of lack/excess which characterizes the instinctual arrangement of the human *Mangelwesen*.

Beyond nomotropism

Johann Gottfried Herder, the founder of philosophical anthropology, was the first thinker to formulate so clearly and explicitly the idea that the human being is a 'sick animal': a creature maladapted to the order of nature. Unlike all other beings that have their place in the natural organization of the world, humans are hopeless misfits, *Mangelwesen*, deficient beings, 'the most orphaned children of nature'. In his *Essay on the Origin of Language*, Herder stipulates the definition of human beings as an 'outcast of nature' which, otherwise a pretty decent caretaker, in the case of humankind behaves as 'the most cruel stepmother'. Humankind is bare life itself, with no inborn skills or qualities that could facilitate its existence and ease the impact of the reality principle. Its drives are indeterminate and, unlike well-defined animal instincts, find no counterpart in the world of natural objects; humankind is thus doomed to remain unfulfilled and maladapted, with no natural place of its own, *denaturalized by nature itself*. Humankind's only way out of this predicament of originary lack is to compensate for its natural deficiency: produce culture which will provide it with substitute symbolic skills ('prosthetic limbs') and thus appease its original anxiety. Humankind, says Herder – very much against Rousseau – must live in culture, because for humans nature is a deadly and hostile environment in which they cannot survive: symbolic forms of culture are their only means of survival. Herder's solution to the problem of human difference is thus clearly a precursor to the one chosen by Canguilhem: humankind is simultaneously continuous with the natural world as its extremely 'experimental' or even 'erroneous' form of life – and discontinuous, because in order to survive it must resort to the innovative products of its own 'imagination', which create the symbolic sphere of cultural institutions. Humans' survival, therefore, is not just a matter of biological instinct of self-preservation: it involves the whole machinery of language, stories, cultural identifications. Neither simply superior, nor simply inferior to the natural beings, humans are just *different*: in a complex and multifaceted kind of way.

The most characteristic feature of the Herderian line of thinkers, which I want to follow here, is that it places human *differentia specifica* in the particularity of humankind's *energetic endowment*: in the singular arrangement of human drives, simultaneously excessive and indefinite. In contrast to all those philosophers (and they are the majority) who locate human difference in the *hermeneutic* moment, i.e. in the moment of initiation of the 'human animal' into a properly anthropogenic symbolic sphere, the Herderian line believes that – only seemingly tautologically – *human beings are born human from the very start*: from the onset, humankind emerges with its characteristic drive-arrangement that determines the vicissitudes of its humanity. A human, therefore, is not so much a being that speaks, endowed with the innate capability to use language, but rather a being marked with a specific mode of life, which Nietzsche, himself steeped in the Herderian tradition, calls simply: *problematic*. It is, in fact, so deeply problematic that it cannot survive without being aided by the symbolic tradition: according to Herder – but also according to the Jewish *torat hayim* which can be translated precisely as the *tradition of life* – human life cannot live unless instructed to do so. The 'origin of language' lies in the early-birther's inability to survive.

Human is born human, which, following the Herderian logic, means: a being *unable to live and survive*. For Freud – who merely draws final conclusions from Herder's philosophical anthropology and presents man as a 'feeble animal' (*schwaches Tierwesen*) which 'must make its entry on earth as a helpless suckling' (FR, 737) – humankind's fundamental vital given consists in a bundle of drive-energy which not only makes it unable to live, but – even stronger – also opposes and threatens its life. The in/de/finite libidinal energy, which constitutes this most problematic – simultaneously natural and unnatural – endowment of human beings, is deprivation and surplus at the same time: it is lacking in surviving skills, but it is also excessive, joy-orientated, and because of that indifferent to the sheer self-maintenance in life. Its first manifestation in the human psyche is thus involuntarily *destructive*. The contrast between the enormous power of the primary drive 'without qualities' and the biological 'weakness' of its fragile vessel constitutes the original tension – or 'living contradiction' – that spurns the evolution of the psychic reality. The vicissitudes of drives (*Triebschicksale*) draw various lines of development and differentiation out of this strange libidinal *datum* that never stops oscillating between lack and excess, and thus never gains an equilibrium. Freud says on the possible origins of culture as deriving from this lack of balance:

In the case of other animal species it may be that a temporar.? balance has been reached between the influences of their environment and the mutually contending instincts within them, and that thus a cessation of development has come about. It may be that in primitive man a fresh access of libido kindled a renewed burst of activity on the part of the destructive instinct.³¹

This *problematic* – powerful, unskilled and destructive – endowment is precisely the reason why humankind becomes a *psychic* being. Psyche is, in fact, nothing but a system of defensive strategies, devised to take care of humanity's primordial incapability to live and survive; the first impulse of what is left in humankind of self-preservatory instincts is to try to tame the primary drive and teach it a skill of staying in life. The lesson of *conservatio vitae*, therefore, is secondary – and precisely because of that lacking the instinctual firmness it possesses in 'other animal species'. The human life is essentially and originally *anarchic* and as such *unliveable*: it must indeed be 'cured' – or taken care of – by the formatting defences that will teach it to survive. Yet, the Foucauldian notion of cure/care does not exhaust the primary dialectical *datum*: although unliveable in its original form, human life also gains the primordial sense of freedom, by preserving a gap or delay that consists in its secondary and non-automatic submission to the fundamental law of self-preservation. In terms of the Hegelian dialectics which, as we have already seen, is the privileged language of life: the primary drive-anarchy must be *opposed* by the necessary submission to 'natural' law and order, so the psyche can survive – but also *preserved* and *recollected* in order to be rediscovered at the higher level, where it will appear as the subjective sense of freedom. Freedom would thus be the third synthetic term sublating both the anarchy of drives and the nomotropism of defences: a more complex, *errotic*, power that accepts the necessity of survival ('erotic' affirmation of existence', yet, at the same time, rejects all seemingly necessary laws imposed by the reality principle and its demand of immediate adaptation (brave investment in the 'error of life'). The Hegelian 'living contradiction', therefore, can be raised to the higher dialectical level only if the nomotropic tendency, orientated towards laws capable of limiting and disciplining the amorphic drives within the finite natural cycle of life, becomes superseded by the *errotic* one, recollecting the original anarchy of drives in the sense of the inner, potentially infinite, freedom. To recall Canguilhem again: 'The fantastic – is the world' (KL, 136).

According to Freud, the immediate effect of the psyche's initial helplessness is its *mimetic* strategy: the in/de/finiteness of the energetic endowment makes it prone to instantaneous imitation in which it learns what it means to be and to survive from other beings that already exist and manage to survive. The whole of humanity's early psychic existence is thus the realm of the 'timid' *mimesis*: a constant quest after a model to imitate, a nomotropic pursuit of the external law that could be assumed as a non-negotiable necessity and thus organize and subjugate the unliveable chaos of drives. Jean Laplanche talks here about the 'dyad stage', in which the newfangled psyche enters into a vital union with the mother's body in order to imitate the indispensable technics of staying alive. The quasi-monistic arrangement of this prolonged primary narcissism does not yet present any alternative, any true otherness to this immediate initiation into life, which imposes itself as a necessity and takes the form of a simple *biomorphism*: a defensive formation of the drives which 'forget' their in/de/finite character and let themselves be taken over and shaped by the 'vital order' of self-preservation. In the biomorphic stage, the exigency of survival is so pressing that everything that puts the precarious life of the infant in danger becomes 'forgotten' and 'erased': overwritten and overruled by the *Lebensordnung* of the elementary *liveability*. The initially unliveable unbound life becomes liveable the moment it becomes repressed as such and, in the strong antithesis to its primary in/de/finity, 'contracts the limit'.

According to Laplanche, *the biomorphic tendency arises in the psyche only because it has no biology*; the weaker the biological functions, the stronger the mimetic drive that chooses 'natural' functionality as its object. Biomorphism, therefore, compensates – still in accordance with the Herderian logic – for the 'lost instinct', by creating an illusion of the 'instinct regained': the biomorphic psyche is engaged in the constant *recherche du instinct perdu*. It presents itself to the psyche as absolute necessity precisely because it is not a necessity at all: it is already a choice and persuasion, merely masquerading as a 'false interiorized biology'.[22]

It is only later that the proper alternative – the first *possibility* to choose – emerges, which questions the first seemingly necessary 'contraction': the first negation of life's original in/de/finity. It occurs only with the intervention of the Father who acts as the first true Other, capable of tearing up the natural self-evidence of the symbiotic union with the maternal body. The moment the Name of the Father penetrates the dyad, the drives are being 'recollected' from their biomorphic path and 'reminded' of their proper destiny (all associations with Plato's anamnesis non-accidental) – which, according to Jacques Lacan, is not the life-clinging Eros, still staking timidly on self-preservation, but the life-negating Thanatos, which remains essentially indifferent to the issue of survival. When, as he states in 'Subversion of the Subject and the Dialectics of Desire', by 'the inverted ladder of the Law of desire' (E, 324), the drive *unlearns* what it means to live and follows its more primordial death-wish – or simply, the *original indifference toward self-preservation* – the psyche becomes initiated into the realm opposite to the biomorphic life, i.e. into the symbolic sphere of language, which can be reached only via the way of the death drive. One set of laws, the *nomos of the Earth*, which teaches all beings natural *conservatio vitae*, becomes thus replaced by another one, the death-governed law of the symbolic. One 'contraction' becomes undone for the sake of another *peras* – this time not natural, but cultural, imposed by the artifice of language. But the cost of this second subordination is the sacrifice of life: the subject initiated into the symbolic sphere no longer lives but, by abiding in death, merely *exists*. By becoming subjects *to* death, we become subjects *of* thought and language – but we also irreversibly lose life.

This is how far the contemporary psychoanalytic theory takes us: to the gates of life and death, Eros and Thanatos, where the choice lies between the *quasi-animality of the biomorphic existence*, with its 'false interiorized biology', on the one hand – and the *humanity of the symbolic existence*, which is conditioned by the law of death, on the other. By assuming that human psyche is fundamentally *nomotropic*, the post-Lacanian psychoanalysis poses in front of us the sole alternative: either we learn to survive, by imitating the self-preservatory 'vital order' and taking on the natural laws of *conservatio vitae* – or we remain faithful to our original inability to survive and follow the sublime law of death, which takes us, its subjects, not only out of nature, but also out of life itself. But my purpose in this book will be to venture beyond that *dualism of biomorphism and thanaticism*, which also means: beyond any nomotropic tendency and into a more dialectical solution where it becomes possible to 'choose life' – this time, choose freely – and once again invert or *turn* the 'ladder of desire' into the life-affirming *errotic* act of *biophilia*.

This second reflexive choice of life is no longer bound by the dualism of Eros and Thanatos and their respective laws; it is beyond both the survivalist imperative of *kata phusein*, on the one hand, and the sublime, anti-naturalist gesture of the withdrawal from life, on the other. In the stage of *biophilia*, life – the true human life – is given new possibilities that could never flourish under either biomorphic or thanatic constraints, but are made possible by the drives' return to their original in/de/finiteness, before they 'contracted' a *peras*, either in the natural or the symbolic form. Now, however, this in/de/finity is no longer just helpless or destructive. No longer opposing life, but affirming it, it subsumes survival and aims at something more, that is, 'more life': a new kind of existence which replaces egotistic self-preservation with other, less necessitarian, goals. This is the moment Hegel calls the 'recollection of freedom', which, in the psychoanalytic paraphrase means: the recovery of the anarchic energy of the drives at the higher 'imaginative' level, when they now *errotically* oppose the nomotropic temptation of the subject which, so far, was looking only for adaptative submission.

It is precisely this *biophilic choice* of which the passage from Deuteronomy speaks: 'I have set before you life and death: choose life' (Deut. 30:19). If the Hebrew Bible narrates its version of a *libidinal theology*, and I will claim that indeed it does – this second dialectical choice constitutes its very gist. The biblical imperative to choose life or believe in life raises above the simple perseverance in life, but also precludes any identification with life-disdaining Thanatos. Neither life-clinging in the biomorphic manner, nor life-negating in the thanatic way – the biophilic option is a free choice of life, life-affirming and life-enhancing, and – this is absolutely crucial here – not just in us, but also in others. The biophilic choice, therefore, is the source of neighbourly love and, as such, the *libidinal foundation of ethics*. The *errotic* freedom loves life which only at first is 'my life': it soon becomes a bedrock of the Wordsworthian 'primal sympathy' which wills and fosters life in all the living.

Seen in the light of this choice, *torat hayim* is simultaneously a *principle* of life, *tradition* of life, *instruction* of life, and the *belief* in life. If, as Laplanche convincingly argues, human life is never just a natural process, then it is always a matter of transmission and instruction that attempts to *persuade psyche into life*. Life, therefore, is never simply transmitted by the biological fact of birth, but must form its own tradition – tradition as symbolic transmissibility – which will format the deficient human being into a living, or rather, in Derridean terms: *living/loving*, entity. But the tradition of life – *torat hayim* – means also that the symbolic sphere is never simply cut off from the 'vital order': it is not based on the thanatic gesture of raising about the 'stupid life',[23] but on *another sublimation* that will continue the elementary instruction how to live, by taking it to the symbolic level. On this account, language, as well as all achievements of culture, religion and philosophy included, could be regarded not as the negation of the natural dimension of *zoe*, but as an *extension* of the tradition of life, or the sublimatory forms of the fundamental *persuasion* into life, which eventually drops the biomorphic pretence of a 'false internalized biology'. For, just as human life is a tradition, so is tradition a life, taking life further, beyond the confines of nature: ever more complex, instruction of 'how to learn to live, finally …'. Creative life and survival do not have to be opposed to one another: once the latter recognizes that it is not a matter of finding the 'lost instinct' of self-preservation, but a matter of symbolic investment into living from the very start, the false dualism between 'mere life' and 'more *than* life' simply collapses. The biophilic *Erros*, therefore, always affirms survival – yet not as a tribute reluctantly paid to our animality, but as a properly human mode of living, all its symbolic articulations included.[4]

The complex *triangulation between biomorphism, thanaticism and biophilism* constitutes the main theme of this book. According to the alternative, more Hegelian, reading of the psychogenetic story, the subject constitutes itself as a gradual recollection (*Erinnerung*) of freedom, which eventually transcends *any* nomotropic/submissive tendency. The real living subjectivity is the formation that ventures simultaneously beyond the necessity of sheer survival and the sublime necessity of self-sacrifice – into a new, always essentially *new*, that is, no longer submissive and mimetic, way of life: it is no longer *initiated*, it *initiates*. Translating this narrative of subjectification into the idiom of late-modern politics, we could say that it wishes to transcend both, the biopolitical paradigm based on the biomorphic law of natural self-preservation – and the sovereign paradigm based on the thanatic law of the 'symbolic suicide'.[5] In order to get constituted as a free living subject, the human psyche has to steer away from nature, or, more precisely, from what presents itself as natural law in the early stage of psychogenesis: the *biomorphic temptation* – but it also needs to steer away from another form of submission, which presents itself as more authentically human, to the Law of Death. *Serving the law* – either in its biomorphic or thanatic variant – is *not* the highest adventure of the subjective life.[6] The true adventure lies in the uncharted territories of *erotic* freedom that chooses life in all its experimental in/de finity, by taking human life *simultaneously* out of nature and out of the dominion of death (which, within the Jewish messianic tradition, both – nature and death – happen to be the synonyms of Egypt, the 'house of bondage').

The denigration of survival

One of the consequences of the late-modern hegemony of the acephalic Neoplatonism is the *denigration of finitude* as a merely privative and vicarious form of being: this default metaphysics also immediately translates into the *denigration of survival* as a merely biological – read: lowest – process unworthy of any symbolic investment. The denigration of survival as falling under the stupid self-contended life-rhythm (Žižek) is the most problematic aspect of the thanatic party, against which my book wants to protest most decidedly, by championing the *torat hayim* as the tradition *of* life in both meanings of the genitive: propagated *by* life, *about* life, and *for* life. Žižek's succinct definition of human subjectivity – 'I am precisely *not* my body: the Self can only arise against the background of the death of its substantial being'[27] – could thus serve as a useful foil against which my version of the living subjectivity will emerge. The coalition, which I want to gather here, can thus also be dubbed as a 'league against death': against the whole thanatic complex of Western philosophy which denigrates survival as a blind animal instinct and extols the inner lack/death/ nothingness of the anthropogenic difference.

Before, however, we close the ranks of the anti-thanatic alliance, the issue of survival must be properly clarified. As we have seen in the previous section, Jewish thinkers often voice their anti-naturalist complaints in which they accuse nature of being too homeostatic, dull, timid, and tautological – in other words, too focused on self-preservation as a 'mere life' which only maintains itself in life. Of all these voices, the most critical belongs to Theodor W. Adorno for whom self-preservation remains a modern nihilistic condition that must be opposed by the proper teaching of life venturing beyond survival. While the epigraph to *Minima Moralia* bitterly states that, in modernity, *life does not live* (MM, 19), the whole positive effort of Adorno's negative dialectics is to prepare historical conditions for the messianic advent of life which would free itself from damage and distortion (*Beschädigung*), and learn to live – finally.

Also in the *Dialectics of Enlightenment*, Adorno and Horkheimer examine the modern construct of subjectivity in constant reference to its relationship with life. On the one hand, they claim that *most* of these constructs are, in fact, nothing but a glorified biological survival based on Thomas Hobbes' doctrine of *conservatio vitae*. On the other, however, they also put whatever hope they still possess into a future subjective formation, capable of exiting the world of natural forces and coining a *happier* way of living, which will have ventured beyond mere survival. If Enlightenment's promise consisted in taking human life out of natural constraints, then modernity did not manage to fulfil it: it merely reproduced the natural conditions of life, in which every singular living being fights for survival, and created the disenchanted 'second nature', imitating the power schemes of the first one. Adorno, therefore, attacks modern 'life which does not live' because, despite all the rhetoric of emancipation, modernity followed the Hobbesian obsession with self-preservation, completely disregarding the other, more 'fantastical' – creative, zetetic, individuating, and joy-orientated – aspect of life. If modern life does not live, it is precisely because it *only* wants to live.

The first part of the *Dialectics*, devoted to the figure of Odysseus as the prototype of the bourgeois ego, serves to demonstrate this paradox: life that defers living infinitely for the sake of the self-defensive maintenance of its own existence and, in consequence, loses itself. The paradox of self-preservation consists, therefore, in what Gershom Scholem, in the different context, called *Leben in Aufschub*: the life-in-deferral that negates real life for the sake of life expected and anticipated, when we will have learned to live and enjoy it – finally.[28] Before that happens, however, the real life is spent in the toil and labour of *conservatio vitae* – also in terms of a meticulous storing of life 'in reserve' for its future consumption – which, the way of the always-cagey Odysseus, walks a thin line between life and death. In order to preserve oneself in existence and store up the potential unused life, the subject must constantly brush against deadly dangers and practise the skills of survival: for a second even, it cannot forget that it can – must, will – die. Firmly tied to the mast of his controlling *ego*, the modern Odysseus resists the temptation of the Syrens, which, for Adorno, represents the forgotten aspect of life: self-questioning risk, hazard, adventure and joy. Of all the figures populating Homeric stories, Odysseus is the most 'natural' and thus boring: despite all the chances to explore and enjoy the uncharted waters he had been offered during the ten years of exile, all he wants is to go home, reunite with his family and reclaim back what was always *his*. Never fully open or attentive to any wonder he encounters in his journeys, he has a deep tendency to see them merely as dangers. Alert only to the possibility of his own demise, he is, in fact, dead already.

This presentiment of dying, which accompanies every representation of the self-preservatory ego, draws life into the pre-established economy of death and turns it, in Freud's formulation from *Beyond the Pleasure Principle* – into 'death's myrmidon'. Adorno's and Horkheimer's account of the self-preservatory life becoming gradually taken over by the thanatic interests parallels Freud's diagnosis very closely:

> *Instinctual life as a whole serves to bring about death*. Seen in this light, the theoretical importance of the instincts of self-preservation, of self-assertion and of mastery greatly diminishes. They are *component instincts* whose function it is to assure that the organism shall follow its own path to death, and to ward off any possible ways of returning to inorganic existence other than those which are immanent in the organism itself. We have no longer to reckon with the organism's puzzling determination (so hard to fit into any context) to maintain its own existence in the face of every obstacle. *What we are left with is the fact that the organism wishes to die only in its own fashion*. Thus these guardians

of life, too, were originally the myrmidons of death. Hence arises the paradoxical situation that the living organism struggles most energetically against events (dangers, in fact) which might help it to attain its life's aim rapidly – by a kind of short-circuit.

FR, 614; my emphasis

Adorno's Odysseus is a subject-slave of his own instinctual ruses and defences which, in the end, turn out only to be the 'component instincts' (*Partialtriebe*) of the death drive: for the sake of the immediate survival, he sacrifices his life and enlists into the service of death. His instinct of self-preservation is so strong that, paradoxically, it makes him unable to live: no longer ready for any living exchange with the world and its 'events', which now appear only as 'dangers', he is already entering 'his own path to death'. He thus embodies the main aporia of the enlightenment which, according to Horkheimer and Adorno, consists in 'the transformation of sacrifice into subjectivity' (DE, 56). Although the enlightenment promised initially to put an end to the mythic practice of sacrifice, which made everything subject to Death, the Absolute Master, it ended up propagating self-sacrifice in terms of a modern hyper-disciplined subject, blindly following the path of self-preservation, once again in the service of the death drive:

> The self rescues itself from dissolution into blind nature, whose claim is constantly proclaimed in sacrifice ... The immense though superfluous sacrifice is required – against sacrifice itself. Odysseus, too, is the self who always restrains himself and forgets his life, who saves his life and yet recalls it only as wandering. *He also is a sacrifice for the abrogation of sacrifice.*
>
> DE, 54–6; my emphasis[29]

Adorno will often come back to the idea of modern subject as a false exit/exodus out of the world of 'blind nature' and its Schopenhauerian principle of universal sacrifice. In *The Jargon of Authenticity*, a pamphlet written mostly against the Heideggerian theory of *Sein-zum-Tode*, Adorno once again attacks the 'idealist' construct of subjectivity as only seemingly free from material constraints. In fact, it is once again determined solely by self-preservation which turns the subject into an empty *tautology*:

> Ever since Spinoza, philosophy has been conscious, in various degrees of clarity, of the *identity between self and self-preservation*. What asserts itself in self-preservation, the ego, is at the same time constituted by self-preservation; its identity constituted by nonidentity ... The Kantian 'I think' is the only abstract reference point in a process of holding out, and not something self-sufficient in relation to that process. To that extent it is already self as self-preservation.[30]

Also the Kantian subject, the product of the most intense 'idealistic sublimation' (ibid.), relies on the empirical given of the non-identical chaotic content of life-to-be-preserved which it merely 'accompanies' and, by accompanying, gathers, collects and protects. Thus, even the Kantian transcendental apperception cannot reverse the relation of priority and establishes itself merely as a more-or-less blind defensive formation, which knows neither what it holds, preserves and defends, nor why it does so – *just* defends. *The self is what preserves itself as preserving itself* – and not the subject that knows itself as knowing. The ground of modern subjectivity is an expression of 'blind nature': a tautological self-defence, more likely to be driven by the Schopenhauerian *Will zum Leben*, than by the idealist self-founding act of a reflexive *Selbstwissen*. The circular form of this empty self-referentiality, which the idealist tradition calls 'the spirit', would thus, in fact, be nothing but the most obstinate remnant of the natural form of existence.

We are thus still in the domain of the modern paradox of 'the life which does not live': the constant focus on self-preservation – the Kantian always vigilant '*I think* accompanying all my representations' – shoves death into the very centre of life. Unceasingly present and turning all 'events' into 'dangers', all 'adventures' into 'hazards', and all 'affective life' into 'pathology', death becomes a guide, a source of existential orientation; this, for Adorno, is the moment of the modern subject's 'thanatic conversion' culminating in Kant, only to be continued by Heidegger. Death, now internalized, functions as a *purge*: it purifies the self by removing all its contents, deemed as pathological threats to the self's formal purity. The 'I', which then 'holds out' as the result of this inner purge, is thus *pure with the purity of the 'new abstraction'* ND, 4): 'dead already' and only in this manner safe – against death. In the end, the subject, far from offering any exodus or respite from the realm of natural forces, turns into a blind tautological machine of self-defence which defends itself so efficiently that it destroys everything it wanted to protect in the first place: indeed, the Schopenhauerian blind impulse of life, now gone even blinder. The self-ascertained and self-secure purity of *cogito* is life so pure that it is life no longer. Or rather, it is a sheer virtual death, unleashing a violent self-purging destruction, a 'monster' of self-preservation: 'The pure tautology, which propagates the concept while at the same time refusing to define that concept – and which instead mechanically repeats the concept – is an intelligence in the form of violence.'[31]

This quotation, which I deliberately took out of its context in order to describe the blind-tautological functioning of the subject, originally refers to Heidegger and his violent style of thinking: this, however, is not an accident. For Adorno, Heidegger, despite all his fervent critique of modernity, must be regarded as the direct heir of Hobbes. The former's *overestimation of death* derives from the obsessive interest in self-preservation that stifles life and paves the way to the sacrificial violence aiming to establish the *pure self* – so pure that, actually, 'already dead':

> Violence inheres in the nucleus of Heidegger's philosophy, as it does in the form of his language. That violence lies in the constellation into which his philosophy moves self-preservation and death. The self-preserving principle threatens its subjects with death, as an *ultima ratio*, a final reason; and when this death is used as the very essence of that principle it means the theodicy of death ... As a limit death not only determines Heidegger's conception of Dasein, but it coincides, in the course of projecting of that conception, with the principle of abstract selfhood, which withdraws absolutely into itself, preserving in itself ... death becomes the core of the self. As soon as it reduces itself completely to itself. Once self has emptied itself of all qualities, on the grounds that they are accidental-actual, then nothing is left but to pronounce that doubly pitiful truth, that the self has to die: *for it is already dead.*
>
> ibid., 133–4, 137; my emphasis[32]

'Constantly affirm survival . . .': the grammar of life

But, would it be possible to think of the survival differently: not as a 'monster' of *conservatio vitae*, which kills life supposedly for life's sake, but rather as this other, Canguilhemian, 'monstrosity' that pushes in the more adventurous and 'fantastical' direction and leads the most intense life, precisely in confrontation with its mortality? And wouldn't it be what Heidegger himself intended to achieve by giving us his first definition of 'being-towards-death' as a life-intensifying condition of finitude?

Such a possibility is offered by late Derrida who most convincingly answers the questions posed by Adorno's critique and, at the same time, realizes the best intentions of Heidegger's project without implicating it in the thanatic syndrome. Unlike the Adornian self-preservation which is always based on the aporia of *self-purification* – aiming at life so pure that in the end it can only achieve death – Derrida's version of survival is based on *contamination*: the originary impurity and insoluble aporecity of all processes building up human life as life-death, *la vie le mort*.

For Derrida – the last, but certainly not the least member of the 'league against death' – survival is *not* rooted in the Hobbesian paradigm of the natural *conservatio vitae*. For him – just as for the whole Jewish tradition of life, speaking the Herderian idiom *avant la lettre* – survival is never a biological *factum brutum* which is to be either accepted as a self-evident cornerstone of modern naturalism, or rejected as 'stupid' or 'unworthy' for the very same reason, but a symbolic object of a *torat hayim*. More than that, the 'teaching of life' gains new significance after the Holocaust: it is the instruction how to live – *again*, as well as *finally* – which deliberately and consciously 'chooses life' in an apotropaic gesture against the thanatic horrors of Shoah. Derrida's claim – 'Auschwitz has obsessed everything I have ever been able to think'[33] – has thus to be taken fully seriously. For Derrida, the right definition of the finite life is not *Sein-zum-Tode*, understood either in biomorphic or thanatic manner, but the *survival* which has a symbolic tradition behind it: it is a *problematic* form of life, which must be taught and learnt. Hence his figure of 'learning to live finally' where the finality of *vivre finalement* refers both to the experience of real finitude and the desire to grasp the symbolic strategy of coping with it:

> Someone, you or me, comes forward and says: I would like to learn to live finally. Finally but why? To learn to live: a strange watchword. Who would learn? From whom? To teach to live, but to whom? Will we ever know? Will we ever know how to live and first of all what 'to learn to live' means? And why 'finally' ... By itself, out of context – but a context, always, remains open, thus fallible and insufficient – this watchword forms an almost unintelligible syntagm. Just how far can its idiom be translated moreover? ... A magisterial locution, all the same – or for that very reason. For from the lips of a master this watchword would always say something about violence. It vibrates like an arrow in the course of an irreversible and asymmetrical address, the one that goes most often from father to son, master to disciple, or master to slave ('I'm going to teach you to live') ... *And yet nothing is more necessary than this wisdom*. It is ethics itself: to learn to live-alone, from oneself, by oneself. *Life does not know how to live otherwise*. And does one ever do anything else but learn to live, alone, from oneself, by oneself? This is, therefore, a strange commitment, both impossible and necessary, for a *living being supposed to be alive*: 'I would like to learn to live.' *It has no sense and cannot have unless it comes to terms with death*. Mine as (well as) that of the other. *Between life and death*, then, this is indeed the place of a sententious injunction that always feigns to speak like the just.
>
> S.M, xvi–xvii; my emphasis

This passage, appearing in the Exordium to the *Specters of Marx*, contains Derrida's latest, messianico-vitalist, project in the nutshell. The *torat hayim*, this 'intangible Jewish principle'[34] concentrates around the 'unintelligible syntagm' or the 'magisterial locution' of the injunction to live and choose life well because 'life does not know how to live otherwise': survival is not a spontaneous biological know-how of *conservatio vitae* but a complex symbolic ratio between life and death, which we all must learn ourselves, only helped by the conceptual props or *prosthesis* of tradition. The phrase *I-would-like-to-learn-to-live-finally* is a 'watchword', a slogan, a shibboleth even, which, for late Derrida, would single out those inscribing themselves into the Book of Life (most of all writers: Hugo, Montaigne, Cixous and Blanchot, as long as he does not philosophize) against the prevalent philosophical Tradition of Death (Kant, Hegel, Heidegger, Lacan and Blanchot-the-thinker). This life, however, is not Life, the new Absolute insinuating itself in the place vacated by the divine transcendence: always posed 'between life and death', it is a finite singular life which must cope with its limitation, yet does not lose ontological significance because of its limits. On the contrary, the 'sententious injunction' forms the very core of the 'religion of the living' which, for Derrida, is simply a tautology, but, unlike in Adorno, certainly not an empty one: a tautological affirmation of life which, in order to live, must affirm itself and *believe in itself* – again and again: emphatically, insistently, *religiously*.[35]

This pre-affirmation belongs necessarily to the phenomenon of life understood as the symbolic effort of living-on, and not as a biological (or biomorphic) process *kata phusein*: *life does not know how to live unless it loves itself*. The Derridean 'living/loving', which replaces the Heideggerian 'living/dying', is his version of *love strong as death*, forming the 'intangible principle' of the Jewish *torat hayim*: 'Living-loving … Life loves itself in the living being, life loves itself, period, it loves to live, it loves itself in living for life. This love is its relation to itself, its self-intimacy with itself, its inevitable self-intimacy with itself, before any other supposed interiority' (DP2, 111).

Living/loving, or the self-preferential essence of all life, is tautological to a T – and yet, its self-referential and self-mirroring nature does not imply the Adornian deadening self-purification: while anxiety is and must be the part of life in survival mode, it is also balanced – 'accompanied' – by the self-intimacy of love in which 'life loves itself, period'. It is precisely this *tautological love*, not bound to any concrete physiological defence, this seemingly abstract 'life loving itself in the living being', which denaturalizes life in the non-thanatic way: as such, it does not belong to the Book of Nature but to the other Book.

No surprise, therefore, that the last words of Derrida were: 'Always prefer life and constantly affirm survival' (*Préférez toujours la vie et affirmez sans cesse la survie*).[36] While the first part of the imperative contains the biblical cryptoquotation – 'I set in front of you life and death: choose life!' – the second appeals to us, late-moderns, to seriously rethink our attitude towards life in its finitude in terms of survival. Choose *vie*, yes – but also affirm it as *sur-vie*, 'more-life'. We will yet see how vitally important, ambivalent and 'double-bound' this *more* can be, but Derrida's aim is to keep it 'in life, and for life': not as a projection of Life infinite and indestructible, the phantasmatic unscathed object of our desire, but as *this* life, ordinary, liveable, which inescapably ends but does not have to be determined by its *finis* (hence *sur*, as the hyper-natural, symbolic dimension of the finite life). This is the last testament of Jacques Derrida that this book wants to follow – the testament in the double sense of: bearing as direct witness to finitude as possible (last words), but also, perhaps, attempting to found a new form of religious sensibility or simply reveal the original core of the ancient messianic belief: *messianic vitalism as the religion of the finite life*. When, in his last seminars, Derrida states that the goal of his new philosophy of life is not to be 'robbed of the finitude' (DP1, 256), as if it were a most precious treasure, he locates himself on the furthest possible pole to the denigration of survival, which still blocks the passage to the future metaphysics of finitude no longer conceived as privation. Here, it is no longer immortality that matters but finitude lived as life, the stubborn 'middle of life', which suspends its own end in the living/loving act of self-belief or self-preference.

The self-preference – the living/loving where love is as strong as death – is Derrida's own coinage that, according to him, should replace the traditional category of self-preservation, too entangled in the natural/biological context of unreflective instinct (no matter whether real or merely 'mimed'). What, therefore, for Adorno and other critics of the modern Hobbesian paradigm, constitutes the empty tautology of pure self-relationality which 'preserves itself as self-preserving', for Derrida becomes the positive fact of life as living and loving itself. The tautology of self-preference, therefore, is not a sign of emptiness as a deadly lack of content, but a beginning of a self-creative subjective process which can only express itself in the narrative form of auto-bio-graphy: if, for Derrida, humans are predominantly 'auto-bio-graphical animals', it is because they write/invent themselves as they go along. There is initially nothing to express: just the primary in/de/finity which can only affirm itself and then begin to assert itself as a new mode of living. Just as the transmission of life is not a simple biological process but a tradition that persuades the recipient into taking up the living, so is the human way of negotiating survival a matter of an incessant symbolic affirmation/assertion: no living-on without loving-on which can only *go with saying* – saying Yes to life, always confirming the original choice.

Already in his early text on Blanchot, called 'Living-On', Derrida spots the *creatio ex nihilo* performative effect of the self-preferential tautology of life:

> narrative as *reaffirmation* (yes, yes) of life, in which the *yes*, which says nothing,
> *describes nothing but itself*, the performance of its own event of affirmation,
> repeats itself, quotes, cites itself, says *yes-to* itself as (to an-) other, in accordance
> with the ring, requotes and recites a commitment that would not take place
> outside this repetition of a *performance without presence*. This strange ring says
> *yes* to life only in the overdetermining ambiguity of the triumph *de* (of, over) life,
> *sur* (over, on) life, the triumph marked in the 'on' of 'living on' [*le sur d'un*
> *survivre*].[37]

Two decades later, in his enthusiastic appraisal of Helene Cixous's literary achievement, Derrida will once again come back to Shelley/Blanchot's *Triumph of Life* and its 'strange ring' of autoteleological yes-saying, which he now – in accordance with the subtle Marrano *clinamen* of the vocabulary that he uses in the dialogue with his Algerian-Jewish friend – calls a 'miracle of a chant of enchantment, which is also a song of songs' (HCL, 79). While positioning Cixous 'on the side of life', Derrida locates himself tentatively 'on the side of death', but then immediately admits that death cannot be treated as a 'side', or an *opposition* to life which indeed resembles a 'middle' or a rounded *medium* with no edges. He thus quotes his favourite paragraph 49 of *Being and Time*, where Heidegger insists that, for him, death must be always kept *Diesseits*, on this side of life, and never be treated as a possible vehicle of *Jenseits*, the 'other side' of the transcendent beyond:

> This [Helene Cixous's] 'for life' is not a *being* for life symmetrically opposed to
> the famous *Sein zum Tode*, being-towards-death, as its other side … Against
> the metaphysics of death, which are interested in the beyond, that is to say
> in the other side (*Jenseits*), Heidegger recalls that one must, on the contrary,
> methodically depart and remain *here on this side*, on the side of *this* side, on the
> side of the here and the here below (*das Diesseits*) … the Here Below and the
> Beyond … Unfortunately, he does not call this 'life', a life before the opposition
> between life and death.
>
>   HCL, 88

But this is precisely what Derrida aims at: to recognize the difficult integrity of the phenomenon called *la vie le mort*, before it bifurcates into oppositions and antitheses, Eros and Thanatos, this side and the other. Seen from the perspective of Here Below, death is to be imagined as a boundary that accompanies life in its adventure in finitude, without pre-empting it from the start as fallen, futile or *lebensunwertig*, not-worthy-of-living: a boundary that can be stretched, hit against in order to expand the 'middle', but this 'against' does not have a force of a full opposition. 'Life death' are thrown in together, almost identical and yet different, but with the difference which yet escapes the dialectics (or, perhaps, cannot even be posed as a contradiction, aporia, or paradox): 'No, life *for* life (and not being-for-life) is therefore nothing else than a living of death, but yes, still living death, living it for oneself, for the other, and for life. Later we will call this experience, or even experimentation: living for the sake of the living, and in order to see – what it feels like, just to try' (HCL, 89).

Derrida will always remain faithful to this project – Heidegger's insistence of rethinking death within the immanence of life – which he also sees as failed and abandoned by Heidegger himself. For, in Heidegger, death inevitably becomes a *beyond* of life, just as in Freud's *Beyond the Pleasure Principle*, where '*for life* would be around here at the service of *for death*' (HCL, 109), or in Kojève's reading of Hegel as the first proper 'metaphysician of death'. No, life can never free itself of death, it is always a survival: a coterminality of life and death so strict that it cannot hope for any dialectical re/dis/solution. And yes, death stays *Diesseits*, which means: death should be acknowledged, but never overestimated. Given room in life – but not *all* the room, so that 'life death' could *still* be *living* death: even if death, still, *nonetheless*, life too. Life not completely deprived of its power – 'might' – of the argument.

Already in *Being and Time*, Heidegger ruins his radical thesis on 'remaining on this side' by introducing the privileged mode of authenticity which once again uses death as the sublime vehicle of *Aufschwung*: the rise above the fallen dimension of Dasein conceived as 'Here Below', *das Diesseits*. Setting himself against this thanatic sublimation and following Canguilhem's definition of life as a constant trial-by-error impromptu, Derrida intuits life as an experience/experimentation, which 'goes in all directions' of the expanded 'Here Below' just in order to try it: what defines life is a spontaneous thrust of *autoteleology*, where life becomes a self-referential and self-preferential process of 'living for the sake of living', *whatever* that may mean or bring. The preposition 'for' in the phrase 'for life' cannot thus be juxtaposed on the same plane with the Heideggerian 'being-for/towards-death', because it announces a different relationship: not of a being as it is, issuing or resulting in its end and thus defined by it, but of a life engaged in autoteleology and autotautology, in which it would most likely wish to stay forever. The 'for' does not refer life 'as it is' to its conclusion/definition; it does not give us a philosophical knowledge of what is life's essence. On the contrary, it encloses life in its own enchanted circle of tautological and autotelic self-preference, which, steering away from any definition, echoes the *la* from the Hebrew blessing of *la hayim*, secretly sent to Cixous and her bright magic of life with love: 'the *for* of *for life* upsets the authority of the "it is," of the essence, of the "what life is"' (HCL, 84). 'Life is life: period', as Derrida will say succinctly few years later (BS1, 307): it must be acknowledged in its originally autotelic and autotautological dimension that defies any deadening-reifying attempt of capture-essentialization. Life is a thing of un-essence, as Rosenzweig originally states (see Chapter 1), and Derrida endorses:

> This 'for', this *pro-* would become the prologomenon of everything, it would be said before any *logos*, it goes in all directions, that of finality or of destination, of the gift, donation and dativity, but also of substitution and replacement: this *for* that, this one *in the place of* the other . . . This 'for' conditions the meaning of 'life'.
>
> HCL, 87

More than that, Derrida is even ready to concede to Cixous that life, in order to assert itself as such, must forget about death, unlearn it, stop believing in it, and then proceed *as if* it *might* [*puisse*] be omnipotent and all-life, all *à côté de vie*, with no impediment in sight, self-raised and self-begotten by its own quickening power, bursting with its performative 'might': this is the reason why the whole essay is written under the redemptive aegis of *sub*junctive/*sub*jective/*sub*versive taking sides – of life, *as if* life might never end, never expire. 'Would that I might . . .', 'I wish I might . . .': this is, to use Rosenzweigian idiom, the wishful – but also stubborn, defiant, subversive – 'grammar of life':

> For she – because she loves to live – does not believe me. She, on her side, knows well that one dies in the end, too quickly; . . . she has the knowledge of it but she believes none of it. *She does not believe, she knows* . . . And I say to myself, on my side: 'Would that I might [*puissé-je*] believe her, I wish I *might*, yes, I wish I might believe her, where she believes none of it, when I say to her that one dies in the end, too quickly' . . . But maybe, maybe it is *as if* I believed her already, yes, if I could, and so she was indeed right – and I wrong in saying and repeating, on my side, because I love living too: 'We die in the end, too quickly'.
>
> HCL, 2; my emphasis

She does not believe, she knows – this sober knowledge refers to the fact of dying, in the end and always too quickly. Cixous knows she is going to die, but concedes to death nothing more: no special intimacy with a death drive and no spiritual investment in any 'metaphysics of death', which would turn her, as it eventually happened with Heidegger (and Freud, Kojève, Lacan, Blanchot, Žižek and so many others) into a death's *believer*. All the 'magic' goes to the other side:

for-life, la-hayim, where it forms 'a singular, almost interminable argument' (ibid.). This argument for-life is indeed singular because, on the cognitive plane, nothing changes: 'We die in the end, too quickly.' Yet what changes and transforms the whole picture from within, is the grammatical mode: the ontological statement, in which death, in the Heideggerian manner, appears as the truth, goal and essence of life, shifts to the subjunctive clause in which life finally finds its defiant means of articulation. And the moment Derrida begins to speak in subjunctives, he is already *converted*: to her side, the side of life which knows death but does not believe it, because it can only believe in itself. He is thus suddenly on the side of the peculiar religion of the finite life, which, as in the quote on Benjamin, does everything for life and in life, in the enchanted circle, the 'song of songs' or 'strange ring' of autoteleology, where life only wants 'more life' (which is one of the possible translations of *la hayim*, offered by Harold Bloom), more life Here Below, *Diesseits*, without any resort to 'more-than-life' in the sublime Beyond. *As if* there were nothing else but life infinitely loving and preferring itself: 'the chance of my salvation, the salvation that I owe and which we probably all owe Helene Cixous here today' (HCL, 69).

So, as long as the finite life understands its inherent subjunctive grammar of *as if* – the way Cixous grasps it – there is no danger of the phantasmatic dimension of life unscathed and infinite alienating itself into a false ontological reality of a divine immortal Absolute. As long as the forgetfulness of death remains a ruse of life and nothing but the ruse, it's fine. *As if*, therefore, of the subjunctive/subjective is the key here, also for an understanding of the 'for' which, for Derrida, determines the meaning of 'life' as a self-performative enterprise, pulling itself (as if) from nothing into something: ' *"might"* [*puisse*] is the absolute performative. Any performative, any phantasmatic omnipotence of the performative draws from the mighty power of this "might". . . . *The subjunctive is mightier, from the subordinate clause, than the ontological main clause*' (HCL, 104–5; my emphasis).

The last sentence can indeed be read as a sophisticated paraphrase of 'love strong as death': love, uttered in the grammar of subjunctive, as mighty or even mightier than death, stated in the constative mode. Life, therefore, is a strange 'magic' that cannot be forced back into the constative language of being and its essences; it somehow manages to escape the ontological clauses and evacuates itself out of being by its own path. And it does so thanks to its own singular grammar of autotelic self-performance, so well captured by Milton's Satan from *Paradise Lost*, whom Bloom with good reasons perceives as the best embodiment of the Hebrew blessing: 'self-begot, self-raised by our own quickening power'. A rich tautology of 'for-life', *la hayim*, in which life tells itself into life and uses the phantasy of omnipotence in order to stretch the boundary called death and achieve, at least, a little 'more-life' Here Below.

For, if life did not have the narcissistic 'might' to imagine itself as omnipotent, it would be immediately crashed by the fateful powers of *Ananke* and violently 'submitted to the supremacy of death', as Freud announces in *Totem and Taboo*.[38] In his apology of Cixous's version of the *Triumph of Life*, Derrida defends her not only against Heidegger's *Todesdenken*, which, despite his own declaration, catapults straight into a new 'metaphysics of death', but also against Freud who in the severe 'recognition of *Ananke*' sees the necessary realistic correction to narcissism and its magic: 'The work and thought of H.C. are and are not a hylozoism, and the omnipotence of thoughts at work in what she writes is nothing but a *modest, loving thought of what the subjunctivity of omnipotence might be*. Call that desire, the sublimated beauty of desire or the desire of sublime beauty if you like' (HCL, 116; my emphasis).

What I am attempting here is in a way nothing but a modest loving midrash to this wisdom that I will also try to defend against Heidegger and Freud alike. The messianic vitalism is not about an ontological display of Life's infinite power or the grandiose 'metaphysics of life' opposed to the 'metaphysics of death', but a *belief* in life, which tests the 'might' of this belief as nothing but belief from the point of view of the singular living: the religion of the finite life. It is all about the self-chosen and self-preferred yes to life as 'living for the sake of the living in order to see – what it feels like, just to try' (HCL, 89). My variant of *torat hayim* is thus also a performative act of re-enchanting persuasion that proceeds along the subjunctive logic of the 'song of songs': *would that life might believe in itself . . . would that it live . . .* For, what might life indeed achieve if it truly believed in itself despite the blows of disenchantment? What would it be capable of?

The grammar of *sur-vie* will thus be the sole topic here: the non-biological, phenomenological and quasi-transcendental definition of the finite life as self-preference or self-belief, taking the autoteleological form of 'living/loving', with which I will attempt to replace the Heideggerian notion of the finite life as based on the principle of *Verendlichung*, i.e. the veri-dictive closure/capture/definition/essentialization of life by death. The Derridean equivalent of Kant's transcendental apperception accompanying all representations, therefore, is not the empty or dead-already 'I think', but 'love in its relation to itself, its self-intimacy with itself, its inevitable self-intimacy with itself, before any other supposed interiority' (DP2, 111). Love which, by affirming the primary in/de/finity, opens the subject to the infinite singularity of the life-narrative which, as Hegel once said of the spirit and its powers of *creatio ex nihilo*, 'magically' converts nothing of a human's original deficiency into something: his or her free reflexive and self-creative life.[39]

This specific choice explains why in what follows I am *not* going to write about or, at least, not analyse in detail: (1) biopolitics, either in its critical or affirmative version (Foucault, Esposito); (2) contemporary revision of *Lebensphilosophie* or philosophy of life which still sports the phantasmatic vision of Life infinite (Deleuze, Agamben); and (3) philosophy of 'undeadness', which, following Heidegger, no longer conceives human existence in terms of life (Kojève, Blanchot, Lacan, Žižek). In fact, somewhat paradoxically, in my defence of messianic vitalism, I want to steer away from *all* late-modern forms of vitalistic approaches which simply do not give justice to the idea of the finite life. If Gilles Deleuze can claim that 'everything I've written is vitalistic', i.e. in the praise of '*A Life*' which neither knows death nor wants to hear about it, and in which 'it's organisms that die, not life'[40] – then, indeed, I don't want to know or hear about that form of metaphysical vitalism. And while the Kojèvian-Lacanian solution would seem the closest to the vision of the originally distorted/denaturalized human animality out of joint, it too will have to be rejected, because, ultimately, it gives up on life altogether, either indestructible or finite. For Lacan, there is no human animal, but there is also no Hegelian 'life of the spirit': the spirit is merely animated by the 'death drive as the "undead" obscene immortality of a repetition which insists beyond life and death'.[41]

My topic, therefore, will be neither *natural* life, nor *phantasmatic* life – but also not the 'obscene immortality' of the undeadness constituting the thanatic reverse of the former. It will be *human* finite life understood primarily as the Derridean *sur-vie*, approached in the combination of three perspectives: phenomenological, theological and deconstructive. It will thus be a certain version of the phenomenology of life, written 'subjunctively' from the first person perspective of the living subject, according to Canguilhem's formula that the knowledge of life is always a knowledge of *the* particular life which wants to know itself – or rather, in my retelling of the story, to *believe* or put *confidence* in itself. A *version*, because it will not follow the 'radical phenomenology of life' as originally created by Michel Henry, but immediately constitute a Jewish *clinamen* from the Christian line and develop *torat hayim* not on the basis of the experience of incarnation but on the basis of the experience of *sur-vie*. Its theological patron, therefore, will not be Christ, the infinite God made finite flesh in order to conquer death, but Jacob, the Jewish hero of survival, who, marked with the wound of finitude, stubbornly limps through the desert.

Although both – Henry's and Derrida's – phenomenological approaches are essentially affirmative towards finite life, they nonetheless stress different aspects. While the former emphasizes God's love for the finite body, or the miracle of embodiment which promises an advent of pure life triumphing over death, a pure shiny 'essence of manifestation' – the latter focuses on the self-love that must sustain the finite life in its 'constant affirmation of survival', and thus in a necessary intertwinement with death.[42] In his polemical footnote about Michel Henry's vitalistic interpretation of Marx,[43] Derrida explains that it is precisely this intertwinement that 'forbids simply opposing the living to the non-living': the very idea of a 'living subjectivity' implies a contamination of life and death, so it simply cannot be captured in terms of a pure vitalistic ontological process with all negativity conquered and dispelled. Instead, therefore, of insisting on the phantasm of life infinite, which, in the Pauline way, would have become life pure and uncontaminated by 'the non-living':

> We are attempting something else. To try to accede to the possibility of this very alternative (life and/or death), we are directing our attention to the effects or the petitions of a survival or of a return of the dead (neither life nor death) on the sole basis of which one is able to speak of 'living subjectivity' (in opposition to *its* death): to speak of it but also to understand that it can, itself, speak and speak of itself, leave traces or legacies *beyond the living present* of its life, ask (itself) questions regarding its own subject, in short, also address itself to the other or, if one prefers, to other living individuals, to other 'monads'.
>
> SM, 235–6, fn; my emphasis

In this book, I will be standing firmly on Derrida's position: the impersonal Life eternal – the highest and most pleromatic life, completely full in its immanentist 'living present', the cherished object of the 'metaphysics of life' – is an 'absolute evil', because, from the perspective of *the* singular living, it equals 'pure death': no separation, no fragmentation, no boundaries between the 'monads' spell the annihilation of every finite particularity for the sake of the monotonous power of '*A* Life' as the new Absolute. In the *Specters of Marx*, Derrida could not be clearer on this point, by reminding us that 'this absolute evil (which is, is it not, *absolute life, fully present life, the one that does not know death and does not want to hear about it*) can take place' (SM, 220; my emphasis).[44] Indeed, it can and constantly does, because it belongs to the strongest *phantasmata* that life constantly dreams about itself, always recreating some ontological variant of life pure and eternal, whether in an openly theological transcendent manner or merely in a cryptotheological immanent one. And if pure life as well as pure death – the uncontaminated vitalistic will-to-power and the nirvanic rest-in-peace – are phantasmatic, it is precisely because of their *purity*: they can never enter the ordinary life tarrying with the necessity of survival. As Derrida says in his last interview, pointing to the internal tensions of *sur-vie*: 'I sometimes see this war [of life] as terrifying and difficult to bear, but at the same time I know that that is life. I will find peace only in eternal rest' (LLF, 47).[45]

There is thus no Shabbath for survival, no seventh day of worklessness, tasklessness and leisurely *désœuvrement*; there are only six days of ceaseless ordeal *bamidbar*. But if limping Jacob, the Hebrew emblem of the finite life, still manages to ramble through the desert, it is only due to the *pharmakon* of death, incorporated into the life process in a small measure that serves the purpose of life's immunization. This is, if you will, a Jewish Nietzsche: Jacob, not killed by the trauma, but immunized by it, made stronger, the ultimate hero of survival, living-on 'the most intense life possible'. In the concluding, particularly dense fragment of *Learning to Live Finally*, Derrida, once again echoing his praise of Helene Cixous, says:

> already from the beginning, and well before the experiences of surviving [survivance] are at the moment mine, I maintained that *survival is an originary concept that constitutes the very structure of what we call existence*, Dasein, if you will. *We are structurally survivors*, marked by this structure of the trace and of the testament. But having said that, I would not want to encourage an interpretation that situates surviving on the side of death and the past rather than life and the future. *No, deconstruction is always on the side of the yes, on the side of the affirmation of life*. Everything I say – at least from 'Pas' on – about survival as a complication of the opposition life/death proceeds in me from an *unconditioned affirmation of life*. This surviving is life beyond life, life more than life, and my discourse is not a discourse of death, but, on the contrary, the affirmation of a living being who prefers living and thus surviving to death, because survival is not simply that which remains, but *the most intense life possible*.
>
> LLF, 51–2; my emphasis

It is not an accident that Derrida refers here directly to Heidegger's Dasein: his emphasis on the positive concept of survival as not 'that which remains', or the nihilizing and finitizing factor 'on the side of death', but as a constant incentive and occasion to 'unconditionally affirm life', is precisely what is missing in Heidegger's own execution of *Sein-zum-Tode*.

Many books have been written about finitude: most of them, following Heidegger's explicit choice, from the perspective of its end.[46] My goal, however, will be different: to rewrite the story of finitude in such a way that it truly turns into a *belief* in the finite life, boosting it with a new self-confidence. Hence the strong connection with the theological – or better, psychotheological – dimension of the messianic vitalism which sees life as most of all an *autoreligion*: there is no life without belief in life as there is no survival without the constant affirmation of survival. Convinced, after Derrida, that 'religion of the living is the tautology' (AR, 85), I want to explore the 'psychotheology of everyday life' in terms of belief, persuasion, confession, promise and conversion, and see if the seemingly impossible – the religion of the finite life – is, 'perhaps, perhaps' quite possible after all.[47]

Part One

Love Strong as Death: Polemics

Falling – in Love

Rosenzweig Versus Heidegger

Could we forget about Heidegger altogether? *Oubliez Heidegger?* The thought appears tempting, especially after all the revelations about his unabashed Nazi involvement in *Black Notebooks*, which bring the fiercest imaginable attack on the figure of the 'metaphysical Jew', and, for some readers, deliver nothing short of the philosophical justification for the Shoah.[1] Yet, if Heidegger's thought continues to inspire today, it is because of what still appears as a valid promise of *der neue Anfang*, the 'new beginning': the new thinking of finitude which will overcome the hubristic 'gigantism' of modern *Machenschaft*, supposedly represented by the 'metaphysical Jew', and return to the 'blessing of the limits', i.e. to the reconciliation with the finite condition of living within the natural immanence.

It is precisely this promise, and the hope that goes with it, that I want to challenge in this chapter. As long as it is not counteracted by an alternative philosophy of finitude, Heidegger's name will persist as a major inspiration for all late-modern thought wishing to get beyond the crisis of modernity, which has been caused by the 'machinating' subject, assaulting the finite world from the transcendent position. *Black Notebooks* leave no doubt that the most pernicious concretization of the hubristic modern subjectivity is the 'metaphysical Jew': the 'principle of destruction', *Seinsvergessenheit*, the forgetfulness of Being, and thus also – last, but not least – *Verfallenheit*, the fallenness that repeats the modern Fall from Being on the existential level.[2]

I thus want to present a possibility of a different thinking of finitude, which – by a twist of irony – derives directly 'out of the sources of Judaism'. Heidegger had been writing against Jews with a vicious consequence, presenting them as agents of machinating 'gigantism' and the deepest *Verfallenheit* – but Jews have been writing again Heidegger too, by attempting to fight him on his own grounds: the philosophy of the finite condition, which – even more ironically – reclaims the 'fallenness' and its 'passion of facticity' as the true and only dimension of human life, which, in Heidegger's own words, is indeed 'completely fascinated by the "world" and by the Dasein-with of Others' (BT, 220). For, contrary to the cliché Heidegger believed in, Jewish thought does not foster the idea of humanity's infinite power over nature, given by God to his absolute disposal; it is not about ruthless and detached calculation based on what Hegel called Abraham's incapability to love. Quite the contrary: *it is all about setting the limits*, but not by the regressive recourse to the natural boundary in the form of death. If the limits prove to be a blessing, it is not because humankind is forced to return meekly to the totality of Being, by becoming its obedient shepherd who hearkens to its call in the humble posture of *Seinsgehören*. The only possible limit for the human subject is the *other*: the freely chosen self-limitation in the form of neighbourly love.

In his critique of Heidegger in *Entre Nous*, Lévinas complains that in his death-dominated and death-orientated thought there is no place for being-with-the-other. *Sein-zum-Tode*, being-towards-death, is a solitary enterprise, and the only *Mitsein* (being-with) which Heidegger envisages in the end boils down, as Lévinas maliciously remarks, to *Zusammenmarchieren*, marching with: an army of isolated Daseins exercising their authenticity in their totally mobilized *Todesbereitschaft*, 'readiness for death'.[3] But Lévinas is not the first and not the only Jewish philosopher who uttered his objection to Heidegger's *overestimation of death* as the factor determining the finite condition. In fact, there is a whole secret alliance of thinkers opposed to what Harold Bloom, himself a member of the group, called somewhat derisively 'Heidegger and his French flock' (AI, xxvii). Despite all the differences between them, Franz Rosenzweig, Hannah Arendt, Emmanuel Lévinas, Harold Bloom and Jacques Derrida form an unofficial coalition of thinkers contesting the Heideggerian mode of thinking finitude solely under the auspices of death.

There is also one further feature that they share: the importance of the intellectual heritage of the *Song of Songs*. *Pace* the clichéd prejudice, both Christian and Romantic, that perceives Judaism as a mechanical – and thus also machinating – religion of the law, *Shir ha-Shirim* proves that indeed, this has never been anything but prejudice. Hegel could not have been more wrong when he famously stated that 'Abraham wanted not to love, wanted to be free by not loving.'[4] Love that is strong as death – this 'privileged formulation'[5] – sheds light on a completely different vision of the finite life in which love, not death, becomes the defining marker of the finitude. Here, the sought-after limit reveals itself through neighbourly love – and it is always and only the other.

In all these approaches, *Shir ha-Shirim* lends itself to the philosophical speculation that offers a different conception of the finite existence, destined to die but no means exhausted by its lethal destiny; determined to resist the final verdict and gain an intense 'life before death', marked by passionate relations with others; limited, yet not by the inner boundary / *peras* of death, but by the existence of those we love. Far from being obedient 'Heidegger's children',[6] Rosenzweig, Arendt, Bloom and Derrida offer instead a promise of a different thinking about the finite life, which is not fated with the Heideggerian thanatic closure: a truly non-privative, open and love-capable *another finitude*. What Nancy summed up in a brilliant stroke of genius – that *finitude is not privation* – is their sole theme and concern:

> Finitude is not the being-finished-off of an existent ... butting up against and stumbling over its own limit (its contingency, error, imperfection, or fault). *Finitude is not privation.* There is perhaps no proposition that is more necessary to articulate today, to scrutinize and test in all ways. Everything at stake at the end of philosophy comes together there: in the need of having to open the thought of finitude, that is, to reopen to itself this thought, which haunts and mesmerizes our entire tradition.
>
> SOTW, 29

If what we are looking for is a philosophy that could do away with the remnants of the acephalic Neoplatonism that continues to measure up everything towards the infinite, *another finitude* constitutes a solid answer. Love as the marker of finitude deprives it of the stigma of privation and negativity, always implicit in death where Dasein is 'butting up against and stumbling over its own limit'. Here, the un-essence, transience, indefinity, contingency no longer emerge as negative features of the finite being *in passing*, but as the condition of the Derridean 'living/ loving' which loves itself infinitely, yet finds the blessing of limits in intense relations with others. As we remember from the previous chapter, Derrida attempts a translation of Dasein as 'Here Below' where the 'belowness' accentuates the *Diesseits*, the *this-side'y* dimension of the analytics of Dasein properly understood, as opposed to *Jenseits*, the 'other side' of death that catapults the existence above the 'fallen' life into the more essential and authentic 'beyond'. Here I would like to see if the 'fallenness' of this 'Here Below' can be revindicated as another kind of a Fall: *falling-for-life* and, at the same time, *falling-in-love*.

A different death?

Rosenzweig was never properly exposed to Heidegger's own thought, but nonetheless reacted to the depressingly thanatic climate of his epoch, by trying to resist it.[7] Rosenzweig's main question, especially in his later period when he began to conceive his New Thinking, was: is it possible at all to think about our finitude differently, not under the auspices of death – the end, the goal, the final destiny, the ultimate verdict? The whole point of Rosenzweig's *Neues Denken* is to venture precisely such an endeavour: to try to think finitude *positively*, against the long philosophical tradition that stigmatized it as privation. Although often seen as a parallel to Heidegger's analytics of Dasein, Rosenzweig's New Thinking is actually the very opposite: despite many deceptively similar formulations, which also portray life as issuing towards death, it is uniquely concerned with the question that could never be properly answered by Heidegger, namely – *Is life before death possible?* Can living assert itself as such and not be immediately identified with dying?

The seeming paradox, therefore, consists in the simultaneous defence of life as *finite* and as *life*: not the shadow of death that informs and paralyses the vital forces at the moment of their inception, but a full 'healthy' life which recognizes the 'sovereignty of death' (USH, 103) and still affirms itself as a separate category of being. The little book of Rosenzweig called *Understanding the Sick and the Healthy* endeavours to teach life the lesson of maintaining itself in this paradox without solving or sublating it:

> By teaching man to live again, we have taught him to move towards death; we have taught him to live, though each step he takes brings him closer to death … There is no remedy for death; not even health. A healthy man, however, has the strength to continue towards the grave. The sick man invokes death and lets himself be carried away in mortal fear. In health, even death comes at the 'proper' time.
>
> USH, 102–3

All appearances to the contrary, this is *not* Heidegger's *Sein-zum-Tode*: it is already a polemical reaction to 'being-towards-death', issued from the perspective of the *torat hayim*, the 'tradition of life' that *teaches how to live* – 'again', i.e. after the late-modern Man has been violently reconfronted with his finitude. The little, yet decisive, difference lies in the emphasis Rosenzweig puts on the active resistance of life against death's chilling influence: on the way the 'healthy' subject *moves* or *continues* towards death, despite the constant danger of 'the paralysis of artificial death', or the 'death in life' that would stop him from moving on. Despite death's declared sovereignty, life, which eventually succumbs to death, is not to overestimate this submission: it is to accept death's presence 'Here Below', but not to allow itself to be overwhelmed by it. Accept the verdict, but not the authority; take on the sentence, but not the wisdom that underlies it. Death may thus be an end, even a goal, but it is pictured here as a limit that is not invited to the centre of life, *in der Mitte des Lebens*, but delegated to the 'boundary', only to intervene in its own 'proper' time.

If Rosenzweig's proposal to 'newly think' finitude is polemical, it is because in Heidegger's original construction of 'being-towards-death' death penetrates into the very midst of Dasein; it is the very motor of its self-transcending exsistence, the teacher of the heroic decision-making which is as groundless, abyssal and pervaded by nothingness as death itself. Here, death is indeed a *telos* of life that runs its course according to this thanatic submission, or as Jean-Luc Nancy calls it aptly, 'sublime self-offering' (FT, 75). Death is let into the middle of life as its thanatic guide; either in the existential function of a catalyst (heroic decision), or, after Heidegger's *Kehre*, as the demobilizing event-horizon which works through the *Gelassenheit*, the quietistic anti-force of appeasement. None of it figures in Rosenzweig's project of New Thinking, which wishes to break with philosophy 'from Ionia to Jena', since Socrates firmly associated with the 'teaching how to die', and replace it with the 'teaching how to live, again' drawing, in Cohen's formulation, 'out of the sources of Judaism'. It thus wants to give death its proper due, but absolutely nothing more: it wants to acknowledge the fact of the finite life without *overestimating* its impact on the process of living. Finding the right measure, the right ratio in death's relationship with life, is the sole purpose here, which makes Rosenzweig's enterprise opposite to Heidegger's one that, from the perspective of *Neues Denken*, may indeed be characterized as a *systematic overestimation of death*.[8]

But before we proceed any further into the difference between Heidegger and Rosenzweig, we have to dispel one serious objection: that it is not Heidegger himself who systematically overestimates death, but rather all those critics who fail to see the vital function of *Todesbewusstsein*, which has nothing to do with any actual death or existential paralysis. According to this line of thought, death in Heidegger's *Being and Time* is a philosophically modified *different death*: just a neutral marker of finitude that works as a catalysing and intensifying factor. All that passes through this narrow 'opening', which is Dasein – aware of its finite existence, acquires infinite urgency and pathos of absolute intensity. As if in the revised reading of Saint Paul, whom Heidegger studied assiduously, this 'opening' is indeed the Pauline 'glass', but not 'darkly', not distorted by the finitude; on the contrary, it becomes a sharp magnifying lens, or a slit in the *camera obscura*, which condenses and refracts the dispersed light, thus forming a microcosmic image of the world. The Heideggerian 'being-towards-death' is thus not about 'dying': it is all about intense living, conditioned into the existential intensity by the awareness of its finite limits, just as in Rosenzweig.

Among many followers of Heidegger, who remain loyal to such a positive account of the death-driven finitude, there is certainly Jean-Luc Nancy with his project of 'finite thinking'. Nancy takes for granted Heidegger's declaration that presents Dasein as a finite *access* to the world: the 'different death' does not function here as closure but as a peculiarly intense type of opening. For, thanks to this finite opening, the world can 'originate' again and again in its *infinite* singularity. The slit of the 'finite thinking' – which, precisely because of its 'narrowing' is also an 'opening' – reveals the countless multitude of beings in ever new light. In *Being Singular Plural*, Nancy defines the Heideggerian notion of finitude as an 'access', carefully avoiding any emphasis on death:

> We only have access to ourselves – and to the world. It is only ever a question of the following: *full access is there, access to the whole of the origin.* This is called 'finitude' in Heideggerian terminology. But it has become clear since then that 'finitude' signifies the infinite singularity of meaning, *the infinite singularity of access to truth.* Finitude *is* the origin; that is, it is an infinity of origins. 'Origin' does not signify that from which the world comes, but rather the coming of each presence of the world, each time singular.[9]

Nancy's 'finite thinking' should indeed be very close – and often is – to my account of *another finitude*. Yet, this affinity could also be quite deceptive. On the one hand, Nancy is an obvious ally: his reading of Heidegger attempts to get back to the *positive* notion of finitude grounded firmly in 'Here Below', first announced in *Being and Time*, but then gradually lost with the mighty – and perhaps not always intended – rise of his *Todesdenken*. In order to prevent this ascension toward a new 'beyond', Nancy will claim that, in his system of the 'finite thinking', freedom occupies the same structural place as death in the systems of Hegel and Heidegger. Freedom is always a positive reverse of the mortal exposure; while death reveals Dasein's ungroundedness and radical contingency, freedom takes up these two negatives and converts them into opportunity. While death tells the privative *truth* about the finite condition closed within the natural cycle of life-and-death, freedom departs from this truth-saying verdict, by deviating into an infinitely free activity of *sense-making*. As Nancy says in *The Sense of the World* with his characteristic apothegmic force: 'Finitude is the truth of which the infinite is the sense' (SOTW, 29). So far, so very good: we will go back to this opening reversal in the chapter devoted to Derrida and his take on Heidegger's 'factical life'.

Even better: in his insistence on collapsing the finite moment of death with the infinite moment of the birth-to-freedom, Nancy can also be said to 'marry'

Heidegger's analytics of Dasein with Hannah Arendt's natalism. For him, this not so unlikely union (I will challenge this claim in the next chapter) announces a wholly new strategy of *infinitization*, where every birth of a new mortal Dasein is also a genesis/creation of a new world which can be 'accessed' only by a new subject, but also 'shared' by him in his practice of communication with everything and everybody that finds a place within the 'opening'. This unique combination of limitation and opening is precisely the 'essence of freedom': not the absolute unconditionality, but the contingent limit which, nonetheless, does not simply restrict and bind, but mobilizes, facilitates, pushes towards creative deviations from the veridictive closure of the 'truth'. The limit embodied in the ontic finitude becomes here a condition of the 'infinite access' to the world, which for Nancy constitutes a 'living sense of life', its palpitating heart:

> There is a negation of sense that is as heavy with sense as the most fulfilled Sense – that is, a negation of sense that, to the precise degree to which it is a negation of sense, is also a confinement to Truth qua pure abyss of sense: *an exposing Death, and not an exposition to death*. Paradoxically, *it is a negation of sense that makes an appeal to life, a living sense of life*. Life becomes the true sense of sense, which as a result no longer has any sense other than the sense of life. The 'living' represents the intimate palpitation that is immediately felt as sense.
>
> SOTW, 161; my emphasis

Nancy's distinction between the *exposing Death* and the *exposition to death* is the crux of his interpretation of Heidegger's *Sein-zum-Tode*: while the latter can and must lead to the Rosenzweigian 'paralysis', the former conditions the sense-making as an immediate and dramatic 'appeal to life'. But can this distinction truly hold?

Nancy's 'finite thinking' may indeed be in harmony with Heidegger's own declarations – according to which death is the fundamental possibility of human Dasein, intensifying the modal dimension of freedom, resoluteness and inventiveness – but it is incapable of reading Heidegger critically, i.e. against the grain. The question – *can we have a truly positive and non-privative concept of finitude with death in its centre?* – still lacks a convincing reply, despite Nancy's ingenious attempt to fuse Heidegger with Hegel and Nietzsche and say to it: *yes*. The opposite interpretation, answering this question with a decided *no*, was offered by Maurice Blanchot, who reread Heidegger's 'being-towards-death' in a different, non-German and proto-deconstructive, context – that is, far away from the heroic overtones of the late *Lebensphilosophie* to which Heidegger remains indebted – and, in consequence, the whole mobilizing effect of death immediately evaporated, together with its alleged highest 'possibility', giving way to an entropic and melancholy sense of incapacitation. The all-pervasive, ultimate, authoritative, veridictive and never-questioned presence of death – all these elements that make for the philosophical overestimation of death, only seemingly challenged by Nancy – constitute a trademark of Blanchot's reading of Heidegger, and Blanchot does not even pretend that this might be a 'different death'. What – perhaps – was intended to appear as a *Lichtung*, a narrowing capable of an intensified opening and access, now definitely turns into *closure*, aporia, blockage, or yet another reiteration of the arch-old topos of death as the *seal*.[10]

Blanchot's deconstruction consists in reversing the original *Being and Time* formula of death as the 'possibility of impossibility' into its very opposite: the 'impossibility of possibility'. Heidegger writes on the ultimate *Möglichkeit*:

> The more unveiledly this possibility gets understood – the more purely does the understanding penetrate into Dasein *as the possibility of the impossibility of any existence at all*. Death, as possibility, gives Dasein nothing to be 'actualized', nothing which Dasein, as actual, could itself *be* … Being-towards-death, as anticipation of possibility, is what first *makes* this possibility *possible*, and sets it free as possibility.
>
> BT, 307

Prima facie, it would indeed appear that death works here as a positive and catalysing factor. Death, the paradigmatic possibility defying any actualization, lies at the core of all other possibilities *as* possibilities: Dasein learns what it means to *be able* to become this or that by understanding the *ability* as such, the pure modal dimension of being. Yet Blanchot insists on inverting the Heideggerian formula to show the essential ungroundedness of its heroic resoluteness. The necessity of death cuts through all of Dasein's projects and reveals their truth as *mere* possibilities, as something possessing only a relative kind of being that pales in comparison to what is truly unconditional: the 'nothing' given by death. Death, therefore, is not something possible in terms of a rich palette of potential actualizations. It is instead a primordial and inescapable 'nothing' that manifests itself as the impossibility of any possibility. For, if possibility is a possibility-to-actualization, then death, by *defying all actualization*, negates also possibility as such. Death signals rather an altogether different way of existing, which, in *Space of Literature*, Blanchot designates as a peculiar *nunc stans* of 'dying':

It is the fact of dying that includes a radical reversal, through which the death that was the extreme form of my power not only becomes what loosens my hold upon myself by casting me out of my power to begin and even to finish, but also becomes that which is without any relation to me, without power over me – that which is stripped of all possibility – *the unreality of the indefinite*. I cannot represent this reversal to myself, I cannot even conceive of it as definitive. It is not the irreversible step beyond which there would be no return, for it is that which is not accomplished, the interminable and the incessant . . . It is inevitable but inaccessible death; it is the abyss of the present, time without a present, with which I have no relationships; it is that toward which I cannot go forth for in it I do not die, *I have fallen from the power to die*. In it *they* die; they do not cease, and they do not finish dying.[11]

In Blanchot, already influenced by Heidegger's *Kehre*, death is no longer enabling: it is disempowering, arresting, paralysing, entropic, privative through and through. It doesn't make us stand authentically face to face with our mortal condition and gain power/potentiality from that bold act; on the contrary, it makes us fall – 'fall from the *power* to die'. The impossibility of possibility announces from the start that all projects-actualizations undertaken by Dasein are essentially futile; the (non)presence of death discloses the fundamental impossibility of the moment of *decision* in which Dasein resolves to be rather something than nothing. This resolution appears not only insignificant when confronted with the verdict of finitude, but also simply impossible; death, instead of mobilizing Dasein to activity, reveals the irremovable *Nichtigkeit* that pervades and therefore *nichtet*, annihilates, its inner possibilities. Hence the step Dasein takes to make a decision to be something rather than nothing appears, in fact, *impossible*: it is a *pas*, a 'non-step'. Overshadowed by the higher truth of death, which 'gives Dasein nothing to actualize' (BT, 317), every step emerges as false, as a *faux pas* and error in need of correction. By problematizing every actualization and every decision, death also invalidates every possibility as possibility, and, above all else, it negates the basic ambition of Dasein to lead *its own*, truly authentic existence. 'Dying' is an abyss of anonymity, which Heidegger associates with the *Verfallen*, the fallen realm of *das Man*, 'they', where it becomes impossible to say 'I'. This very step, the most fundamental among Dasein's projects, which strives to confirm the *Jemeinigkeit* of all its doings and moods, now meets the strictest prohibition: *pas* (step) turns into *pas* (no). There is no escape from the verdict of anonymity, from the 'unreality of the indefinite': '*I* never die but *one dies*', says Blanchot. The 'Here Below' can only dissolve/fall further and further into the *Abgrund* of universal entropy.[12]

Blanchot's deconstruction of Heidegger's *Sein-zum-Tode* is thus based on one fundamental suspicion: that Heidegger, despite all the declarations to the contrary, cannot in fact face and look straight in the eye what he himself discovered – namely, the full scope of negativity implied by Dasein's finitude. One of the aspects of Heidegger escapist tendency is, as we have just seen, his critique of the 'fallen existence', which, according to Blanchot, is the real element of death's 'unreal indefinity'. The other closely related one is Heidegger's demand of authenticity, which cannot leave Dasein's 'opening' truly open and indefinite, and anxiously presses towards both, elevation and closure – out of the 'belowness' and its entropic dissolution. Although ready to redefine human existence as an 'open question', Heidegger can hardly tolerate such a level of indefiniteness and surreptitiously shoves death into the emptied centre in order to present it as the *missing essence* of Dasein. Blanchot's reading is thus faithful to the *arcana* of the deconstructive art, as formulated mostly by his friend, Paul de Man; on the performative level, Heidegger's text does precisely the opposite to its intended and stated meaning, where the crux of this aporia is located in the secret bifurcation of the concept of death: the real 'dying' occurring in the 'indefinity' and the hypostatic/ideological notion of Death as the defined end and essence of Dasein's existence. While 'dying' is an entropic element that counteracts any 'step' toward essentialization, Death is meant to do precisely the opposite: become 'constitutive' to Dasein's way of being as its essence-firming 'apodictic evidence' (BT, 309):

> Dasein, as thrown Being-in-the-world, has in every case already been delivered over to its death. In being towards its death, Dasein is *dying* factically and indeed constantly, as long as it has not yet come to its demise ... 'ending', as dying, is constitutive for Dasein's totality ... Dying is not an event; it is a phenomenon to be understood existentially ... Factically, Dasein is dying as long as it exists.
>
> BT, 303, 284, 295

In the *Introduction to Metaphysics*, Heidegger will say explicitly: *Aber das Sein des Lebens ist zugleich Tod*, 'The essence of life is death' (IM, 100). But is this death the same as dying? The indefinite living/dying can never become authentic: in order to gain *Eigentlichkeit*, it must 'step beyond' its fallen 'belowness' and acquire essence. There is, therefore, no such thing as an *authentic life*; it is either authenticity – or life. Or rather, to be more precise: either Death, the hypostasis of the 'beyond' – or dying, the entropic element of Here Below.

Blanchot's suspicion consists in not taking Heidegger at face value when he declares that he is giving us the true account of the proper *Sein-zum-Tode*, which, on Blanchot's account, can never be either *proper* or *authentic*. Just as Bataille with his memento against any *emploi* of death (issued against Hegel, but also his master Kojève),[13] Blanchot also dismisses the Heideggerian use of the 'different death', which allegedly essentializes and authenticates human existence, as an illusion. The aporia lies here in assuming that only constant awareness of death can give Dasein the taste of the authentic existence, whereas 'dying' *as such*, before it is ideologically hypostatized as a possibility of 'stepping beyond', is nothing but *falling* into the abyss of expropriation, non-propriety, non-ownership, powerless dissipation in the anonymous element of 'they': *dying stronger than death*. So, when Heidegger stubbornly insists on maintaining his 'different death' as the gate to *die eigentliche Existenz* full of heroic self-actualizations, he in fact does the very opposite: he surreptitiously smuggles in a living element of *Sein-gegen-Tode*, in which Dasein not so much adopts the death-dominated mode of being (which, in truth, is the fallen anonymous 'dying') as defends itself *against* the verdict, as any living thing would, by resolutely trying to become *something* against the tide of the overwhelming abyssal nothingness. All Dasein does, all his projects and decisions, springs not from his intimacy with death, but from the 'passion' or 'affection' of life resisting death, which Heidegger overtly rejects as fallen, inauthentic and – because it is just fleeting *life* – unfit to describe 'what is proper to man', his fixed essence. Despite all the efforts to eliminate the last remnants of life for the sake of the existence focused on its 'nothing', life, with its defiant *gegen-Tode*, is still there, albeit unacknowledged and unrecognized. More than that: it is all that there *is*; all that gives Dasein *something* rather than nothing.

Could it be that Heidegger – irony of ironies – would still be a secret *vitalist*, 'too much in thrall to the biological life', as Adorno suspected him of being (MCP, 132)?[14] Or, that his hypostasis of mine, always mine (*jemeinig*) death as opposed to the 'indefinite reality of dying' would still be nothing but a *ruse of life*, trying to resist the entropy? The following quotation could indeed confirm such scandalous suspicion:

> Death, as possibility, gives Dasein nothing to be 'actualized', nothing which Dasein, as actual, could itself *be*. It is the possibility of impossibility of every way of comporting oneself toward anything, of every way of existing. In the anticipation of this possibility it becomes 'greater and greater'; that is to say, the possibility reveals itself to be such that it knows no measure at all, no more or less, but signifies the possibility of the measureless impossibility of existence. In accordance with its essence, this possibility offers no support for becoming intent on something, 'picturing' to oneself the actuality which is possible, and so

forgetting its possibility. Being-towards-death, as anticipation of possibility, is what first *makes* this possibility *possible*, and sets it free as possibility.

BT, 307

This is Heidegger's own emphasis, enhancing the active and the positive: *being, making, possibility*, which open Dasein 'measurelessly' to ever 'greater and greater' tasks. But for Blanchot, the emphasis lies elsewhere, on negativity and arrest, on Dasein's failure to assert itself: *nothing, impossibility, non-actualization*. The 'impending' (BT, 294) and 'measureless' impossibility of existence, which is forbidden to be pictured in any actualized shape (all affinities with the 'jealous God' of the Second Commandment non-accidental), immediately dissolves any actuality, which Dasein has happened to assume, into *nothing*. Having been 'delivered over' to this new deadly divine, Dasein can never assert itself in what it actually *is*, but is always forced to be-no-longer, to undergo constant and constitutive 'dying' in the service of this unpicturable and measureless – ever 'greater and greater' – abyss of pure possibility that defies any concrete actualization. Thus, when read semi-theologically (and this is certainly Blanchot's perspective), Heidegger's death steps into the traditional role of the 'beyond' in relation to which no other being can assert itself in existence and has to sacrifice its actuality; the possibility so immense and infinite that it excludes and actively opposes any finite actualization.[15] So, if Dasein resolves to become something rather than nothing, it goes against the grain of its deadly creed and asserts itself – as life, for life and in the 'middle of life'. If it *wants* anything: to be proper, authentic and heroic – it must betray its inner calling, and thus fall into inauthenticity. Hence the aporia.

And, indeed, against his own belief in death-inspired positive resoluteness, Heidegger readily admits that: 'Anticipation discloses to existence that its uttermost possibility lies in *giving itself up*, and thus it *shatters* all one's tenaciousness to whatever existence one has reached' (BT, 308; my emphasis). Therefore, if Dasein decides to become *something*, the 'anticipatory resoluteness', formed in face of the impending certainty of death, immediately 'takes it back', because death, as precisely 'taking back' everything, is not just an end of the process, but its very medium, the constant and constitutive 'dying' as *deactualization*: 'The certainty of resolution signifies that one *holds oneself free for* the possibility of *taking it back* – a possibility which is factically necessary' (BT, 355). And even if Heidegger adds immediately that such certitude of 'taking back' and 'shattering' only strengthens the resolute will to repeat itself,[16] Blanchot will treat it merely as a defensive evasion of what to him seems inevitable, namely the entropic dissolution into 'irresoluteness'. To be authentic, for Blanchot, is not to leap into decisions resulting in passing actualizations, but to stay 'dying' and 'irresolute', to let death truly take power over life, that is, to become *inauthentic* and '*fall* from the power to die'. It is again, fully in accordance with Heidegger's own letter (if not the spirit): 'Anticipatory resoluteness is not a way of escape, fabricated for the "overcoming" of death; it is rather that understanding which follows the call of conscience and which frees for death the possibility of acquiring *power* over Dasein's *existence* and of basically dispersing all fugitive Self-concealments' (BT, 357).

For Blanchot, however, *all* decisions to be something rather than nothing belong precisely to the realm of 'fugitive Self-concealments', fabricated not *zum* but *gegen Tode*: even the very figure of Death as the semi-divine *telos* of the heroic life is one of them, a ruse of life and an escape from the Real of 'dying'. If there is an 'unshakable joy' in serving 'Death, the absolute Master' (we have to remember that in his reading of Heidegger, Blanchot already fuses him with Hegel whom he learnt through Kojève), then it consists in staying rather nothing than something. And again, Heidegger provides the textual evidence: 'The ecstatical character of the primordial future lies precisely in the fact that the future *closes* one's potentiality-for-Being ... Primordial and authentic coming-towards-oneself is the meaning of existing in *one's ownmost nullity*' (BT, 379; my emphasis).

In the end, it is precisely this 'ownmost nullity' that substitutes for the initially open indefinity of Dasein: death, far from opening and enabling, becomes the privative essence of human finitude which now 'takes back' all its actualizations and focuses on its own 'nothingness' – a pure possibility, so vast and measureless, that it turns into a blocking impossibility. Mindful of Bataille's objection, Blanchot will always remind us that death cannot be mastered, disciplined, domesticated, made use of: despite all Heidegger's ruses to force it serve the authentic existence, 'dying', the original entropic-privative matrix of the hypostasis of Death in *Sein-zum-Tode*, proves more powerful and, in the end, disambiguates the equivocation. Indeed, dying stronger than death.

Pace Nancy, therefore, Blanchot would argue that Heidegger's proposition is not a philosophy of the *finite life*, in which finitude does not emerge as privation. If Heidegger's project was to give us a new positive view of finitude with death in the centre, it collapses on all fronts: whether as 'dying' which insinuates constant entropic *Verendlichung* into the 'midst of life', or whether as a hypostatic death offering a false 'beyond', it leaves Dasein as either dissipated in anonymity or frozen in nullity. Blanchot's deconstructive commentary destroys the hopes which Nancy binds with the 'exposing death': there is either life, but then wrenched against death, *gegen-Tode*, oblivious to and ignorant of the lethal truth of its finitude – or the awareness of death, but then dissolving into the deactualizing element of 'dying', where no project or 'step' taken by Dasein makes any sense, Nancy's *faire-sens* included.

Life of un-essence: in/de/finity of love

Blanchot's proto-deconstructive reading of Heidegger allows us to see the vast shadow thrown by his thanatic spirit; in Derrida's words, death, instead of forming Dasein's 'most proper possibility', turns into a seal of absolute *aporia*: 'the most improper possibility and the most ex-propriating, the most inauthenticating one'.[17]

This aporetic tendency is precisely the reason why Rosenzweig's project appears more promising: it liberates the notion of *positive finitude* from the dubious supremacy of death and focuses it *instead* on love. This *instead* is the clue of the whole operation: while love bears some affinity to death, it also brings an irreducible difference. While it may not have a well-defined essence, it does not slide back into 'nullity' or 'nothingness'. Love works better as the mobilizing factor within the condition of finitude; *instead* of sealing the finite life with the non-negotiable *arrêt*, which, as Blanchot had demonstrated, is always its latent potency, love actually offers an opening in the form of an affective mood that creates 'access' to as many beings as possible, knowing that there will be no infinite time given for their contemplation. Thus, if finitude exerts a pressure on the subject who then simply must make a decision, this narrowing expresses itself better in the *decisionism of love*.[18] While for Heidegger, the role of death will always be central – whether as the mobilizing factor of *Entschlossenheit* or the appeasing factor of *Gelassenheit* – for Rosenzweig, on the contrary, it will always be downplayed, almost to the point of indifference.[19]

This confrontation never took place in reality, but we can nonetheless attempt to stage it retrospectively. First, *enter* Heidegger. In the series of lectures composed in 1935 and then edited under the title *Introduction to Metaphysics*, Heidegger indeed confirms Blanchot's later diagnosis on the aporetic nature of the concept of death within his system. He openly presents death as the *ultimate aporia*, by drawing on the original Greek meaning of the word as 'no way-out', 'no exit', the unsurpassable 'blocking of the passage'. Man, who likes to see himself as *pantoporos*, the most resourceful creature which 'begets in itself its own un-essence, the versatility (*Vielwendigkeit*) of many twists and turns' (IM, 168) deep down appears to be, in fact, *aporos*: a priori blocked and thwarted:

> There is only *one* thing against which all violence-doing [of the *pantoporos* hubristic human Dasein] directly shatters. That is death. It is an end beyond all completion, a limit beyond all limits. Here there is no breaking forth and breaking up, no capturing and subjugating. But this un-canny thing, which sets us simply and suddenly out from everything homely once and for all, is not a special event that must also be mentioned among others, because it, too, ultimately does occur. *The human being has no way out in the face of death, not only when it is time to die, but constantly and essentially.* Insofar as humans *are*, the stand in the *no-exit of death*.
>
> IM, 168–9; my emphasis

But for Heidegger, the aporia of death is not something to be deplored: by setting 'a limit beyond all limits', death curtails the hubris of human Dasein who – just as Odysseus, to whom this fragment actually refers – perceives itself as indefinitely plastic and, because of that, capable of becoming anything and everything and conceiving of every possible ruse in order to bend the fate and adjust the world to its needs. Thus, even the most *pantoporos* Odysseus must eventually meet the *aporos* death that will put an end to his clever subterfuges. It is not an accident that Heidegger applies exactly the same characteristics – cunning, limitless resourcefulness, lack of essence, versatility, intermixing, cleverness of calculation – to Odysseus and to the 'world-Jewry'. Among the Hellenists of Heidegger's time, Odysseus, this least tragic of all Greek heroes, was widely assumed to be a late Semitic import to the Greek mythology: an alien influence that soiled its purity, best represented by the most tragic of all Greek heroes, the beautiful Achilles who, despite all the efforts to make him immune to death, proved nonetheless to be mortal – as everything else.[20]

This is precisely the moment of Rosenzweig's first retort. For him, just as for Heidegger, human life is with no pre-established essence: indefinite, open, question-like. The latter, in the *Introduction to Metaphysics*, states firmly that 'the determination of the essence of the human being is *never* an answer, but is essentially a question' (IM, 149). Yet, the two thinkers play it out very differently. Heidegger, as we have already seen, *nolens volens* gravitates towards the closure, the seal, the dead-assuredness of death, which then substitutes for the missing essence of Dasein: *Seinsdenken* and *Todesdenken* become in the end undistinguishable synonyms. It is, after all, death that tears away Man from the familiar homeliness of the world of seeming and throws him in the nearness of

Being, the most un-canny – *un-heimlich* – of all thoughts. It is the annihilating, *nichtende*, power of death, which puts Man in touch with the *Nichts des Seins*, the nothingness of Being's pure potentiality, which underlies – but also undermines – the realm of actualized beings. Death, therefore, becomes the vehicle of the highest spiritual transport which defines the destiny of human Dasein. *The human being has no way out in the face of death, not only when it is time to die, but constantly and essentially*; this, for Rosenzweig, is precisely the sickness – 'sickness unto death' – that pushes death into the very centre of human life, as its defining moment, giving it fake constancy and essence. In Heidegger, no being, no positive content can ever fill the gap of nothingness that constitutes human being and thus offer an answer to its glaring questioning abyss; this *Nichts* can only be matched by the *Nichts* of death that helps to disclose the abyssal *Nichts* of Being.

Rosenzweig's intention is precisely to counteract the mastery of this deadly triad that turns the ordinary 'un-essence' of human life into a fetishized, fixed, sublime 'Nothing'. In order to avoid this fixation, the life must agree to be just the thing of 'un-essence', a flow without form, a meandering story with many twists and turns, precisely the way it is described by the Odyssey: a 'life which is content to be an in-between state, merely a *transition from one thing to another*' (USH, 80). Rosenzweig explores the essential *Nichts* of human life in the form of a horizontal narrative that evolves only thanks to its indefiniteness; by refusing to turn the singular life into something easily definable, he lets it assume a meandering structure, containing many *peripeteias*, the resourceful twists and turns, that postpone the final verdict; here the *erzählendes Sprachdenken* becomes a synonym of *Lebensdenken*, life-thinking. As in Heidegger, the human life emerges here as indefinite, with no pregiven essence, but all this seemingly privative characteristic merely serves as the canvas for a new narrative philosophy: the open drama of temporality, which can only evolve in the living exchange between human being and the world. In the narrative approach, the *nullity* of Dasein's essence transforms into a *futurity* of a being that exists in an open-ended time. Just as the Heideggerian essentialization, the story also delivers a *form* to life, but this form, unlike the sublimated and fetishized 'nothing', is a horizontal form-in-the-making, supple and plastic. It draws its arabesque line unconcerned with the criterion of *Eigentlichkeit*, which, despite Heidegger's intention to go beyond it, still pertains to the arsenal of traditional – Neoplatonic – metaphysics. *Human beings do not have one essence – they have stories. One thousand and one stories.*

There is a clear parallel between Rosenzweig's interest in the narrative form and Walter Benjamin's essay, *Storyteller*, which mentions Scheherazade's one thousand and one tales as the paradigmatic case of the storytelling practice that not only postpones but also complicates the death sentence: unlike in Nancy's static opposition between truth and sense, where no story can ever modify the naked lethal truth of finitude, the main function of this *récit* is to create a 'middle' space of deferment that makes room for the living unpredictability despite the inevitable finale in the dead-assuredness of death.[21] The complication of this dead-simple sentence consists in the way in which the story includes the finale on its own right and terms, and *appropriates* it to such an extent that it indeed comes in the 'proper' time, so that the singular life may end up by 'dying in its own fashion'.[22]

In the end, therefore – for this is *the* end, yet no longer so adversarial and necessitarian – death approaches life as life's brother, as the last line of the *Büchlein* declares. For many commentators, this conclusion sounds terribly disappointing and indeed very Heideggerian, if not simply *lebensphilosophisch* Schopenhauerian.[23] But one can also interpret this brotherhood of death as the sign of the confrontation with the Hegelian-Heideggerian line of thinking which elevated death to the highest status of *Meisterschaft* with its unquestioned dominion over human life, the 'death, the Absolute Master' syndrome, so succinctly summed up by Paul Celan in his ominous phrase from *Todesfuge*: *Tod is ein Meister aus Deutschland*. When Rosenzweig says – 'Life's eloquent lips are put to silence and the eternally Taciturn One will speak: "Do you finally recognize me? I am your brother"' (USH, 103) – he not only distances himself from Hegel, but also enjoins death in the dialogic practice and drags it onto the side of life (*das Diesseits*), by letting it speak, which here is not just a metaphor. While in the metaphysical night of the Heideggerian *Todesdenken*, the dead-mute silence reigns, in Rosenzweig's living day the dialogue never ceases; once life is unable to talk, the death takes over the 'flickering torch' of speech in the neighbourly-brotherly fashion. Just as in Derrida's *la vie le mort*, where survival keeps both life and death on *this side*, Rosenzweig's 'brotherly' account of death blocks any attempt to turn it into a sublime representative of the 'beyond'.[24]

When commenting on affinities and divergences between Rosenzweig and Heidegger, Karl Löwith (who actually argues that they have much more in common than I want to claim), spots one crucial difference: while they both emphasize the *Endlichkeit* of human life, Heidegger dissolves it in the immanent temporality, offering no resistance to transience, yet Rosenzweig insists on the infinite moment: the perfect fulfilment of life which truly and finally comes to be and thus eternalizes itself.[25] True, but this eternal completion is possible only on the grounds of the more fundamental form of infinity that plays itself out in human life, despite its finitude. This infinitization takes the form of *in/de/finity* or *infinitiveness*, deriving from the grammatical concept of the infinitive that alludes to the infinite potentiality of uses into which the verb may be put: the peculiar condition of human life that refuses to be forever a fixed and concrete 'something', yet without slipping into the Heideggerian 'nothing' of pure possibility or the Blanchotian 'unreality' of deactualization – 'we must daringly seize upon a life which is content to be an in-between state, merely a transition from one thing to another. Let us reject the ever-present answer, "Life is," "Man is" – and let us become part of the onward-moving life of man. Here life "is" not, it simply occurs [*geschieht*]' (USH, 80).

This is an outright apology of the *inessential life*: something very adversarial to Heidegger, who called it a wrong type of 'un-essence', superficially resourceful as Odysseus and, because of that, incapable to plunge metaphysically into the abysses of Being – but also to György Lukacs whose famous essay 'Metaphysics of Tragedy' Rosenzweig actually had read, unlike Heidegger. In this essay, devoted to the philosophical essence of tragedy and published in 1914, Lukacs, at that time still a doctoral student of Georg Simmel, attempts to get out from the morasses of *Lebensphilosophie* thanks to the 'transport' (*Aufschwung*) offered by the death of the tragic hero. Unlike life, which is a chaotic anarchy of light and darkness that can never be lived to the end and always evades any form, death is a 'chisel' (the Simmelian *Gestalter*): it carves life into a statuesque stony structure by arresting its flow and thus giving it a definite character:

> Life is an anarchy of light and dark: nothing is ever completely fulfilled in life, nothing ever quite ends; new, confusing voices always mingle with the chorus of those that have been heard before. Everything flows, everything merges into another thing, and the mixture is uncontrolled and impure; everything is destroyed, everything is smashed, nothing ever flowers into *real life* . . . Real life is always unreal, always impossible, in the midst of empirical life. But suddenly there is a gleam, a lightning that illumines the banal paths of empirical life; something disturbing and seductive, dangerous and surprising. The *accident*, the great moment, the *miracle*; an enreachment and a confusion. It cannot last, no one would be able to bear it, no one could live at such heights – at the height of their own life and their own ultimate possibilities. One has to fall back into numbness. *One has to deny life in order to live.*[26]

Lukacs and Heidegger go thus hand in hand: they both want to get out from the stream of life in which being and seeming, truth and mere appearance, clarity and dispersion, *Dichtung und Wahrheit*, are forever intertwined and there is no way out of this ambivalence apart from what at first seemed like a no-way-out, a

total blockage and aporia: death, the *thanatic miracle.* Just as Heidegger wishes
for the forces of the uncanny and incidental to break through the covers of the
ordinary into the truth of Being, Lukacs wants to step out from the *Lebensstrom*
in order to experience the Real, which is denied to him in the normal course of
life. This is precisely the most pernicious kind of wonder Rosenzweig warns us
against at the beginning of his *Büchlein,* a truly dark *metanoia:* the deadly
paralysis that imagines that it *steps* beyond the flow of life into something
transcendent and more real, but, in fact, it only *stops:* becomes idly arrested,
without discovering anything outside life. It is precisely this false transcendence
that Maurice Blanchot puns as *pas au-delà,* 'the step not beyond', which is held in
check by the *arrêt de mort,* the arrest-sentence of death.[27]

In order to avoid this deadly miracle, the life must agree to be the thing of
'un-essence', a flow without form, a meandering story with many twists and
turns: a 'life which is content to be an in-between state, merely a *transition from
one thing to another'.* Life must flow, retaining its indefiniteness and,
simultaneously, the integral 'fluidity of the whole'; it must always be in the state
of *flux* keeping up 'vital mobile energy' (USH, 92). Life must flow and assume the
transience, but this kind of transience/transition will have nothing to do with the
Pauline 'sting of death' that impregnates life with the stigma of dying. In this
transience, life does not succumb to morbid passing *away,* but is the lively
passing *from one thing to another,* always confronting the challenge of otherness,
always overreaching – beyond any fixed identity, towards ever richer self-
differentiation. Only then, in the ultimate vital appropriation of transience, can
it be called life: the living condition truly separate from death, a properly distinct
category in which 'living' means really something else than 'dying' and thus turns
into an argument of its own.[28]

But we also remember from *The Star* that this, only seemingly derogatory,
characteristic of a non-essential *transition from one thing to another* was given to
what Rosenzweig regards as the highest and most valuable content of the
revelation: *love.* Love goes from one neighbour to another and paces restlessly
the whole world in constant transition, oblivious to its own 'essence'. Love, in
Goethe's words, 'connects all' without creating a hypostatic *Allheit* [totality], itself
indefinite and because of that infinitely open to embrace each being, one after
another – nominally and nominalistically – just like God himself who knows
every creature by name as a unique singularity.[29] For Rosenzweig, therefore, the
life-in-transition, life-in-between, does not indicate anything *privative* –
dispersion, dissolution, decay, impurity, incompleteness, fall – as it does for
Lukacs and Heidegger (but also Blanchot, even if he affirms it). It is inessential so

it can fill itself with intense neighbourly relations; it is *lacking essence*, so it can be *full of love*. As Jean-Luc Nancy puts it in his *Finite Thinking*, in the fragment clearly inspired more by Rosenzweig than Heidegger: 'Love cuts across finitude, always from the other to the other, which never returns to the same – and all loves, so humbly alike, are superbly singular. *Love offers finitude in its truth*; it is finitude's dazzling presentation' (FT, 264; my emphasis).

Before, it was the 'exposing Death' that demonstrated the truth of the law of the finite life – now it is love that, equally strong as death, takes over the same function. It is the same function, the one of the most fundamental marker of finitude – but the result is very different. Instead of *death, truth, silence – love, sense, story*.[30]

Love cannot do without the narrative *Sprachdenken*, because its basic manner of operating, thanks to which love attaches itself to all the neighbours it encounters, is *language*: 'it is language which erects the visible bridge from man to that which is not man, to the other' (USH, 80). If life means love, then love means also living speech – naming, addressing, calling, that is, cultivating the *passion of relationality*:

> The bond of the consummate and redemptive bonding of man and the world is
> to begin with neighbour and ever more only the neighbour, the well-nigh nighest
> ... (Love) glides from one bearer to the other, the next one, from one neighbour
> to the next neighbour. It is not satisfied until it has paced off the whole orbit of
> creation; ... it leaves its traces everywhere in its migration by providing the
> plural of things everywhere with the sign of singularity.
>
>   SR, 235

But this process of 'gliding from one bearer to another', this gradual 'pacing of the whole orbit of creation' cannot happen all at once, for no shortcuts are allowed here; no jumps to general categories that would circumvent the singularity of every concrete neighbour which the Rosenzweigian love encounters. Love is a life-long, continuous and always incomplete process of solving the 'living contradiction' between the infinite and the finite, where the endlessly open, transitional and relational nature of love offers a dynamic synthesis in the form of *in/de/finity*: not the infinity of essence, which human life does not possess, but the infinity of 'un-essence', a virtual non-being that can *fall for* – and thus become, if only for a moment – everything. If, according to Heidegger, life of 'un-essence' is *Verfallenheit*, then indeed the finitude spent under the sun of love is constantly *falling*: falling-in-love with all those things it cares about. In this manner, Rosenzweig pioneers the rhetorical reversal that constitutes the guiding theme of my book: an affirmative twist on the Heideggerian notion of *Verfallenheit* which in existential terms repeats the default Neoplatonic metaphysics of the Fall. Yes, we are fallen and still falling – in love.[31]

We could thus sum up the difference between Rosenzweig and Heidegger by once again evoking the biblical line, which is also the guiding motif of *The Star*: *azzah hamavet ahavah*, love strong as death. The vital, incomplete, exposed in/de/finity of love, which falls and disperses in un-essential transience – versus the definite closure of self-possessive authenticity, sealed by the verdict of death. Both these visions of life are finite, but while the Heideggerian overestimates the defining moment of the ending as 'constant and essential', the Rosenzweigian evades it as merely secondary, because Rosenzweig is not looking for *any* definition of human life. Agreeing that human life must remain a 'thing of un-essence', he goes rather for love that thrives on everything non-essential: strictly singular, transitory, non-identitarian, exposed. For him, a human being is not a death-bound 'nothing', collapsing into his inner nothingness, but a lively bundle of energy which easily flows into 'the energies of the world' (USH, 92). The Herderian lack/deficiency, which decides about the anthropological difference, does not congeal here into a fixed hypostasis of 'nullity', but remains a flux that carries the diffusive and transitory acts of loving which can form relations in the most plastic-Protean fashion – with anything and everything. *Love turns the negativity of 'un-essence' into the positivity of intense singular relations.*[32]

This is what Rosenzweig calls *die Umkehr*: the 'turn', but also, more theologically 'conversion'. A conversion to a truly new 'metaphysics of finitude' that no longer dishonours finite life.

Love: a perfect affect for the imperfect world (contingency)

In *Minima Moralia*, Theodor W. Adorno recommends that we look at the world from the vantage point of redemption which allows us to see it as potentially happy and satisfied, though still finite. A responsible use of the compassionate 'despair', which we feel towards the suffering of all contingent beings here and now in their unredeemed and distorted state of things, should consist in the disinterested care for their finite condition: this caring sentiment, this 'felt contact', is what complements, but also motivates, our knowledge. Adorno does not call this affect explicitly 'love', but the light without which the technical skill of philosophy remains blind can only be conceived as the loving affect for the fellow creatures:

The only philosophy which can be responsibly practised in face of despair is the attempt to contemplate all things as they would present themselves from the standpoint of redemption. Knowledge has no light but that shed on the world by redemption: all else is reconstruction, mere technique. Perspectives must be fashioned that displace and estrange the world, reveal it to be, with its rifts ad crevices, as indigent and distorted as it will appear one day in the messianic light. To gain such perspectives without velleity or violence, entirely from felt contact with its objects – this alone is the task of thought.

MM, 247

This messianic affectivity, in which love lends light to critical knowledge, emerges for the first time in Saint Paul's *First Letter to Corinthians* where love appears as the perfect affect for the imperfect world. And if love alone is perfect within the created reality, it is because it has a unique capacity to anticipate the perfection of the future redeemed state of things:

Love is patient, love is kind. It does not envy, it does not boast, it is not proud. It does not dishonour others, it is not self-seeking, it is not easily angered, it keeps no record of wrongs. Love does not delight in evil but rejoices with the truth. It always protects, always trusts, always hopes, always perseveres. Love never fails. But where there are prophecies, they will cease; where there are tongues, they will be stilled; where there is knowledge, it will pass away. For we know in part and we prophesy in part, but when completeness comes, what is in part disappears. When I was a child, I talked like a child, I thought like a child, I reasoned like a child. When I became a man, I put the ways of childhood behind me. For now we see only a reflection as in a mirror; then we shall see face to face. Now I know in part; then I shall know fully, even as I am fully known. And now these three remain: faith, hope and love. But the greatest of these is love.

1 Cor. 13:4–13

Both these recommendations refer to an alternative affective horizon surrounding the notion of finitude: not deadly fear, but love that grasps the finite without trying to 'dishonour' it. In this non-thanatic vision, contingency appears in a different light: it is not just the negative – the miserable transience given over to the destructive power of time – but also not just the fully positive to be left as it is. The perfect affect for the imperfect creation contains a good dialectical tension which does not allow love to passively affirm the contingent existence: *contingency, having no ultimate reason for being the way it is, opens itself to the possibility of transformation.* At the same time, love does not condemn contingency to the shame of illegitimacy: it does not plunge it into the 'dishonour' of a lesser being whose destiny is to merely pass away in the lower spheres of emanation. Its compassion is active, not *vanitative*.

Love, therefore, is the affect perfectly attuned to the contingent existence that constitutes, as Freud would have it, its first object choice. Love does not look for *Grund*, the Heideggerian justifying reason for contingency, but, precisely because of that, it does not treat contingency as statically given in its ontic status quo. Unlike the Platonic Eros, which only temporarily chooses contingent beings in order to abandon them for the sublime heights, the Pauline-Adornian love fully accepts creatureliness in its transient condition. The term 'creatureliness' – Franz Rosenzweig's *Kreatürlichkeit* – does not appear here accidentally: love as the perfect affect maintains within the created world the satisfaction of the Creator, who himself commented on his work – *ki tov*, 'and it was good'. Love, therefore, is the trace of transcendence within the immanent reality: it watches over creation, by pushing it towards *creatio continua* here and now. The Rosenzweigian non-sublime acts of earthly messianism are the daily works of neighbourly love which, in its passion of relationality, 'connects all'.

The passion of relationality is the opposite of the affective position dominated by fear and anxiety. *The Song of Songs* talks about love strong as death, which also means that love is as strong as fear. Psychoanalytically speaking, love and anxiety are the interchangeable affects which constitute two different forms of the same *libido*: the indefinite and simultaneously excessive, unique human drive. In the Introduction we have seen how Freud introduces his own version of the Herderian anthropological difference: while animals possess instincts with their well-defined goals and destinies – human beings posses only *drives*: the pulsional *Sturm und Drang*, which does not have its a priori established orientation and because of that can connect with everything and nothing at the same time. When this excessive libido chooses nothing, it disperses into the halo of anxiety, a non-concrete and non-objectified fear that troubles the psyche with a notorious sense of unfulfilment and detaches it from the world of objects. The anxiety dominated psyche plunges thus into solitary depression and melancholy.[33]

Love as the passion of relationality occupies the opposite affective pole. Its passionate will to cathect everything without 'dishonouring' it (Saint Paul again) orientates itself towards all elements of reality which it tries to grasp in the net of intense relations. In this perspective, the language itself would be the opposite of the demential muteness, but also, as such, a derivative of the loving affect: the 'living speech' (Rosenzweig's *lebendige Sprache*) connecting the self with all that surrounds it – the being-here of *Da-sein* with the being-there neighbourhood of *Fort-sein*, as in favourite Freud's play of *Fort-Da!* – appears to be the libidinal bedrock of language in which all can be bound to all. Thus, just as the Goethean love connects all – so does language. In its libidinal passion of relational binding, love, which 'does not boast and is not proud' and language, which strikes far-reaching connections between naturally unrelated designates, would be one and the same thing.

Love strong as fear: this peculiar equivalence does not refer to the content of the affect, the way it was wrongly understood by Augustine who, as we shall soon see, identified love with death. It refers merely to the formal – or, better, energetic – aspect of the affect, where the life-giving love and the death-bringing fear emerge as the two forms of the same human libido and its indeterminate excess. The libido constantly oscillates between fear, in which the psyche withdraws from the object-cathexes and falls into dead silence, and love, in which the psyche encounters and binds objects thanks to the 'living speech'. The human libido, therefore, always transcends the animal link to the niche, determined by instinctual needs: it is characterized either by the lack of relation to anything or by the passionate excess of relationality, which would like to cathect and connect everything.

Yet, the relation between love and language grows more problematic once language begins to emancipate from its affective source. Although love, as Rosenzweig has it, strives to 'pace the orbit of the creation' (SR, 235), it is also strictly nominalistic: it can choose its objects only 'one by one' and never via general categories. Language, however, swiftly detaches from the concrete thing and, rather like the Platonic Eros, chooses the 'icy abstraction' of general ideas, with their sublime aloofness towards anything sensuous and concrete (ND, 4), where the original affect which gave birth to speech, possible only between the two living singularities, dies. Love thus simultaneously gives rise to language and subverts it, by constantly 'breaking the wholes' – this is how Rosenzweig puns on the Kabbalistic *shevirat ka-kelim*, by turning it into *shevirat ha-kolim* – the aim of which is to once again nominalize the general abstractions and turn them back towards the contingent. The living, nominalistic, affective source of speech undermines language as an abstract system and does not allow it to close upon itself in the hermetic realm of Platonic ideas. The living relation which connects all (or, as E.M. Forster put it, '*only* connects') can thus never be simply identified with the linguistic structure where the connection ossifies into a systemic reference.

But love not only simultaneously creates and subverts language. The loving affect for the world also changes the perception of contingency itself, by subverting the Neoplatonic negative approach to transience, temporariness and finitude. Philosophy has always defined the contingent as something non-necessary, which can come into existence but does not have to. *Contingentia* does not possess sufficient reason, which Leibniz regarded as the minimal condition of a being worth its name, i.e. a being that is better than nothing. Hence still in Hegel, contingency as such is pure negativity close to *nihil*, which must be forged into rational necessity: the 'reduction (*Abkürzung*) of all immediate content of experience'[34] is the Hegelian task of philosophy.

Yet, in the world where all contingency would be eliminated for the sake of the rationally grounded necessity love would become simply spurious and inoperative. This is why in Hegel's system, love is only a transitory stage used by the cunning of reason that strives towards its ultimate goal: freedom as necessity made conscious. Hegel makes room for love solely on the level of the familial ties where it prepares the first binding; later these ties will be handed over to reason, which will give them the final form of systemic necessity. Thus, similarly to language, which tends to forget about its living/loving source and freezes into an abstract sublime structure, the philosophical system, too, forgets about love by seeing in its acts merely a camouflage for the works of reason. To attempt to recover the true meaning of contingency, therefore, equals the deconstructive attempt to recover the proper meaning of love as – to recall Saint Paul again – a perfect affect for the imperfect world, which lies at the bottom of our linguistic/cognitive activity.

Precisely: *activity*. To see the world through the light of redemptive love means to see it predominantly as an arena of action, *not* contemplation with which love has been wrongly associated for far too long: a being which has no sufficient reason to exist is also a being which does not have its pre-established *telos*, so it can be fashioned according to love's will. Part of the redeeming force of love consists precisely in this radical *conversion*: in turning the vice of negativity (lack of ground and justification) into a virtue of chance (positive futuristic project of a better being). Here, contingency is neither a veil for necessity nor an object of a passive contemplation, but offers itself instead as an infinite plasticity: unfinished work, still open to the ongoing *creatio continua*.

This, however, is not the plasticity of chaos, where contingency is 'let loose' and thus abandoned to the 'ontology of accident'.[35] Love for the contingent world is driven by the Adornian compassionate 'despair', which responds to the suffering and tries to prevent it. It does not see the suffering as the 'irreparable' kernel of existence, but merely as a clash or, in Spinoza's terms, 'bad encounter': a wrong set of elements that collide instead of cooperating and which could be repaired with one messianic 'slight adjustment', *mit einem geringen Zurechtstellen*.[36]

This, for Adorno, is precisely the Archimedean point of support that allows the whole globe to move, as well as the ultimate criterion of all serious thought: the suffering of the contingent being which is, just as contingency itself, never necessary. The contingent suffering, unnecessary by principle, opens thus to change, adjustment, transformation, or – simply – *work*.[37]

The Hegelian tradition considers work as the derivative of fear – more specifically, the fear of death. Unlike the Master, who does not fear death and looks negativity straight in eye, the Slave is in the grip of mortal anxiety: he is forced to work only because he fears death from the hand of the Master. 'The fear of the Lord is the beginning of all wisdom', says Hegel by paraphrasing the sentence from the Book of Job: this is also the beginning of work and the civilizational transformation of nature (PS, 117). In his early theological works, young Hegel still experiments with the idea of love, but only to abandon it at the stage of *The Phenomenology of Spirit*, where he rejects it as a passive and ineffective sentiment. The Christian community, which he describes in 'The Spirit of Christianity and Its Fate', realizes the Pauline ideal of love with a swiftness of a 'pistol shot', and then rests on its affective laurels: instead of working, i.e. transforming the natural reality, the Christian *Gemeinde* turns out to be satisfied and lazy in its sectarian seclusion. Lulled by the vision of the advancing redemption, the members of the Christian sect do everything *hos me*, 'as if', lovingly waiting for the apocalypse that will end time, while beings lie there untouched as indifferent lumps of matter that only block quick access to the realm of immortality. Hegel, who, in his private notes, called himself, somewhat immodestly, the 'Aquinas of the Protestant world', cannot agree with such a triumph of passivity and holy laziness: as all Lutherans, he wants a *theological justification of work*.

And Hegel indeed succeeds in his endeavour, but under the aegis of a different religion which he changes as if imperceptibly – until Alexandre Kojève reveals the hidden trumps of his cunning theological game. According to Kojève, the new Hegelian religion consists in the *revelation of death*, since only fear of death can be the source of work: first slavish, then more and more autonomous. More and more, but never fully so: members of Western civilization can work only under coercion fuelled by the fear of losing their life – first because of the direct external threat coming from the Master, and subsequently because of the internalized drive towards self-preservation. The source of work, therefore, is the traumatic revelation of pure negativity: the deadly anxiety of the contingent being who knows that he is issuing inevitably into death. In the Kojèvian understanding, which may be seen as precursory and paradigmatic for the whole 'thanatic strain' of late-modern thought, it is death and nothing else which makes humanity human: the experience of death is the necessary *anthropogenic* moment which raises the human animal above its 'stupid life':

> It is death that engenders Man in Nature, and it is death that makes him progress to his final destiny, which is that of the Wise Man fully conscious of himself and therefore fully conscious of his own finitude. Thus, Man does not arrive at Wisdom or at the fullness of self-consciousness so long as, in the way of the vulgar, he feigns an ignorance of the Negativity that is the very source of his human existence, and that is manifest in him and to him, *not only as struggle and labor, but moreover as death or absolute finitude.* The vulgar treat death as something of which one says: 'It is nothing, or it is false'; and by turning away from it most quickly, they hasten to pass on to the order of the day. But if the philosopher wants to attain to Wisdom, he must 'look the Negative full in the face, and [must] abide with it.' And it is in discursive contemplation of Negativity revealing itself through death that the 'power' of the Wise Man, conscious of himself, [and] who incarnates Spirit, is manifested.[38]

Yet, if we try to look differently at contingency and finitude, we also gain a new understanding of the idea of work. Perhaps, we don't even have to go beyond – or against – Hegel in order to find a theological justification for what Kierkegaard used to call 'the works of love'.[39] The anti-Kojèvian and more Kierkegaardian reading of Hegel was offered by Emil Fackenheim in his *Religious Dimension of Hegel's Thought*, which discusses Hegelian variant of Judaeo-Christianity as a religion of the active transformation of the world. According to Fackenheim's interpretation of Hegel, Christianity (which he, partly against Hegel, draws 'out of the sources of Judaism') is – unlike 'pagan' religions regarding reality in terms of the necessities of fate – the first religion of radical contingency. It perceives the world not as a Stoic 'iron cage' that can only be escaped by mystical contemplation, but as the Pauline 'passing figure' which, precisely because of its transience, is infinitely malleable. For Hegel, the Pauline transience/passing is thus merely a reverse of the radical malleability of the contingent being which can either 'pass' in its figure passively or be actively 'trans-figured': transformed by the Spirit itself which penetrates matter and works through it from within. Hence, in Hegel's system, contingency is a necessary moment of the plan of creation: 'According to Hegel's theory, contingency itself is necessary without qualifications. On account of the necessity of the Notion there must be contingency in the world.'[40] Conceived as such, love, incarnated by the all-active, all-reaching and all-penetrating Spirit (*der angreifende Geist*) has nothing in common with either simple escapist negation of the contingent realm or its passive contemplation:

But faith by itself – the pristine faith of New Testament – only begins the confirmation. The believer who first hears the good news of the transfigured world exists in a world still untransfigured. Therefore, to begin with, he can only be in this world and not of it, negating it like Stoics and Skeptics. *But the quality of his negation differs from theirs. He does not flee from the world, abandoning it to the control of untransfigured worldliness. Rather, he must dispute that control, and indeed, radically 'invert' the world with all its untransfigured values.* Only when this inversion has become wholly actual will the divine confirmation of the human have penetrated the whole of the human being . . . Hegel's Christianity will be not New Testament Christianity, but rather the life of a church only initiated by New Testament faith. This life will be . . . of the modern Protestant rather than of the medieval Catholic church. *Even the life of the Protestant faith will be fragmentary unless it is in creative interrelation with secular life . . .* The life, death, and resurrection of Christ has initiated a process which seeks completeness until an infinite, transcendent heaven has descended to a finite, transfigured earth.

ibid., 143; my emphasis

This other Hegelian concept of the 'work of love' – attaching itself to contingency in order to transform it with the regulative ideal of paradisiac *happiness* descending to earth – seems to be in perfect accordance with Duns Scotus who, having wrestled with the last powerful system of contemplative Neoplatonism created by Thomas Aquinas, inaugurated the modern world, by declaring: 'I say that contingency is not merely a privation or defect of Being like the deformity which is sin. Rather, contingency is a positive mode of Being, just as necessity is another mode.'[41]

On this reading, contingency is not being reduced to necessity, just as the immediate living concreteness is not to be sublated into 'icy abstraction' of the ideal concept. On the contrary, contingency itself becomes necessary *as such*: as a malleable 'figure of the world' which offers itself to the continuous transfiguration – until it 'paces the orbit of creation'.

For Rosenzweig, love indeed is an action which harbours a creative power: without love, all the neighbours/creatures – the multitude of contingent beings who just happen to spring into existence next to us – would indeed be 'like those who go down to the pit' (Ps. 28:1) or like the Pauline 'clanging cymbal' (1 Cor: 13.1), that is, nothing but automata briefly animated by a mechanical trick. Love, however, bestows the spectacle of creaturely being with autonomous and autotelic meaning. Love's goal is not to give those creatures life after death, but to give them *life before death*: to offer them active and affirming light thanks to which – as Franz Rosenzweig claims – they will be able to see their life again and say *ki tov*, 'yes, it is good'. Love, therefore, lifts existence to the second power in which the ephemeral phenomena of the contingent being raise to the dignity of 'essences'.[42] Thus, if David's Psalms are so full of fervent invocations to God who gives life, it is not because of the future possibility of life immortal, but because of the fear of death in life, in which contingent creature recognizes its negative fate and 'becomes like those who go down to the pit'. To have faith in active love means to believe in another finite life which will be able to *live* – instead of waiting for its end in the fearful mode of *imitatio mortis*.

As Franz Rosenzweig demonstrates in his *Star of Redemption*, whose second book is wholly devoted to the 'grammatical analysis' of *The Song of Songs*, this poem is, in fact, about a *disenchanted* love – yet, disillusioned for its own good. At the beginning, indeed, love strives towards God, but becomes rejected and, thanks to this fortunate frustration, comes back to the creaturely world where the one great unattainable object (as if the Lacanian *objet A*) becomes diffused into a metonymic sequence of small objects (*objets a*): the neighbours. In the psychoanalytical terms of D. W. Winnicott, the Rosenzweigian God could thus be said to resemble 'a good enough mother' who gently rejects the passionate possessiveness of her child and teaches it a lesson of the 'positive frustration'. For Rosenzweig, 'disenchantment makes love only stronger ... Love cannot be other than effective. There is no act of neighborly love that falls into the void' (SR, 269), because it is precisely the disenchantment that shows love its proper trajectory: away from the elusive Grand Object and towards the contingent beings of the world, which just happen to be next, in the most direct concrete vicinity (*Platzhalter*, or in Duns Scotus' idiom, *locum tenens*). In consequence, love – the active affect turned away from the false path of sublimation and back, towards the contingent beings – assumes the task of 'connecting all' and 'pacing the orbit of creation' (SR, 235).

Thus, after the commandment to love fails to reach its divine target and, due to this fortunate fiasco, *falls* back to earth, the soul, still seized by the loving fervour, no longer looks for the Great Other, but only for the others – *anything* – that happen to be nearby. Taught not to focus on one object only, frustrated in its desirous possessiveness, diffused and decentred (all in positive way!), the soul embraces *whatever* comes close. But the soul embraces it not in the Augustinian spirit of deadly indifference, operating without distinction or exception. It addresses its neighbours as singular *this* or *that* which occupies a place next to it. The real other can thus emerge only as an object of the *falling down, diffused and diffusing, love*: as a meta-ethical remnant of the broken conceptual totality, that is, only when he or she (or it) no longer figures as just *a* neighbour:

> [Love] is very unlikely really to reach the object toward which it was running. It was, after all, blind. Only the sense of touching the nighest had provided it with knowledge of the object. It does not know where best to penetrate the object. It does not know the way. Seeking it thus blindly, unguarded, *unpointed* – what is more likely than that it should lose its way, than that it should never get to see the object for which it was originally intended? Granted that it arrives somewhere, indeed at more than a single Anywhere is consequence of its *broadside diffusion*.
>
> SR, 269; my emphasis

But this dialectics of falling, effective as it is in its indefinite 'broadside diffusion', cannot be left to its own devices: it must be organized and disciplined under the supervision of the Law, which changes the emphasis of the blind love-action and makes it concentrate precisely on what initially only seemed to be its unintended consequence or 'side-effect' (SR, 269): the neighbour. It is, in the end, the Law, which explicitly chooses the *second* object for love, thus formatting its infinite diffusion; it is the Law that preserves God's lesson of frustration and further teaches love to choose, instead of one metaphorical Great Other, the innumerable small others, lining themselves up in an infinite metonymic series: of *whatever* simply comes next, close, nearby as a touchable, ostensible *das Diese*. Blind love acquires sight only thanks to Halakhah; it can only truly function when instructed by the Law. For, instead of stumbling, it can now 'walk' (where *hlkh* is the Hebrew root shared both by the verb 'walking' and the name of the legal codex). Love must proceed methodically, disciplining its diffusion in the infinite series of 'small' object choices that eventually will exhaust the horizontal 'plurality of things' (SR, 235). However, methodical or not, it is not a sublime act of reaching out towards the Absolute – the God, the Essence, the Truth itself – but, to the contrary, it is an act of *falling*: falling of and in love, towards and with the contingent world of the ontic objects.

This is what Rosenzweig designates as being *in der Mitte des Lebens*, in the middle of life, where the true business is happening, 'occurring' (USH, 80), that is, *in media res* of what is important – but also, literally, *in the middle*, in the healthy forgetfulness of the end, and in the falling in/of love, which Heidegger would have summed up with one contemptuous term: *Verfallenheit*. Rosenzweig's New Thinking covers exactly the same area as Heidegger's existential analysis, but constantly gives it the reverse spin: all those phenomena which *Being and*

Time describes and subsequently dismisses as *fallen*, Rosenzweig picks up and endorses as the real stuff of the 'middle of life'. Let's read Heidegger's fragment on fallenness from *Being and Time* through the Rosenzweigian lens:

> This 'absorption in . . .' [*Aufgehen bei . . .*] has mostly the character of Being-lost in the publicness of the 'they'. Dasein has, in the first instance, fallen away [*abgefallen*] from itself as an authentic potentiality for Being its Self, and has fallen into the 'world'. 'Fallenness' into the 'world' means an *absorption in Being-with-one-another*, in so far as the latter is guided by idle talk, curiosity, and ambiguity. Through the interpretation of falling, what we have called the 'inauthenticity' of Dasein may now be defined more precisely . . . 'In-authenticity' does not mean anything like Being-no-longer-in-the-world, but amounts rather to a quite distinctive kind of Being-in-the-world – the kind which is *completely fascinated by the 'world'* and by the Dasein – with of Others in the 'they'. Not-Being-its-self [*Das Nicht-es-selbst-sein*] functions as a positive possibility of that entity which, in its essential concern, is absorbed in a world. This kind of not-Being has to be conceived as that kind of Being which is closest to Dasein and in which Dasein maintains itself for the most part . . . Idle talk *discloses to Dasein a Being towards its world, towards Others, and towards itself* – a Being in which these are understood, but in a mode of *groundless floating*. Curiosity discloses *everything and anything*, yet in such a way that Being-in is everywhere and nowhere. Ambiguity hides nothing from Dasein's understanding, but only in order that Being-in-the-world should be suppressed in this uprooted 'everywhere and nowhere'.
>
> BT, 220–1; my emphasis

The 'absorption in being-with-one-another', betraying a 'complete fascination by the world' would not be dismissed as endangering Dasein's 'being-its-self': on the contrary, Rosenzweig endorses it as a right kind of affect orientating itself toward the series of the ontic objects which love encounters as simple whatever beings, *locum tenens* (*Platzhalter*), which Heidegger rejects as a shallow mode of 'they'. The 'idle talk', suspected of proliferating a 'groundless floating' of superficial 'curiosity', transforms in Rosenzweig's conversion into a 'living speech' of everyday life, which indeed 'discloses to Dasein a Being towards its world, towards Others, and towards itself'. The 'groundless floating', the sign of being 'in the middle of life', reflects for him the in/de/finite nature of love that can attach itself to 'everything and anything'. And if love can eventually pace the whole orbit of creation, it is only because it is 'uprooted' thanks to language and thus 'everywhere and nowhere' at the same time. If this is *fallenness*, then indeed, it is 'closest to Dasein' and for good reason. As Derrida could have said: 'This is life, *period*.'

The 'inauthentic' love: *Verfallenheit*

So, perhaps, instead of fighting against the idea of the Fall, there is another way to approach the lapsarian trope and say: *yes, finite being is a Fall, but a Fall-in-Love?* What if love, this perfect affect for the imperfect world, is the missing factor of the 'finite thinking', which has the Hegelian magical power of a true conversion of nothing into something? What if love is more than able to fulfil the function that Nancy designates to the Heideggerian 'exposing Death'? Seen in this alternative light, where it is rather love than death that tells the truth of our finitude, the universe of contingent beings is indeed constantly *falling*: falling *from* grace of the pleromatic perfect existence – but also falling *in* love, with itself. '*To lack nothing*, despite everything that's lacking: this is what it means to exist' (FT, 12): the finite being may thus be incomplete, shattered and groundless, but *not* hopelessly thrown into a cold abyss. It has accepted its in/de/finity as the source of love and, in that sense, indeed lacks nothing: it certainly does not crave 'nothing' as its missing essence, as in Heidegger. It is, therefore, the same *incompleteness* of the finite being, this time however described in its alternative aspect: while love as the marker of finitude shows it exposed, shattered and sharing its fallenness – death as the marker of finitude reveals a hard aloof monad of pure thinking that boldly stares its negativity straight in the eye.

The best illustration of what it means to substitute love for death as an alternative marker of our finitude comes from Walter Benjamin's early essay on 'Two Poems by Friedrich Hölderlin'. This brilliant miniature, so characteristic of Benjamin's style, demonstrates the crucial passage – *from Heidegger to Rosenzweig* – in an exemplary way. Benjamin sketches here a trajectory of evolution between the two versions, earlier and later, of the same poem by Hölderlin, which characteristically changes title from *Dichtermut* (*The Poet's Courage*) to *Blödigkeit* (usually translated as *Timidity*, but meaning also *stupidity*) and moves away from the theme of death and poetic myth towards the theme of love and poetic singularity. While the first version models poet's activity on the courageous *amor fati*, which allows him to embrace a semi-divine visionary position, the second is far more modest and 'timid' in its poetic aspirations, which now know how to limit themselves and stay 'in the midst of life'. What before appeared as *fallen* and because of that unworthy – now still remains *fallen*, but no longer to be contemptuously dismissed or 'dishonoured'.

The contrast between these two versions of the same poetic theme – Hölderlin's earlier *Dichtermut* and later *Blödigkeit* – serves Benjamin to illustrate the favourite motif of his own thinking which only then begins to take its shape: the passage from the life subdued to the mythic generality to the singular life challenging myth, while still using mythic images.[43] Both poems tackle the same subject: the relationship between the poet, who epitomizes a singular life (*das Lebendige*), with the whole of life (*das Leben*). The earlier poem, *Dichtermut*, emphasizes a need for courage (*Mut*) in the face of the deadly power of Parca who runs the totality of life; the poetic singularity feels endangered and on the defence when confronted with the rest of the living creatures to which it can relate only via the common condition of mortality. 'Doesn't Fate herself raise you to serve her hands?' asks Hölderlin, and this line, for Benjamin, is the axis of the first poem, expressing the gist of its vision: life's finitude conceived solely *sub specie mortis*. The later poem, however, is a site of a significant change or, as Benjamin calls it, *dislocation*: the sublime mood of the poetic courage gives way to a seemingly naive *Blödigkeit*, stupidity or distraction, as if *oblivious* of the true limit-conditions of a singular life, its emerging out of and returning back to the dark abyss of Fate. 'Don't your feet treat the truth as they do on soft carpet?' is now the sentence that replaces the former one, and overcomes the former's vertical-sublime-lethal mood with the more horizontal, diffused and extended one, more affirmative towards the creaturely world: 'Aren't all living creatures kin to you? / Doesn't Fate herself raise you to serve her hands? / So then wander defenseless / Through life and fear nothing!'[44] 'Aren't many living creatures known to you? / Don't your feet treat the truth as they do on soft carpet? / So then, my genius, just step / Boldly into life without care!'[45]

In the earlier poem, the mood was passive, dependent, waiting, sublimely arrested by the vertical dimension setting a metaphysical frame for the world of the living: its abyssal origin and its deadly end – but in the later one all this is gone: the poet forgets about life's limiting poles and actively strides into the very middle of creaturely life, positing it as 'true', not just a shadow of the more powerful metaphysical reality. Before the poet stood in fear as if *arrested* by the Blanchotian *arrêt de mort* – now he is *walking* 'without care', in the Rosenzweigian Halakhic manner of stumbling-yet-moving that combines Jacob's limping/wandering steps with the childlike first walking attempts. In *Dichtermut*, the poet contemplates the relation of his life to the life in general with a subdued horror – yet in *Blödigkeit*, the poet enters into this relation, walks straight into it, and then strides upon the world as if on an extensive carpet woven out of the singular lives (*die Lebendigen*): a complex pattern of existences, where all single threads remain visible, exposed and none is given over to the abstract notion of life as such. Benjamin calls this passage from the abstract generality of myth to the nominalist concreteness of poetic experience a 'dislocation of the mythological', characteristic of the mature romantic poetry:

> The association with mythology gives way to the context of a myth of one's own. For here, if one sought to see nothing more than the conversion of the mythological vision into the more sober one of walking, or to see nothing more than how dependency in the original version ('Does not the Parca herself nourish you for service?') turns, in the second version, into a positing ('Does not your foot stride upon what is true?') – all this would mean to remain only on the surface of the poem . . . It is the same procedure – *a dislocation of the mythological* – that everywhere constitutes the inner form of the revision.
>
> SW 1, 26, 28

The first life, therefore, remains in the grip of powerful 'gloomy mythology', which leaves no room for a singular invention and is governed by death as the force of an abstract generality – but the second life, though also availing itself of the mythological motifs, is already an individual, nominalistic, poetized creation and a deliberate *clinamen* from the general myth, stealing myth's elements for the sake of its own unified expression. Hence the second life constitutes itself as 'the poetized', *das Gedichtete*, a new form of a story/*récit* as if 'bricolaged' from the scraps of the deconstructed myth: 'One could say that *life is the poetized of poems* . . . The analysis of great works of literature will encounter, as the genuine expression of life, not myth but rather a unity produced by the force of the *mythic elements straining against one another*' (SW 1, 20; my emphasis).

This passage – from the integrity of myth, in which the singular *Lebendige* submits to the sublime wisdom of fate, to the antagonistic poetic use of the mythic elements, in which the singular life seeks its unique articulation – corresponds to the shift from the Greek to the Oriental, which is also the way Hölderlin saw it himself (SW 1, 35). The first poem 'lives in the Greek world': 'a structured world, whose mythological law is death' (SW 1, 23). But the second poem indicates a move from the fated life to the intimation of a redeemed life, already anticipated but not yet fully realized in the earlier version: 'a nonperceptual concept of life, an unmythic, *destiny-less concept of life* stemming from a spiritually exiguous sphere', thus forming 'a new cosmos of the poet . . . in an arrangement far removed from the mythological' (SW 1, 24–5). What for Benjamin counts as a redemption, or at least, an index of the messianic direction, is life's *destiny-lessness*, or *fatelessness*: the Hölderlinian *Shicksallosigkeit*, constituting the most cherished treasure of *die Unsterbliche*, the divine immortals.

But the finite life can also taste this ambrosia, yet only when it *forgets*, as if by a silly distraction, its destiny in the inevitable death. *Blödigkeit* is a moment of 'falling' in the Heideggerian sense of the word, fully endorsed by Rosenzweig: falling into the middle of life which then extends itself indefinitely, oblivious to its origin and its end. The singular life, therefore, does not thrive on *intensity* and all its sublime modes – its true element is diffusion and extension (*Erstreckung*), that expands the middle by postponing the finale which, albeit inevitable, gets removed from sight. Man, though finite, in this 'stupid' and *verfallen* mode of *das Man*, can thus also become *fateless* – but it would be a *bêtise* to dismiss it as a simple illusion.[46] We shall yet see, in the Chapter 3, on Derrida, how this *bêtise*, far from being 'just stupid', is capable of shaping a new affirmative attitude towards the creaturely world. Benjamin too, as if already anticipating the thanatic-heroic developments of the Heideggerian strain of thought, warns against any blithe dismissal of the 'stupid life'. *Blödigkeit* is not just falling, lack, illusion, purely negative deficiency; it has a positive structuring power. Thus, while in the earlier poem, 'Life was still the precondition of death; the figure sprang from nature . . . In this poem the danger of death was overcome through beauty. In the later version, *all beauty flows from the overcoming of danger.* Earlier, Hölderlin had ended with the dissolution of the figure, whereas the new version ends with the pure basis of structuring' (SW 1, 33; my emphasis).

This fragment can also be read as a direct polemic with Hegel's critique of the feebleness – or stupidity – of Beauty, which he opposes to the deadly power of Understanding, deriving from the bold 'tarrying with the negative' (PS, 19). While the old beauty served merely as an aesthetic veil, anaesthetizing the painful sting of death with its soothing 'images' – the new beauty, emanating from the fateless structuring of the finite life, emerges as *love*, the power of binding: '*Temporal existence in infinite extension,* the truth of the situation, binds the living to the poet' (SW 1, 27; my emphasis). Fateless, loving, walking horizontally upon the soft carpet of the living, the poet, no longer an isolated self in need of the existential courage to face the All, is now 'nothing but a limit with respect to life' (SW 1, 35), a 'supreme sovereignty of relationship' (SW 1, 34), which provides a common point where singular lives – only *some*, never *all* – intersect and enter into the 'bonds of love' (Hölderlin's *Liebesbande*). As Benjamin asserts, the 'innermost identity of the poet with the world' (SW 1, 34) *calms* the death anxiety, because his newly acquired love of the living appears at least as strong as the fear of death. The transformation, which the poet undergoes, is thus very much like the Rosenzweigian *Umkehr*: the reversal, conversion, or Exodus out of Egypt, the distressing 'narrow place' (*mitsraim*) of isolation. The moment love replaces death as the mark of the finitude, *die Erstrickung*, the oppressive narrowing of life paralysed in front of its lethal destiny, which appears as a condensed ending point, gives way to *die Erstreckung*, the 'stretching' or the extension, where love proceeds in a generous diffusion. The sublime intensity of the death as 'the point of existence' relents in favour of the mundane extensity of love, 'unpointed' (SR, 269), stretched out and diffused to embrace the living: not *all* the living, as in the first version, but only *many* [viele] living, i.e. only those the poet truly encounters, not in an abstract gaze of *die Allheit*, but concretely, meeting them on his way one by one. The poetic language has no force to connect all in one stroke, but it strikes many relations with the living and finds 'happiness' in the fulfilled passion of relationality (or, as Heidegger puts it dismissively: 'the absorption in being-with-one-another' (BT, 220)). Although finite, the poet's life opens thanks to the carpet-like extension of language to the practice of *infinitization*: it will not make him infinite, yet will also allow him to break the isolating barrier of his finitude.[47]

Thus, awakened from the sublime *Rausch*, the poet enters the stage of a serene sobriety which gives new shape and structure to his life: 'sobriety is now allowed, is called for, because this life is in itself sacred, *standing beyond all exaltation in the sublime*' (SW 1, 35; my emphasis). And then Benjamin immediately adds: 'Is this life still that of Hellenism?' (ibid.). Clearly not any longer, for all the mythic elements are now rearranged according to the 'Oriental fashion'. Hölderlin has reached his 'Hebrew moment'.[48]

Being-Towards-Birth

Arendt and the Finitude of Origins

Philosophy is indeed, as Nancy put it, 'marked as deadly': in Hegel, Rosenzweig's main adversary, as well as in Heidegger, the later enemy of Lévinas, human finite life is spent under the solitary auspices of death.[1] Nancy, who follows the analytics of Dasein only to a certain point, knows it well and for this very reason enlists for his 'finite thinking' another ally, coming from the corner opposite to Heidegger: Hannah Arendt. As he rightly points out, Arendt is the first thinker to consciously and deliberately move away from Heidegger without regressing into an idealistic illusion of the Husserlian infinite 'transcendental life': the first thinker to elaborate a parallel project of *another finitude* which does not exclude infinity but transposes it into the original plurality of love relations, 'the infinite singularity among others'. Thus, in the footnote explaining the idea behind *Being Singular Plural*, Nancy announces that his 'finite thinking' is not going to be just a commentary on Heidegger but also a 'move on from him': 'in the relation to Heidegger, one must remember the singular role played by Hannah Arendt and her reflection on "human plurality".[2] This singular role comes to the fore most spectacularly in Hannah Arendt's doctoral dissertation, *Augustins Liebesbegriff*, 'On the Concept of Love in Saint Augustin', written in the 1920s under Karl Jaspers' supervision.[3]

In birth we trust

The first part of Arendt's dissertation is devoted to the critique of Augustine's idea of love which, in her interpretation turns out to be merely a *Thanatos in disguise*: it is hard not to see that this is, in fact, a thinly veiled critique of Heidegger himself.[4] Arendt shows how Augustine, caught in the terminological net of Neoplatonic thought which defines love as craving (*appetitus*), runs into trouble with his account of the concept coming from a different tradition: the neighbourly love (*caritas*). Augustine's thinking would be thus wholly inscribed into a metaphysical craving for the eternal and the infinite, which completely disregards the finite dimension of the creaturely life. In the passage which strongly recalls Blanchot's analogical take on Heidegger, Arendt states that for Augustine, 'life on earth is a living death, *mors vitalis*, or *vita mortalis*. It is altogether determined by death; indeed it is more properly called death' (LA, 11).

But then, she also detects another stream of thought in Augustine – less 'Greek' and more 'Pauline' – that connects love not with the Platonic lack of being and craving, but with a *fullness of being* as given by the Maker in the moment of birth. Arendt writes:

> The decisive fact determining man as a conscious, remembering being is birth or 'natality,' that is, the fact that we have entered the world through birth. The decisive fact determining man as a desiring being was death or mortality, the fact that we shall leave the world in death. Fear of death and inadequacy of life are the springs of desire. In contrast, gratitude for life having been given at all is the spring of remembrance, for a life is cherished even in misery: 'Now you are miserable and still you do not want to die for no other reason that you want to be.' *What ultimately stills the fear of death is not hope or desire, but remembrance and gratitude*: 'Give thanks for wanting to be as you are that you may be delivered from an existence that you do not want. For you are willing to be and unwilling to be miserable.' *This will to be under all circumstances is the hallmark of man's attachment to the transmundane source of his existence.*
>
>   LA, 52; my emphasis[5]

And as the primary attachment to the giver-of-life which, by definition, must be transmitted from the outside, this will also constitutes the canvas of religious belief: its immediate basis is the sense of 'createdness' (*Kreatürlichkeit*). Arendt does not treat life as a natural/biological category. Life for her is a philosophical notion, just as being and thinking: *whatever tarries with the negativity of one's finitude is alive.* The living being is not a natural being, not even necessarily an organic one: it is a being that has to cope with its being finite, either instinctively or consciously – and one of these strategies, perhaps the most efficient, is to counteract the fear of death by 'remembrance and gratitude' for the 'gift of life' which always, necessarily, presents itself as a *gift*. This is why the condition of creatureliness (or createdness), brought in by Arendt, fits such description of life more aptly: a condition of life *given*, of life which constitutes a gift that can be essentially *trusted*, accepted with love and gratitude, unlike in the case of Heideggerian Dasein who reacts to the *datum* of its factical existence with the horror of *Geworfenheit*.[6] This *datum* can never become completely *mine*, never fully appropriated – but not because life is only lived 'by proxy' (as in Marion's reading of Augustine); life cannot be owned, because, as we already know from Rosenzweig, it is always 'in transition', always in passing from the donor to the donee, always in 'flow' and 'transmission'. Yet, at the same time, it must also be granted generously, i.e. not immediately expropriated, 'taken back' or 'shattered' in its fragile resoluteness, as in Heidegger's account. Derrida, whose contribution to this idea of *transitive life* we will soon explore, would also add that the creaturely condition is the one of the life given, but only in the *given time*, which is inescapably finite: not an eternity of self-secure ownership, but also not a nothing. Later on, in *The Life of the Mind*, Arendt will attribute this particular stance towards one's finitude to finite creatures determined by the moment of their birth and which she, in the deliberate distinction to the Greek tragic tradition, calls *natals*: 'Every man, being created in the singular, is a new beginning by virtue of his birth; if Augustine had drawn the consequences of these speculations, he would have defined men, not, like the Greeks, as mortals, but as *natals*'.[7]

For both, Arendt and Derrida, to believe in life as given – if only for a 'given time' – is the belief per se, and as such, the universal source of all revelatory religions that perceive the gift of life as deriving from the outside of the immanent cycle of nature (to recall again Derrida's 'Is not the religion of the living a tautology?'). As Hölderlin already knew, anticipating Arendt's focus on the potentials of *homo natus*: 'birth namely / Accomplishes the most, / And the ray of light, / That meets the new-born'. But if that is the case and natality indeed is the locus where life starts to learn the lesson of faith and trust, then, perhaps, the atheism – or, at least, atheism in its modern purely rationalist version – derives from the *denial of natality* as the rejection of the creaturely condition (or, simply, any conditioning per se). Indeed, such denial found the best expression in the figure of Satan from John Milton's *Paradise Lost*, the sacred patron of all modern atheists, who in his famous speech to the angels, trying to motivate them to rebel against their alleged Maker, famously declares: 'Who saw / When this creation was? remember'st thou / Thy making, while the Maker gave thee being? / We know no time when we were not as now; / Know none before us, self-begot, self-rais'd / By our own quick'ning power'.[8]

This is a different set of questions, which thrives on the reverse of every belief or the radical doubt: if you were not present at the moment of your inception, how can you *really* know that you were given the 'miracle of existence'? Hence Milton's Satan is the poetic incarnation of the Cartesian *cogito* who also does not know time where it was not as now, because it has always existed without life. Self-enclosed, self-begotten and self-raised, the 'thinking subject' knows none

before him, because he owes nothing to the chain of life's transmission. Even if he
dies, he has never lived; he has never been born. He does not start from 'home'
with all the anterior set of 'givens', which he is invited to accept as a *gift*[9] – he
simply starts from nowhere. Just as Epicurus dismisses death as an event that
cannot be witnessed – so does Satan dismiss birth as unwitnessable and therefore
invalid as a source of our existential self-determination. The element of
transcendence, necessarily inscribed in the bestowment of the gift of life, becomes
eliminated, together with life itself: the elimination of life, which is a characteristic
feature of modern philosophy (we will come back to this issue in the next chapter,
on Derrida), equals the elimination of transcendence, which is a characteristic
feature of philosophy as such.[10] In that sense, the pure 'thinking subject' of
modern philosophy – who might die, even if he never lived – indicates absolute
rejection of the creaturely condition that Arendt tries to recover, together with
her *belief in natality*: the fact of birth that cannot be witnessed, known, or
remembered, but precisely because of that must be believed in. In birth we trust.

Arendt's theologico-philosophical notion of the *natal life* harbours the most
promising opposition to the renaturalizing tendencies of late-modern biopolitics,
because, from the very beginning, creatureliness means *denaturalization*.[11] It is
in order to emphasize the difference between creature and natural being that
Augustine draws his distinction between *principium* and *initium*: the beginning
of the world and the beginning of man. Arendt quotes the famous fragment
from *The City of God* (XII, 20): *Initium ut esset, creatus est homo, ante quem
nemo fuit*: 'That a beginning be made, man was created.' Whereas *principium*
grounds the universe in the manner of the Greek *arche*, i.e. as the first arch-
principle of perpetual order of being, *initium* allows for a creative disruption of
the cosmic monotony, into which there suddenly enters a *novitas*, something
radically new. 'The child is born': this sentence announces a revolution of
newness disturbing the natural *nihil novi sub sole*:

> The beginning that was created by man prevented time and the created universe
> as a whole from turning eternally in cycles about itself in a purposeless way and
> without anything new ever happening. Hence, it was for the sake of *novitas*, in a
> sense, that man was created. Since man can know, be conscious of, and remember
> his 'beginning' or his origin, he is able to act as a beginner and enact the story of
> mankind.
>
> LA, 55

The finite being, therefore, does not have to think about itself as running
towards its death; it can also think about its moment of springing into being,

its *whence*, where it was bestowed with life, and revert the sequence of expectation by *substituting the beginning for the end*; or, in other words, by eliminating the obsessive thinking-of-death and replacing it with the grateful and trusting remembrance of one's origin. In Arendt's rendering, the Augustinian man says: I want to return to where I came from, for in my beginning is my end – the promised fullness of life. Remembrance and gratitude, therefore, are not strictly opposed to hope and desire; rather they engender their own structure of hope and desire, this time not driven by the recognition of death, but by the wish to cherish the original gift of life, to intensify it, to hope for 'more life' yet to come:

> Since our expectations and desires are prompted by what we remember and guided by a previous knowledge, it is memory and not expectation (for instance, the expectation of death as in Heidegger's approach) that gives unity and wholeness to human existence ... Only man, but no other mortal being, *lives toward his ultimate origin* while living toward the final boundary of death ... *By virtue of man's quest for his own being, the beginning and end of his life become exchangeable.*
>
> LA, 56–7; my emphasis

It is, therefore, this fundamental *reversal* that makes human finite existence truly human. Arendt's notion of exchangeability between the beginning and the end structurally resembles the Rosenzweigian *Umkehr* where love, given by the Maker, replaces death, sealing the creaturely existence with the heavy mark of mortality and, given the fact that Arendt knew *The Star of Redemption* at the time when she wrote about Augustine, her natalism may indeed be derivative from Rosenzweig's lesson on the existential conversion.

We will find some later variants of this reversal in other thinkers inspired by the Jewish heritage of *torat hayim*. In Levinas, it is precisely this reversed temporality which creates a countercurrent against death, a human life as *Sein-gegen-Tode*: instead of running straight towards its end, the human life creates an 'eddy' – or an 'interiority' – in the stream of time, which resists the flow of transience, and by reaching freely towards its origins in memory it separates from a being's general participation in the *flux*, thus making itself free. In *Totality and Infinity*, in the openly anti-Heideggerian fragment, Levinas defends human life's own dimension of delaying death and creating a realm of the middle: '*This is why the life between birth and death is neither folly nor absurdity nor flight nor cowardice*. It flows on in a dimension of its own where it has meaning, and where the triumph over death can have meaning.'

Yet, the acknowledgement of the separate 'in-between' of life cannot be reconciled with the remnants of the acephalic Neoplatonism that constitutes the default mode of Western thinking, still so tangible in Heidegger. In order to conjure away its hovering shadow, Lévinas, in the distinctly Arendtian gesture, points to the moment of natality when the subject immediately 'enters in the relation with the Other': it is precisely this relation that makes his life meaningful, though in a different sense than the 'meaning' allegedly acquired by an eternal infinite being:

> The postponement of death in a mortal will – time – is the mode of existence and reality of a separated being that has entered in the relation with the Other. This space of time has to be taken as the point of departure. *In it is enacted a meaningful life which one must not measure against the ideal of eternity, taking its duration and its interests to be absurd or illusory.*
>
> ibid., 232; my emphasis

In Lévinas, therefore, human life is consciously finite, not aspiring to eternity: it derives its meaning from entering in the relations with others, made possible in the 'space of time' of life's self-extended *medium*. Its finitude is not determined solely by mortality, at least not directly: death is mediated here through the *resistance against death*, drawing from the sources of memory which pulls against the time's seemingly irreversible 'it was'. Lévinas' vision of the triumph over death, ultimately exercised in the love of the neighbour, remains strictly within the confines of the finite life. Once our subjective separated being enters in the relation with the Other and acquires meaning thanks to it, the lethal threat comes also mediated via the death of others whom we love precisely because they can – and will – die (as Derrida says apropos Cixous: 'in the end, too quickly'). *Pace* Heidegger, for whom man is defined by the intimate relation with his 'ownmost death', Lévinas claims the opposite: we learn about death and experience its sting not through some internal intimation of *Verendlichung* that constantly 'shatters' the core of our being, but through the demise of the living creatures we love. In *God, Death, and Time*, in the conclusion of his lecture on Ernst Bloch and his 'principle of hope', Lévinas says:

> Thus we come back to the love 'strong as death.' It is not a matter of a force that could repel the death inscribed in my being. However, it is not my nonbeing that causes anxiety, but that of the loved one or of the other, more beloved than my being. What we call, by a somewhat corrupted term, love, is *par excellence* the fact that the death of the other affects me more than my own. *The love of the other is the emotion of the other's death.* It is my receiving the other – and not the

anxiety of death awaiting me – that is the reference to death. We encounter death in the face of the other.

GDT, 105; my emphasis

...and thus become even more determined to take a stand *gegen-Tode*: love has not power to 'repel death inscribed in my being', but it has a power to expose the ethical scandal of the death of the others, which makes us want to oppose it.

Poising himself against Heidegger even more explicitly, Harold Bloom also argues for the powers of the *medium* of life. For him, the poetic life (which here serves as the intensified *pars pro toto* of human life as such) is structured according to the rhetorical trope of *metalepsis* or the 'reversal': the substitution of an origin for an end, which allows for the emancipation of a creative impulse from the thanatic repetition of 'more of the same'. Only when cause and effect are metaleptically reversed and the poetic self, instead of going with the flow 'towards-death', works stubbornly towards his own origins, a new creation can happen at all; only when the poet dwells within and elaborates on the powers of *origination*, can he hope to become truly *original*, not just a copy or replica of what was before. The Arendtian-Levinasian-Bloomian focus on the origins is thus the necessary precondition of freedom, creativity and – according to what we have said previously about Heidegger's hidden dimension of *Sein-gegen-Tode* – 'resoluteness', which, in Nietzsche's words, rebel against the time's 'It was' or against the time's empty accumulation and repetition.

This is where, it seems, Hegel, Heidegger and Kojève, the three masters of modern thanaticism, get it wrong: it is not *just* the consciousness of death which acts as an anthropogenic factor that makes human being truly human. A mere consciousness of death only adds a reflexive dimension to the animal way of living, which inevitably ends with dying; as indeed in Hegel's description of the Master who once challenged death fully consciously but then leads an idle life of a *verblödet*, stupefied, beast. What truly constitutes the anthropogenic moment is the *reversal of temporality*, which ignores the end for the sake of a *doubled origin*: the renewal of the gift of being exercised in the spirit of biophilia, or the Derridean synonymization of 'loving-living', which affirms every moment of life as a repetition of the beginning, the incessant *birthing*. For Paul and Augustine, due to this reversal-renewal, death as such completely dissolves by showing its true face of a *rebirth* into a truly eternal way of living. But this is only one extreme – Christian – version of the anthropogenic reversal, which goes so far as to annul altogether the initial condition of finitude; by turning death simply into a new birth, this time giving life eternal and infinite, the Christian 'impatient heart' (Rosenzweig) evacuates itself from the realm of creatureliness, inescapably marked with death.[15] What Arendt – but also Rosenzweig, Lévinas and Bloom – have in mind is more modest, and more in harmony with the limits of finite being: the reversal does not prolong the moment of 'natality' ad infinitum, offering a birth without death and life without loss, but complicates the temporality of human finite existence by giving it a non-natural, or reverse, *causa finalis*. It lets human origin shine on and organize the whole of life by deprivileging the natural end. Contrary to the thanatic condition, which overestimates death as the ownmost, organizing and defining, goal-centre-essence of human life, this vision of finitude, focused on natality, ignores the natural end by replacing it with the counter-rhythm of a constant renewal, working on and through the original 'gift of life': a gift not be defined, possessed and pinned down to its 'essence', but to be lovingly shared, told and diffused, as precisely a Rosenzweigian 'thing of no-essence', in a constant 'transition from one thing to another'. Thus, the very idea of the gift itself immediately implies sociality inherent in the moment of origin – versus the absence of others, obliterated in the solitary (*unbezüglich*, 'regardless') moment of dying, so often emphasized and extolled by Heidegger. The focus on the beginning of human life, rather than on its end, brings in the *original heterogeny* of human existence: the constant company of others who gave me life and sustained its precarious growth with their love, summarized in the ideal image of the Augustinian 'God, who made me'. Seen from the perspective of its beginning, the finite human life is immediately relational, sustained by the exchange of love and gratitude – while seen from the perspective of its end it sinks into the soliloquy of death, always too *jemeinig* and *einzig* to be shared.

This *love of life*, as finite and given, is based not on fear and expectation of death, but on remembrance and gratitude that manage to form a new imperative: to work upon and augment what had been offered here and now, in the innerworldly condition of creatureliness: a 'given time'. What we therefore love in our neighbours is not the spark of an infinite, indestructible life fallen into the creaturely realm, but the finite share of life that comes from the same source, the 'God who made me'. It is precisely this dependence and gratitude that shapes the Lévinasian 'covenant of creatures' who share the same enterprise of a *given life*: offered as a gift and a task at the same time.

This combination of gift and task – a 'given time' of a single creature who is not asked to complete the enterprise of life, but also asked not to desist from it[16] – constitutes the gist of what Wallace Stevens calls 'a constant effort to be born'.

Love is not a passive mood of an all-embracing contemplative *Ja-Sagen*; it is an active affect, the task of which is to awaken in every newborn creature a sense of gratitude that will override the anxiety of separate existence, or, in Otto Rank's formulation, the 'trauma of birth' (on which more in a moment). As Laplanche's close associate, Jean-Bertrand Pontalis says, in the distinctly anti-Lacanian vein which echoes the anti-Heideggerian tones of Arendt's and Lévinas's *torat hayim*: it is the *transmission of life* – and not the *initiation through death* – that constitutes the anthropogenic secret of human existence. *It is only natural that we all should die, but it is not at all natural that we all should want to live*:

> To be a *living person*: a *task* carried out, programmed for the animal organism, but which is always in need of invention for humans; a contradictory task, if one thinks about it, but one which gives humans individual tension and mobility, the ability to be not normal but normative, and which makes repeated encounters with others a necessary event. *For what both biologically and psychologically defines life is that it is transmitted.*[17]

To instil in a newborn human being a wish to live, despite all the anxieties caused by life's finitude, is not enough just to enkindle the instinct of self-preservation. It is only due to a symbolic bond of love, which presents the newborn as a 'lovable creature', that it can begin to participate in the characteristically human enterprise of finite life and *transmit life further*: not only – not even predominantly – in furthering the species, but in spreading the gift of life in the acts of neighbourly love, precisely the way it was envisaged by Rosenzweig. It is not 'by imitation (*mimesis*) that man's essence comes to share in the eternal being' (L.A, 74), adjusting itself as a part to the whole, but by *initium*, the power of a new beginning, which renews – always afresh, always singularly – the experiment of the finite life that knows and accepts its creaturely status. Transmissibility of life, far from being self-evident and spontaneous, is thus a matter of the non-natural 'tradition of life'.

The miracle of natality versus the machine of nature

All this, according to Arendt, can be deduced from the *philosophical concept of birth*. Just as are *Mangel*, 'deficiency', in Herderian terminology, or 'monstrosity' in Canguilhem's approach, so is 'natality' a borderline category that situates human life at the very fringes of the natural; where nature deconstructs itself as the system of life and gives way to the freedom of the living, based on the canvas of creatureliness. The birth, therefore, is both natural as a biological fact, and at the same time, *denaturalizing* as a caesura that throws the individual human life out of joint, determined by the natural system of self-preservation – and into a different set of relations implied by the creaturely 'gift of life'. Birth is a *miracle* spelling the radical beginning, the very possibility of possibility and of breaking the fatal boredom of the natural cycle which, to 'mortal beings' like us, can only mean the Schopenhauerian doom. In one of the most powerful fragments of *The Human Condition*, in the chapter devoted to 'Action', Hannah Arendt says:

> If without action and speech, without the articulation of natality, we would be doomed to swing forever in the ever-recurring cycle of becoming, then without the faculty to undo what we have done and to control at least partially the processes we have let loose, we would be victims of an automatic necessity bearing all the marks of the inexorable laws which, according to the natural sciences before our time, were supposed to constitute the outstanding characteristic of natural processes . . . *to mortal beings this natural fatality, though it swings in itself and may be eternal, can only spell doom.*
>
> HC, 246; my emphasis

Once again, we can hear here a clear voice of protest against the Heideggerian verdict of *Sein-zum-Tode* which sentences us, 'mortal beings', to death which, beginning its work with the moment of birth, subsumes everything potentially new under the inexorable law of the natural cycle. More than that, we can also hear the voice of protest against thinking in terms of *sola immanentia* which 'leaves men to themselves', shuts their life in the predictable boredom of the 'law of mortality' and brings all their daring projects to ruin:

> If left to themselves, human affairs can only follow the law of mortality, which is the most certain and the only reliable law of life spent between birth and death . . . The life span of man running toward death would inevitably carry everything human to ruin and destruction if it were not for the faculty of interrupting it and beginning something new, a faculty which is inherent in action like an ever-present reminder that men, though they must die, are not born in order to die but in order to begin. Yet just as, from the standpoint of nature, the rectilinear movement of man's life-span between birth and death looks like a peculiar deviation from the common natural rule of cyclical movement, thus action, seen from the viewpoint of the automatic processes which seem to determine the course of the world looks like a miracle.
>
> HC, 246

Yet, what is also significant here, this deregulation/deviation does not spell a break with life: this is not the thanatic caesura of the sublimated *bios* which soars above *zoe* and despises the needs of biological being. Arendt does not follow the Greek (but also Hegelian-Kojèvian) line in which *bios*, by having negated *zoe*, catapults human being into a non-natural existence of 'pure thinking'. Although reluctant towards nature as the 'automatic system of repetition', in which, as in Kohelet's vision, nothing new emerges under the sun (see the reference to Ecclesiastes in HC, 204), she is also highly aware of the 'tyrannical' element in the Greek model of *bios* as *eu-zen*, the 'good living' that violently submits to itself the vital order. In her note from 1952, apropos Marx and his praise of natural necessity (which she also opposes), Arendt writes: 'The Greeks do the opposite: they "derive" freedom out of the "rational" or *violent domination* of the necessary. This is one of the reasons why the logos becomes tyrannical … *Eu zen* = to live in freedom = to dominate *tyrannically* over necessity.'[18]

Possibly having in mind the sentence of Heraclitus, which elaborates on the ambivalence of *bios* – 'The name of the bow is life; its work is death' – Arendt distances herself from the vision of 'good living' based on the thanatico-sadistic principle of domination, symbolized by the 'deadly Apollo', the divine archer and the god of intellect. Arendt's reluctance towards nature[19] combined with her enthusiasm for life which knows and tolerates no tyranny, may appear as aporetic to those commentators who want to locate her within the Aristotelian opposition between *bios* and *zoe*,[20] but, as she herself openly admits, her *Natalität* is not of a Greek origin, it follows the Gospels, Saint Paul and to some extent Saint Augustine:

> The miracle that saves the world, the realm of human affairs from its normal, 'natural' ruin is ultimately the fact of natality, in which the faculty of action is ontologically rooted. It is, in other words, the birth of new men and the new beginning, the action they are capable of by virtue of being born. Only the full experience of this capacity can bestow on human affairs faith and hope, those two essential characteristics of human existence which Greek antiquity ignored altogether, discounting the keeping of faith as a very uncommon and not too important virtue and counting hope among the evils of illusion in Pandora's box. It is this faith in and hope for the world that found perhaps its most glorious and most succinct expression in the few words with which the Gospels announced their 'glad tidings': *A child has been born unto us.*
>
> HC, 247; my emphasis[21]

Just as in Derrida's definition, we are dealing here with a different movement – not of Thanatos fighting against Eros, not of *bios* rising out of the contempt for and negation of *zoe*, but of the dialectical tension of 'life against life', but always in and for life', which characterizes messianic vitalism. In Arendt's theological imagination, life is always a *given life*; if she may often come across as hostile to the notion of sheer survival which she (wrongly) associates only with the biological self-preservation of *animal laborans*, it is only for the sake of life as reflecting on its givenness, life articulated and maintained by the tradition of life. Life conceives of itself as offered – transmitted, handed over, and thus rooted in the 'chain of tradition' – which excludes any 'Satanic' self-conception as *causa sui*, on the one hand, but also as, at least, partly exempt from the 'iron cage' of natural necessity. The living, therefore, is principally a *dependent being* and as such the opposite of the philosophical Absolute, but this is not the kind of dependence that would clash with its sense of freedom; it is not modelled on Milton's Satan, the *birth-denier* who claims that his autonomy must be either self-caused or it does not exist at all. The concept of the *gift* allows for a dialectical *tertium* between the full submission to the natural Ananke and the equally absolute subjective freedom: a different sort of 'chain' – the 'chain of tradition' – which transmits the 'persuasion into life' in order to teach every singular birthling to dispose of the gift freely, the way he or she sees it fit, yet not without gratitude and respect. The gift is always a surplus towards any necessity – it cannot be accommodated into the 'the overall gigantic circle of nature herself, where no beginning and no end exists and where all natural things swing into changeless, deathless repetition' (HC, 96) – but it also gently 'chains' by its persuasion: that it is worth while to believe in life, despite its finitude.

With life lived as *given* being becomes *transitive*: no longer a fixed essence, as in Heidegger, but, as in Rosenzweig, released – or *leased out* – to be acted out and told in the infinite number of ways. 'To lease' indeed chimes closely with 'to re-lease', which, on its part, shares the 'liquid' family resemblance with the words signifying redemption as, for instance, the German *Erlösung*: liquidation of the solid and petrified, absolution as *solvency* which, in Arendt, constitutes the main function of love. In *The Human Condition*, love emerges mostly as forgiveness: 'forgiving and acting – she says – are as closely connected as destroying and making' (HC, 241). By the power of 'undoing of what was done' (ibid.), the exonerating love releases from fixations and rigid cycles of retribution; it makes those who pardon one another in the act of love *solvent* again, capable of moving on and going on with their lives – which, as we have seen in the previous chapter, is also the essential motif in Rosenzweig. *Life must flow* – and it cannot maintain its liquid solvency without the neighbourly acts of mercy.

On Arendt's teaching, which in my reading forms an ingenious continuation of *torat hayim*, the Augustinian *initium* is an active *initiative* – the opposite of the passive *initiation*, implied by the Heideggerian horror of *Geworfenheit* which throws unprepared Dasein in the midst of the hostile world. The birth throws too -- but into a solvent/fluid element of commencing, initiating, and, as antithetical to the Heideggerian *Verendlichung*, never-ending. The life seen from the point of the natalist beginning – the only moment that truly gives an intimation of life *almost* pure, the least touched by death, not yet 'ready for dying' – is always, as Dante called it, a *vita nuova*: novelty and innovation is part and parcel of its paradoxical Rosenzweigian 'un-essence' – never accomplished, always promising. *The natalist life, therefore, is a constant promise.* Death cannot be promised: it is a dead-sure axiom and because of that so cherished by Western philosophy. Life, on the other hand, can only be promised, and because of that forms a favourite mirage of Western messianism. Life always begins and never ends, just as Scheherazade's stories; its non-ending nature constitutes the very opposite of the being defined by its end. But if every young life is most of all an *initium*, that also means that life cannot be initiated by any external ritual of formatting. The *torat hayim*, the tradition of life, proceeds in a different way than the *rites de passage* based on simple submission: the transmission is successful only if the 'gift of life' is not received in the passive spirit of grateful surrender, but if it is immediately taken over in the active and free, initiating initiative. The initiative here is not heteronomous: it belongs to each and every new life itself, precisely as in Derrida's description of the paradoxical autodidactic nature of life: 'And does one ever do anything else but learn to live, alone, from oneself, by oneself?' (SM, xvii).

The permanent *initium*, therefore, is like permanent neoteny: the repetition of the act of natality, an open *being-towards-birth*, which must be strictly opposed to the closure of 'being-towards-death', where death functions as a defining 'chisel' or *Gestalter*, forming the in-de finite life into something 'lived to the end', and because of that 'authentic' and 'real'. In Heidegger, as well as Lukacs, we can still hear the echo of the archaic model of initiation in which the law of life must come from the outside of life: Dasein becomes 'authentic' only when *ver-endlicht*, i.e. defined from the beyond of life, which only can give life a form. From the natalist perspective, however, life is not expected to be 'real' in the sense of being 'lived to the end'. It is seen as always beginning – and because of that un-finished, in-finite. Arendt's natalism, therefore, gives us a very Rosenzweigian answer to the Hegelian problem of the 'infinite-in-the-finite' or, in original theological formulation, *finitum capax infiniti*: the moment of infinity lies in life's deliberately in/de-finite 'un-essence', i.e. in its power of commencing that actively opposes the thanatic closures and opens to a potentially infinite chain of transmission. Just as Rabbi Tarphon says in *Pirke Aboth*: 'You are not required to complete the work, but neither you are free to desist from it' 2, 21). This work, the work of life, is all about beginning, renewing, revising, continuing, where the whole 'chain of tradition' – *shalshelet ha-kabbalah* – is as alive as the smallest link which it contains. This image of the chain – strictly horizontal and strong with the strength of all the singular lives that form it – is particularly apt to describe the 'tradition of life', which remains 'in life and for life'. *Pace* the common prejudice that sees Jewish Law as the epitome of the sovereign imposition from 'beyond', it is far more inherent to life itself.

Arendt's *Sein-zum-Geburt* is a close structural equivalent of Heidegger's *Sein-zum-Tode*: just as death and its special place in human existence singles Dasein out of the continuum of worldly beings – so is birth in Arendt a possibility of a radical break with the continuum of natural cycle. Yet, while in Heidegger the break is absolute and transports Dasein 'above biological life', in Arendt the caesura appears more dialectical: it is after all still a life, or rather, *the* life, where life condenses into its most intense singular manifestation. Natality breaks with nature, but it does not break with life.

Life, the permanent birthing

But to leap straight into the *media vitae* and initiate, instead of being initiated, means to be able to get over the traumas caused by those 'overspecified poles' that threaten to collapse the precarious middle: the 'trauma of death', of which I have spoken here copiously, but also the symmetrical trauma of which I have been silent so far – the 'trauma of birth'.[24] Melanie Klein, who – together with Otto Rank – pioneered psychoanalytic research into postnatal anxiety, says:

> The first external source of anxiety can be found in the experience of birth. This experience, which, according to Freud, provides the pattern for all later anxiety-situations, is bound to influence the infant's first relations with the external world. It would appear that the pain and discomfort he has suffered, as well as the loss of the intra-uterine state, are felt by him as an attack by hostile forces, i.e. as persecution.[25]

Hannah Arendt's take on natality would thus appear a bit one-sided: while she emphasizes only positive aspects of the fact of being born – the radical beginning, love of and for the others, following the active gratitude of the child thankful for the gift of life – she ignores the psychoanalytical discovery of persecutory anxiety and anger linked to the *loss of the prenatal bliss*. We shall see in a moment that this omission is far from accidental and that it belongs to a specific psychotheological set-up, closely related to *torat hayim*, which does not even consider the idea of the prenatal life as life, hence does not dwell upon its loss. But it does not mean that Arendt is wrong. In her *Envy and Gratitude*, Melanie Klein also makes room for love and gratitude which, in a healthy psyche, eventually balances and compensates for the deadly anxiety. Writing about maternal care, she says:

> The gratification and love which the infant experiences in these situations all help to counteract persecutory anxiety, even the feelings of loss and persecution aroused by the experience of birth. His physical nearness to his mother during feeding – essentially his relation to the good breast – recurrently helps him to overcome the longing for a former lost state, alleviates persecutory anxiety and increases the trust in the good object.
>
> ibid., 63

In this section, I would like to put Arendt's natalism in the wider context of what Derrida, apropos Benjamin, calls 'the awakening of Judaic tradition'. According to Hermann Cohen, who pioneered this awakening in the twentieth century, its foundational moment is the deliberate 'choice of life' that opposes the 'metaphysics of death', prevalent in the so-called 'pagan' religions. This reverse and contrary drive of Judaism can indeed be summed up as the *affirmation of the fact of birth*. All other elements of Judaism's contrariety listed by Freud in his essay on 'Moses and Monotheism' – separation, persistence of traumatic memories, guilt, irreconciliation, proleptic movement towards futurity – derive from this one fundamental decision to say *yes* to the simple fact of being born: of leaving the blissful bondage of the womb and enter the risky desert of autonomous self-constitution. Hence, in Jewish imagery, the mythologem of the painful expulsion from Paradise interferes with the joyful narrative of the Exodus from Egypt. When Paradise acquires Egyptian features of constriction and 'narrowing' (*mitsraim*) indicating obstacle to maturation, then the act of getting out of this original cosmic womb can only mean abandoning the state of infantility, which, paraphrasing Marx, we could easily call the 'idiocy of the paradisiac life'. When we remember that, in Jewish theology, both rabbinic and Kabbalistic, the expulsion from Paradise is definitely much less dramatic and deplorable than in the Christian narrative, where the trespass of Adam and Eve grows into an unpardonable original sin, bearing all the marks of the tragic *hamartia*, this *pronatalistic* – and with it, proleptic and progressive – thrust becomes even more visible. The Augustinian Christianity, steeped in the pagan idiom of Greek tragedy, expresses its *antinatalistic* wisdom in the idiom of the original sin, which repeats the famous words of Sylenus, quoted by Nietzsche in the introduction to *The Birth of Tragedy*: *me phynai*, 'it would be better for you never to be born'. Judaism, on the other hand, could easily borrow the most prophetic lines from Milton's *Paradise Lost*, which describe the adventurous mood of the exiled first couple after they had overcome their 'natural' tendency to nostalgic sorrow: 'Some natural tears they drop'd, but wip'd them soon; / The World was all before them, / Where to choose / Their place of rest, and Providence their guide: / They hand in hand with wandering steps and slow, / Through *Eden* took their solitary way.'[27]

I want thus to argue that, psychoanalytically speaking, the narrative of the Jewish Exodus, *yetsiat mitsraim* – coupled with the principle of life, *torat hayim* – delivers a great code containing a unique, but also universal, strategy of dealing with the 'trauma of birth'. It urges us to accept it and *get over it*, so that life can establish itself as quickly as possible in its own autonomous 'middle'.

By claiming that the most significant traumatic event in human life was *not* of a sexual nature, as Freud famously insisted, Otto Rank, the inventor of the 'birth trauma', poised himself on the verge of psychoanalytic heterodoxy. Controversial still today as a prodigal advocate of 'anti-Oedipal heresy', Rank nonetheless provides key insights into the psychology – or, better, in Santner's phrasing, *psychotheology* – of birth experience: the lingering memory of the prenatal bliss, the traumatic rupture of the intrauterine existence, the ambivalent figure of the mother who simultaneously gives shelter and expels from it, and the paternal function that consists of tearing the child away from its regressive infatuation with the womb.

In Rank's somewhat exaggerated account, all symbolic and culture-forming achievements of human race 'finally turn out to be a belated accomplishment of the incompleted mastery of the birth trauma' (TB, 5). Myths, marking the 'pagan' stage of the development of mankind, are nothing but 'the most sublime attempts to *undo* the birth trauma, to *deny the separation from the mother*' (TB, 105; my emphasis). According to Rank, the vast majority of cultures choose the 'pagan' way, i.e. maintain the high level of maternal ambivalence that 'rests on the protection given by the mother (womb), but on the other hand is due to the fear of her caused ultimately by the birth trauma' (TB, 90) and as such constitutes the insoluble enigma of natality: *the* enigma itself, the alpha and omega of all mysteries. Attracted by its fascinating ambiguity, the 'pagan' economy of pleasure seems unable to leave this mystifying knot of ultimate bliss and at the same time lethal threat: 'just as the anxiety at birth forms the basis of every anxiety or fear, so *every pleasure has as its final aim the re-establishment of the intrauterine pleasure*' (TB, 17; my emphasis), 'naturally' imagined as 'the best of all worlds' (TB, 63). The very idea of separation, on the other hand, is unanimously associated with evil, sin and the negation of life: 'To be dead has the same meaning for the child as to be away – that is, to be *separated* – and this directly touches on the primal trauma' (TB, 24). Hence the 'pagan' solution understands augmentation of life as *restitutio ad integrum*, that is, as a symbolic reconciliation with the totality represented by the life-giving womb, which undoes the traumatic occurrence of birth and its incipient evil of the deadening separation. The *trauma* of birth is thus being removed – together with the very *fact* of birth. The child is thrown out with the bathwater – literally.

There is, however, a possibility of the 'reversal tendency'. The spell-binding ambivalence of natality may prevail and preserve its mesmerizing status in later cultural formations, but it may also strive towards the resolution that Rank calls the *heroic conversion* and which indeed chimes closely with the reverse tendency, of the Judaic model: 'By means of the reversal of feeling (hate) towards the father, the entire situation of the mother's protecting womb, in its cultural and cosmological significance, becomes a *unique, gigantic, hostile entity*, which pursues the hero, identified with the father, and ever challenges him to the new battles' (TB, 72; my emphasis).

Yet, in Rank's psychoanalytically rather conservative interpretation, the 'hero conversion' is, in the end, doomed to failure: the vindictive Mother figure takes its inevitable revenge by meeting the hero with his final destiny being also her final manifestation – death. Here we touch on the pagan limitation of psychoanalysis itself which did not take the name of Oedipus as its guiding aegis in vain. In absolute fidelity to Freud's orthodoxy, Rank says: 'The Unconscious can think of separation, departure, and dying only in terms of the wish-fulfilling regression to the womb, because it knows and can portray *no other* wish tendency' (TB, 81; my emphasis).

Thus, whenever the 'reversal tendency' of a 'forward movement' (ibid.) emerges, it must be reinterpreted, quite acrobatically, as a disguised or displaced desire for regression. Psychoanalysis, described by Freud himself as a new powerful 'gloomy mythology', pays thus its due to the 'pagan' psychotheology: any attempt to go 'in the other direction' reveals itself ultimately as futile and illusory. On this account, a Jew would be only suffering from an 'eternalized' hero syndrome, taken out of the context of psychic development and then frozen in the vacuum: while he *converts* from hating father to hating mother, he ultimately fails to reconcile himself with the maternal element, which will always remain the proper goal of the heroic circuitous journey.

Yet, in Sandor Ferenczi's *Thalassa* (published in the same year as the *Trauma of Birth*, 1924, in close collaboration with Rank), the tables already begin to turn, however timidly. For the most part of the book, Ferenczi explains coitus in terms of a secret regressive wish to return to the maternal womb, but he also makes room for another, quite opposite, desire to progress: to leave the matrix for good and celebrate the fact of birth as the exodic moment of emancipation: 'We too consider coitus as such a partial discharge of that still unassimilated shock which is the legacy of the birth trauma; at the same time it appears to be like a game, or, more exactly expressed, a commemoration celebrating a *happy liberation from the bondage*.'[28]

It is not an accident that the last phrasing of this quote, although referring to the successful completion of sexual act – 'a commemoration celebrating a happy liberation from the bondage' – could have come directly from the *Pesach Hagadda* and, considering Ferenczi's Jewish orthodox background, it very well might indeed. In Ferenczi's psychoanalytic speculation, Exodus figures as the paradigmatic emblem of the reverse movement, strongly opposed to the womb nostalgia which he, following Otto Rank, perceives as the predominant 'default' tendency of human psyche. While the 'natural' vector of human desire orients itself regressively towards the bliss of the primary narcissism, the 'exodic' movement pushes in the other direction, wishing for another fulfilment that would not cancel out the fact of being born, i.e. of becoming a separate individual.

A similar praise of separation as a unique feature of the Judaic tradition was uttered by Eric Santner who in his seminal work on Rosenzweig and Freud, pioneering the psychoanalytic approach to Jewish religion, stated that:

> The losses correlative to the advent of monotheism ... can be understood as a *series of traumatic cuts or separations*: of the deity from plastic representation; of spirituality from magic, animism, and sexual ecstasy; of thinking from the fantasy of the omnipotence of thoughts; of death from the cult of the afterlife (call it separating from 'Mummy' and all forms of 'mummification').
>
> PEL, 105–6

In this clever punning, Santner makes an imaginative shortcut linking Egypt as the realm of death ('mummification') with Paradise as the lap of mother-nature, signifying the prenatal blissful existence ('Mummy'). This pun, which on the deeper structural level identifies life-before-birth with death (the Beckettian horror of *womb-tomb*), makes it absolutely clear that in Judaic tradition *there is no life before birth*: the true life begins only *after* we are finally and irreversibly born. The peak of life does not reside in the pleromatic experiences of primary narcissism, but in in the affirmation of the very trauma that constitutes birth: the violent destruction of the dyadic union between mother and child, followed by the latter's ultimate separation. The traumatic character of this event can never be denied by any reparatory or re-enchanting magic: the violent rupture, which disenchants and cuts the umbilical cord linking with the magical pleroma, is the necessary ingredient of life understood in the Jewish way. Thus, what Santner calls the 'losses correlative to the advent of monotheism' are, in fact, traumas converted into affirmative, though hesitant and 'wandering', steps of a liberated and separated living being – precisely as in Milton's prophetic vision, in which Adam and Eve enter the world with the limping walk of Jacob.

The original affirmation of the trauma of birth results in the affirmation of all other consecutive traumas, immediately converted into stepping stones of maturation and progress: the loss of the immanent sense of the sacred embodied in the immediacy of plastic representations; the loss of the magical omnipotence, characteristic of the primary process that cannot yet differentiate between phantasy and reality; the loss of unbound sexual ecstasy, where no obstacle bars the entrance back into the cosmic womb; and the loss of immortality, which is the necessary cost of gaining a self-knowledge of one's separation as a mortal finitude. These traumatic losses, which thanks to the act of affirmation ('and God saw that it was good': *ki tov*) turn into *advantages* and because of that into *advances*, pave the way forwards: they open the very possibility of a proleptic, future-oriented development that breaks from the regressive, circulatory movement characteristic of what Rank calls the 'denial of birth'. By giving up on the nostalgia after the prenatal existence in the womb, the Jewish version of monotheism institutes a *break*, a trauma as a positive way of life, which cuts itself loose from the regressive circle and *passes forth* – in the manner of Jacob whom Harold Bloom very aptly called the 'restless crosser' and because of that the paradigmatic – post-traumatic – Hebrew hero.

Jacob, the first Hebrew hero who broke loose from the determinations of nature, by having challenged his older brother's right to progeniture and then wrestled victoriously with the Angel of Death, is the original bearer of *trauma converted into a way of life*: his lameness marks the loss which nonetheless does not stop him from 'passing forth'. On the contrary, being able to walk away from one's birth, walk forward, step into the realm of separation must be marked by a limp, the sign of traumatic limitation and curtailment, both, however, fully accepted as a deliberate resignation from the pleromatic life for the sake of the finite life of a separated fragment. In the figure of Jacob, therefore, Judaism emblematizes this new, pronatalistic and proleptic, notion of life that radically departs from the 'pagan' sense of insatiable vitality; it is no longer the prenatal phantasy of what Hegel calls *das unverletzte Leben*, the 'unscathed life' beyond any harm, but the harsh reality of the separated, fully born fragment, for ever cut off from the phantastical source of unwounded vivacity. Thus, while Christianity, as Hegel himself very perceptively attests in his *On Christianity*, still sports the phantasy of *life unwounded*, Judaism breaks for good with this pagan matrix and decides to choose the different direction. For, as Freud famously remarks at the end of *Beyond the Pleasure Principle*, by quoting one of his favourite German poets: 'Wither we cannot fly, we must go limping, / The Scripture saith that limping is not sin.'

The decision to accept the fact of birth – as, only at first trauma, but then as a simple *fact*, no longer to be questioned – allows us to walk away, even if by limping or by 'wandering steps', from the place of one's origin and forget the womb that no longer determines the point of reference of all later existential development. This act of *displacement*, which shifts Jewish people away from the moment of birth as no longer enigmatic/mesmerizing, marks Judaism as absolutely one of its kind: unique and peculiar, going against the grain of the 'default' mode of human psyche which 'naturally' privileges the 'birth denial' and hence cannot budge from the spot of *wo es war*, 'where *this* happened', i.e. the inexplicable enigma of leaving the prenatal bliss and entering the hostile world. Judaism's psychotheological set-up prevents the Jewish psyche from too much libidinal investment in this fateful *wo es war*, by displacing it onto the middle of life; it does not foster any symbolical means of undoing either the trauma or the fact of birth.

The natalist desire

According to Santner, who uses Franz Rosenzweig's *neues Denken* as his springboard, this very refusal to do what other people do, i.e. to negate the facticity of being born and keep the pretence *as if* birth never happened, makes Jews distinct in terms of their deep structure of desire. While 'pagan' cultures attempt to translate the tragic principle of *me phynai* ('I wish I'd never been born') into elaborate symbolic edifices whose function is to maintain the illusion of non-natality, i.e. a prolonged continuous existence within a cosmic-national-ethnic-familial womb (however we name those supraindividual Rankian 'entities'), usually represented by one's native motherland, Jews do not put down roots and never invest symbolically in any already given 'primary libidinal objects. Just as they walk away from their place of origin, accepting the futility of any symbolic strategies of 'birth denial', they also do not form attachments to anything that links itself to the moment of birth by a nostalgic metonymy:

> Jews, Rosenzweig asserts, do lack the passionate attachment to the things that constitute the primary libidinal 'objects' of other historical peoples and nations, attachments that ultimately constitute their vitality and endurance as peoples and nations: land, territory, and architecture; regional and national languages; laws, customs, and institutions founded and augmented in the course of a people's history. In Rosenzweig's view, Jewish difference is fundamentally a *difference in the structure of desire*, in the relation to the void around which desire orbits. That the objects of Jewish desire – the land of its longing, for example – are deemed 'holy', means that desire is *infinitized*.
>
> PEL, 110[30]

The infinitization is the direct result of voiding the desire from its primary – essentially maternal – attachments which are formed in the human psyche at the stage still closely resembling the oneness of primary narcissism. Although primary attachment is no longer a union, it still preserves the compulsive force of the early narcissistic monism; as such, the primary attachment expresses both separation, which had already happened, and the undoing of separation, which symbolically cancels out the fact of birth and reverts the subject back to the bliss of non-differentiation. Santner implies that the 'pagan' solution privileges primary attachments as an illusory (yet symbolically quite real) strategy of 'birth denial' and thanks to this secures for the psyche a maximum of joy, deriving from the imitation of the prenatal existence. He also suggests that Judaism, by not investing in the strategies of reversal and forfeiting the prenatal ideal of pleromatic life, denies 'pagan' people their share of *jouissance*. By insisting on breaking the 'bonds of love', which form the primary attachments, Judaism empties the desire, by turning it into a 'desert-desire' which defers, delays and complicates its fulfilment into infinity, and which I here call *Erros* (the drive-in-the-desert, combining *Erros, error* and *errance*). In consequence, the pleasure becomes infinitely postponed: it becomes a matter of promise, of the futuristic *not-yet*, but restrained here and now.

So, all this *taking time*, which invests in the future, also means: no pleasure *now*. This 'reversal tendency' voices a severe prohibition of the illusory joys flowing from the fake strategies of 'birth denial': a ban on *jouissance* which no 'pagan' psyche can ever forgive. No one expressed his objections against this prohibition more strongly and clearly than Jean-Francois Lyotard. In his emotional polemic against Emmanuel Levinas, *Figure Foreclosed*, Lyotard accuses Levinas, and *pars pro toto* the whole Jewish tradition, of propagating a psychotic attitude towards reality, based on the foreclosure of the maternal figure of nature. Jews, says Lyotard, are psychotic because they cannot reconcile themselves with natural necessities of life; by not being able to come to terms with conditional limitations, they simply ignore and exclude them from thought by means of a typically psychotic manoeuvre Freud called *die Verwerfung*, 'foreclosure'.

Lyotard's objection boils down to just one criticism: it reverses the accusation of 'pretence', by implying that it is not the 'pagan' mind but the Jewish one that actually attempts to erase the memory of birth and then go on pretending that it never had happened. In Judaism, therefore, we do not really encounter a positive affirmation of the trauma of birth but merely a *double denial*: by pretending that they never proceeded from the maternal womb, Jews also deny the existential necessity of the 'denial of birth'. They simply *refuse* to engage with the traumatic separation from the womb – and this leads directly to psychosis. There is nothing *new* here, only the psychotic blockage and destruction of the *old*: of the pre-existing, age-proof and universally efficient ancient ways of the 'pagan' mediation, which Lyotard associates with the more liveable psychic attitude, i.e. neurosis. For, contrary to psychosis, which moves violently on the basis of foreclosure (*Verwerfung*), neurosis moves more subtly on the basis of repression (*Verdrängung*), which has more capacity to negotiate with the repressed content: 'The latter represses, or in other words symbolizes, the instinctual representative; the former excludes it, and rejects it through foreclosure' (ibid., 77). Yet, in Lyotard's account, both psychosis, projected by him on the Jewish religion, and neurosis, represented by 'paganism', share the same point of orientation that we have designated here as the trauma of birth: the moment of separation from the maternal body which is then reinterpreted retrogressively as *castration*, the loss of vitality issuing from being cut off from the pleromatic source of all life. For, 'where does the site of frustration lie, if not with the mother?' (ibid., 77). The eternal problem with the Jews is that they 'deny *that*', trying to erase what simply cannot be erased: 'We can see in this configuration an erasure of the female element, a denial of castration, in other words foreclosure . . . This is the kind of madness into which rationality plunges us' (ibid., 76).

The point of Lyotard's fervently 'pagan' critique is that Judaism merely forecloses the context of birth from the womb, giving it no thought or consideration. The greatest trauma of human life, giving us the inexhaustible food for constant re-elaborations and *nachträglich* figurations, becomes ignored and thus made inactive – yet Judaism gives *nothing* instead. It is, therefore, a religion of pure Thanatos that feeds only on the 'loss of objects' (or what Santner calls 'primary attachments') that are subsequently replaced by only one 'pseudo-object' in the form of the Torah: Judaism is a 'discourse without things' (ibid., 82) which in the end produces a 'civilization of non-mediated discourse and power' (ibid., 85), where 'the voice of the Father' commands absolute fanatical obedience. Despite the conviction of Jews themselves that their religion is all about *torat hayim,* the result is precisely the reverse: it is the *religion of death.*

Lyotard only repeats in a new form a staple argument, known since the time of Marcion, if not Paul himself, then only reinforced by Luther and the whole Lutheran tradition, which also includes Hegel: Lyotard's main source of inspiration. But is it really so that the *désintéressement* in the birth enigma must necessarily lead to the thanatic consequences? *Sometimes* it does, indeed. Hannah Arendt's objection to Heidegger consists precisely in reproaching him for foreclosing the context of birth and producing a strange hybrid called Dasein which dies, although it has never been born and never lived, that is, was never really introduced into life – which, in Lyotard's terms, would make Dasein psychotic. But we have already seen that things are not that simple, and that the overestimation of one of the 'overspecified poles of life' – either birth or death – leads to the erasure of the middle which is life's proper element. There is thus something else involved in this formation of the middle region – and this is precisely what eludes Lyotard. What he misses in his accusatory fervour is the positive stake of this enormous effort of *decathexis,* which tears subject away from the 'natural' object of his desire, the Mother-Nature, in order to push desire on the way forward, towards the *infinitization,* thanks to which desire will be able – in the future – to form *relations with everything and anything.* In Lyotard's interpretation, this traumatic break takes the form of a pure rejection, only thinly disguised by later attachment to 'pseudo-objects'. For him, Jewish religion, by treating mother and nature *as if* they never existed, has nothing to say about the only issue that should consume all our speculative efforts: the secret of being born, of becoming separate, of breaking 'natural' ties with mother and what she represents, the whole of nature. But while Lyotard insists on Judaism's ineptness manifesting itself in the psychotic incapacity to deal with the most challenging mystery of birth, I would say rather that Judaism actually fully affirms the moment of natality, by getting over it once and for all and in such a way that it no longer bothers and disturbs the flow of human desire, ready to reach for other goals. What, therefore, Lyotard perceives as Judaism's poverty, sterile negativity, inadequacy and lack, I would like to see as Judaism's mature achievement which consists precisely in not investing too much of libidinal energy in the enigma of birth.

In response to this alleged inadequacy, Lyotard launches an apology of 'pagan' polytheism which, according to him, provides a much better chance of working through the traumatic relationship with nature, so fiercely denied by Jewish monotheism, together with all pleasure: 'The pleasure principle is given free rein in Homerism, but not in the Moses religion ... Does it not signify the exclusion of the mother and the disavowal of castration? The *Vernichtung* of the figurative is also a *Verneinung* of the maternal' (ibid., 77, 105).

Jewish iconoclasm, waging war on figures and images, is thus a part of the psychotic movement of foreclosure – 'the rejection without symbolism' (ibid., 103) – which, instead of solving the problem, pretends it never existed in the first place.[32] Pagan iconophilia, however, expresses an enormous effort of symbolization whose goal is to repair the traumatic break caused by the moment of birth. This reparation does not aim at the factual but merely virtual undoing of the trauma: the 'pagan' man does not actually regress to the pre-castrational and blissfully incestual relation with the maternal body, but also does not give it up as his highest ideal of happiness, which now he only tries to achieve *in effigie*. No wonder, therefore, that for Lyotard the most perfect embodiment of 'pagan religiosity', which plays out this neurotic ritual of breaking and repairing, of conflict and reconciliation, is realized by Hegel: the most 'erotic' philosophical thought which resigns on oneness and plenitude on the level of experiential immediacy, but regains it on the symbolic level of Absolute Knowledge. The neurotic strategy of sublimation, which Lyotard endorses as the most productive civilizational force, is possible only when the repressed content – the return to the fullness of the prenatal existence in the womb – is both repressed in its direct form and then reinstituted in its all so numerous symbolic avatars. Contrary to this, Jewish monotheism remains culturally barren, because, by foreclosing the Mother Figure, it also dries up the vital sources of energy without which no sublimatory process can ever take off:

> Detachment from reality is, then, essentially a detachment from myth, and this confirms the above analyses: neurosis has to be classified as a form of myth, as, that is, a form of integration of libido and reality; but detachment from reality, which already has been identified as one of the features of psychosis, implies that the ego gives up its compromise functions and allies itself with formations of the libido against the outside world.
>
> ibid., 95

By contrast to this psychotic 'stuckness', isolation and paralysis – all signs of 'death-in-life', frozen in hostile relations with the outside (Hegel's portrait of the

ugly and unloving Abraham, eagerly taken up by Heidegger in his description of
the Semitic Odysseus) – the Hegelian dialectic is 'the expanded form of the
neurotic symptom known as compromise formation' (ibid., 95). For the symbolic
reconciliation – the second chance of happy return to the maternal union offered
by sublimation – is indeed a question of a wise compromise shared by myth,
dialectic and neurosis.[33] At the same time, however, it is completely absent from
the fanatically uncompromised Jewish mind.

And uncompromised it is. Lyotard's instinct in finding his privileged adversary
is indeed right for no one demonstrates its stubbornness better than Lévinas, the
fiercest opponent of all things pagan, who in *Difficult Freedom* dismisses the
child-like seductions of neurotic symbolism, by saying: 'This, then, is the eternal
seductiveness of paganism, beyond the infantilism of idolatry, which long ago
was surpassed. The Sacred filtering into the world – Judaism is perhaps no more
than the negation of all that.'[34] Negation – but also a radical reversal, a game-
changing *conversion* to the natal life, which no longer can be described in terms
of a psychotic foreclosure.

For, what is an error in one game (psychosis) does not have to be an error in
another (liberated life). The whole point of the Jewish strategy of dealing with
the 'enigma of birth' is that it leads precisely to the moment of *teshuva*, 'turn',
Umkehr – after which things begin to look radically different. However, we have
to be aware of psychoanalysis's own limitations which force Rank to define this
'turn' as a 'gradual substitution of the mother by the form of the father' (TB, 122).
While indeed turning away from the maternal ambivalence might require help
from the paternal side, this switch of loyalties and obedience does not constitute
the very gist of this conversion, which can be properly understood only in terms
of the radically liberating *decathexis*. The psychotheological act of Exodus, of
walking away from the Egyptian swamps of the birth enigma, does not mean to
fall under an equivalent sway of the Father Figure; this is but a transitory phase
on the path of psychic evolution which leads towards the radical decathexis of
the 'time and place of origin': mother as well as father, these two 'overspecified
poles' of libidinal life, and their tiringly repetitive 'family romance'.

This is precisely what Santner calls a 'violent reorganization of our drives'
(PEL, 65): violent because it is sudden, producing an abrupt *Gestaltswitch*, which
completely gives up on *any* backward-looking nostalgia and formats the drives
strictly according to the vector of futurity and permanent birthing. If, as Otto
Rank claims, 'the birth trauma is the ultimate biological basis of the psychical'
(TB, xiii), then the Jewish *torat hayim* offers one of the most fundamental
interpretations of what it means to be human; by elaborating on the biology of

the neotenic birth, which in human beings is always premature and because of that traumatic, it provides its own anthropogenic model that stands in a stark opposition to the 'pagan' nostalgic solution relying on the reparatory power of symbolic compensation. *While the latter aims at the undoing the trauma of birth, by undoing the birth itself – the former aims at the undoing of the trauma of birth, by undoing its traumatic aspect.* Its sober factual affirmation of birth – as the positive act of separation inaugurating life proper, i.e. *the middle of life* – delivers a canvas for a psychotheological agon that repeats itself in perpetuity with every single individual being born.[35] The exciting novelty of the Isaiahian/Arendtian *A child has been born unto us* consists precisely in not knowing which route the child is going to take: whether it will invest symbolically into the pre-natal *reditus* or choose, in Wallace Stevens' formulation,

> The accent of deviation in the living thing
> That is its life preserved, the effort to be born
> Surviving to be born, the event of life.[36]

Part Two

Erros, the Drive in the Desert

Derrida's *Torat Hayim*, or the Religion of the Finite Life

In light of everything we have said so far about life as the non-essential 'thing of the middle', the Derridean imperative – 'to learn to live *finally*' – can only sound ironic and that's certainly the way this phrase was intended. The learning of life can never realize itself in full because of the permanently liminoid structure of life, always birthing itself and lingering on the threshold of initiation, *before the law*. Just as Arendt, who saw life as always initiating, never initiated, Derrida too believes that there can be no initiation into life, because *life is an indefinite postponement of initiation*; anything *final*, which would put an end to hesitation and taking time, equals the dead-assuredness of death. One can only be initiated into the law of the finitude through and into death. But as long as one lives, one is a fool: the *am ha'aretz*, the Kafkan man from the country, the eternal apprentice remaining in *Blödigkeit*, stupidity, *bêtise*. By avoiding finality of any sort – something that angered Lukács complaining that 'nothing can be lived to the end' – we still persist in living, this process of 'un-essence'.

Yet, although there is no final learning how to live, there is nonetheless a 'teaching of life': the 'great intangible Judaic principle of *torat hayim* (ATTIA, 112). Great and intangible – but also precarious, aporetic, exposed to a complex dialectic that always threatens it with a self-annihilating double bind. In this chapter, I will follow the arabesque meanders of Derrida's engagement with the 'principle of life', which, especially in his later phase, became a new foundation for rethinking practically everything: religion, law, social bonds, ethical responsibilities, neighbourly love, the definition of humanity and – last but not least – finite life itself. This is where the lesson of *another finitude* finds its most advanced elaboration.

The beast and the hunter

There is something paradoxical about this complexity, because the starting point of Derrida's *torat hayim* is precisely the opposite – stupidity, *bêtise*, *Eigensinn*,

Blödigkeit, or foolishness of the Kafkan 'man from the country' who stands before the law. Yet, at the same time, it is a very contrary and sophisticated version of 'stupidity' that Derrida aims to defend against all too easy dismissals of life as always automatically a 'stupid life', which abound in the Western philosophical tradition. His understanding of stupidity is closest to what Heidegger calls *Eigensinn*, 'stubbornness', which involves also certain hard-necked self-assertion: a stubborn refusal to get initiated into the final truth of life, a stubborn evasion from taking the final lesson, a stubborn abiding in the liminoid paradox, and a stubborn denial to face the truth-saying verdict of death.

In *The Beast and the Sovereign*, wholly devoted to the reappreciation of *bêtise* as the basic mode of 'non/learning to live', Derrida once again chooses Heidegger as one of his favourite sparring partners, especially when it comes to the issues of life and death. In *The Introduction to Metaphysics*, Heidegger says: 'Den Eigensinnigen ist Leben nur Leben. Tod ist ihnen Tod und nur dieses. Aber das sein des Lebens ist zugleich Tod. Jegliches, was ins Leben tritt, beginnt damit auch schon zu sterben, auf seinen Tod zuzugehen, und Tod ist zugleich Leben.'[2]

Having in mind what Heidegger thinks about the bestiality of *nur-Lebende*, that is, animals that 'merely-live', Derrida comments: 'it is *bête* to think that life is simply life, without asking oneself the question, as Heidegger will immediately do, of a death that is life, a life that is death, a death that belongs to the very being of life ... the stubborn *bêtise* consists in not asking questions' (BS1, 306). Since the whole seminar is about the complex relation between the beast and the sovereign – the *bêtise* of the beast versus the 'wisdom' of the sovereign master, their inner affinity (both are beyond law) and their hierarchical opposition (one is below, the other is above the law) – Derrida's sympathies go naturally towards the 'beastly paradigm' and against all those philosophical tropes that foster the hierarchical structure of sovereignty. And one of these tropes, perhaps the most fundamental, is the belief that 'only Dasein has an experiential relation to death, to dying to *sterben as such*, to his *own* death, his own being-able-to-die, to its possibility, be it the possibility of the impossible, whereas the animal, that other living being [*zoon*] that we call the animal, perishes but never dies, has no relation worthy of that name to death' (BS1, 307–8) – the belief which Derrida vehemently rejects.

Although Derrida does not mention Rosenzweig here, we can see how, in his defence of *bêtise*, he takes on the latter's common sense approach to language. For Rosenzweig, the main source of philosophical malaise is precisely not being able to see things as they are, which results in the confusing series of reductions and substitutions, as in Heidegger's paradigmatic attempt to find life's essence: *Aber das Sein des Lebens ist zugleich Tod* [But the essence of life is nothing but death] (IM, 100). This indeed is a model for philosophical reduction: *aber* suggests rhetorical opposition to the naive first appearance; *Sein,* understood here as *essence,* pretends to reach for the deep core behind the mere appearance, *Schein;* and *zugleich* emphasizes that in philosophy things end up always precisely the opposite of what they seemed at first. *Eigensinn,* therefore, when rehabilitated in the mood of New Thinking, would be a stubborn effort to stay at the surface, with the transient flow of things. More than that, we could ironically subvert the pseudo-etymological hermeneutics of Heidegger himself and interpret *Eigensinn* as 'to sense [*sinnen*] one's own [*eigen*]': to *arrest* the speculative mirroring and stick to the phenomenon itself, *give it time,* so it can reveal its unique identity. '*Bêtise* is perhaps positivity itself' (BS1, 307), says Derrida tentatively and hesitantly, being aware of all the dangers that come from the too-simple affirmation of this position.³ Yet, *especially* in the question of life and death, it seems like a good point to start. *Leben ist Leben,* full stop; there is nothing in life but life.

But it is only in the beginning – the necessary *bêtise* of the original positivity – that the teaching on life is stupid and reluctant to ask questions which would easily demonstrate that life is not an argument. Once the all-too-easy reduction of life's essence to death is avoided, life immediately assumes the structure of the paradox: *Nur-Leben,* although indispensable as life's self-assertion against the defining imminence of death, is far from simple. Let's remind ourselves of the crucial passage from 'Force of Law' written in reference to Benjamin's notion of 'mere life' (*blosses Leben*), which they both criticize as relying precisely on this deceptive simplicity, where Derrida says:

> This critique of vitalism or biologism ... here proceeds like the awakening of a Judaic tradition. And it does so in the name of life, of the most living of life, of the value of life that is worth more than life (pure and simple, if such exist and that one could call natural and biological), but *that is worth more than life because it is life itself, insofar as life prefers itself. It is life beyond life, life against life, but always in life and for life.*
>
>   AR, 289; my emphasis

At first glance, it would be hard to find a greater contrast between the stubborn *bêtise* of the starting point, which says 'life is life, period' – and this most dialectically complex formula of *torat hayim.* Derrida's stubborn life-long *Lebensdenken* seems indeed very far from the traditional vitalist line of thinking about life in terms of a simple *zoe*, reconciled with its finite cycle of birth and decay. For Derrida – just as for Hegel – life is a 'living contradiction' that can live on only by *negating its own finitude*: first, by projecting the image of the infinite 'more-than-life', and then by bringing it back into the condition of the immanent 'more-life'.[4] His vitalism is, as all messianic thought, *antinomian*: it attempts to incorporate the elements of transcendence – *life beyond life, life against life* – without losing anything in the immanentist translation. The antithetical, i.e. self-transcending, self-opposing and self-challenging aspect of life, which expresses itself in the category of transcendence venturing beyond here and now as its 'counter-principle'[5] immune to suffering, fate and death, is not rejected here, but reinterpreted in such a way that it finds place back *in life and for life*. It does not make life *straight*, by demanding that it overcomes its antithetical aspect which presses towards the projection of 'the unscathed' – but rather allows for its dialectical denouement that accommodates the transcendence within the immanent realm. It wants to live the transcendent possibility *in the middle of life*: between the simple *zoe*, which too naturally accepts the 'rhythm of transience', and the phantasmatic life immortal, which transcends all natural limitations. If it still needs the transcendent counter-principle, therefore, it is only in order to gain distance from the natural cycle of being and create a new mode of *more life*, in which it will be able to achieve the kind of freedom and happiness that are impossible within the natural constraints.[6]

Yet, Derrida's confrontation with Heidegger is not merely negative. It is quite tempting to see his own enterprise of *Lebensdenken* as a continuation of Heidegger's early project, conceived when he was still intensely exposed to *Lebensphilosophie*, and only later on abandoned for the sake of the strict *Seinsdenken*: the project of the *factical life*. In his Freiburg lectures on the hermeneutics of facticity (1915–23), Heidegger says:

> *Facticity* is the designation we will use for the character of the being of 'our' 'own' Dasein . . . Being-there in the manner of *being* means: not, and never, to be there primarily as an *object* of intuition and definition on the basis of intuition, as an *object* of which we merely take cognizance and have knowledge. Rather, Dasein is *there* for itself in the 'how' of its ownmost being. The how of its being opens up and circumscribes the respective 'there' which is possible for a while at the particular time. *Being – transitive: to be factical life!* Being is itself never the possible object of a having, since what is at issue in it, is what it comes to, is itself: *being* . . . If we take 'life' to be a mode of 'being', then 'factical life' means: our own Dasein which is 'there' for us in one expression or another of the character of its being, and this expression, too, is in the manner of being.[7]

In life being becomes transitive: what does it mean? By becoming transitive in the mode of life – as *lived* in this world, here and now, factically, before 'life' becomes captured by life sciences – being opens itself to singular and unique interpretations, *Auslegungen*, coming from everything that exists in the mode of living. *Being, the intransitive infinite, becomes lived as the transitive finite* – and with this crucial *conversion* into transitiveness, it also acquires *polivocity*. The Aristotelian principle, according to which being can be interpreted in many ways, fulfils itself in the way being becomes imparted to beings as their life which lays being out in the infinite palette of colours refracted by a living care, each time singular, singularly resisting death, telling its own story to postpone the demise. This is also the point in which the polivocity of being – *life lived each time singularly* – and the literary narrative/*récit* converge as one and the same project: to be able to tell one's own story of being means to *have lived being in the transitive mode of factical life.*[5]

Later on, however, already in *Being and Time*, Heidegger will drop the concept of the factical life in favour of the concept of Dasein, and the whole project of the transitivity of Being *actualizing* itself in the living singularity will be abandoned too. As Derrida says in the already quoted commentary on section 49 of *Being and Time*, which promisingly describes the this-side (*Diesseits*) facticity of human way of dealing with being: 'Unfortunately, he [Heidegger] does not call this "life," a life before the opposition between life and death' (HCL, 88). From this time on, 'life' will rather become the name of the difference separating humankind's way of existing from the organic way of being-present. For, Dasein no longer lives: now it *exists*. Instead of cultivating its *intimate relation with life* – a possibility opened by the self-reflexive structure of being implied by the factical life – it acquires an *intimate relation with death*, which Heidegger evacuates from the biological realm and bestows with ontological meaning. With this move, Heidegger discards his own concept of life alternative to the *lebensphilosophisch* notion of life as the *intransitive* overarching structure (which then, once again, will be echoed in Heidegger's own *Seinsdenken* as Being's excess undermining all actualizations), as well as to the *possessive* notion of life as we know from the Hobbesian proprietary paradigm: a third promising notion posed between *intransitivity* and *possessivity*. That is, between Life that defies any appropriation and discards any particular actualization of the living for the sake of new vast possibilities – and life that can be fully owned by self-preservatory interests sticking to what life already is; between the overruling power that precludes ontological independence of a singular being, on the one hand – and the possessiveness that grants independence in a too proprietary manner, turning being into an object of self-preservatory care, on the other.

It is thus not improbable to see Derrida's concept of life as deriving precisely from the project abandoned by Heidegger, where *life is being lived but not owned*; where being (at that time still being: not Being, and certainly not yet Beyng, *Seyn*) opens itself to polivocal *récits* on 'this side' of the multitude of the living, without ever becoming 'mine' in the form of a property; and where life, far from just meeting its end (Heideggerian *Verenden*, 'perishing'), has a life-forming non-oppositional relationship with death, called 'originary mourning'. This would be also a *subjective life*, as long as it is a *lived* life, i.e. life reflexive thanks to the transitivity of the verb, which allows the living to seize its life in reflection without objectifying it: as something that can be 'assisted by the discourse', constantly accompanied by the autoaffection and the *récit*, which – unlike the Blanchotian 'constant companion' envisaged as death – helps life to live-on, that is, strengthen its antinomian odds against the assuredness of dying.[10]

For Derrida, therefore, subject would be a living subject structured as a constant vigilance and care circling around the intimate relation with life of which, at the same time, I can never say that it is fully 'mine'. It rather has to be 'followed' – as *suivre* hidden in *Je suis* meaning 'I am', but also 'I follow' or 'I fall for' – 'traced', even 'hunted', and this is what language is for: to articulate life as *lived*, to create in the autobiographical narrative the fleeting and evasive sense of 'mineness' which can never take the form of secure possession. This non-possessive lack of certainty derives from the gap between the hunter and the hunted beast: between the language, which never fully adheres to the living process, because it can go on 'even were it to be already a dead thing speaking', and the ever elusive living 'I', the prey that cannot be captured:

> Whether it is pronounced, exposed as such, thematized or not, the 'I' is always posed autobiographically. It refers to itself. The 'I' shows itself, it speaks of itself and of itself as living, living in the present, in the living present, in the moment in which 'I' is said, *even were it to be already a dead thing speaking* . . . We are here analyzing the sign of life within the very structure of the auto-position of the *I* or of *ipseity* . . . I would say what follows, namely that henceforth *I am (following), while reading, quoting myself, deciphering my traces*.
>
> ATTIA, 56; my emphasis

This indeed is the 'factical life' in all its complexity, to which also the fragment on *torat hayim* in the 'Judaic tradition' alluded: the constant overlapping of the living immanence with the transcendence of language, *within* and *beyond*, but always in life and for the sake of life; life felt as mine, but never owned as such. The whole late corpus of Derrida's texts could thus be seen as the 'Jewish *clinamen*' on the Heideggerian idea of the factical life where being becomes transitive, i.e. caught in the passage between transcendence and immanence: no longer divine, but also not fully appropriated; no longer 'belonging to Him' (according to Kafka's aphorism: *Das Wort 'Sein', bedeutet im Deutschen beides: Dasein und, Ihmgehören*), but also never quite belonging to us. *In and out*: always on the liminoid borderline, lingering on the threshold, *in-transition*. This is yet another dimension of the preposition 'for' which Derrida, in his book on Cixous, sees as the 'meaning of "life"': life is never a neutral mode of being, it is always being 'lived *for* oneself, *for* the other, and *for* life' (HCL, 89; my emphasis) in the subjunctive/subjective declension 'of the gift, donation and dativity' (HCL, 87).

Yet, at the same time, the more Derrida praises early Heidegger, the more severely he criticizes his philosophy since *Being and Time*, which abandoned thinking of life completely. For Derrida, this is not an accident: to think life means also to constantly and vigilantly resist the temptation to *think life away*. Life, an uneasy middle term, has a tendency to conjure itself away, by either falling back into *being* or by leaping forward to *thinking*: the dual evasion that makes Heidegger see greater affinity between the *denkensfähig* Dasein and a non-living stone than between Dasein and a merely-living, animal, *ein nur-lebendes Tier*. In both cases, whether degraded to the inorganic existence or sublimated to the level of pure thinking, life runs away from itself and its inner aporia. Either as an indifferent being or as pure spirit, *die fühlende Seele*, the Hegelian 'middle soul', escapes the liminoid aporecity of the living which, while living, must constantly face its end.

First of all, by abandoning the idea that being can become transitive in the factical singular life, Heidegger regresses into the intransitive relation of dominance, in which Being recuperates all the features of the general *Leben* which can never be 'lived' by or for us: it is rather us who are 'lived' by it, according to Georg Groddeck's ominous sentence from *Das Buch vom Es* (also quoted by Freud): *Wir leben nicht, wir sind gelebt* [We do not live, we are lived]. Simultaneously, on the other hand, Heidegger regresses into the proprietary paradigm of bare self-preservation, in which *Jemeinigkeit* of the 'ownmost' death becomes the defining mark of Dasein's intimate relation with its mortality. Instead, therefore, of the one new entity called 'factical life', there emerges a duality which from now on will plague the Heideggerian *Seinsdenken*: on the one hand, *Sein* with its *expropriating* power of the *Er/Ent/eignis*, capable of throwing the actual Dasein out of joint any time – and, on the other, Dasein which *appropriates* its essence and assuredness in the moment of its *eigenst*, ownmost' death. And even if Heidegger does not describe this duality in such antagonistic terms, the way in which Dasein clings to its 'one certitude' and *claims* it as, both, its own individual essence – a deadly *heacceitas* – and the essence of humankind as such, defined by what is most proper to being human, appears self-preservatory and defensive against the vertiginous power of *Ereignen* exercised by *Sein*. Which – completely against Heidegger's intentions – brings him back into the Cartesian fold, where the singular *cogito* constitutes itself as a defensive mechanism built on the one certitude against the arbitrary power of the malicious demon, or simply, without any further disguises, the nominalist *Deus Fallax* himself.[13] Instead of the *neuer Anfang*, which promised a more open and generous relation with being, we are back into Cartesian trenches in which the subject/Dasein clings to its one dead-sure possession, *safe from any harm*, and defends it against the expropriating higher power of *Seyn* which then can only become an object of a vague masochistic mystique.

The key to this shift in Heidegger's thinking is the strange twist on the idea of mortality, which, instead of exposing Dasein's living precariousness, leads it to the gates of the 'negation of finitude' and renders Heidegger's later project much more Cartesian than he himself intended. For Derrida, it is an element of a broader philosophical game which consists in the *elimination of life* – for the sake of either pure dying or pure thinking – as the elimination of precariousness, the purpose of which is a gain of *indemnity*. The first occurrence of the paradox – *mortality without life* – has its classical locus precisely in Descartes's *Meditations*:

> Descartes' prudence not only incites him to abstract from the 'I am' of his living body, which, in a way, he objectivizes as a machine or corpse (these are his words); so much that his 'I am' can apprehend and present itself only from the perspective of his potential *cadaverization*, that is to say, from the perspective of 'I am mortal' or 'already dead' or 'destined to die,' indeed 'toward death' ... The presence to itself of the present of thinking ... that is what excludes everything detachable constituted by life, the living body, animal life ... If I want to hold onto and present what I am, and who I am, it is necessary to begin, therefore, by suspending this common definition of the 'rational animal.' 'I am,' in the *purity* of its intuition and thinking, excludes animality, even if it is rational. In the passage that follows this bracketing of the rational animal, Descartes proposes abstracting from his 'I am,' if I can put it this way, *everything that recalls life*.
>
> ATTIA, 71–2; my emphasis

Mortality without life is thus the dead-assuredness of *cogito ergo sum* without the precariousness of the animal process that sustains a brittle life. *Sum* becomes a property of *cogito* that controls and owns its being – but only and insofar as it is thinking; any other impurity or colour contaminating this transparent parcel of 'my own being' would again reopen it to loss and vulnerability. Mortification or cadaverization serves, therefore, as the vehicle of the purifying sublimation whose ultimate stake is *indemnity* – just as in Blanchot's equation *dead – immortal*,[14] in which dying, being-already-dead, saves and protects from death:

> Even if it is not necessarily signed by a dead person, this *cogito ergo sum* should not, all the same, have anything to do with the self-affirmation of a life, of an 'I breathe' that would signify 'I am living, I have breath in me [*anime*], I am animal'...'I breathe therefore I am,' *as such does not produce any certainty*...And 'I think' is something that an animal cannot utter. No more than 'I' in general... The indubitability of existence, the autoposition and automanifestation of 'I am' does not depend on being-in-life but on thinking, an appearance to self that is determined in the first place not as respiration, breath, or life, indeed, on a thinking soul that does not at first appear to itself as life.
>
> ATTIA, 86–7; my emphasis

'I breathe therefore I am' does not produce any certainty – and it should *not*. The quest after certainty destroys the liminoid tensions of the autobiographical narrative, by turning it into an 'autoimmune disease': the more it tries to capture life in the movement of archivization and indemnification, the more it threatens to become deadening and, as such, counterproductive; instead of saving life, it eliminates life as, paradoxically, the greatest danger to life. If Descartes's *Meditations* can indeed be regarded as belonging to the genre of autobiography (and Derrida, similarly to Blumenberg, insists on it), then they may serve as the limit case in which the anxious *urge to indemnification* becomes so powerful that it annuls all life that produced this impulse in the first place:

> Autobiography, the writing of the self as living, the trace of the living for itself, being for itself, the auto-affection or auto-infection as memory or archive of the living would be an *immunizing movement* (a movement of safety, of salvage and salvation of the safe, the holy, the immune, the indemnified, of virginal and intact nudity), but an immunizing movement that is always threatened with becoming *auto-immunizing*, as is every *autos*, every ipseity, every automatic, automobile, autonomous, auto-referential movement. Nothing risks becoming more poisonous than an autobiography, poisonous for itself in the first place, auto-infectious for the presumed signatory who is so auto-affected.
>
> ATTIA, 415; my emphasis

The same defensive 'neutralization of life' (ATTIA, 87) reappears in Heidegger, but in an even more aporetic manner. Here again, we deal with the syndrome of *mortality without life*, which suggests a different, truly *intimate* relation with death that initiates into 'pure thinking', unknown to animals who 'merely-live'. Just as the Hegelian *wirkliche Seele*, which becomes pure spirit by letting in the deadly 'tremendous power of the negative', Dasein cultivates its relation with death, by simultaneously cutting all former attachment to life. By doing so, it enters into the sublime sphere of the 'anthropological difference' or 'what is proper to man', which is marked by a *different mortality*: death not as the negation of existence but as a manner of thinking and cognizing existence, or in Nancy's formulation: the *exposing Death*.

Death not as the *peras*, the limit that ends the breathing brittle life – but as the *de-finition* of existence, the vehicle of *Seinsdenken* and its pure abstract conceptuality, no longer linked to the polivocal – autobiographical and literary – expressions of the 'factical life'. It is the same abstract conceptuality which – since Descartes, via Hegel and Kojève, up to Lacan – disassociates itself from the vital element and becomes capable of stating, only seemingly paradoxically – as Mr Waldemar in E.A. Poe's story, analysed by Derrida in *Voice and Phenomenon*[15] – 'I am dead':

> Heidegger's Dasein which, however much it may first appear as (possible-impossible) being-towards-death, does not in the first instance declare itself to be a living thing. Paradoxically, it is a mortal, indeed, one who is dying without essentially having anything to do, in its being-there, in its 'I am', with life . . . At the heart of all these difficulties, there is always the *unthought side of a thinking of life.*
> ATTIA, 110–11; my emphasis

Unthought, or rather deliberately left aside. Heidegger does not simply forget about life.[16] For the thinkers of the 'anthropological difference' traditionally conceived, to whom Heidegger belongs – with Descartes, Hegel, Kojève, Lacan and, to Derrida's grief, also Lévinas (at least to some extent) – it is only natural to skip life in the *Todesdenken* which extols humankind's intimate relation with death: intimate to the point of the Lacanian identification with the mechanical and inorganic power of the death drive, indeed making Dasein closer to the stone than to the living plant or animal. For, if Freud was right in *Beyond the Pleasure Principle* (and Derrida very much hopes that he wasn't), what makes human psyche a unique phenomenon in the world of nature is that it is able to give voice to Thanatos which drives towards the total erasure of all life and presses *beyond*, towards the nirvanic transcendence of nothingness.[17]

Derrida insists on recalling our attention to the paradox – *mortality without life* – in order to deconstruct the apparently self-evident edifice of human exceptionality, which seems to be founded on 'nothing' or on the 'lack' rendering man a *Mangelwesen* in the world of the organic nature. The discourse of lack as the original sin, then compensated by the idea of *felix culpa*, seems most suspicious to his deconstructive ears. Derrida, therefore, in a move parallel to Agamben's 'jamming of the anthropological machine', wants to disturb the seemingly obvious Herderian mechanism of compensation, which eventually forgets about its defensive origin and presents itself, in a triumphant and victorious manner, as a *mastery* over nature (this 'cruel stepmother'). The 'machination' in which the 'anthropogenic' swindle – the phantasmatic reversal from the orphan of nature to the king of nature – takes roots precisely in the first compensatory manoeuvre, in which mortality suddenly emerges with no life behind it and lo: the *lacking animal*, endangered and precarious, transforms into a *lack of animality*, taking man out from the land of the living and making him safe from harm. By turning vice into a virtue, the natural deficiency becomes a glorious default:

> Its analogous or common traits are all the more dominant given that their formalization, that to which we are devoting ourselves here, will allow us to see appear in every discourse concerning the animal, and notably in the Western philosophical discourse, the same dominant, the same recurrence of a schema that is in truth invariable. What is that? The following: what is proper to man, his superiority over and subjugation of the animal, his very becoming-subject, his historicity, his emergence out of nature, his sociality, his access to knowledge and technics, all that, everything in a nonfinite number of predicates, that is proper to man would derive from this *originary fault*, indeed from this *default in propriety, what is proper to man is default of propriety* – and from the imperative [*il faut*] that finds in it its development and resilience.
>
> ATTIA, 413

At the same time, however, Derrida is not willing to simply deny the 'anthropological difference' and engage in some kind of 'biologistic continuism'. He is in favour of presenting the *limen* between man and animals as 'more than one' and not so well defined as in all ideological models of anthropogenic initiation; rather blurred, abyssal, hard to cross and hard to trace, that is – *liminoid*:

> I have thus never believed in some homogeneous continuity between what calls itself man and what he calls the animal ... The discussion becomes interesting once, instead of asking whether or not there is a discontinuous limit, one attempts to think what a limit becomes once it is abyssal, once the frontier no

longer forms a single indivisible line but more than one internally divided line, once, as a result, it can no longer be traced, objectified, or counted as single and indivisible. *What are the edges of a limit that grows and multiplies by feeding on an abyss?*

ATTIA, 398; my emphasis

The issue, therefore, is not the negation of the discontinuity between humans and animals; the issue is the critique of the phantasmatic narrative of Man becoming Man by turning his lack into sublime nothingness: the death looked straight in the eye, which then demands full sacrifice of the 'beast', so that the weak lacking animal can transform into a powerful, no longer precarious, lack of animality. We shall yet see that this story can be told in a different way, without recourse to the sacrificial logic which, in the last decade of his life, remained the main target of Derrida's deconstruction. What he designates as *originary fault, default in propriety*, or *what is proper to man as default in propriety* does not have to be thought of in terms of deficiency, pathology and Fall of *conditio humana* as an 'ailment' – *Krankheit*, pathology, sickness – that needs to be cured, compensated or simply removed by the sacrificial trick. The lack of propriety/property, the in/de/finiteness that constitutes human life as such does not have to generate the compensatory quest for certainty, property and propriety, in which Man would come into possession of his own essence. As in Rosenzweig, whom we have already confronted with Heidegger, it can remain the originary condition realized in a different way, that is, lived – as well as loved and told – in the infinite number of ways: the one thousand and one stories.

The deconstruction of the sacrificial logic involved in the choice of 'mortality without life' constitutes the *pars destruens* of Derrida's *torat hayim*. The gist of this sacrificial logic is the 'break with life' (DP1, 4): a phantasmatic claim that it is possible to rise above the polivocal 'clamour of being' into a sublime sphere of pure Truth. For Derrida, the strongest representative of this claim in late-modern thought is Lacan.

Derrida criticized Lacan's phantasmatic attachment to the 'anthropological difference' at least twice: in *The Animal That Therefore I Am*, and again, with only small variation, in the first part of the seminar called *The Beast and the Sovereign*. As always, the target of Derrida's critique is Lacan's particular use of the Herderian concept of man as *Mangelwesen*, 'deficient being', which lies at the centre of the anthropogenic mirror-stage: 'the datum of a true specific prematurity of birth in humans' which corresponds to an 'intraorganic mirror' or, as Derrida calls it, 'autotelic specularity of the inside, linked to a defect, a prematurity, an incompleteness of the little human' (E, 96; BS1, 115). In 'Variations on the Standard Treatment', Lacan calls the human neoteny 'a fact in which one apprehends this dehiscence of natural harmony, demanded by Hegel as the fecund illness, the *happy fault of life*, in which man, by distinguishing himself from his essence, discovers his existence' (E, 345). In 'Subversion of the Subject', Lacan formulates this principle of creative deficiency, which denaturalizes human beings, in an even more Kojèvian manner: 'The struggle that establishes him [man] is indeed one of pure prestige, and what is at stake is to do with life, well placed to echo that danger of the generic prematurity of birth, unknown to Hegel, and which we have made the dynamic mainspring of specular capture' (E, 810).[38]

Exposure to death – desired and feared at the same time – is the compulsory repetition of the original trauma caused by the premature birth, in which the anthropogenic moment consists in recognizing the constitutive lack: something the animal can never do. The human subject, therefore, gains merely a relative mastery – over human and non-human animals – but himself bows down to the Master Signifier and his royal insignium of the 'right to kill', which belongs truly only to 'Death, the Absolute Master' himself. To become a subject means thus to negate one's deficient finite life and enter the Blanchotian 'space of death': above and beyond life, in which the *default*, no longer attached to life, stops being the sign of weakness and transforms into the masterly *nothingness* of death. Once the subject 'resurrects' on the other side of the anthropogenic divide, it is no longer a *deficient being*, the Herderian *Mangelwesen* disprivileged by life, but a triumphant *existence*, reinforced by its previous default. The lack, now truly central and constitutive, becomes glorified as the most sublime 'purity of Non-Being', throwing its bold 'No' to the lowly business of life – not just *my* life, but all life as such. The lack, therefore, does not go away, but is transfigured into a black sun engulfing the whole of being, the transcendent nothing and the anthropogenic essence *per se*. The revealing of this essence, which is 'most proper to man', is the moment of *jouissance*, best expressed by the words of the Serpent, Mephisto from Paul Valéry's poem: 'I am in the place whence it is shouted: "the universe is a defect in the purity of Non-Being." And this is not without reason, for *in being maintained, this place makes being itself languish*. This place is called Enjoyment, and it is the lack of this place that would render the universe vain.'[39]

Without man who recognizes his true essence – and detaches his glorious lack from the process of life, where it can only figure as a weakening 'deficiency' – the universe as such would be *vain*, the *kol hevel*, one big useless vanity from Kohelet's vision. It is only the negative *regressio*, in which worldly beings languish, that dignifies the existence of the cosmos which, despite all its naive investment in the business of life, is also capable of creating a human being which is in a sovereign power to reverse it. This power, greatest in the whole universe, is the infinite power of the death drive: the all-nihilizing self-recognized *lack*. Derrida comments:

> The real human sovereign is the signifier. *The entry of the subject into the human order of the law presupposes this passive finitude, the infirmity, this defect that the animal does not suffer from* ... What the animal lacks is precisely the lack in virtue of which man is subject to the signifier, subject subjected to the sovereign signifier. But being subject of the signifier is also to be subjecting subject, a *master* subject ... This sovereignty is the superiority of man over beast, even if it is based on *the privilege of the defect*, lack, or fault, a failing that is referred to the generic prematuration of birth as well as to the castration complex ... *The animal self lacks the lack.*
>
> BS1, 125, 132; my emphasis

It probably won't be an exaggeration to say that *everything* Derrida has written, especially in his later period, goes against the grain of this *logo-nomo-centric* complex based on 'the privilege of the defect', which found the ultimate articulation in Lacan's teaching. This complex forms a dangerously integral whole, containing not just anthropology (the 'fecund illness' of the originary lack), but also metaphysics (transcendence of the death drive beyond the pleasure principle of life) and ethics (no neighbourly love, just a deadly struggle for prestige and recognition). The importance of this *Auseinandersetzung* cannot be overestimated: it is *the* agon of Derrida's life, done 'for the sake of life' or simply *for-life*. *To say No to the sublime No of the deniers of finite life, or, better, to shout it against their negative Enjoyment* – is late Derrida's battle cry. It is precisely here, in his highly polemical *torat hayim*, that he will find the alternative to the phantasmatic anthropology of the glorious lack.

Life's double bind as two sources of morality and religion

The Death Penalty Seminar, conducted right before *The Beast and the Sovereign*, brings a new definition of deconstruction: 'Deconstruction ... is perhaps, *perhaps* the deconstruction of the death penalty, of the logocentric, logonomocentric scaffolding in which the death penalty is inscribed or prescribed' (DP, 23).

This new definition puts the death penalty and the sovereign violence that administers it into the very centre of the deconstructive enterprise. The logocentric and logonomocentric scaffolding is *the* locus of sacrificial cruelty; a place from where the highest sovereign power, which is always a 'power to kill', rules by distributing guilt, fear and punishment among the living, itself exempt from the precarious condition of the finite life and because of that – *unscathed*, beyond any hurt or harm, indemnified, *indemne, unverletzt*. To deconstruct – literally, to dismantle – this scaffolding would mean to bring down this instance of exemption, which situates itself above life as *more-than-life*, and throw it back into the condition of the living: horizontal, universal and already immunized against any vertical sublimations which produce sovereign exceptions. When thus in *Rogues*, Derrida defines democracy to come in terms of his mysterious notion of *khora* – as "the *khora* of the political" (R, 44) – he implies precisely that: a strictly horizontal 'republic of the living' in which nothing and nobody will ever be able to assume the exceptional position of the unscathed; or, in a slightly different idiom, a 'covenant of creatures' who will finally conjure away the spectre of God, the absolute Lord and Master, soaring above the living and punishing them according to his violent caprices. *Khora*, which Derrida defines as 'the opposite of the unscathed', embodying scathedness and vulnerability itself, is here a 'principle of life' that will have liberated itself from the rule of death as an enigmatic signifier obliquely referring to the transcendent dimension of something 'more-*than*-life' – infinitely more significant, powerful and durable, which dwarfs any actual life in comparison.

The task of deconstruction, therefore, would consist in blocking this sublimatory mechanism that creates lofty scaffoldings of the highest and unscathed, and keeps life on the low level of *khora*: the *fallen*, imperfect, corporeal, precarious, but also fully reconciled with its finite condition, with no contempt for or despair over one's fragile body 'again, *fallen* – but *in love*). It is, therefore, *khora* – the ultimate name of the 'republic of the living' and the 'covenant of the creatures' to come – that gives a sense of destination for Derrida's messianic project of getting 'beyond the sovereign violence'. In the realm of *khora*, life may be finite and thus die – but no life will ever be sacrificed. In the Kingdom of *khora*, there will be no longer any power coming from either above or below – neither the transcendent God, nor the deep-immanent Life/Being – but only the neighbourly friendship, the last incarnation of the Pauline *agape*, operating horizontally and flatly, with no scaffolding or underpinning, just Here Below: love which bears all things, believes all things, and endures all things, the infinite *patience* watching over the universal effort of survival.[29]

The seminar on *Death Penalty*, in which Derrida delivers the most philosophically elaborate defence of the abolitionist position in history, can justifiably be regarded as the culmination of his *torat hayim*. Here, the analysis of all the arguments in favour and against the death penalty offers Derrida a chance to ponder speculatively on the abolitionist perspective and its central concept: the *right to life*. The 'right to life', as opposed to what Maurice Blanchot used to call the 'right to death' founding the logic and politics of sovereignty, belongs to a different paradigm which Derrida, in his other writings from the similar period, associates with *messianicity*: the attempt to think beyond the sovereign law and its sacrificial demands, towards the notion of a self-governing happy life, which derives from the certain religious tradition but is by no means reducible to it. The connection between the Death Penalty seminar and Derrida's 'messianic' writings helps to reveal a positive stake of the deconstructive work undertaken in the former, which is precisely the new concept of the *finite life* and its inherent 'right to live'. We could thus sum up Derrida's effort in the Death Penalty seminars with the paraphrase of the title of the next series: *more beast, less sovereign*. This would imply that the abolitionist doctrine can indeed find a proper justification in the messianic teaching of 'more life' and, thus reinforced, more effectively oppose the political theology of sovereignty, in which the superior legal and logonomocentric structure always constitutes a power *over* life, never *of* life itself.

Thus, while Michael Naas is right in claiming that: 'Derrida's main objective in the seminar is to criticize or deconstruct certain abolitionist discourses of modernity in order to develop his own, let us call it, more "philosophical," less theological, less strictly Judeo-Christian, more universalizable, maybe even more "Enlightened" abolitionism',[21] I want nonetheless to show that what he ultimately drives at is *not* a complete refutation of the Judaeo-Christian heritage. Although this heritage is indeed troubled with the confounding aporia on the issue of *sanctity-versus-sacrificability of life*, Derrida does not wish to reject it altogether in order to reach a purer secular abolitionist discourse: rather he aims at a deconstructive distillation of the messianicity, no longer simply Jewish or Christian, which he strongly associates with the 'literary intervention' and which, when opposed to the logonomocentric philosophy, could help to solve the ambivalence and let us move beyond the sovereign paradigm for good. The seminal essay 'Faith and Knowledge' already outlines this 'beyond' as a peculiar *religion of the finite life*: not the infinite unscathed life, which very easily turns into its thanatic/sovereign reverse of 'more-than-life' and then strikes back the living by demanding sacrifices, but always and only the *finite* life which, precisely because it is precarious and finite, must believe in itself and claim a separate 'right to live'. This messianic religiosity, by combining the imperative of 'getting beyond sovereignty' with the messianic/Pauline injunction of 'no more sacrifices', attempts to reformulate the religious interest in terms of the *belief in the finite life* which can no longer be sacrificeable to anything seemingly higher. So far, political theology has been firmly associated with the defence of sovereignty as representation/incarnation of the infinite life as the very 'essence of living'. Derrida's deconstruction, by substituting the sublime 'life unscathed' with the ordinary 'finite life', demonstrates that there is still a possibility of *another* political theology that knows nothing higher than the precarious and vulnerable existence of a singular living thing.[22]

The Death Penalty seminar, therefore, gives Derrida a chance to explore one of the most notorious double binds – if not *the* original double bind *tout court* – which is the structure of religious belief as grounded in the equally aporetic concept of life itself. For Derrida, the holy constitutes most of all a self-projection of life while religion is the first language of life's self-articulation. It is an image of *life unscathed* – always safe and sound, holy and whole, pleromatic and unharmed – in which the finite and precarious life of the actually living things deposits its hopes for indemnity: the invincible 'more life', untouchable by fate, suffering, and death:

> *The religion of the living – is this not a tautology?* Absolute imperative, holy law, law of salvation: saving the living intact, the unscathed, the safe and sound (*heilig*) that has the right to absolute respect, restraint, modesty . . . that which is, should remain or should be allowed to be what it is (*heilig*, living, strong and fertile, erect and fecund: safe, whole, unscathed, immune, sacred, holy and so on). Salvation and health. Such an intentional attitude bears several names of the same family: respect, modesty, restraint, inhibition, *Achtung* (Kant), *Scheu*, *Verhaltenheit, Gelassenheit* Heidegger), restraint or holding-back (*halte*) in general.
>
>   AR, 85

The source of religion, therefore, is the finite life that vehemently negates its finitude – its precarious exposure to the 'slings and arrows of outrageous fortune' – and *projects*, as well as *protects*, what is 'the most living in life itself' in the figure of the transcendence: the unscathedness itself which transcends any condition of damage and danger.

Yet, the unscathed, although created by the desire to live, is itself no longer living: it is the 'fantasy of the dead as the principle of life and of survival'. This projective sublimation is the seemingly most obvious, smooth, purely mechanical process, but precisely because of that it must be stopped, jammed, deactivated, *arrested*:

This mechanical principle is apparently very simple: life has absolute value only if it is worth *more than* life. And hence only in so far as it mourns, becoming itself in the labour of infinite mourning, in the indemnification of a spectrality without limit. It is sacred, holy, infinitely respectable only in the name of what is worth more than it and what is not restricted to the naturalness of the bio-zoological (sacrificeable) – although true sacrifice ought to sacrifice not only 'natural' life, called 'animal' or 'biological,' but also that which is worth more than so-called natural life. The price of human life, which is to say, of anthropo-theological life, the price of what to remain safe (*heilig*, sacred, safe and sound, unscathed, immune), as the absolute price, the price of what ought to inspire respect, modesty, reticence, this price is priceless. It corresponds to what Kant calls the dignity [*Würdigkeit*] of the end in itself ... This dignity of life can only subsist beyond the present living being. Whence, transcendence, fetishism and spectrality; whence, the religiosity of religion. This excess above and beyond the living, whose life only has absolute value by being worth more than life, more than itself – this, in short, is what opens the space of death that is linked to the automaton (exemplarily 'phallic'), to technics, the machine, the prosthesis: in a word, to the dimensions of auto-immune and self-sacrificial supplementarity, to this death-drive that is silently at work in every community, every *auto-co-immunity*, constituting it as such in its iterability, its heritage, its spectral tradition ... Religion, as a response that is both ambiguous and ambivalent is thus an ellipsis: *the ellipsis of sacrifice.*

AR, 87–8; my emphasis

But does the *negation of finitude* always have to proceed that way? Must it always mean to reject life as such, because it is always precarious and vulnerable, and go for something 'more-*than*-life', no longer alive and thanks to that no longer exposed to harm: *dead-immortal*? Or, perhaps, it may also mean to reject life at the extreme of its mortal exposure, the natural 'mere-life', in search of 'more-life', another mode of living that will find a way to relax the natural limitations and manage to 'linger' within their confines a bit longer, bit more worthwhile? The negation of finitude, projecting the figure of 'life unscathed', would thus create the originary locus of ambivalence or the blind spot of indecision between 'more-than-life' and 'more-life': between the 'unscathedness', which gives up on life because it is always 'lacking', on the one hand – and the 'livingness' [*vivacité*] that wishes to enhance life, even if it means giving up on the ideal of absolute indemnity and embracing the 'originary lack', on the other. The 'unscathed life' would be, in fact, a deeply aporetic figure that demands to be unpacked by the 'doubling' that will then reflect on the future religious choice of: either *absolute indemnity* or *happier life*. The first channel creates the series of religious metaphors linked to the idea of *sovereignty* – the second, closer to Derrida's heart, creates a series of religious metaphors linked to the idea of *messianicity*.

Within the sovereign paradigm, religion is the cult of the absolutely indemnified and thus absolutely powerful: the power transcending the vulnerable condition of the living, *beyond* life-and-death, as well as *over* life and death. Freed from the precariousness of life, it has no weakness in itself: it is the unflinching power of 'Death, the Absolute Master', whose unwavering reliability offers a model for the functioning of the law (see again Derrida's critique of Lacan). The model of the cultic behaviour is thus *sacrifice*: the finite imperfect and precarious life has to be given up in the 'sublime offering' for the sake of the transcendent 'more-than-life' which negates life in its feeble finitude. In the *Death Penalty*, Derrida says:

> The dignity of man, his sovereignty, the sign that he accedes to universal right and rises above animality is that *he rises above biological life*, puts his life in play in the law, *risks his life* and thus affirms his sovereignty as subject or consciousness. A law that would refrain from inscribing the death penalty within it would not be a law; it would not be a human law, it would not be a law worthy of human dignity.
>
> DP1, 4

Derrida alludes here to the same philosophical lineage as in *The Animal That Therefore I am*, which subscribed to the sovereign paradigm. It begins with Descartes, who eliminated life for the sake of the dead-sure certainty; continues with Kant, for whom the sanctity of the law consisted in the ascetic rejection of the 'pathological' sensuous living process; proceeds via Hegel read in the Kojèvian manner, as the ultimate philosopher of 'Death, the Absolute Master' who ascribed subjective dignity only to those who 'risked their lives' in deadly confrontation and thus rose above their immediate vital interests; and ends with Maurice Blanchot and Jacques Lacan, the two Kojève followers, who elevated the cult of the Thanatos to the most sublime theoretical heights.[23]

This is also the main lineage of modern Western philosophy: the thanatic, as well as logo-nomo-centric strain, which Derrida seeks to oppose by mobilizing the alternative tradition of messianicity. The main messianic thinker to whom Derrida alludes in his seminar is Saint Paul who, in the Epistle to Romans, famously advocated the full sublation of law into love, or the dissolution of law's hardness into a fluid and supple element of mercy. For Saint Paul, the law simply equals death, because it deadens the soul which should live solely in a state of loving grace. And indeed, Derrida's readings of the Western legal tradition shows that the very idea of the law had *almost* always been based on the sovereign power of death: it is via the death penalty that the human *Gesetz* touches upon the mightiest law of nature, according to which all that lives is destined to die.[24] Although, as he often emphasizes, the death penalty differs from the natural verdict, there is also a point of affinity between them: the 'right to kill' represents the absolute order of justice, which, without this recourse to death, would lack ultimate authority as a merely constituted and conventional human legal system. Thus, despite all the difference, there is more than just an analogy between Derrida's investigation into the idea of the legal pardon, which releases the convict from capital punishment, and the figure of the messianic pardon in which life becomes exonerated and forgiven in order to exercise its inherent 'right to live' – against the 'law of death' which condemns all the living to the same bitter end. In fact, this difference vanishes once the 'law of death' begins to hover over the heads of the mortals in the form of a persistent *memento mori* – as in Heidegger, Blanchot or Lacan. Once it becomes a *verdict*, which fixes the prospect of dying into a tangible, almost concrete entity of the inevitable, the so-called natural death begins to resemble the death penalty and the distinction 'between all the meanings of condemnation (condemning to death, condemning to die as a result of so-called natural death, or condemning to die as a result of illness)' becomes impossible (DP2, 242).[25]

Within this religious complex, death becomes the model of the Absolute, as well as the mystical foundation of all authority: virginally pure, ideal, ultimate, unflinching legality that knows no exception, no extenuating circumstances. It is the groundless grounding of the law, which is dead-sure; the measureless foundation of all measure, which never founders. Whenever life wants to 'regain virginity' – regain what it never had in the first place – it always reaches for *imitatio mortis*; if it wants ultimate solution to its 'troubles' [*peines*], it achieves it by dissolving itself into death: 'the death penalty, the supreme punishment, the absolute castigation, would have as its end the reconstitution of a *castitas*, the redemption of an immaculate purity' (DP2, 230). In Kant, therefore, if law is to be law, by definition it cannot make any exceptions: it must be as intransigent as death itself. Or, to cut short the analogy: it must be *death, period* – because it is only death that operates on the basis of the perfect *jus talionis* (life for life; everything else is a compromise). Death is thus also the ground of the natural law: non-artificial, non-made by human hands and minds, and because of that non-negotiable and irreversible: '*this is where law is natural law*; the fact that the death penalty is a criminal law . . . one that is universal and thus eternal, confirms that this instituted law, as law, is in fact natural law' (DP2, 258; my emphasis).

This thanatic syndrome, in which life achieves ideal perfection only in death, is what Derrida calls 'death penalty *as* religion' (DP1, 2): the sacred dimension of the intimate and unique relation to death which decides upon 'what is proper to man' (DP1, 1). And, as we already know, this is also the central myth of the 'anthropological difference', which he aims to deconstruct: 'the idea that the death penalty is a sign of the access to the dignity of man, something that is proper to man who must, through his law, be able to raise himself above life (which beasts cannot do), this idea of the death penalty as a condition of human law and of human dignity' (DP1, 9).

But, even more than that, Derrida wants to deconstruct the double bind of religion which, on the one hand, avails itself of the death penalty and, on the other, issues the commandment *thou shall not kill*, suggesting an 'absolute right to life' (DP1, 11) – the glaring contradiction which went as if unnoticed for the most of the history of the Greco-Judaeo-Christian West and its main institutions: churches and states which 'put to death a speech, the body of a speech that claimed to be the presentation of a divine speech' (DP1, 24). The negative purpose, therefore, is to counteract the 'theologico-political system as a system of sovereignty in which the death penalty is necessarily inscribed' (DP1, 23) and oppose it with the *resurrected* 'body of a speech' which spoke in the name of life and which sovereignty condemned to death. Hence also the choice of those heroes who revealed the theologico-political double bind in the most spectacular way: Socrates, Jesus, Hallaj, and Joan of Arc. And, especially in the first volume, the writers: most of all, Michel de Montaigne and Victor Hugo.

But, why the writers? Because, as Derrida soon reveals, literature applies a peculiar tactic which, in the Introduction, I called, after Benjamin, the *Scheherazade strategy*: it plays with, postpones and softens the verdict of the law, so extolled in all its duress by philosophy. Philosophy, which demonstrates absolute attachment to the law and the sovereign paradigm, demands that the subject *submits* and submits *immediately*; literature, on the other hand, insists on 'buying time' and because of that appears more conducive to relativization, forgiveness, pardon, exceptionality and extenuating circumstances. Derrida's messianic antinomianism, as it presents itself in the Death Penalty seminar, is a subtler version of the Pauline critique of the law. For Derrida, the literary narrative becomes the privileged expression of life which, as long as it lives, asks for the pardon from the blind and all-levelling hardness of the law. It wants to be *this life*, unique and singular, indissoluble in the generalities of the system: 'it is writers who, before abolishing the death penalty or "destroying" it, have imposed the concept of extenuating circumstances. Not innocence, but the means of exculpation by sheltering from the blind hardness of the law, by attenuating the punishment' (DP1, 104).

Derrida's concern, therefore, is *not* the Nietzschean 'innocence of becoming' that would exonerate life altogether and relieve it from any 'restraint' of the legal system; *not* the uncontaminated 'beastly' element or bare life 'outside the law'. This is not a desirable outcome for Derrida who fights simultaneously on two fronts: against the absolutism of death and the deadly initiation, on the one hand, but also against the vitalist image of life lawless, unscathed, and happily prelinguistic, on the other. What is at stake here is a *pardon* that softens, bends, mollifies and attenuates the law, the Shakespearian 'mercy which seasons justice' without relieving of the law altogether. This is 'the writer's right, a right no less *sacred* than the legislator's' (DP1, 105) – to speak in the name of the finite life that knows that it cannot escape the law of death for good, but can nonetheless postpone the verdict and exercise its autonomous 'right to live' and the possibility of 'more life' in the time of delay, deferment and temporary release. Derrida's sole object of interest is the finite life which, despite its finitude, is not defined by its end and asserts itself in its right to difference, to be a 'living-on' and not just a pre-established dying, *Sein-zum-Tode*, issuing towards the inevitable death, *always already sacrificed*. What he thinks about is *another finitude*, freed from the philosophical overestimation of death as the inner law of human existence, dictating the cruel sacrificial *rite de passage* of the anthropogenic initiation. In *The Animal That Therefore I Am*, Derrida, in the Rosenzweigian broad gesture of condemning the whole of Western philosophical discourse 'from Ionia to Jena', says:

> at the heart of all these discourses *sacrifice* beats like a vital impulse. They [Kant, Heidegger, Lacan, Lévinas] represent four varieties of thinking sacrificial experience ... Not necessarily of sacrifice as ritual sacrifice of the animal ... but of sacrifice as fundamental, indeed, of a founding sacrifice, within a human space where, in any case, exercising power over the animal to the point of being able to put it to death when necessary is not forbidden.
>
> ATTIA, 91

The writer's right is here as *sacred* as the legislator's precisely because it appeals to the other – more spectral and hence more repressed – aspect of religiosity which, because of the rebellion against the sacrificial 'yoke of law', Derrida calls messianic. *No more sacrifices!* – this paradigmatically messianic call of Saint Paul can thus also be understood as *No more initiations!*: no more cruelty of self-offerings, no more flirting with the sublime fetishism of death, no more disdain for life, no more denigration of survival. The literary subject, lingering 'before the law' (*avant de la loi*), stands for all these 'beastly' elements of existence that resist becoming a sacrificial lamb on the altar of sovereignty: be it the sovereign law of language or the sovereign law of the state.

So, although the content of the seminar is death-as-penalty and penalty-as-death, on its performative level it is structured as a literary narrative which, in the manner of Scheherazade, postpones the lethal verdict, relieves us of the sacrifice, and lets the singular life live on in the *time of delay*:

> We would begin by pretending to begin before the beginning. As if, already, we wanted to delay the end ... It is indeed of an end, but of an end *decided*, by a verdict, of an end decreed by a judicial decree [*arrèt e par un arrèt de justice*], it is of a decided end that decidedly we are going to talk endlessly.
>
> DP1, 1

Endlessly and *against*. Mercy granted by the messianic narrative of literature, as opposed to the *dura lex* of the legislative philosophical discourse, consists here in a *given time*: a gift of temporality that creates a separate and idiosyncratic time of the finite living-on spun between the two absolutes to be evaded by the 'softening' literary touch: death as pure law, on the one hand – life infinite and lawless, on the other.

Both these Derridean motives – literature as a mouthpiece of life, as well as its piece of resistance, and as the Scheherazade strategy of postponement – derive from Walter Benjamin's essay on Nikolai Leskov, 'The Storyteller', which I have already mentioned apropos Rosenzweig. Here, the storyteller is the *Fürsprech der Kreatur*, the 'mouthpiece of creation', while his story becomes a plastic form, radiating from the nether side of this life: a form that mediates/oscillates between the anarchic bare life, spent in the extension of the worldly immanence, and the rigid order of the law which is of an alien transcendent origin. While it must progress by the very nature of the narrative itself, it also postpones and procrastinates, due to which it can stay within the flux of life and its law-defying indefiniteness. In his early talk on Kafka in German radio, from July 1931, Benjamin already sees the antagonistic use of the haggadic element against the halachic order as the most distinctive feature of Kafkan parables:

> Like the haggadic parts of the Talmud, these books, too, are stories; they are a Haggadah that constantly pauses, luxuriating in the most detailed descriptions, in the simultaneous hope and fear that it might encounter the halachic order, the

doctrine itself, en route ... The fact that the Law never finds expression as such – this and nothing else is the *gracious dispensation of the fragment.*

SW2, 496–7

This is also the leitmotif of Derrida's reading of *Before the Law*: thanks to the meandering and evasive nature of the narrative itself, the Gorgon of the Law and its 'severe radiance' [*strenge Licht*] can never be approached directly. Thanks to the 'gracious dispensation of the fragment' within the story which looks with curiosity 'in all directions' and luxuriates in aside details, but never straight ahead, the divine Law does not have to be confronted 'face to face' – which could only mean death. Singular life is thus 'given time' in the narrative art of evasion, which finds the longest, most roundabout, and *extended* route to its finale, instead of issuing directly *zum Tode.*[27]

This permanently liminoid realm – the realm of the living middle described by literary narratives in between the 'overspecified poles' – is precisely the Kingdom of the Derridean *khora*. She is like harlot – 'open to all men', and not just men: also beasts, rogues and all sorts of singular *animot.*[28] It/she does not judge; it postpones all judgement, so that the *voyou* life with its 'living accent of deviation' (Stevens again) can live on in the mode of self-delighting self-preference, without being automatically *accused* and made *guilty*. In the Kingdom of *khora*, the rogue living being may be slightly 'deviant', but is not an automatic trespasser: against Kant and Hegel, who claimed that every singular life is a 'criminal' as long as it deviates from the one stream of the 'uninjured life', by causing to it a temporary harm – the *voyou* is released from this fundamental form of guilt. It is free of the original sin.

In the second volume of *La peine de mort*, Kant and Hegel become the main adversaries, instrumental in yet another philosophical swindle: the general *criminalization of life*. The very term of 'life uninjured', *das unverletzte Leben* – the prototype of the Derridean *vie indemne* as the name of the major religious phantasm – derives directly from Hegel. In his early unfinished essay on 'The Spirit of Christianity and Its Fate', Hegel, closely following Kant, develops his theory of criminal behaviour as causing a harmful division within the oneness of life:

> Only through a departure from that united life which is neither regulated by law nor at variance with law, only through the killing of life, is something alien produced. Destruction of life is not the nullification of life but its diremption, and the destruction consists in its transformation into an enemy. It is immortal, and, if slain, it appears as its terrifying ghost which vindicates every branch of life and lets loose its Eumenides. The illusion of trespass, its belief that it destroys

the other's life and thinks itself enlarged thereby, is dissipated by the fact that the disembodied spirit of the injured life comes on the scene against the trespass, just as Banquo who came as a friend to Macbeth was not blotted out when he was murdered but immediately thereafter took his seat, not as a guest at the feast, but as an evil spirit. The trespasser intended to have to do with another's life, but he has only destroyed his own, *for life is not different from life, since life dwells in the single Godhead.* In his arrogance he has destroyed indeed, but only the friendliness of life; he has perverted life into an enemy.[29]

The criminal is the one who attempts to appropriate life for himself and thus injures the unity of life, which dwells in the single Godhead: the 'Most Living Thing', the Sovereign Source of all that lives, but also the ultimate Phallic Father from Freud's *Totem and Taboo.* This association implies that *all* that lives partakes in the criminal predicament of the patricidal sons from Freud's 'anthropological fantasy': to be alive means to have *stolen* the vital power which rightfully belongs only to the One; to be alive is to engage in the criminal act of appropriation, which implicates every *Lebendige* automatically into what Benjamin calls *Schuldzusammenhang,* the 'net of guilt'. *To be alive is to be guilty, period.*

In the second volume of *The Death Penalty,* therefore, Derrida focuses on the theme of the 'criminality' of every singular life; accordingly, the role of literature as opposed to the harsh philosophical discourse of punitive thanatophilia is taken over by psychoanalysis (although, as we shall see, not as successfully). While reading closely Theodor Reik's pro-abolitionist essay,[30] Derrida interprets psychoanalysis as a deconstructive exorcism on the unconscious that looms in all of us as the abyss of primordial guilt. What Hegel sees as the original sin of every singular life which, in the manner of a metaphysical criminal, detaches itself from the homogenous stream of life and thus makes it 'injured' – dispersed, fragmented, scathed and finite – turns out to be a deep syndrome of the unconscious, which imbues us with the a priori wish to induce guilt and to punish, preferably by death penalty: 'One can, then, of course wish to prohibit killing. Never kill! Never put to death! Never put to death another living being, whether the other or yourself. But can one prohibit the conscious or unconscious desire to kill? What presides over this desire?' (DP2, 8).

Life is not innocent, it comes with a price – *peine,* which means fee, *poena,* penalty, but also trouble and pain: 'If there is a *peine* to pay to live life, it is because life has something like a price'.[31] This price, however, is nonetheless worth paying, and, according to the strictly talionic law, the repayment of it must be life itself: the gift of life is never properly owned and extended in perpetuity, it is always to be duly paid back in the moment of death. So, just as Derrida does not believe in the happy anarchy of a wholly liberated life (which is still Benjamin's position in his 'Critique of Violence' (SW1)), he also doubts in the absolute outcome of the psychoanalytic exorcism: the guilty feeling of life can never be completely dispelled for the sake of the anarchic 'innocence of becoming', because life cannot be turned into a property, it can never be simply and only 'my life'. Derrida thus asks rhetorically, while alluding to the founding gesture of the liberal legislation, based on the full individual appropriation of life: 'Can we consider life a property? Is one the owner [*propriétaire*] of one's own [*propre*] life, as some modern law texts seem to imply when they speak of the right to life or the right to one's own life, as if it were an inalienable right?' (DP2, 98).

No, I can never enjoy *my* life as if it only belonged to me and I owed nothing to anybody else. But life can still be *less* guilty than is implied by the dark morasses of the unconscious which sees every singular life as a 'criminal' always already punished by the death sentence: always already paying back to the source of *life unscathed* which, as in Hegel's vision, is one, uninjured and knowing no internal negations. Life can thus be *less* guilty if it becomes released from the original sin of separation, which dares to say No to the oneness of life. The exorcism on the unconscious is thus successful enough if it manages to break its pleromatic principle of never-saying-No: if it affirms separation and fragmentation, which occur in the moment of birth, as free of the a priori sense of guilt and sin, or if it allows us to constitute a singular finite life as 'free of charge' (*peine*) in this one – absolutely crucial – respect. If, in other words, the singularity of the 'natal' is released from its traumatic, guilt and anxiety inducing, aspect.

Thus, even if we indeed, as Freud formulated it tersely, 'owe our death to Nature/God',[32] it does not mean that by dying we return the living spark to some divine treasury that guards it as a precious jewel: the very time of *lease* – 'given time' – is not criminal appropriation or theft. The unconscious tells us that we have robbed life of life in order to get born and lead our singular life, because it imagines life as something infinitely valuable, while every living thing is something infinitely unworthy, leading its life only 'by proxy' (see Augustine and Marion again). The psychoanalytic exorcism cuts into this aporetic *Traumnagel*, in which life bifurcates for the first time into the potential, always one Life and the actual, always divisive living – and judges against the latter. We thus need to be constantly telling ourselves that, as living singular creatures – living-loving and lovingly leading our own lives, we do not have to imagine the preciousness of life in terms of a stolen good. Although the unconscious equally constantly prompts us to believe that we are bunch of criminals to be hanged immediately on the scaffolding of *peine du mort*, this is not the only way in which 'love of life' can express itself: we, as living beings, may indeed be *voyou* – deviant, idiosyncratic and law-bending – but not criminals *tout court*. 'The accent of deviation in the living thing' may in fact be the only way in which life can be lived at all. Even if *torat hayim* is a tradition, there is no orthodoxy in this discipline, which, as Derrida often emphasizes, can never be 'learned finally'.

Here we touch again on life's primordial double bind, the very worth of life's preciousness which bifurcates into the two series of images: the sovereign line of instant punishment and the messianic line of original pardon. While in the political theology of Sovereignty, which stands for the Highest Living Being representing Life As Such, everybody and everything is a criminal, not just potentially, but actually, as a thief-of-life, stealing what rightfully belongs only to the One – in the political theology of *khora*, which patiently gives without expecting a return, everybody and everything is a *voyou*, allowed to disseminate freely and guiltlessly. While in the Sovereign edifice, which is the structure of the unconscious, life can only be *taken* – first stolen as a precious treasure (Lacan calls it very aptly with the Platonic term: *agalma*) and then, with death as the rightful punishment, taken back again – in the Kingdom of *khora*, which occasionally shines through the patient work of deconstruction, life is *given*: given without debt, guilt and return, although merely for a while.

But the finitude of the gift is *not* a punishment for the hubris of separation: it is part and parcel of the gift itself. Life would not consider itself as worth loving – and thus preserving and perpetuating itself – if it were securely infinite, i.e. given absolute insurance in immortality. The gift, therefore, can only be a 'given time': temporary and transient, and precisely for that reason – so valuable. We already know from Hannah Arendt that creaturely life considers itself as a *gift*: the precious object of self-appreciation, always in transition, never to be owned for good. In Derrida's rendering, however, this self-appreciation constitutes life's most fundamental double bind: the gift may appear as a stolen treasure, so precious that it cannot ever be deserved unconditionally by a newborn individual – or a free gift, freely disseminated without guilt, debt and expectation of return, which leases life to the individual for his or her own self-delight. The second option, however, can only be reached through the deconstruction of the former *Schuldzusammenhang* into which life implicates itself as if mechanically, with the assuredness of the 'machine' whose Satanic Mills turn day and night in the tireless repetition of the unconscious – against the 'miracle' of forgiveness.[33] For, if I love life the way I do – more than anything else – then how could I possibly *deserve* to be alive? How could I merit such gift? In order to deserve life, I would

have to deserve it before I came alive, and since it is blatantly impossible, I am
born already guilty, always already in debt, with the unmerited gift on my hands.
The need of self-justification, with which my unconscious troubles me, giving
me a constant *peine*, can most easily be satisfied if I also agree to die even before
the actual death: if I internalize the just punishment for my hubristic
unworthiness, by paying back the gift of life while in life and with my life,
according to the precise calculation of *jus talionis* which is the only law
recognized by the unconscious.[34]

But there is – 'perhaps, perhaps. . .' – another way in which this self-justification
can proceed: not via death, in which I return all that I 'owe Nature/God', but via
the intense relationship with others who, by loving me in return, alleviate my
sense of undeserved existence. Unlike Agamben, therefore, who would like to
solve the puzzle of life by deactivating its inner structure of self-preference – life
must stop loving and willing itself and just be, without any extra 'task' of self-
affirmation – Derrida does not believe that such 'un-troubled' life, *la vie sans
peine*, could still be called 'life'. Life necessarily lives itself as troublesome,
problematic, burdened with *peine* which immediately translates into 'auto/
hetero/punishment', coming from the deepest, still pre-subjective layers of the
extimate unconscious, where *peona forensis* and *poena internalis* can no longer
be distinguished: '*Je peine* [I'm at pains] and *j'ai de la peine* [I'm in pain]; *je suis
peiné* [I'm pained/punished]' (DP2, 29). Again and again, Derrida dissects the
phantasmata of simple vitalism which insists on regaining life's absolute
innocence: no such thing can ever be possible. Life must justify itself, but it does
not have to do it by turning its *peine*/trouble into *peine*/penalty: immediate
paying-back of the gift. It can just as well give it *forward*; share it with others and
assist them in their *peine*/burden in order to experience gratitude (*merci*) and,
with it, forgiveness (*mercy*), grace and dispensation. Thus, while 'to the
unconscious, gratefulness is as foreign as is forgiveness',[35] the ethics of neighbourly
love turns against the merciless economy of the guilt-inducing unconscious
'machine' and insists on the idea of life as a 'miraculous' gift which does not have
to be returned, with an exact talionic calculation, to the donor.[36]

But does love turn against the unconscious *in vain*? If Freud and Reik are
right, then 'all of this would be nothing but an appearance or a ruse of
consciousness . . . while, at the same time, the unconscious keeps on counting,
exchanging, reconstituting the economic calculation' (DP2, 171):

> Forgiveness comes to disavow in consciousness the talion, the harsh law of
> the talion, which continues to operate in the unconscious. In short this means

that, according to Freud and Reik, talionic law never stops governing the unconscious. Forgiveness would be an illusion, a simulacrum, at most a reaction formation of consciousness that would merely confirm the *violence of the unconscious talion.*

DP2, 173

Yet, at the same time, Freud and Reik also believe in 'an evolution that is less cruel, more civilized, that would not only abolish the death penalty but also substitute confession for punishment' (DP2, 179) – yet, on the basis of what?[37] If the ethical 'reaction-formation' is nothing but a symptom that still serves the economy of the unconscious, then what can be the real *force* behind the enlightenment? For Derrida it is – again – the 'living-loving', the 'miraculous' secret of life's self-preference, seen from the other side of life's aporia, where it truly wants to exercise its biophilia, without the intimate implication with guilt and death. The wish to become free of the unconscious is thus a real and powerful drive: a *voyou* desire that strays away from the pleroma of drives, deviates from their vengeful purposes, and actually wants less cruelty and more civility: more regard for myself as well as others. A desire for *my* life, which 'errotically' wanders out of the Egypt of the id fused with superego, where the latter's rational 'an eye for an eye' is just as cruel as the talionic drive of the unconscious.

This desire for *my* life – akin to what Derrida calls *pulsion du propre* in his earlier essay on Freud, *The Postcard*[38] – would be the very opposite of the desires craving for the unlimited expression of pulsional cruelty, be it an immediate 'wish to kill' or a more mediated, yet equally violent, wish to execute moral law with an ideal and unflinching purity. Again, the *leben-und-lebenlassende*, the 'live-and-let-live' patience of *khora*, which welcomes the living rogues – the 'suppleness' of an ethical approach which always takes into account extenuating circumstances – stands here in contrast to the cruel impatience of sublime idealization, best represented by Kant. And it is precisely this 'suppleness' that unites the best part of psychoanalysis and literature in their participation in the civilizing process which 'seasons' and 'softens' the 'violence of the unconscious talion'. Not, however, when psychoanalysis advocates to substitute confession for punishment, for 'this becoming worldwide of repentance, confession, and/or psychoanalysis, would simply reaffirm the interiorization of guilt or shame for an indestructible criminality, for an ineradicable originary sin, for a drive that would be impossible to eradicate . . . simply a process of absolute interiorization, of autoverdict and autopunishment' (DP2, 227). Psychoanalysis and literature converge only on the subtler language of merciful *souplesse*:

> Not that one forgive, since forgiveness is a reaction formation, but that *one become benevolent, tolerant, flexible, in order to avoid the rigidity of the ideal* ... No excessive rectitude in law, in short, no absolute correctness. For inflexibility, rigidness, correction are essential attributes of what is right ... *Flexibility is incalculable*; it is that for which there is no objective rule, as there is for law. But this is perhaps what Reik is suggesting: without an objective rule, one must be benevolent toward the other as other, by finding each time, and this is perhaps what benevolence is, by each time inventing the flexibility, the form and degree of flexibility, of *relaxation of the law*, the good rule (without rule, then) of flexibility. Otherwise we get cruelty; *the inflexible law is what produces cruelty.*
>
> DP2, 205–6; my emphasis

Is it, therefore, possible to have the law, which could be less cruel and more 'relaxed', deriving from the supple and fluid medium of life itself? And, accordingly, could we have *another* religion believing in the singular finite life, with all its aporetic dialectics to which only literature can give proper testimony [*récit*]? The ultimate stake of Derrida's project of enlightenment – the *new* enlightenment – is to begin to understand that all the cruel phantasms of ontological infinity, sovereignty, unscathedness and ideal perfection derive from the instability of the finite life itself, which is bound to negate its own finitude, but – and this brings us a bit of hope – does so 'always in life and for life'. Derrida's new proposal differs from the old formula, still operative in psychoanalysis, which equates enlightenment with disenchantment: Derrida knows that life cannot be completely made free of all fantasies, because life is a process coterminous with self-preference and self-belief. What, however, can be deconstructed is the status of this *autoreligion*: when it no longer sustains the projection of the ontological 'beyond', but stays *Diesseits*, on *this* side of the finite life, life's belief in itself transforms internally. *Wo es war, soll ich werden*: where there was the unconscious phantasm either of life unscathed or perfect death, the finite living awareness shall enter, choosing life as a gift 'in transition' in which 'being becomes transitive': 'lived for oneself, for the other, and for life' (HCL, 89). Never to be owned, but nonetheless generously leased out.

A non-simple human life: contamination

The negative stake of the seminar is to speak against the death penalty, but its main positive stake is to conceive of a new universal ethics based on the 'right to life' – this time, fully consciously *always in life and for life* – which can at the same time be rooted in the particular self-preservatory 'interest': the love of life deriving always and inevitably from the desire/love of *my* life.

Derrida starts his deconstruction of the logonomocentric logic by attacking its main presumption at least since Kant: the claim that all ethical behaviour as such must be grounded in abstract *disinterestedness*, capable of detaching itself – by a lofty sublime sacrifice – from the 'pathology' of the concrete life. It is only according to this logic that universality comes with the resignation of 'my own vital interests'; that it must be bought with submission to the absolute heteronomy of the law, always arriving from the sphere *beyond* life (one has to remember that the Kantian ethical autonomy is, in fact, a radical heteronomy when seen from the perspective of the sacrificed bodily existence). Derrida's position here is, again, very subtle. He is neither in favour of the universal law imposed on life from its beyond – nor in favour of a 'happy lawless life' which would know no 'restraint'. He aims, rather, at a universal law that would emanate from life and itself and then become accepted by it as binding and restraining. The moment of universalization, therefore, should rather be *inherent* to the self-reflexive living process, thanks to which the self-preservatory interest can transform into a generalized sense of autopreference: the *biophilia* as the proper choice of life:

> And I say straight on: yes, I am against the death penalty because I want to save my neck, to save the life I love, what I love to live, what I love living. And when I say 'I', of course, I mean 'I', me, but also the 'I', the 'me', whoever says 'I' in its place or in mine. That is my interest, the ultimate resource of my interest as of any possible interest in the end of the death penalty, every interest having finally to be 'my interest' . . . well, *neither disinterested nor interested in this sense* ('to save our skin' – ABR), the abolitionist struggle, in my view, must still be driven; it cannot not be driven, motivated, justified by an interest, but by another interest, by another figure of interest that remains to be defined . . . *I can put the living before the dead only on the basis of the affirmation and preference of my life, of my living present, right there where it receives its life from the heart of the other.*
>
> DP1, 255; my emphasis

Against the disdainful comments of the Kantian defenders of the law – and contempt is always a powerful weapon of distinction among 'human animals' – Derrida defends the self-preservatory interest of each and every living being: yes, I am in favour of the abolition of the death penalty, because *I* wouldn't like to end this way. Yet, already the very fact that this interest is stated in language, it immediately opens to universalization: 'And when I say 'I', of course, I mean 'I', me, but also the 'I', the 'me', *whoever says 'I' in its place or in mine.*' The shifter 'I' works here as a universalizing vehicle; as we know from Derrida's *Speech and*

Phenomena, it can almost completely lose its living bearer on the way to pure enunciation (which then takes the form of the paradoxical *I am dead*, uttered by Poe's Mr Waldemar), but it can also *shift* the concrete living experience – the Rosenzweigian '*I* want to live, *I* want to remain' – to a place of articulation where it can be shared and recognized by others. The strangers in the creaturely night can still exchange their sense of vital concerns. The autobiographical stories of co-survivors are driven and motivated by the desire 'to save the life I love' – just as the work of all those writers, who have spoken against the death penalty.[39]

In the previous sections, we have seen how Derrida opposes the 'sacred right of the writers' to the dark logonomocentric logic of philosophers. But in what way would such law of the affirmation of life be *sacred*? *To what religion would it belong?* If belief in the sacred means to be ready 'to espouse [its cause] *at the cost of life*' (DP1, 270), then we are in the very heart of the paradox: the absolute right to life 'has no price', which again means that it is 'worth more than life, on the surplus value of life, on the "sur-viving" that would be *ultra-life, more than life in life*' (DP1, 270; my emphasis). Thus for Kant, the exponent of the death penalty, *just as* for Beccaria, the opponent of the death penalty, 'justice is above life, beyond life or the life drive, in a sur-viving of which the *sur*, the transcendence of the 'sur' – if it is a transcendence – remains to be interpreted' (DP1, 271). *Der Gesetzgeber ist heilig* [the legislator is sacred], says Kant – and Beccaria, though of the opposite opinion as to the meaning of his legislation, agrees. The highest laws – in favour either of death or life – can be conferred only by a true sovereign who, as any true sovereign, in the end demands sacrifices. If you fight for the cause of life, you must be ready to lay down your life: thus, once again, *Life against the living*.

The situation would be, frankly, hopeless, unless there is some way out, some *clinamen* from this religious logic of sovereignty, in which the sacred always calls for 'burnt offerings'. And if such *clinamen* were possible, its chance would have lain uniquely in the complex doubling resulting from life's negation of its own finitude, which we have discussed in the previous section. Again, Derrida's fragment on Benjamin from 'Force of Law', which defines life as an inherently unstable process that cannot sustain itself on the purely biological level, comes here infinitely useful. According to Benjamin/Derrida, life is bound to transcend the condition of the naked *zoe* and, because of that, inevitably create religion. It cannot rest in itself as a flat 'simply human life' that does not care about anything greater than itself. Life, as Bergson has remarked, is indeed a machine that automatically projects images of gods and cannot be arrested, as long as it is life. In the end, these *Ur*-images of unscathedness and indemnity as opposed to the equally primal images of harm and exposure lead Derrida to conceive the mechanism of auto/immunity which, only apparently organicist, reaches far deeper, into the very core of *the phenomenon of life understood philosophically*. In *Rogues*, he says:

> Why did I think it necessary in order to formalize this strange and paradoxical revolution to privilege today something that might look like a generalization, without any *external limit*, of a biological or physiological model, namely, autoimmunity? It is not, you might well imagine, out of some excessive biologistic or geneticist proclivity on my part. On the one hand, I began by noting that the circular or rotary movement of the self's return to itself and against itself, in the encounter with itself and countering of itself, would take place, as I understand it, before the separation of *physis* from its others, such as *tekhne*, *nomos*, and *thesis*. What applies here to *physis*, to *phuein*, applies also to life, understood before any opposition between life *(bios* or *zoe)* and its others (spirit, culture, the symbolic, the specter, or death). In this sense, if autoimmunity is physiological, biological, or zoological, it precedes or anticipates all these oppositions. My questions concerning 'political' autoimmunity thus concerned precisely the relationship between the *politikon*, *physis*, and *bios* or *zoe*, life-death.
>
> R, 109[40]

Now, if we read the former passage in the light of the latter, the Benjaminian *blosses Leben* will emerge precisely as 'bare life' which, itself aporetic and unstable, precedes all later stabilizing qualifications and dualisms. Bare life, being neither *zoe* nor *bios*, finds itself in the state of constant oscillation in which it is bound to transcend itself and – as Bergson said in the conclusion to his *Two Sources of Morality and Religion* – inevitably 'make gods'.[41] The juxtaposition of these two passages demonstrates that, indeed, the best language to capture the dialectic of life thought philosophically is *metatheological* – hence in Benjamin, Rosenzweig and Arendt 'bare life' is also a 'creaturely life'. While the above fragments explains the mechanism of auto/immunity that governs life even before it is conceived biologically – the passage on Benjamin reveals the religious meanders of life as a process which 'prefers itself'. Following partly Spinoza and partly Rosenzweig, Derrida defines life as a being which wants to remain/linger in being, or a being which, in even the shortest and most minimal reflexive circuit, comes back to itself to say Yes to its own existence.[42] The idea that *biophilia* – love of life – is an essential mode of finite life and that living and loving engage in a constant synonimization, is Derrida's own way of working-through the 'privileged formulation' of *torat hayim*, i.e. 'love strong as death': '*Loving-living. Loving: living* ... This love is its relation to itself, its self-intimacy, its ineluctable self-intimacy, before any other supposed interiority' (DP2, 83: my emphasis). This is perhaps the most important message coming from late Derrida: loving-living as *one* act, absolutely self-intimate, effecting itself as a centre of life before any splits resulting from reflection; an affective self-intimation which 'tells' itself only one thing – that it wants more what it has, or wants more of what it already is, and thus *loves itself into life [elle s'aime à vivre]*.[43]

Fichte (whom we mentioned in passing in the Preface, and who will also return in the last chapter) had already discovered that the best model for the *intellektuelle Anschauung*, the 'intellectual intuition' of the transcendental self, in which subject and object do not undergo a mutual alienation and which, because of that, constitutes the essence of *Ichheit* [selfhood], is not intellectual at all: it is love. In the lectures on *The Way Towards the Blessed Life*, Fichte praises love of live as that inner auto-affective attitude which heals the split with an immediate reunification:

> Love *divides* an existence which is in itself dead, as it were into a two-fold being, holding it up before its own contemplation – and thereby makes it an Ego or Self, which beholds and is cognizant of itself; and in this personality lies the root of all Life. Love again *reunites* and intimately binds together this divided personality, which, without Love, would regard itself coldly and without interest. This latter unity, within a duality which is not thereby destroyed but eternally remains subsistent, is Life itself.[44]

If we now juxtapose these two quotations – from Derrida and from Fichte – we will immediately see their close affinity and, at the same time, a distance towards Hegel who, in the preface to *Phenomenology of Spirit*, famously criticized love as an 'idle play' not allowing the true element of negativity come to the fore.[45] We could also further extrapolate the difference between Fichte and Hegel on the issue of selfhood to the difference between Derrida and Lacan: while for the former, living-loving is the indivisible self-intimacy of a living being – for the latter, the inner split, forming the ex-timate core of the psyche, can never be cured. While for Derrida, the self-preference of life is what keeps the subjective process together – for Lacan, the self is forever lost in the mirror-game of self-representations, which can only be arrested (again, the ubiquitous *arrêt de mort*), but never healed.

The analogy with Fichte continues: just as in Fichte, the primordial selfhood cannot remain at the blessed level of *intellektuelle Anschauung* and plunges into the *mise-en-abyme* of endless alienating self-objectifications, although the reason for this fall remains unclear – in Derrida too, living/loving is bound to lose its unperturbed self-intimacy. This time, however, we know why: the minimal oscillation of love and life grows into the aporetic *Schweben* because of the internal conflict of the interests that tear them in opposite directions. It is precisely the *autopreference of life* which becomes the source of life's most troubling aporia which turns it into a 'living contradiction'. Life, *insofar as life prefers itself* (AR, 289) constantly oscillates – *schwebt* – between the two extremes, yet can live-on only if it maintains itself between them: to arrest the movement at any of the extreme poles can only spell death. Life, therefore, is a deviant being, a *voyou*, which proceeds with the drunken limping step of Jacob who wanders through the desert in search after the promised *more-life*. These extremes from which life/love bounces off can be synonimized in a number of ways: as a tension between the thesis of self-identity and the antithesis of self-alienation (Hegel), between dogmatism and freedom (Fichte), between self-preservation and creativity (Bergson, Canguilhem, Deleuze), between actuality and potentiality (Heidegger, Agamben), between 'fear of life' and 'fear of death' (Rank) or, as in Derrida, between overprotection and defencelessness, i.e. between the hermetic self-enclosure of pure *autos* and the full exposure to the heterological element of the other. In any of the 'overspecified pole' of this oscillation life *dies*: either because it kills itself by too much defence, which begins to attack its own system, never as pure and *auto ipse* as it 'should' be – or it is killed because of the uncontrolled invasion of otherness. Yet, at the same time, life is always bound to meander in between these two suicidal poles: it needs simultaneously to raise the immunological guard in order to protect its self-centring sameness, if it wants to *survive* – and to lower it in order to keep in touch with environment (e.g. to receive nutrition), if it wants to stay *alive*.

This is also the point where the Fichtean analogy breaks: life can never be *pure life*. In Derrida, life is always *the realm of contamination*. All the time, life must contaminate itself with death and make itself impure in order to keep itself *in* life and *as* life. If it prefers itself as life, it must welcome a degree of 'self-deadening' into its midst, which means that it must give up on the life eternal which, as Fichte claims, knows no death – but this happens ultimately on life's conditions: always *in life, and for life*. Thus, although one can never 'learn to live, finally', one can nonetheless become aware of life's insoluble inner aporia, which Derrida calls *life-death*. It would be a grave mistake, however, to understand life-death in the manner of the Heideggerian/Blanchotian/Agambenian *Gelassenheit*, in which life, refused the blessedness of *zoon aionios*, gives up on living completely and abandons itself to the privative mode of 'dying'. Similarly to Rosenzweig, who reclaimed for life the concept of the Fall and *fallenness*, and similarly to

Arendt who uncoupled the notion of finitude from being-towards-death, Derrida also makes a move beyond the default acephalic Neoplatonism and its lingering conceptual prejudices, and revindicates the idea of *impurity* as a necessary contamination of any liveable life. Essentially non-essential and impure, life avails itself of self-deadening technics in order to survive and keep on as life. To be able to lead life-death without overestimating death would thus mean to take some final lesson of life, but also – 'perhaps, perhaps' – to modify life's spontaneous tendency to produce religion as the cult of life pure and infinite, and shift it to another form of religiosity, in which *the finite life would (finally) be able to believe itself as finite.*

Derrida ascribes this prophetic position to Michel de Montaigne whose 'enigmatic hand-to-hand combat with Christianity' – and particularly with the Augustinian emphasis paid on the immortal life at the cost of the earthly one – might have derived from 'the Marrano Judaism that haunted his filiation on the side of his mother' (DP1, 276). Derrida professes to have a 'great compassion' for Montaigne, perhaps also in the sense of a deep *Einfühlung*, because these two formulas could just as well be used in his Marrano self-portrait from 'Circumfession'.[46] Montaigne's meditations on death, in which he, again and again, resists the sacrificial 'higher wisdom' of religion and praises a certain condemned man who refused the last confession (just as Derrida refused to accept Reik's 'compulsion to confess') 'signal thereby that he preferred to love life, to live while loving, and to die while loving, *to die while loving life, to die alive,* in short, *to die in his lifetime, to die while preferring life,* or even *die from loving life* rather than to let himself be delivered from it by the analgesic trap of confession' (DP1, 277–8; my emphasis).

There are thus two parallel variants of the finite life-death: *to live dead* – and *to die alive.* While Montaigne (and Derrida) prefers the latter, the philosophical line prefers the former: to give up, in Lacan's words, 'the phantasm of livingness' and assume one's own non-existence, even before the actual physical death. But not just philosophy. On Montaigne's critical reading, *all* religions, not just Christianity, feed on this sacrificial logic: 'Every religion is *capable* of preferring something else to life, at the cost of life ... the religious of religion is always the acceptance of sacrificial death and the death penalty, in the shadow of a surviving that supposedly is worth more than life' (DP1, 279).

But there is a slight hesitation in this seemingly very apodictic verdict that literally sentences all religions *to death,* to their death-bound essence: the word 'capable'. Does it suggest that there could also be another 'religious of religion' that awakens *another* tradition which, led by the messianic choice of life, proclaims the principle of 'no more sacrifices'? The last paragraph of the seminar talks indeed of its *spectral* – exemplary, exceptional, non-imitable, antinomian – presence which offers an alternative that proceeds along the lines from the Song of Songs: *love strong as death*. Although preferring life and its restless livingness to the perfect stillness of death, this is still *religion* because it also has its version of the unscathed, the perfect affect for the imperfect world – *love*. Of all things in the universe that are finite and perishable, love, as Paul says, is the greatest because, as *love falling for the finite and perishable*, it is always 'safe and sound': invincible, indemnified to all disappointments (which, as Rosenzweig claims, only make it stronger), infinite in its readiness 'to pace the orbit of the whole world', absolute in its lack of discrimination, the all-embracing 'strangely love' – immune to fall precisely in its constant falling. Not the hyperbolic, sublime and hypostatic force of death, which catapults 'beyond and above life', but resolutely horizontal and anti-hypostatic force of love, which stays 'in life', Here Below, is the name of the only unscathed in which I (and all 'I's as well, universally) can truly believe: 'love as love of life, of my life, of the "my life"' (DP1, 283) – *insofar life prefers itself*.

The final note, therefore, is not without hope: the death of God *exemplified* by the Passion, although so lonely and singular when juxtaposed with the vast history of world religions and churches, is a stopper which blocks the sovereign flight 'above life', *Jenseits*, beyond, and points in another direction – 'Love itself has need of it, of this granted grace, in order to save itself, to attempt forever to come through safe and sound. It must keep watch [*veiller*], it must mount sur-veillance over survival' (DP1, 283).

But if Derrida curbs his (and our) enthusiasm in dealing with this unique holiness of safe and sound love, it is also because he wants to keep his 'cold-blooded', warry type of antinomian messianism, which will avoid the Pauline far too optimistic hot-headedness, believing that love has already prevailed and triumphed over death (see again Derrida's rejoinder to Michel Henry). The double bind of religion will always continue, by doubling the structure of religious belief into belief in the divine legislation and belief in the divine love, which also means that the 'right to life', granted to all creatures, will always be accompanied by the 'law of death', in the disposal of the sovereign creator. There will always be law, just as there will always, hopefully, be love. As long as Abrahamic religions continue, there always will be the 'death *of* God', the event announcing the end of all sacrifices and universal pardon – and, at the same time, 'death *as* God', demanding 'sublime offerings' for the sake of justice, as inflexible and firm as death itself.

There is, however, yet another possibility to approach the religious aporia, which may facilitate grasping of the – seemingly unthinkable – 'religion of the finite life'. In the crucial moment of his reasoning, Derrida vehemently rejects a 'consolation' supposedly deriving from the *knowledge* of the Blanchotian 'instant of my death': 'some quasi-suicidal mastery of my death, ... this phantasm of omnipotence over my own death' (DP1, 219). Derrida speaks here in unison with Rosenzweig who, at the beginning of *The Star of Redemption*, emphasizes the difference between normal life destined to die one day, on the one hand – and an abnormal life reduced to a suicidal track of *Sein-zum-Tode*, which embraces the fact of death as always already happening, on the other. Writing mostly against Hegel, but also in anticipation of Heidegger, Rosenzweig says: 'In fact, Man is only too well aware that he is condemned to death, but not to suicide. Yet this philosophical recommendation can truthfully recommend only suicide, not the fated death of all' (SR, 4).

Neither Rosenzweig nor Derrida resort to the gambit of immortality: life is *scathed* by definition, yet it is *life* only insofar it has a *future*. The indefinite horizon of futurity, of 'given time', is the source of the infinite-in-the-finite which cannot be hypostatized into any sovereign unscathed entity/essence, but is a temporal futuristic mode in which scathed life is lived. Derrida's critique of Blanchot, Lacan and, partly, Heidegger derives from their fetishization of the 'instant of my death', of the *arrêt de mort* understood as the arrest that abstracts death in the form of a sovereign hypostasis. It is, therefore, not just *overestimation* of death that kills life prematurely, but also – if not predominantly – the hyperbolic *hypostasis* which turns 'the instant of my death' into a transcendent instance 'in abeyance': 'already dead' and because of that 'immune to death'. Derrida calls it *bad infinitization*: 'This is the infinite perversity, properly infinite and infinitizing. Of the death penalty. *It is this madness – to put an end to finitude*' (DP1, 257; my emphasis). The madness, therefore, is the belief that the negation of negation – putting an end to the end itself – could reverse the process of finitization and thus (re)produce infinity. In one of the most insightful fragments of the seminar, targeting the very source of this thanatic attraction, Derrida says:

> Fascinated by the power and by the calculation, *fascinated by the end of finitude*, in sum, by the end of this anxiety before the future that the calculating machine procures. *The calculating decision, by putting an end to life, seems, paradoxically, to put an end to finitude; it affirms its power over time; it masters the future, it protects against the irruption of the other.* In any case, it *seems* to do that, I say; it only seems to do that, for this calculation, this mastery, this decidability, remain phantasms. It would no doubt be possible to show that this is even the origin of

phantasm in general. *And perhaps of what is called religion* . . . This is one of the places of articulation with religion and with theology, with the theologico-political. For *this phantasm of infinitization at the heart of finitude*, of an infinitization of survival assured by calculation itself and the cutting decision of the death penalty, *this phantasm is one with God*, with, if you prefer, the belief in God, the experience of God, the relation to God, faith or religion.

DP1, 258–9; my emphasis

Sure, but *all* religion? Then what about the absolute right to life, exposed as such by the scandalous 'death of God', who submitted to the death penalty only in order to abolish it and thus became the first abolitionist himself? By focusing on the phantasm of infinitization or indemnification – the originary phantasm of phantasms – Derrida can clearly see the spot of the bifurcation, the very dynamic of the double bind that splits religion into, on the one hand, belief in the unscathed sovereign being, and, on the other, belief in the transcendence defined as 'beyond sovereignty', in which it is the finite life that gains the status of the unconditional. Having his eye on this spot, Derrida defines 'the impossible task of this seminar' as precisely outlining the religion of the finite life: simultaneously scathed *and* unconditional. More than that: scathed and *because of that* unconditional – the unheard of grounding of religious intuition in extreme precariousness and vulnerability of 'what is most living in life' and what, just as *khora*, this living open flesh, is the very opposite of the infinitized and insured: 'Radically heterogenous to the safe and sound, to the holy and the sacred, it never admits of any *indemnification*' (AR, 58). For what is most living in life, the livingness itself, *vivance, Belebtheit*, is precisely its transience, exposure, perishability.[47]

But if there is a difference between the 'condemned life', in which all living share the lot of 'criminals', and the finite and perishable life that can nonetheless enjoy its 'given time', it lies in the gap that the Latin proverb formulates simply as *mors certa, hora incerta*. Death is sure, it's time, however, unknown: not to know and not to want to know is the condition of a finite life lived from the perspective of the middle. In the concluding passage of the whole seminar, Derrida binds his *torat hayim* precisely with this refusal to know *when*:

The insult, the injury, the fundamental injustice done to the life in me, to *the principle of life* in me, is not death itself; it is rather *the interruption of the principle of indetermination*, the ending imposed on the opening of the incalculable chance whereby a living being has a relation to what comes, to the to-come and thus to some other as event, as guest, as *arrivant*. And the supreme form of the paradox, its philosophical form, is that what is ended by the possibility of the death penalty is not the infinity of life or immortality, but on the contrary, the finitude of 'my life.' *It is because my life is finite, 'ended' in a certain sense, that I keep this relation to incalculability and undecidability as to the instant of my death.* It is because my life is finite, 'finished' in a certain sense, that I do not know, and that I neither can nor want to know, when I am going to die. *Only a living being as finite being can have a future, can be exposed to a future,* to an incalculable and undecidable future that s/he does not have at his/her disposal like a master and that comes to him or to her from some other, from the heart of the other.

DP1, 256–7; my emphasis[48]

What matters, therefore, is to keep the ending open as long as possible, as in the *Scheherazade strategy*, applied by all writers, the masters of deferment and delay, who really know how to 'linger awhile': it is precisely this subtle operation that makes the ending, the Rosenzweigian 'fated death of all', different from the suicidal closure.[49] This also happens to be the very definition of *another finitude*: destined to die but not to the verdict of death, not immortal but having a future, finite but also in/de/finite in its given mode of temporality.[50]

But the last line suggests an even bolder manoeuvre which Derrida tested for the first time in *Aporias*: the *messianization of death*. Seemingly contrary to his religion of the finite life; seemingly giving in to Heidegger's teaching of *Sein-zum-Tode* (and usually read that way), this move is the most daring *Gegenzug* against the deadly 'master from Germany'. For the messianization of death does not consist in simply turning Death into Messiah/God, the way it was criticized by Leo Strauss apropos Heidegger. Far from it. Rather, it is an operation of making death as *indeterminate* as possible: of removing its arrival from the dead-certain realm of philosophy which shifted the intimate relation with death into the centre of human existence. Just as one cannot be intimate with the Messiah who is the figure of radical otherness – the very 'heart of the other' – so one cannot be on intimate terms with one's own death; the whole idiom of deep knowingness, certitude and ownership, turning *der eigenste Tod* into a property, in terms of both possession and the essential feature, must be deconstructed and discarded. The messianization of death does not indicate that death has power to redeem us, only that it should remain transcendent to the course of our life, just as the Messiah, simultaneously dreaded, kept at bay – and awaited. Precisely as in this wish expressed in tractate on the Messiah in the Talmud, which nicely sums up the rabbinic contribution to the *torat hayim*: 'may I not live to see Him coming' (note the messianic-vitalistic grammar of the subjunctive!). For, if one understands the messianic intervention as the final verdict passed on the world, one lives only if the Messiah postpones his coming. For Derrida, the truly messianic – *merciful* – Messiah is the one who postpones his coming *indefinitely*.

And when he does so and thus allows life to forget about death, the living is granted its small moment of grace. While depicting the 'bright magic' of Cixous's 'song of songs' and its subjunctive incantations as the only magic he is willing to subscribe to (*may I not live to see death coming*) – Derrida also offers the best account of what the future religion of the finite life could look like:

> *Live! Would that you might live!* ... This mighty tautology [of life always preferring itself] that knows how to make the address itself arrive, can always be called magic, incantation, animism, phantasm of omnipotence. Certainly, but this baptism is no use as long as one has not clarified what these words mean ... what decides here *for life* is not a wish for immortality or eternity, at least in the accepted sense of these two words ... For this appellation ... there is a time of survival that is life itself, life in life (a life that is no more death than the opposite of death, a life that does not know death), but there is neither immortality not eternity, in the old sense of these words – unless [*sauf si*] the unharmed [*sauf*] being, the spared [*sauvé*] and thus pardoned [*graciée*] life, in its finite moment of life, deserves to be called immortality or eternity, in the grace of the finite instant; and it is probably this appellation of life that we are and will still be enchanted by, an appellation of life that knows equally neither death nor immortality, namely eternity outside time. Everything takes place in the instant.
>
> HCL, 76, 81

Neither death, nor immortality; neither damnation, nor salvation; neither nothingness, nor infinity – only a gentle pardoning *sur-veillence sur sur-vie*, watching over the survival (DP1, 283) in the never-simple *symploke* of life believing in itself: 'life beyond life, life against life, but always in life and for life' (AR, 289).

Another Infinity

Towards Messianic Psychoanalysis

Derrida's discovery of auto/immunity – the condition that necessarily affects all life, organic or not, insofar as it prefers itself – must be confronted with Freud's equally fundamental theory of drives. Moreover, it must be confronted polemically, especially with Freud's late dualism of Eros and Thanatos. The aporetic dialectics of self-preferring life radically opposes the dualistic distinction between the life-drive and the death-drive, by insisting that we always and only deal with 'life-death' in which the elements of self-deadening are necessary for survival. There is no such thing, therefore, as the death drive pure and simple, at least not in the fundamental position of the psychic *arche*, which is now taken over by the aporia of autopreference. Just as Rosenzweig could be said to accuse Heidegger of the systematic *overestimation of death*, so does Derrida object to Freud's ungrounded supremacy of the death drive.

As Derrida suggests in *Rogues*, this aporia constitutes 'the logic of the unconscious' which contains the 'pharmakon of an inflexible and cruel autoimmunity that is sometimes called the "death drive" and that does not limit the living being to its conscious and representative form' (R, 157).[1] The gift of life, therefore, is indeed also a *Gift* [poison], which never allows life to be pure – despite the enormous investment in the phantasm of unadulterated Erotic liveliness/vivacity, made by religions and philosophies of all times. The alleged death drive, therefore, is one of the complex expressions of life which, at the level of self-consciousness, appears to itself as inescapably aporetic. In that sense, Derrida would have rather agreed with Rank saying that 'the opposite of the positive life instinct would be not the death instinct, but fear, whether it be of *having to* die or of *wanting* to die' (MBH, 269), i.e. an ambivalent 'blocking agent' that derives from the primary life awareness taking the form of anxiety (a hypothesis Freud scornfully rejects as non-scientific, while discussing it towards the end of 'The Ego and the Id'). Yet, although adversarial to Freud's late dualism of Eros and Thanatos, Derrida's dialectics of autopreference-auto/immunity can nonetheless be reconciled with Freud's first theory of drives, in which the original libidinal energy immediately bifurcates into sexuality, on the one hand, and the vital order, on the other. To show that such reconciliation is possible and – moreover – that, again, it can 'proceed as the awakening of the Judaic tradition' of *torat hayim* will be the task of this chapter.

Situating Freud on the map of the Jewish thought is a notoriously difficult problem. Psychoanalysis came under the attention of many thinkers who, despite all the disparities of their positions, ended up with a similar conclusion, differing only in the finality of their verdict. They all, rather unanimously, tend to perceive psychoanalysis as essentially non-Jewish, because immersed in the tragic paradigm which closes the life of the individual in the past-oriented, cyclical and fatalistic eternal return of the same and, as such, offers *no future* and *no hope*. Thus, in 'Reflections on Jewish Theology', Gershom Scholem claims that psychoanalysis is a science that 'occupies a throne of mercy without justice'; it sports a vision of therapeutic forgiveness which is based on the tragic imperative of reconciliation with the naturalistic world as it is, deprived of any strong normative imperative to move 'beyond nature'. Jacob Taubes, in a similar vein, in a few essays from the collection *From Cult to Culture*, criticizes Freud for the tragic conservatism which manifests itself in the overdetermination of the human psyche by the past and the parallel obliteration of the future, ultimately sealed by Freud's final choice of the arch-Greek dualism of Eros and Thanatos. Yosef Yerushalmi, continuing this line of critique in *Freud's Moses*, reproaches Freud for choosing the tragic Oedipus as his main hero – instead of going for a different possible candidate of psychoanalytic treatment, who, according to Yerushalmi, could be much better represented by a non-tragic, more hopeful figure of Job. And Theodor Adorno, the most hesitant of them all, in *Minima Moralia* accuses Freud of being too timid with his new psychoanalytic theory and thus unable to see its potential daring messianic uses which could reach beyond the conformist 'disgrace of adaptation'.

All these Jewish critics see the *messianic potential* of psychoanalysis but, at the same time, are disappointed with Freud's tragic, fatalistic and, finally, ultra-conservative handling of his own discoveries. My purpose will be to push their critique into a more positive direction and show how the messianic potential of psychoanalysis can be enhanced and, perhaps, also realized. I will thus try to read Freud in a non-tragic manner, moving his conclusions away from the fatalistic model of therapy towards the messianic model of redemption. By using the works of Jonathan Lear and Eric Santner (although not without some modifications), I will focus on Freud's theory of libido, especially from the middle period of *Three Essays on the Theory of Sexuality*, and read it alongside the pronatalistic conversion advocated by Rosenzweig, Arendt and Derrida. Perhaps, we can indeed find there a psychoanalytic equivalent of what Walter Benjamin used to call a 'slight adjustment': a sudden messianic transformation which revolutionizes the organization of human psyche and liberates her from her tragico-fatalistic overdetermination by the past.

From vinegar to wine, or the psychoanalytic miracle

In his essay on Franz Kafka, Benjamin defines the messianic master move in the following way. First, he introduces the idea of distortion: the distorted form life 'assumes in oblivion'.[3] Kafka's strange animals – from Odradek to the half-lamb, half-kitten – are distorted erroneous creatures whose prototype is the hunchback, the figure of a forgotten, curtailed, unfulfilled and ultimately *unlived* life: 'This little man is at home in *distorted life*; he will disappear with the coming of the Messiah, of whom a great rabbi once said that he did not wish to change the world by force, but would only make a slight adjustment in it' (ibid., 134).

This 'great rabbi', of whom we in fact know that he was no other than Gershom Scholem, compares Messiah to a 'golden hand' who, instead of using a forceful solution, merely plays a tiny trick on the created reality which then, quite unexpectedly, sheds all distortion and appears in its full potential glory. Ernst Bloch, already providing a midrash to the sentence of the 'great Kabbalistic rabbi', Scholem, explains: *Alles wird sein wie hier – nur ein klein wenig anders* ['All will be like here and now – just a little bit different'].[4] The 'slight adjustment' would thus be a sort of magical repair, the one we manage when we kick the TV set in hopeless despair – and lo, it suddenly plays again, better than ever. It involves certain violence but of a much more delicate kind that does not destroy wholesale but targets only the specific wrong within the creaturely reality: the distortion of life. It is life, lived in a distorted, self-oblivious, encumbered form, which is the precise target of the messianic operation. The slight adjustment, therefore, would consist in *correcting the error of creaturely life*: in letting life live without distortion.[5]

This transformation – Rosenzweig and Benjamin would say: *die Umkehr*, conversion – can also be paraphrased in psychoanalytic terms. In the realm of psychoanalysis, the slight adjustment, correcting the distorted condition of the creaturely life, translates into a shift in which a psychic mode most pertinent to the tragic condition, i.e. as Freud himself characterizes it, a 'common human misery',[6] in one abrupt manoeuvre breaks into a psychic mode pertinent to the messianic state of happiness. In other words, this adjustment would involve a sudden *turn from anxiety to joy*; an operation Jonathan Lear calls the 'lucky break'.

Freud, in his tragic register, gives anxiety a special status within human psyche, by saying, in the Kantian manner, that it constantly accompanies every conscious representation. In Freud's account, anxiety functions as a manifestation of 'libidinal excess', i.e. an energetic surplus that characterizes human drives. Unlike animal instincts able to find immediate natural fulfilment, human drives are indefinite and have no matching counterparts in the surrounding world; in consequence, they can never be 'properly' satisfied and as such produce a halo of restlessness, a certain anxious reverse which accompanies – and thwarts – every attempt to achieve gratification.[8]

The analogy with Kant is not just accidental. Anxiety may indeed be a reaction to the lingering, background presence of the original libido which Freud signifies as the Kantian X: an indeterminate, yet objectless, purely quantifiable energy which constitutes psyche's instinctual endowment – 'The simplest and likeliest assumption as to the nature of drives would seem to be that *in itself a drive is without quality*, and, so far as mental life is concerned, is only to be regarded as a measure of the demand made upon the mind for work' (TETS, 46).[9]

Anxiety marks the remnant of this energetic X which hovers above all fixations and cathexes that bind and pacify libido in object relations; is it the psychic sign of the energetic surplus which has not been neutralized in the so-called object choices, or – to use more Judaic terminology, very adequate in this case – it is the indication of what remains of the iconoclastic force in the natural reality of material images. In *The Three Essays* Freud, in order to describe the relationship between the libidinal excess and anxiety, uses a telling metaphor of wine and vinegar. Just as wine turns into vinegar, its sweetness into acid, the excessive libido turns inevitably into anxiety: 'One of the most important results of psycho-analytic research is this discovery that the neurotic anxiety arises out of libido, that it is a product of a transformation of it, and that it is thus related to it in the same kind of way as vinegar is to wine' (TETS, 102fn).

And, further on, writing about nocturnal anxieties of small children and adult neurotics: 'In this respect a child, by turning his libido into anxiety when he cannot satisfy it, behaves like an adult. On the other hand, an adult who has become neurotic owing to his libido being unsatisfied behaves in his anxiety like a child' (TETS 102).

The question now – and this is precisely the messianic question we have in mind – is whether the irreversible can be reversed, or, to use Eric Santner's formulation, *a miracle can happen* and the vinegar can turn once again into wine.[11] Can this energetic excess be regained and then accommodated within the human psyche in a different, more positive way, without just being a cause of permanent *Angst*? Can anxiety, this constant depressive 'creaturely cringe' of ontological unease, error, distortion and maladaptation be solved into what it came from: the excess of energy?[12]

We have just characterized the messianic slight adjustment as an attempt to correct the error of creaturely life. But not all attempts to correct the error of life can be called messianic. There is a *differentia specifica* which makes the messianic slight adjustment stand out as a unique way of solving the error or reversing the distortion. The key to this specific difference lies in exposing a peculiar way in which messianic tradition treats the *creaturely anxiety*.

The notion of creaturely anxiety constitutes the main theme of Walter Benjamin's reflections on the nature of modern melancholy. In his essay *On the Origins of German Tragic Drama*, Benjamin explores the anxious condition of an early modern individual who longs to live in a properly historical time, but is still doomed to remain within the 'natural history', which thwarts the messianic promise offered by Christianity, by turning it into yet another 'pagan' cycle of becoming and perishing. Living in the monstrous distortion of time called 'natural history', the early modern man cannot make sense of either nature or history: he thus undergoes a Job-like experience of unexplained suffering and vainly summons the distant-absent God to justify his ways to men. He lives a distorted, curtailed life within the frames of the thwarted promise and absurd cycles of waste and ruins, which he cannot accept or embrace in a manner of the tragic Greeks: the 'natural history' is the worst of the two worlds – the failed messianic expectation of 'more life' and the crushing aspect of fate levelling all back to 'mere life' – coming together and fusing into a particularly poisonous combination. Finding no way out, as well as no direct expression, the creaturely anxiety freezes into permanent melancholy, a crippling and deadening symptom of tormented life, which since then accompanies every conscious representation of modern man.

Humankind, therefore, once again proves to be chosen, but this time it is a purely negative election of the one who is the most exposed, most vulnerable to the creaturely crisis: being thrown completely out-of-joint, simultaneously out of nature (no longer) and out of history (not yet), in the paradoxical nowhereland of *Naturgeschichte*. But also because of that man becomes a *Fürsprech der Kreatur*, a Job-like spokesman – advocate of all creatures, abandoned to the 'night of the world' and its melancholy 'death-in-life'. The human being becomes a *paradigmatic creature*, whose problematic 'aliveness' locates itself on the more basic level than the life of animals, the one of 'creatureliness': while animals can still feel secure and fulfilled in their natural niches, the human life falls beneath them, to the most fundamental ground of *Kreatürlichkeit*, before any distinction between nature and history. The human being, this anxiety embodied, is thus the living truth of the *created* reality, earlier and more primordial than the system of *phusis* (in that sense, Benjamin's notion of creatureliness forms a negative counterpart to the one offered by Arendt). Eric Santner interprets Benjamin's insight in the Hegelian manner and says that, exposed as 'bare life', *Man is the truth of the animal*. He is a walking deconstruction of every quasi-natural 'fixedness' and ontological security, showing a gaping abyss underneath: 'What ultimately subjects man, in an emphatic sense, to the destructive forces of natural history is precisely his aberrant place in the "great chain of being" ... What I have been calling creaturely life, then, does indeed mark our resemblance to animals, but precisely to *animals who have themselves been thrown off the rails of their nature*.'[13]

Off the rails, out of joint, down into the spiral of bare life (*blosses Leben*), deprived of any vector or direction – that is the essence of this vertiginous experience Benjamin calls the creaturely anxiety: the most direct reaction to the ontological error that constitutes human existence. The 'spiritual supplement', which traditionally characterized a human being as a chosen creature and a crown of creation (ibid.), oscillates strangely between *more* and *less*, depending on the perspective we take. On the one hand, it shows itself as nothing but bare and naked life, deficient in comparison to better equipped natural beings – on the other, however, it reveals the dynamic, experimental aspect of life which can also be thrown off the rails and, in this manner, made creative.

With this Herderian diagnosis, we enter into the sphere of reflection which Eric Santner, in his comparative ruminations on Rosenzweig and Freud, calls *psychotheology*: a form of thinking that combines psychoanalysis and religion, by seeking to describe the peculiar mode of functioning of the human psyche in terms deriving from sacral traditions. Similarly to Derrida, it binds the origin of theological language to the fundamental self-discovery humanity makes about its Janus-faced condition of, alternately, primary 'lack' and primary 'excess'. In reference to the indeterminate nature of human drives as discovered by Freud, Santner writes: 'Psychoanalysis differs from other approaches to human being by attending to the constitutive 'too muchness' that characterizes the psyche; the human mind is, we might say, defined by the fact that it includes more reality than it can contain, is the bearer of an excess, a too much of pressure that is not mere physiological' (PEL, 8).[14]

This 'excess' opens a whole gamut of possible religious interpretations that we were already widely discussing in this book, but it can be roughly divided into two opposite groups. The one approach, which I call here tragic, condemns this energetic excess as a sign of humanity's maladaptation to nature, interprets it as a *lack of meaning* within well-ordered and otherwise meaningful 'great chain of being', and thus confirms the original diagnosis of Man as a mere ontological error. The other approach, here associated with the messianic vitalism, invests in this *excess of energy* as a promising factor of ontological disturbance, shaking the balance of the natural order and pushing it out of joint from its repetitive cycle of becoming and perishing; it will therefore put trust in the human error as such, hoping to turn it into a new principle of life and thus build a positively valued 'tension of election' (PEL, 8). Santner, whose main aim in his *Psychotheology* is to create a link between Freud and Rosenzweig, concentrates mostly on the latter option, by locating in it the emergence of the Jewish doctrine of revelation: 'If there is a "Jewish" dimension to psychoanalytic thought, it is this: the cure is indeed a kind of "exodus," only not one out of Egypt; it offers rather an exodus out of the various forms of Egyptomania that so profoundly constrain our lives, and, while sustaining a level of adaptation, keep us from opening to the midst of life' (PEL, 45).

The 'Egyptomania' is Santner's own term for what he calls a 'too much of demand that most powerfully captures life, undeadens it, makes it rigid with energy' (PEL, 64), while this energy, remaining unused, causes nothing but anxiety. But where does it come from, this *Zuviel vom Anspruch*? It is the 'wrong' answer to the *Zuviel vom Leben*, which is perceived as a mere error to be corrected: corrected by a compensating legitimation that will renaturalize this vital excess and find it a proper place within the great chain of being. Creaturely anxiety, therefore, arises as most of all the issue of *legitimacy*: a self-imposed demand of the psyche which reacts to its own original *excess of energy* as the *lack of meaning*, or, more precisely, the lack of place within the hermeneutic order of being or ontological homelessness. 'Egyptomania' is thus a compromise formation which at the same time appeases anxiety, by delivering ideologico-religious structures of meaningful support for the surplus flow of indeterminate energy, but also sustains anxiety, by setting the psyche on the course of seeking the ready-made sense where it simply cannot be found.[15] The messianic role of psychoanalysis consists then in the repetition of the gesture of Exodus, *yetsiat mitsraim*, which exempted Jews from the tragic rule of nature and made them elected in their exceptional-excessive way of living – and take the analysand out of his 'own private Egyptomania' in which he exerts his doomed attempts to give meaning, justification and legitimacy to himself as an always doubtful member of the cosmic order.

By Santner's account, psychoanalysis equals the effect of revelation by offering a chance of liberation from the creaturely anxiety of legitimacy – yet not through an illusory reconciliation with the totality of being, but through a recognition of the originally erroneous status of human life as ambivalently plagued/blessed with an excess of negativity. The 'Jewishness' of this strategy, according to Santner, manifests itself precisely in the alternative dealing with the anxiety of legitimation: if it is to go away, it is not thanks to some hermeneutical satisfaction, which manages to compensate the original lack of meaning, but thanks to a sudden switch of perspectives – *conversion* again – which releases us from the hermeneutic tyranny of sense-giving or the 'signifying stress'. However – and this is a crucial point in this dialectical reasoning – anxiety constitutes an absolutely necessary stage of the psychic development, where the energetic excess freezes into a 'creaturely cringe', thus being prevented from a chaotic dispersion in the world of natural objects. Anxiety would thus constitute an essential *memento* that reminds human being of its status as an ontological misfit and outcast and does not allow it to return, or attempt to return, to the world of natural fulfilment. Anxiety's role would be to *preserve* this excessive energy in the 'undead' and, in that sense, distorted and pathological way, so – eventually – it can be used for a different purpose than just a trivial (Adorno would even say: disgraceful) goal of natural adaptation. The anxious distortion, *Entstellung*, therefore, is not just an error which has to be simply *undone*: it is a stage which should be traversed towards a new solution.

To stretch a little bit the physico-mechanical rhetoric, which Freud himself sanctioned as a legitimate way of describing the works of human psyche, we could say that anxiety works here as a *capacitor*: it collects, condenses and preserves the surplus of energy which then waits to be used in a way different than natural, object-oriented fulfilment.[10] The anxiety, therefore, would be also a vessel retaining – and restraining – the energy in the state of pure potentiality with no objectual match in the outside reality. In *The Star of Redemption*, Franz Rosenzweig describes this retainment of energy in terms of an inner enclave or a 'crypt' where the very essence of the human soul survives untouched by the current of being: 'In Judaism man is always somehow a *survivor*, an inner something, whose exterior was seized by the current of the world and carried off while he himself, what is left of him, remains standing on the shore. Something within him is waiting' (SR, 404–5).

The second joy

Young wine, therefore, must turn into vinegar: this souring experience is an indelible share of the human condition and it cannot be *simply* reversed. The slight adjustment does not just undo the process with the magical trick of

Ungeschehenmachen. The messianic conversion, which turns the curse of the original lack into a blessing of excessive energy, is not regressive; it is proleptic, because the 'new happiness' (as Nietzsche calls it) can emerge only *after anxiety*, and never through its simple erasure. But the special role assigned to anxiety differentiates the messianic strategy from the Nietzschean one, which insinuated itself as an attractive third in between two traditional basic models. 'Now you must only dare to be tragic human beings, for you will be released and redeemed', says Nietzsche in *The Birth of Tragedy*,[17] thus translating the messianic idiom of redemption into the tragic idiom of reconciliation. We are to shed all anxiety of legitimacy and signification by learning to love life as an abyssal process, the more enchantingly beautiful, the less meaningful – but the way to this paradise regained leads to reconciliation, *Versöhnung*, with the natural world. Here, redemption becomes a *releasement*: a superhuman gesture of relinquishing all fear in face of the Dionysiac dispersion.

If we were to use Benjamin's conceptuality, we could say that this Nietzschean strategy consists in just flattening the creaturely cringe of the hunchback: in a simple unleashing of its condensed and unused energy, not to be saved and preserved for any special or 'miraculous' use. Whereas the messianic tactic aims at a different solution: the hunch, the monstrous mark of the distorted life, is to reveal its other, so far unexpected, aspect – of a *wing case*. Just as vinegar is to turn into a better wine than the original – the second joy or, as it is sometimes put, 'the second fire'[18] – the hunchback is to transform into an angel, akin to the strange angel from Walter Benjamin's feverish vision, called Agesilaus Santander, whose shadow, according to Gershom Scholem, accompanied him all his life as a mark of a potential and unfulfilled promise. In his description of a cringing posture of Benjamin, Scholem – and then Santner – could have used the words of Saul Bellow who, in *More Die of Heartbreak*, gives a portrait of an old Jewish botanist, Benn Crader, the favourite uncle of the protagonist: 'his hunch always gave an impression of being actually a wing case, but as if the wings simply could not spread in this world'.[19]

In *Happiness, Death, and the Remainder of Life*, Jonathan Lear addresses precisely this *turn* as the ultimate therapeutic goal of psychoanalysis: the halo of anxiety, bearing the frustrated remnant of indefinite energy – as Bataille could have named it in reference to pure negativity, *sans emploi*, without any objectual use and because of that frustrated – must turn into libidinal excess, this time finally finding its way towards delight and happiness: the Blakean joy which is pure energy.[20] The energetic surplus, so far causing only a 'cringe', must find a volatile outlet – a way out of the symbolic systems of fixations. This is what Lear calls a *lucky break*:

From a psychoanalytic point of view, this is the deepest form of human helplessness: *helplessness in the face of too much energy*. As Freud points out, we are vulnerable to repetitions of such helplessness from the beginning to the end of our lives. But this is a peculiar kind of 'repetition' – because it is a *repetition of something that is in itself without content*. It is *the breaking-through of quantity without quality* . . . Whether it becomes a repetition, in the psychoanalytic sense of a repetition compulsion, *depends on what happens next*. What appear as repetition are the mind's attempts, at varying levels of failure and success, to inform this breakthrough with meaning . . . *Life is too much*.

HDRL, 109; my emphasis

The mechanism responsible for souring the psychic experience of the contentless, purely energetic libido and for turning its potential joy into anxiety, wine into vinegar, is precisely this: the excessive remnant comes back all the time in a staccato rhythm of repetition without content, thus putting a 'signifying stress' on the mind, which feels extremely anxious to inform these breaches with meaning. The 'slight adjustment' proposed by Lear consists, therefore, in blocking the mechanism of repetition and allowing for a *next* move: in establishing a different therapeutic approach to the purely energetic and quantitative 'too-muchness of life'. While traditional, more conservatively minded psychoanalysis usually supports the analysand's psyche in her attempts to bestow this excess with meaning, and in this sense merely strengthens the compulsion to repeat – Lear's psychoanalytic method does the messianic reverse: it allows us to reveal the sheer meaninglessness of our drives and come to terms with this finding, which then works as a breaking point, relieving the psyche from its compulsive desire to bind, give sense, and create integral symbolic totalities. The 'lucky break', therefore, resembles Arendt's emphasis on the essentially natal nature of human life: always birthing/initiating, pressing for something *next* and *new*, and thus breaking out of the cycle of repetition, this excessive energy is in/de/finite and contentless – and must be acknowledged precisely as such.

The 'lucky break' comes when a person, so far encumbered by the heavy task of giving a retrospective symbolic rationale and justification to her every motivation, affect, word or behaviour of her past, suddenly gains a distance to this compulsive obligation and, with a deep sigh of relief, exclaims – *this is crap!* (HDRL, 117). This moment of crisis, instead of darkening her misery, makes the analysand paradoxically happy. For happiness, opened by such a lucky break, means nothing more than the acceptance of life in its undistorted manifestation, i.e. as always excessive in regard to meaning – a 'too much' of sheer energetic quantity, disrupting the qualitative field of sense, now dismissed as a pile of crap.

Happiness, therefore, is all a matter of *happenstance*: of turning what seemed as weakness into strength, absurdity into joyful unprincipled anarchy of more life, error into a new way of living:

> The analytically minded person – in contrast to the *phronimos* – takes advantage of breaks in the structures. Instead of referring the break back to a structure of repetition ... one treats it as an occasion for opening up new possibilities, possibilities not included in any established structure. In this sense, analysis begins when the analysand declines the role of *phronimos* – and branches off in ways that do not fit any established virtue ... It is, as it were, an *existential sabbath from ethical life*.
>
> HDRL, 127–8

In depicting a vision of perfect happiness as a 'sabbath from ethical life' – a break from symbolico-rational wholes, radically opposed to the Greek vision of happiness as Aristotelian *sophrosyne*, a balanced and harmonious self-satisfaction of reason producing meaningful totalities – Lear assumes a messianic tone, chiming closely with Rosenzweig, Benjamin and Arendt. But also Lévinas as criticized by Lyotard who, taking firmly the side of the neurotic suturation of the structure, regards such attitude of inner-psychic 'sabbath', in which the psyche says a light-hearted farewell to her past family romance, as nothing short of the psychotic foreclosure. For Lear, however, the 'lucky break' is not psychotic: it is an exodus out of the dualism of neurosis and psychosis, rigid structure and void, Eros and Thanatos, in which none of these categories matter any longer. The desert of the 'lucky break' is not a void cleared by the death drive so often praised by Lacan and Žižek:[22] it is only a freedom from anxiety and its Egyptomaniac 'signifying stress', which overcharges the psyche with the obligation to give sense and justify. The original libido – the purely quantifiable, indefinite energy that means nothing in itself – can thus become either the source of eternal symbolic frustration or the source of eternal delight which breaks every system of meaning in order to create 'new possibilities'. Then, instead of collapsing into itself, the libido opens to free relations with 'anything and everything' (BT, 220), which, not at all incidentally, is for Heidegger the synonym of the worst kind of *Verfallenheit*.

But how is this passionate relationality ready to embrace 'anything and everything' to be achieved? A lot depends here on the right interpretation of this intermediary stage I have called half-jokingly the *stage of capacitor*: the condensation of energy which becomes withdrawn from unsatisfying natural cathexes and, from this time on, lies within the psyche, causing indefinite anxiety and waiting to be used in a 'miraculous' kind of way. This highly ambivalent

formation, which Santner associates with 'undeadness', needs to be traversed –
yet *not* in the regressive direction, but only dialectically forward, thanks to the
event of 'lucky break'. The next step for the libido to take is thus to come into
relations with objects that will not be based on the model of gratification. Not
attachments, therefore, but true *relations* which, as Rosenzweig says, have an
inbuilt component of necessary and positive disappointment: 'It must be an act
of love wholly lost in the present moment. Disillusionment can only help it to
this end by ever and again dis-illusioning it against the natural expectation of a
success . . . Disillusionment keeps love in condition' (SR, 215).

What it means is that in the *post-phantasmatic relation with the neighbour*,
which can be 'anything and everything' in our vicinity, there is a place for a
real transcendence that reaches infinitely beyond our possible needs and
expectations.[23]

When translated into Santnerian idiom, which situates itself closer to the
Lacanian field, this development takes the form of the following sequence. First,
because of its original indefiniteness and nothingness, libido *must* become over-
cathected on a contingent *something* that just happens to offers itself at the initial
moment of drive's manifestation. Then, right after the inevitable disappointment
of this first love 'choice', libido faces only one, essentially tragic, alterative: it either
gets 'stuck' in the nostalgic circle of futile attempts to 'refind the object' it never
properly had and forever chase the elusive *objet a* – or it renounces this pathetic
game of 'hide and seek' and closes proudly on itself, by discovering that, from the
very beginning, it always only wanted *nothing*. The Lacanian subject, therefore,
has only two ways of expressing its frustration: it can either engage in the
hopeless games of Eros, or choose the more sublime path of Thanatos.[24] The
messianic 'slight adjustment', however, adds here a third option: the possibility of
unpacking the libidinal energy in such a way that it becomes capable of striking
a new type of relation with every single thing around, this time without
obfuscating its contingency. This peculiar attentiveness, able to love 'whatever
comes next', not despite but *through* disillusionment, disenchantment and
unfulfilment, means that the subject approaches 'anything and everything' in its
status of a remnant – 'out of joint' (PEL, 140) and 'singled out' (PEL, 65), being
there for itself, and not as a potential object of any libidinal gratification. Being,
in a way, not an *object* at all; rather a counterpart – partner, relation – of the
Erros: the originally objectless drive.

This return to life – the Rosenzweigian final *into life!* – augmented and
extensified, where the objectless *Erros* finds its non-objectifying relation with
'anything and everything' (or, more modestly, just 'many', as in Hölderlin)

constitutes the final aim of the vicissitudes of the *messianic drive*. In the last chapter of his *Psychotheology*, devoted to the Hölderlinian motif of *was aber bleibt*, but interpreted – similarly to Benjamin's reading of the author of *Blödigkeit* – in the messianic terms of the remnant, Santner writes:

> What remains is precisely that: the remnant, the part that is not a part of a whole but rather the opening beyond the 'police order' of parts and wholes. What poets establish is not some sort of vision or consciousness of the All; rather they introduce into the relational totality of social existence – into the social body divided into parts – the perspective of 'non-all'. This refers, once again, not to some place or experience of exception, some locus of authentic life outside the part-whole logic of social relations, but rather, to use a Kabbalistic formulation, to the sparks or blessings of 'more life' *within* those relations, which can be liberated from their undeadness by the intervention of the right word.
>
> PEL, 142

And this right word, pushing liberated energy – imagined here as the Kabbalistic spark of 'more life' – on its messianic path towards the neighbours, is the *imperative to love*: the paradoxical 'interpellation beyond interpellation' which should not be confused with a 'metaphysical seduction', creating a fake, sublime and mesmerizing, *beyond* made of what Derrida calls 'more-than-life'. This time, the dimension of transcendence occurs within immanence, incarnated into the objectless other, the other who transcends all 'object cathexes' and presents itself as the remnant:

> To conceive a radical shifts of direction in life – of a genuine *exodus* from deep individual and social patterns of servitude – human beings, both individually and collectively, require the notion of an interpellation beyond (ideological) interpellation ... which means a kind of love that exceeds any sort of mere 'object cathexis', a love that is no longer tied to representation ... *We don't need God for the sake of divine things but for the sake of proper attentiveness to secular things.*[25]

Yet, one has to remember – in favour of more dialectical Derrida and *pace* Santner[26] – that this final transformation of libido would not be possible without the previous dialectics of interpellation. Before it is 'properly understood' as the non-sovereign injunction to love, it must be first necessarily *misunderstood* as the sublime authority which gathers and hypercathexes the libidinal energy, by issuing the Law of prohibition, forbidding the libido to disperse in a pursuit of accidental love-objects and making it freeze into anxious and undead 'creaturely cringe'. The first *law-giving* interpellation *ex*-cepts and *ex*-empts the subject from the creaturely reality, taking him out of the biomorphic patterns of 'discharge/ release' and thus keeps in reserve the energy that can later on be called upon by the *love-giving* interpellation and transform into 'non-cathected' neighbourly love, no longer governed by an image, a concept of totality, or a phantasmatic representation of an ideal choice-object. Only then, after the stage of necessary erring, which projects libido's strangeness and indeterminacy into some transcendent 'beyond', this energy can once again return to earth and begin to navigate in between the two dangers – of *renaturalization,* on the one hand, and *metaphysical abstraction,* on the other. As I have already indicated in the Introduction, where the concept of libidinal theology was first mentioned: the psyche must first steer from her biomorphic temptation, by falling into thanatic disdain for life – or, in a complementary version I have proposed in Chapter 2: in order to free himself from the maternal attraction, the subject has to 'convert' to the paternal side. This, however, is but a stage which does not end the process and does not exhaust the alternative. There is yet another *conversion* in store which allows the subject to reassume his original 'errotic' energy on the level of the *messianic love*: love without choice, not particular about any object, able to touch everything, yet without converting it into an abstract *Allheit.* Love able to love without any additional exciting, justifying, and sense-seeking work of hermeneutic fantasy.

On Lear's and Santner's readings, the Freudian trajectory of human libido would thus be analogous to the Rosenzweigian 'path' of the soul, which he depicts in *The Star of Redemption*: the path that leads from the death-dominated creaturely proto-cosmos (*Vor-Welt*), where the subject closes upon himself; through the world of revelatory Love, where he responds to the one object only that 'ex-cites' him, i.e. God; to the hyper-cosmos of all-encompassing redemption, where all things encountered become objects of his neighbourly kindness – *from nothing, through something, to everything.* In a very similar way, the vicissitudes of human sexual drive lead it from its initial nothingness, to which it can always return by means of the thanatic release; then, through the stage of accidental fixations on various objects, crowned by the hypercathexis on the grand, elusive, privileged object – Big Other; to a final realization in its open relationship with 'anything and everything', conceived as our equal, fully singularized, neighbours.

And in Lear's account, this love is indeed as strong as death – because, in the end, there is no such thing as the death drive. Jonathan Lear is one of those rare thinkers who dared to challenge the Lacanian hegemony and openly claimed that Thanatos is nothing but a hypostasis: One wants to say, of course the death drive works in silence – not, however, because it is a mysterious principle, but because *it is not a principle at all* (HDRL, 136).[27]

But, what is it then? Lear and Santner again go here hand in hand: the thanatic hypostasis is the projection of *beyond*, caused by the excessive 'too-muchness' of human drive (or, in Derridean terms: a surplus of life that projects itself as the metaphysical more-than-life). This projection, however, can hardly be avoided, because 'there is an inchoate sense that there is a remainder to life, something that is not captured in life as it is so far experienced. Thus there is pressure to construct an image of what lies outside' (HDRL, 163). This pressure cannot be resisted – it *must* at first produce a rigid image of transcendence – but it can be deconstructed afterwards, *nachträglich*. Here, Lear joins Derrida for whom deconstruction is also a necessarily *after-the-fact* method, which can attempt to deactivate only those structures that have already formed spontaneously. For Lear (as for Derrida), the paradigmatic case of the metaphysical projection of the *beyond* is Plato's myth of the cave, where not just immanence, but also transcendence becomes imprisoned in a spatial image and, in this manner, distorted. While criticizing the hermeneutical structures that issue a pressure to conform, i.e. to find a *place* within their system of meaning, Lear says:

> The whole theoretical structure is only one more instance of the cave, and if psychoanalysis has taught us anything, it is that the *wealth of human possibilities cannot be contained by any variant of this image*. To live with human possibility, one has to tolerate a peculiar kind of theoretical anxiety: *the willingness to live without a principle*. Only then we can begin to grasp the peculiar possibility for possibility that human being opens up.
>
> HDRL, 164–5; my emphasis

The real *beyond*, therefore, is beyond all principles – not just 'beyond the pleasure principle' – and as such fosters a properly non-nomotropic and iconoclastic attitude which goes hand in hand with the originally objectless drive whose 'errotic' quality cannot be *placed* anywhere:

> What *Beyond the Pleasure Principle* introduces is, as it were, the need for an outside to this outside. I say 'as it were' because by now it should be clear that *we do not need another place – even in a metaphor*. What we need to grasp is not another place but a peculiar kind of possibility: *the possibility of disrupting the field of possibilities*. . . Ironically, when it comes to human living, the field of possibilities is not a field. Or, to put it less paradoxically: any purported field of possibilities is always a somewhat restricted fantasy of what is possible in human life.
>
> HDRL, 160–1; my emphasis

Transcendence, therefore, is not a place; it is *ou-topos*, or *a-topos*, just as the 'desert in the desert', imagined as *khora* in Derrida: a no-place of pure potentiality or, as Winnicott would like to call it, an infinite *play* in which all reality with its ontological rules becomes suspended. By advocating the next move – the 'beyond of beyond' – Lear shows us the passage beyond death as a quasi-principle into *more life*: the true transcendence of infinite, an-archic possibilities, non-restricted by any Image. Paralleling Santner's intuition of life rebelling against nomotropism, Lear conceives 'more life' as essentially *iconoclastic*: 'limping forward' in Jacob's way, without any pre-existing pattern and lucky-breaking for good with the principle of repetition/imitation.

Happiness, when transcending just the fleeting moment of 'lucky break', would thus mean to be capable of 'living life without remainder' which, in Lear's idiom, equals 'living life without a principle' (HDRL, 106), where 'the remainder' no longer manifests itself as a destructive repetition of original 'helplessness', but as a source of a new life – or, in Rank/Arendt's natal terms, no longer as a 'trauma of birth', but as permanent natality with its traumatic aspect removed. The removal of this trauma, carried in the form of a 'creaturely cringe', would thus be the very gist of 'the slight adjustment', allowing our psychic energies to 'flow into the world' and 'into the midst of life', finally synchronized with life's 'happening' – precisely the way envisaged by Rosenzweig (USH, 92). Happiness would thus be the outcome of the series of reversals/conversions achieved in the lucky *happenstance*: helplessness turning into freedom; sense of absurd meaninglessness turning into joyful unprincipled anarchy of more life; obedience to the transcendent law turning into releasing break (*this is crap!* HDRL, 117); and badly hooked, fixated and seduced desire turning into desire infinite and liberated from the need of its own justification.

Thus, if the black star of the death-drive stands for the hypostasis of the dimension which is transcendent and hostile to life – the Derridean deadly Absolute as more-than-life – the happy life spent 'in the midst of life' runs under the an-archic sun of love. Just as Santner, and perhaps even more so, Lear speaks the language of Rosenzweig for whom the commandment to love is *not* the law uttered by a life-threatening external divine instance. Love is *not* an 'enigmatic signifier': it does not bind and seduce the excess of psychic energy, but liberates it and thus deactivates the 'creaturely cringe'. Love is not a *meaning*, but is synonymous with the break itself which simply ends the hermeneutical, find-your-place-in-the-hierarchy games of sovereignty. Love is transcendence itself, the purest 'outside of the outside' of which there can be no Image. Love is a non-principle of life: just as in Derrida, it supplements and 'softens' every law by its inherent an-archy –

Let us count the ways of love. Love is active. It flows through humans, but it is larger than human life. It is through love that humans, and the rest of living nature, acquire form. Love tends toward higher organization and form, but humans do not acquire form by passively being affected by love. What it is for love to run through a person is that he himself becomes a locus of activity. That is what it is for love to permeate our nature.

L, 219

So, do miracles really happen? After all, monstrosity and miracle are just two faces of the same *Ungeheuer*, the derailed creature out of joint and out of hand. The vinegar of anxiety, say Lear and Santner, can thus be turned into wine of delight, provided we understand the nature of the 'signifying stress' which imbues us – as it turns out, quite unnecessarily – with the *fear of meaninglessness*, or the *privation of meaning*, captured for the first time by the Platonic myth of the cave, the founding image of the Neoplatonic conceptuality, still prevalent today, even in acephalous forms. To be able to tolerate life in its energetic bareness and also to be able to live it 'without remainder' means to be no longer anxious: to turn anxiety, this shadowy reverse of 'creaturely bare life', painfully lamenting its lack of legitimate ground and sense, into a surplus of energy which – to resort to the Marxian idiom at its messianic highest – melts into air everything solid and profanes everything holy as nothing but 'crap'. This turn – from fear to joy, from anxiety to delight – is thus like a *Gestaltswitch* between the two aspects of human indeterminacy: the tragic and the messianic. What from the tragic perspective manifests itself as a *lack*: the hermeneutic lack of meaning, legitimacy or proper place in the order of nature – from the messianic perspective manifests itself as an *excess*: the energetic surplus of undistorted life that transcends every systematic closure and enters into intense horizontal relations with 'anything and everything'.

Another sublimation, or *Erros* in language

If we are looking for the clues to *another Freud* – to a more vitalist-messianic and less tragic psychoanalysis – we will find them – buried and distorted, but nonetheless present – in his *Three Essays on the Theory of Sexuality*, the work published as early as 1905. Again, Jonathan Lear comes in very handy here, which is no surprise: as a 'death-drive-negationist' (Žižek), he refuses to see Freud's *Beyond the Pleasure Principle* as his definitive last word on the nature of human drives. But he does not just simply rely on the *Three Essays*, in which Freud formulates his first non-dualistic drive theory; he also pioneers the reading of Freud's contributions 'against the grain', trying to uncover their truly revolutionary message with which Freud himself felt somewhat uneasy.

The gist of Lear's critical interpretation of *The Three Essays* is the full *affirmative* acceptance, with all consequences, of Freud's major discovery: the indefiniteness of human drive which is 'in itself, without quality'. Full acceptance means here: the human drive must be taken as it is, as simultaneously lack and excess – *without* any efforts to domesticate its strangeness, which is precisely what Freud wants to do. When Lear says that Freud 'did not know what a drive is or what it is for a drive to be sexual' (L, 121), he does not mean it pejoratively. On the contrary, he rather wishes that Freud had managed to remain in his *docta ignorantia* or 'negative capability' and did not attempt to cover it with too hasty definitions, of which the first – and most confusing – consists precisely in calling the drive *sexual*.

According to Lear, the 'aim' in the form of sexual gratification is merely grafted on the drive that, in its original state, must be *aimless* – which explains why it should be defined by Freud merely in quantitative terms as *Drang*, the pure pressure and demand without purpose and without a clue how to ease it. But – and this constitutes the true find of Lear's analysis – if there is no 'natural' or pregiven sexual aim, which the original drive would wish to realize, *there is no sublimation either*, at least not in its orthodox Freudian variant which sees it as a diversion of erotic libido into other culturally more acceptable channels. *There is no sublimation understood as the conversion of sexuality into a desexualized type of enjoyment.*

But it does not mean that the human psyche does not sublimate at all. It does, but it involves the indefiniteness of the original drive, which – after the stage of compulsive attachments it undergoes because of its helpless postnatal 'adhesiveness' – becomes recovered and then accepted on the higher level of libidinal development. Once the psyche works through its initial 'helplessness' and learns to live with it, it is also ready to accept and affirm the indefinite character of its energetic endowment, and then use it outside the mechanism of object-seeking and object-cathexes. From our analysis of Rosenzweig in Chapter 1, we already know that this is the characteristic of love that remains as in/de/finite as the drive of which love is manifestation: it has no privileged object, although, at the same time, it can become known to us only through the most concrete 'works of love', i.e. through the parade of objects, through which it *flows* and *runs*, never to be *arrested* or *fixated*. What, therefore, Freud calls 'sexual energy' is not necessarily bound by all the limiting and disciplining practices of adhesion, attachment and cathexis, which he rigidly ascribes to sexual behaviour.

The so-called *desexualization*, which in Freud's system takes place almost immediately, with the early emergence of the 'ego-functions', occurs in too easy a way, thus showing that, perhaps, there was nothing to desexualize in the first place. Lear says:

> Freud began with the idea that sexuality is a drive. The problem is that he did not know what a drive is or what it is for a drive to be sexual ... Perhaps, *sexual energy is not at bottom sexual energy*; that is, perhaps sexuality is a manifestation of a more fundamental force permeating nature. After all, once Freud discovered that the sexual drive can invest normal I-functions and thus exist in a 'desexualized' form, the question must arise as to whether the sexual drive is best conceived of as a distinctively sexual drive.
>
> L, 121, 144

For Lear, this more fundamental force permeating nature is, as we have already seen, *love*. Love, however, is the late sublimated avatar of the original drive which, *in the beginning*, is not love, *not-yet*. It is actually the very opposite of love: a pure destruction of helpless 'too-muchness' which endangers the very survival of the psyche. If we are questing, therefore, after *another sublimation*, we need to understand the mechanism in which the infinitely intensive drive, violently pushing towards the destruction of any finite vessel, eventually *converts* into an infinitely extensive love, ready to embrace and affirm 'anything and everything' finite that comes near as a *Platzhalter*.

The thinker who helps to understand this ultimate conversion is Harold Bloom who, after all, popularized the translation of the Hebrew blessing – *l'hayim* – as *more life*. All his work can be regarded as one incessant revision of Freud's work: a deep misreading of the father of psychoanalysis, which deliberately follows the Jewish 'principle of life'.[28]

It is self-evident from the start that the concept of 'more life' Bloom has in mind differs fundamentally from what Freud in his *Three Essays* calls 'the vital order', i.e. the most basic natural system of the instincts of self-preservation; it is much closer to the originally indeterminate energy of libido, which cannot be contained within a well-defined, homeostatic system of natural needs and their objectual gratifications. If one reads Freud's speculation in *The Three Essays* against the grain, it becomes immediately clear that 'human sexuality', precisely because of its indeterminacy, is always *in danger* of falling under the rule of the better organized vital order – but it can also use its original indefiniteness to free itself from the latter's mechanical functionality, once it learns to protect itself against this danger. Human sexual drive may thus be inchoate, premature and deficient when compared to well-determined self-preservatory instincts – yet, this can also be turned to its advantage.

The story told by Freud in *The Three Essays* concentrates on the first stage of libidinal development, in which the original libido – of 'no fixed abode' (as Kafka says on Odradek), no purpose and no object – begins to imitate the better formed self-preservatory instincts and *lean on* – via *anaclisis, Anlehnung* or 'adhesiveness' – their vital functions, as feeding or defecating, to use their objects for its autotelic form of enjoyment. Soon, however, this seemingly subservient 'propping' turns into 'wrestling', and *anaclisis* takes on the form of *agon*. In one of his most powerful pieces, 'Wrestling Sigmund' from *Breaking of the Vessels*, Bloom boldly juxtaposes the story of wrestling Jacob from the biblical writer J with Freud's account of the beginning of human sexuality, thus giving a peculiar agonistic twist to the Freudian notion of *Anlehnung*. The picture that emerges out of the striking interference of these two images – Jacob wrestling with the Angel of Death and a human infant suckling the maternal breast – presents human sexuality as a drive that fights with the vital order, by refusing to be imprisoned by its mere natural functionality, or the dull homeostasis of *phusis*. According to Bloom, life fights against life, or, to be more precise, human sexuality, forming the daring figure of 'more life', opposes the system of self-preservation, which forms a humble figure of 'mere life'. It may thus seem that 'wrestling a divine angel is rather a contrast to sucking one's mother breast, and achieving the name Israel is pretty unrelated to the inauguration of the sexual drive',[29] yet, Bloom insists, these two narratives tell the same story:

> *All human sexuality is tropological,* whereas we all of us desperately need and long for it to be literal . . . As Laplanche says, expounding Freud: 'Sexuality in its entirety is in the slight deviation, the *clinamen* from the function.' Or as I would phrase it, *our sexuality is in its very origins a misprision, a strong misreading, on the infant's part, of the vital order* . . . I call Freud . . . 'Wrestling Sigmund,' because again he is a poet of Sublime *agon*, here an agon between sexuality and the vital order. Our sexuality is like Jacob, and the vital order is like that among the Elohim with whom our wily and heroic ancestor wrestled, until he had won the great name of Israel. Sexuality and Jacob triumph, but at the terrible expense of a crippling. All our lives long we search in vain, unknowingly, for the lost object, when even that object was a *clinamen* away from the true aim. And yet we search incessantly, do experience satisfactions, however marginal, and win our real if limited triumph over the vital order. Like Jacob, we keep passing Penuel, limping on our hips.
>
> ibid., 69–70; my emphasis

This *clinamen*, however, is deliberate: it wants to make an error of mistaking objects of the vital order with the most exuberant and perverse phantasies. What is *human* in 'sexuality' (if, as Lear rightly observes it can be called 'sexuality' at all), is from the very beginning *perverse* – a literal object of the vital order turned into a trope. The emphasis on perversion is precisely the clue of the distinction between drive and function, as made by Laplanche, who, in *Life and Death in Psychoanalysis*, writes:

> *Function, need,* and *instinct* characterize generally the vital register of self-preservation in opposition to the sexual register … Thus the sexual object is not identical to the object of the function, but is displaced in relation to it; they are in a relation of essential *contiguity* which leads us to slide almost indifferently from one to the other, from the milk to the breast as its symbol … Sexuality in its entirety is in the slight deviation, the *clinamen* from the function. It is in the *clinamen* insofar as the latter results in an autoerotic internalization … The drive mimics, displaces, and *denatures the instinct* … The whole of sexuality, or at least the whole of infantile sexuality, *ends up by becoming perversion* … Now sexuality, in its entirety, in the human infant, lies in a movement which *deflects* the instinct, *metaphorizes* its aim, *displaces* and *internalizes* its object, and concentrates its source on what is ultimately a minimal zone, the erotogenic zone.[30]

In other words: sexuality is the *figure of function* – while function is the literal basis, on which the figurative work of sexuality 'leans on'. For Laplanche, who follows Freud faithfully, this deviation is the mark of *perversion* which, in its longing after the *fetish*, the perfect object, still betrays nostalgic desire of the impossible literal gratification. If it were only perversion, therefore, the figurative *clinamen* would have to remain nothing but an error, for ever caught in the rigid ritual of fetishization, thus only emphasizing functionality of the vital order, from which it allegedly deviated. Bloom's revision of Laplanche, however, consists in one simple manoeuvre: *in the absolute rejection of any nostalgia after literalness, which allows him to pass the stage of perversion to a more promising stage of sublimation.* This passage becomes possible once the psyche invests in the error as such – the glitch in literality – and turns it into a 'willing error'.[31]

Bloom offers here a Jewish version of sublimation which differs considerably from the teachings of the 'divine Plato', as Freud calls him deferentially in the introduction to *The Three Essays*. Instead of a winged Eros that flies above its abandoned material objects to become unencumbered and purely spiritual, we get an image of an impaired, limping hero who managed to detach himself from the lethal embrace with the vital order and *survived*; now he restlessly 'passes forth, though severely damaged in his natural vitality, but fortified as an error which has no ideal object of fulfilment and no model to imitate: as in Paul Klee's another famous painting, an angel with one wing. His survival acquires shape through his struggles: first with Esau and then with Sammael, who in Bloom's interpretation symbolize two closely intertwined aspects of the vital order: self-preservation and submission to the rule of death. Instead of a Spirit, which rises above matter in a triumphant ascension towards the supranatural sun, we see an anxious quester, walking through a horizontal desert away from the Egypt of nature, but always 'limping', always endangered by the fall into the snares of *Lebensordnung*.

In this version of sublimating antithesis, nature is not so easily abandoned. The Exodus from nature, from the seduction of 'propping' (*Anlehnung*) on the certainties of the vital order, is a hard-won victory that accepts the fundamental dissatisfaction of the 'sexual' drive (Rosenzweig's and Lear's disappointment): in not being able to find its true object, which never existed in the first place, it transforms everything natural into eternally vague object of desire – into a *figure*, something else than it actually is – and, as such, it also gives birth to the symbolic sphere of language. *Anaclisis*, therefore, is a critical phase both of the greatest danger and the greatest chance: it is an agon which may be either won or lost. It may either bow down the sexual drive and turn it into a quasi-natural force imitating animal instincts, condemned to their naturalistic model of homeostasis and 'health' of what Laplanche calls *instinct mimé*, a biomorphic instinct regained via imitation – or, to the contrary, surrender the vital order to the excessive in/de/finite libido and allow vital instincts to be 'troped' beyond its boringly literal mere functionality into the realm of figurative fulfilment: something Nietzsche, in his subtler phases, used to call the 'abundance of tender Yeses'.[32] The drive may thus either fall into embrace of self-preservation, or – due to the superegoic repression – give up on its early fixations, renounce all (dis) satisfactions offered by natural objects, and expand into a figurative force, creating a new set of desires in the domain where previously there was nothing but literal functionality.[33]

This agonistic Eros, therefore, is not just an instinct of life as opposed to the instinct of death, closed within the repetitive circle of *phusis*, but a power of figuration wrestling both with life and death as a cycle of mere functions. It is no longer sexuality forced to conform with the natural need of self-preservation, but an *Erros*, Eros and error fused: an energy of primordial *libido* that regains its original 'erring' in/de/finity which now serves not as its deficiency, but as its main advantage. For, once it detaches itself from the vital order, it immediately begins to *err*: it crosses the limits of the functional system of *phusis* and wanders out from the Egypt of nature into the desert of open possibilities. *Erros* refuses to be closed within the boredom of natural life, but it does not reject life altogether. Quite the contrary, instead of negating life, it regains its original an-archic libidinal form and, by liberating it from the confines of natural repetition, transforms life into a 'quest romance' of continuous 'crossing' and 'passing forth' that began with the most paradigmatic of all Hebrew heroes: Jacob at Penuel. This is also where our *libidinal theology* begins.

Anxieties of the Young Libido: Freud's *Three Essays* against the grain

We can now undertake a close reading of Freud's *Three Essays* in the lights of libidinal theology formed by Santner, Lear and Bloom. Its main hero will be the Young Libido – indeterminate, helpless, yet powerful – and its first anxieties; a true *monster* the education of which is the only *Sorge* of Freud, acting here in the role of the Kafkan *Hausvater*, or the guardian of the paternal order, dismayed over the antics of Odradek, the quicksilver agile and ever-spinning living spool which represents the restless human drive.[34] The more Freud tries to put and pin it down; the more he disciplines the Young Libido – the more it flies away, into the margins and outskirts of *perversion*. This is not at all accidental that the first theory of human libido is thus also the first Freudian tractate on the human infant as a 'polymorphous pervert'.

The first essay, entitled 'Sexual Aberrations', purports to answer the question: what can we know about human libido from the objects it chooses? The manner in which Freud formulates his main problem follows his methodological decision which imitates the scientific methods of physics: just as physical forces can be observed and measured only through the material objects with which they interact, libido, the psychic energy, can only be seen via its objectual materialization. At the beginning, therefore, Freud lists a huge variety of object-choices made by libido deemed by him 'pathological', i.e. realizing itself not in the 'normal' heterosexual and genital intercourse, but in all sorts of 'deviations' [*Abweichungen*], with a special emphasis paid on homosexuality. And already the first conclusion, in which Freud generalizes on the nature of the homosexual models of 'inversion', is quite surprising. It directly undermines the thesis implied by his method, namely – that there is a strict connection [*Verknüpfung*] between libido and its chosen object:

It has been brought to our notice that we have been in habit of regarding the connection between the sexual instinct and the sexual object as more intimate that it in fact is. Experience of the cases that are considered abnormal has shown us that in them the sexual instinct and the sexual object are merely soldered together – a fact which we have been in danger of overlooking in consequence of the uniformity of the normal picture, where the object appears to form part and parcel of the instinct. We are thus warned to loosen the bond that exists in our thoughts between instinct and object. It seems probable that the sexual instinct is in the first instance independent of its object; nor is its origin likely to be due to its object's attractions.

TETS, 26

Freud firmly rejects the theory of an innate object that would be linked to the drive in a necessary manner. It is only the powerful norm of heterosexual relations, against which all other sexual orientations are seen as aberrant and abnormal, that causes us to think that there exists a pre-established object of human sexuality. This illusion turns us blind towards the fact that *all* libido binds with its object merely contingently, through an artificial act of soldering [*Lötung*], and that 'in the beginning' and in its original form [*zunächst*], it remains independent from the object. This is the first aporetic tension that begins to explode the *Three Essays* from within: although Freud's chosen methodology tells him that all we can know about libido derives from its object-cathexes, the original libido appears to retain a certain surplus which can never become fully exhausted by any object-choice.

Does this 'independence' or this surplus character mean that libido is simply *objectless* [*objektlos*]? Freud uses this dangerous, methodologically forbidden term only once, in the description of the autoerotic sexuality of young children, 'at first' [*zunächst*] marked by anarchy and amorphy, i.e. a lack of unity and a lack of purpose: 'The excitations from all these sources are not yet combined; but each follows its own separate aim, which is merely the attainment of a certain sort of pleasure. In childhood, therefore, the sexual instinct is not unified and is *at first without an object*, that is, auto-erotic' (TETS, 110).

In all other parts of the text, however, Freud never goes as far as that: the 'objectlessness' functions merely as an asymptotic borderline which the object-attachment approaches without ever radically severing the link with its materialization. Still, the link [*Verknüpfung*] appears here more loose and because of that different than the internal or intimate [*innig*] link which binds the self-preservatory drives with their objects, such as thirst or hunger. Thus, although the comparison between the drives of *conservatio vitae* and sexuality will become the explicit theme only of the second essay, already at this introductory stage we learn about the crucial difference in relation to the object. While libido can find gratification in practically everything – not only without forming a strong attachment, but also allowing for a degradation [cheapening, *Herabsetzung*] of its passing object-choices – the self-preservatory drive attaches itself to the object much more strongly and never treats it as a dispensable 'ersatz': 'Nevertheless, a light is thrown on the nature of the sexual instinct by the fact that it permits so much variation in its objects and such a cheapening of them – which hunger, with its far more energetic retention of its objects, would only permit in the most extreme instance' (TETS, 27).

At this stage, however, Freud does not contemplate the idea that the sexual drive might indeed be *objektlos*, let alone non-sexual: determined by his 'scientific' methodology, he is looking for an object cathexis which would be able to explain the essentially *non-cathected* character of the original libido, responsible for the whole variety of 'aberrant' love-choices. The first hypothesis, therefore, that he formulates to elucidate the difference between these two types of attachment – contingent and necessary – refers to the difference between their respective *aims*. While the 'normal sexual aim' consists in joining the sexual organs in the coital act, the 'perverse aberrations' result from the drive's fixation on the 'temporary sexual aims' and thus its choice of accidental objects. Perversions, therefore, are 'sexual activities which either (a) *extend*, in an anatomical sense, beyond the regions of the body that are designed for sexual union, or (b) *linger over* the immediate relations to the sexual object which should normally be traversed rapidly on the path towards the final sexual aim' (TETS, 28; my emphasis). The first outline of the theory of partial objects [*Partialobjekte*, or in Klein's formulation, *Teilobjekte*] is thus also the best explanation of the mechanism of perversion. The partial (or component) object, when it emerges on the drive's path, slows down its progress towards its proper and integral 'natural destiny': sexuality, instead of rushing to fulfil a procreative function, indulges in extension [*Überschreitung*] and procrastination [*Verweilung*] and, in its self-indulgence, which denies the biological service, becomes strangely independent. As if hanging in the air – without either specific source, object or aim.

We could thus say that in perversion sexuality behaves exactly as the life which meanders, deviates and lingers over, and in this manner delays its end/fulfilment: the way Freud will describe later on the living process in *Beyond the Pleasure Principle*.[35] It uses the whole spatio-temporal arsenal of deferment in order to prolong what, according to its 'natural destiny', should issue, quickly and effectively, into the service [*Dienst*] of procreation. The deviation [*Abweichung*] and the lingering [*Verweilung*] are, therefore, two major sins from the perspective of a smooth biomorphic process: they are, in Freud's own words, the 'dangers of fore-pleasure' (TETS, 90). But can't they be also regarded as the original manifestation of the biophilic act of living/loving: of staying in life a little longer and, in the Derridean liminoid manner, 'lingering on the threshold'?

Verweilen is not a neutral word in German: it bears the Goethean connotation of Faust's famous *Verweile doch, do bist so schön!* – *Stay awhile, you are so beautiful* – where 'lingering' signifies a precious moment of joy, which detaches itself from the normal course of life, as if arrests time and lets it stay for a while (*verweilen* and 'awhile' share the same root).[36] Moreover, Freud uses here the same word as Heidegger in the 'Anaximander Fragment' where he, in the tragic manner, accuses the hubristic life for 'lingering', i.e. remaining in life too long, beyond the right due of time, which he also calls with the neologism deriving from the verb *verweilen*: *die Erweilnis*, staying-for-awhile, or, following Hölderlin, *die Weile*. To linger would thus mean to remain within the 'whileness' of life against the 'just ordinance of time' and to enjoy the self-expanded 'middle' taken out of the natural transience.[37]

Already here we can see the tension which will reverberate through all three essays: although Freud wants to speak as a responsible *Hausvater*, eager to discipline the Young Libido and enchain it to the service of its 'natural destiny', his repressed Schopenhauerian self comes to the fore in the numerous moments of doubt. The nexus of mortality and sexuality – Schopenhauer's obsessive motif – checks also Freud's enthusiasm towards the genital stage of sexual development with its fixed object choice, in which life pays homage to death, by prolonging the existence of the species at the expense of living individuals. Perversion, therefore, would be the first act of resistance towards sexuality properly sexualized and its entanglement with death, and, in that manner – prima facie quite surprisingly – would indicate a certain degree of libido's capability of *desexualization*. For, as Ernest Becker rightly points out: 'Resistance to sex is a resistance to fatality'.[38] By lingering on its way towards sex-and-death, libido pauses and joyfully luxuriates in the 'side-currents' of perversion, so it can avoid encountering its 'natural destiny' en route. By paraphrasing Benjamin even further,[39] we could say that perversion indeed offers a 'gracious dispensation of the fragment': the partial objects which perverse sexuality annexes are precisely those 'fragments' which allow libido to hide for a while and defer its fate.

Freud, however, does not want to give in to his Schopenhauerian temptation, at least not this time. Again and again, there recurs in his essays the same disciplining pattern: although clearly presenting itself as *almost* objectless and independent from its fleeting attachments, the Young Libido is forced to lie down on the Procrustean bed of object cathexis. Although it manifested a merely loose connection to its objects, which it would rather see 'degraded' and 'cheapened' than slowing down its diffusion – now it is bound, and very tightly, with *Partialobjekten*. The partial objects and temporary aims appear thus all of a sudden to throw a net over the agile libido, not so free as it might have seem *zunächst*, at the beginning. Its freedom is now shown as merely apparent, a *Schein* of what is, in fact, the very opposite of a free flow: it is rather 'inhibited' [*gehemmt*] and 'arrested' in its development which should run directly, without any delay to the discovery of the normal object of heterosexual desire. The partial objects, therefore, may not be the ones on which libido should 'linger', but for Freud there are still *objects*, targets capable of cathexis, and this is what he chooses to emphasize. What, for a moment, glimmered as an excess of an energy fleeting over its non-essential attachments and resisting to follow the 'path' of genital normalization, now turns into a reverse image of an 'inhibited development' which slows down the progress of maturation. The polyperverse remnant of the original libido – 'the constituents of which are rarely absent from the sexual life of healthy persons' (TETS, 39) – becomes literally a *per-versio*: a deviation from the main path, a blind alley of the drive declining to fulfil its procreative destiny and because of that 'blocked', arrested – 'In these cases the libido behaves like a stream whose main bed has become *blocked*. It proceeds to fill up collateral channels which may hitherto have been empty' (TETS, 48).

Accordingly, the idea of contingency, which originally suggested a more loose attachment between libido and its object, now transforms into a blind accident in which the child 'happens to hit on one of the predestined regions' (TETS, 62): a fixation on a contingent object which, despite its contingency, binds as strongly as the 'normal' and 'ultimate' object (or, as the 'necessary object' of the self-preservatory drives). *What first appeared as the contingent attachment to the object – now transforms into contingency of the object itself.* This seemingly minor shift will result in far-reaching consequences: in his conception of *tuche*, Lacan will adopt Freud's object-orientated tendency and shift it into the very centre of his theory of drives. According to the Lacanian theory, the determining choice of the primary contingent object makes libido totally dependent on its first super-strong attachment, the power of which can only be opposed by Thanatos, the only remainder of the truly unbound and objectless drive. Thus, what for Freud was still merely a methodological diagnosis – we can know libido only from its object-choice – in Lacan transforms into ontological statement: libido *is* its object choice. And, if libido can only exist in and through its objectual materializations, then the only representative of the free energy can be the death drive, wanting *nothing*, therefore – no object. While libido must always be object-orientated, it is only the death drive that can remain *objektlos* – hence the necessary career of Thanatos as the only libidinal energy capable of breaking bonds and clearing voids, which, as we just have seen, are indispensable for psychic health.[40]

Yet, when we read Freud's text against the grain, we immediately see the ambivalence which Lacan's interpretation ignores: Freud cannot help but admire the wayward skills of the Young Libido, which evades all disciplinary practices that want to turn into a law-abiding procreative desire for the member of the other sex. So, just when it would seem that libido's amorphy and anarchy has been dealt with and bound in hyper-strong cathexes – better perverse than none at all – Freud suddenly lapses in formulations so openly *antinomian* that they could indeed satisfy the most demanding Lurianic Kabbalist: 'Certain of them [perversions] are so far removed from the normal in their content that we cannot avoid pronouncing them "pathological." This is especially so where (as, for instance, in cases of licking excrement or of intercourse with dead bodies) the sexual instinct goes to *astonishing lengths* in successfully overriding the resistances of shame, disgust, horror or pain' (TETS, 39; my emphasis).[41]

This fragment boldly anticipates the clue of the next essay, being also the climax of all three contributions: the agon between libido and vital order, which consists partly in overcoming the 'natural' resistances created by the latter, as abomination, shame, fear and pain. There is yet another important suggestion embedded here: the 'astonishing achievements' [*ernstauliche Leistungen*] listed by Freud, although 'perverted', are as *admirable* as the achievements reached by libido at the stage of sublimation. It is essentially the same *work* in which libido engages, both in perversion – and in sublimation. When writing about the former, Freud says, again in the antinomian vein:

> It is impossible to deny that in their case a *piece of mental work* has been performed which, in spite of its horrifying results, is the equivalent of an idealization of the instinct. *The omnipotence of love is perhaps never more strongly proved that in such of its aberrations as there.* The highest and the lowest are always closest to each other in the sphere of sexuality: *vom Himmel durch die Welt zur Hölle.*
>
> TETS, 40; my emphasis[42]

Note, by the way, Freud's own peculiar version of *love strong as death*: the omnipotence of love – or rather omniviolence, *die Allgewalt* – manifesting itself in the many-coloured halo of sublimations/perversions, is the weapon which *Three Essays* readies against the Thanatos who will soon replace the polyperverse Eros as the candidate to all-powerfulness within the psychic life. And if libido falls from heaven, through the earth, down to hell – from the free spark to the most confused [*verirrt*] kind of bondage, and from the highest bliss 'sweet as wine' to the most poisonous vinegar of anxiety and horror – can it also be reverted from its mighty fall? Is the affinity between the horrors of perversion and the most virtuous works of sublimation the tipping point where the same 'instinctual path' bifurcates into up and down? Or, perhaps, in this weird domain there is *no* up and down, and, consequently, no difference between perversion and sublimation? Indeed, in the general summary, Freud seemingly innocently attests that 'the multifariously perverse sexual disposition of childhood can accordingly be regarded as the *source* of a number of our virtues' (TETS, 116; my emphasis). The question is – *how* this occurs.

No one has better expressed the ambivalence that underlies Freud's theory of drives than Adorno. In *Minima Moralia*, he simultaneously praises psychoanalysis for discovering the common root/source of sensual joy and spiritual achievement, and criticizes Freud for building a fence around this path-breaking discovery, which does not allow the adepts to enter the sacred place:

> In Freud's work, the dual hostility towards mind and pleasure, whose common root psycho-analysis has given us the means for discovering, is *unintentionally* reproduced. The place in the *Future of an Illusion* where, with the worthless wisdom of a hard-boiled old gentleman, he quotes the commercial-traveller's dictum about leaving heaven to the angels and the sparrows, should be set beside the passage in the *Lectures* where he damns in pious horror the perverse practices of pleasure-loving society. Those who feel equal revulsion for pleasure and paradise are indeed best suited to serve as objects: the empty, mechanized quality observable in so many who have undergone successful analysis is to be entered to the account not only of their illness but also of their *cure, which breaks what it liberates*.
>
> MM, 61; translation slightly altered; my emphasis

Freud, therefore, has found the key to the 'energetic paradise' of free libidinal energy – simultaneously hellish and heavenly, marrying the hell of the lowest perversions with the heaven of highest sublimations – but, driven by his control-freak 'arid wisdom' of a Talmudist building the 'hedge around the Torah', he immediately hides it deep in his pocket. By paraphrasing Heine, he implies that while heaven should be left to angels and sparrows – the joy, the 'eternal delight' of a free-flowing life, must be left to the perverts: stigmatized, reduced and ridiculed. Although not indifferent to the 'magnificence of our drives', Freud nonetheless uncovers it only for a moment – as if only in order to reveal his mighty enemy. Instead of ushering us into the libidinal pleroma, he merely 'breaks what he liberates'. And all of it – unintentionally.

It is precisely this troubling ambivalence that accompanies the most important definition of the drive, formulated by Freud towards the end of the first essay:

> By an 'instinct' [*Trieb*] is provisionally to be understood the psychic representative of an endosomatic source of stimuli which are in continual flux, as contrasted with a 'stimulus', which is set up by *single* excitations coming from *without*. The concept of instinct is thus one of those lying on the frontier between the mental and the physical. The simplest and likeliest assumption as to the nature of drives would seem to be that *in itself a drive is without quality*, and, so far as mental life is concerned, is only to be regarded as a measure of the demand made upon the mind for work. What distinguishes the instincts from one another and endows them with their specific qualities is their relation to their somatic sources and to their aims.
>
> TETS, 46

Usually commentators focus on the first two sentences of this passage, where 'drive' emerges as a borderline concept between body and psyche. But I would like to emphasize the tension that arises between the idea of *one* drive defined as a constantly flowing force without qualities, *der Trieb ohne Eigenschaften*, on the one hand – and the idea of *many* different drives which differentiate according to their somatic sources, on the other. Is the original psychic energy indefinite and, because of that, homogeneous – or does it differentiate from the very beginning, depending on the bodily place it comes from? This dilemma comes to the fore very strongly towards the end of the third essay, in the section entitled 'Theory of Libido', which was added in 1915 as refutation of Carl Gustav Jung's concept of *one undifferentiated libido*. Deeply reluctant about this idea, Freud now claims that *his* notion of sexuality has nothing to do with the 'transcendental X' of energy which allegedly underlies all psychic processes:

> We have defined the concept of libido as a quantitatively variable force which could serve as a measure of processes and transformations occurring in the field of sexual excitation. We distinguish this libido in respect of its *special origin* from the energy which must be supposed to underlie mental processes in general, and we thus also attribute a *qualitative* character to it.
>
> TETS, 94; my emphasis

The problem, however, is that libido – the way it has been defined so far – has no 'special origin', because there is no one single bodily organ with which human sexuality would be 'strictly bound'. In the three subsequent editions of the third essay until 1920, there was a passage openly stating that 'we do not know with what organ or organs sexuality is connected', while in the latest version, presumed as ultimate, Freud says that 'the analysis of perversions and psycho-neuroses has shown that the sexual excitation is derived not from the so-called sexual parts alone, but from *all* the bodily organs' (TETS, 94; my emphasis), which may play erotogenic role. It would thus seem that there is absolutely no reason why libido should differ from the original, truly quality-less energy, because it is impossible to turn it into something more *qualified* – either in regard to its source ('no organ' or 'all organs'), or in regard to its aim ('general appeasement'), or, finally, in regard to its objects ('contingent object of choice').

We could thus say that, methodologically speaking, Freud oscillates here between Kant and Hegel. On the one, Kantian, hand, he is ready, though somewhat reluctantly, to accept the hypothesis of the free indefinite and boundless energy as the 'transcendental X' of his theory of drives, which – just as the Kantian thing in itself that cannot be known empirically, but is nonetheless a necessary premise of all cognitive activity – cannot be the object of research, but must be assumed. Yet, on the other, Hegelian, hand, Freud struggles with the scandal of the drive *in itself* and wants to give it, already *in the beginning*, the objective character, which would make it accessible to his investigations. For, as he himself admits: 'we are faced by the difficulty that our method of research, psycho-analysis, for the moment affords us assured information only on the transformations that take place in the object-libido' (TETS, 95).

It is at this most aporetic juncture, where a new hypothesis springs into being: the one of the 'ego-libido'. The 'ego-libido' functions as a peculiar borderline or compromise concept which emerges in the space between the objectless and object-orientated libido: it is simultaneously a synonym of the original energy without qualities (the Kantian moment) and its later avatar, already accessible to empirical research, which binds itself with the ego as its first object (the Hegelian moment):

> We can follow the object-libido through still further vicissitudes. When it is withdrawn from the object, it is held in suspense in peculiar conditions of tension and is finally drawn back into the ego, so that it becomes ego-libido once again. In contrast to object-libido, we also describe ego-libido as 'narcissistic' libido. From the vantage-point of psycho-analysis we can look across a frontier, which we may not pass, at the activities of the narcissistic libido, and may form

some idea of the relation between it and object-libido. Narcissistic or ego-libido seems to be the great reservoir from which the object-cathexes are sent out and into which they are withdrawn once more; the narcissistic libidinal cathexis of the ego is the original state of things, realized in earliest childhood, and is merely screened by the later extrusions of libido, but in essentials persists behind them.

TETS, 95; my emphasis

So, how many forms of libido are there – three (autoerotic objectless libido, ego-libido and object-libido) or just two (ego-libido and object-libido)? The ego is designated to become a *primary object*, somewhere between object cathexis and its lack, which Freud defines as narcissism. Yet, if libido is narcissistic, it is only in the sense of the primary narcissism where there is not yet a clear distinction between various objects, the ego included. And if, as Freud also suggests, it is autoerotic, then not via object relation, but rather, in the manner of the Fichtean *intellektuelle Anschauung* – which forms a *tertium* between Kant and Hegel – where it can enjoy itself in one undifferentiated stream of auto-affection.[43] It would seem, therefore, that if libido is 'dragged away from objects', it does not simply return to the 'ego-libido' as its primary object, but rather *recollects* its original form of autoerotic and objectless delight, which hovers as a spectral halo over each and every object choice.

But why does Freud not pursue this 'Fichtean' solution, which offers itself as a promising third hypothesis regarding the status of the original drive? The most probable answer is that he, now acting more than ever as the Kafkan deeply concerned 'family man', tries to defend his own paternal version of psychoanalysis, which relies on the dense understanding of the term sexuality. At all costs, therefore, he wants to distance himself from Jung's theory of *Libidowandlungen* formulated in 1913, in which, as Freud says, Jung 'watered down the meaning of the concept of libido itself by equating it with psychic instinctual force in general' (TETS, 96). But let's be fair here: *Jung is right*. None of the disciplinary strategies that Freud imposes on the Young Libido can really bind it. What Jung does later on with his quality-less libido, by imposing on it his own dubious strategy of spiritualization, is another matter, which does not concern us here. Yet the very core of Jung's diagnosis saying that *human sexuality is less sexual than we think because it is a libidinal form closest to the original indefinite drive* – remains true. Jonathan Lear would have consented too: the role of psychoanalysis is not to search into the way in which libidinal energy exhausts itself in object-fixations, but also to quest after elusive manifestations of the primordial libidinal freedom, spectrally present in the form of a 'remainder' in all, only seemingly so tight, cathexes.[44]

So, 'why not become Jungian'? The answer is simple: with Jung's absolute monism we lose the whole dimension of the inner-psychic conflict without which there would be no formation of subjectivity – the agon between sexuality (or *however* we call this autotelic, autoerotic, autoeudaimonic drive which drives at absolute joy) and the vital order that cares only for self-preservation. In the quarrel between Freud and Jung, therefore, we need a compromise which Laplanche calls 'a constant tension between monism and dualism',[45] which, on the one hand, allows for the hypothesis of the original energy manifesting itself as extremely *plastic* sexuality or 'sexuality expanded' (*sexualité élargie*) – and, on the other, makes room for the conflict between this primordial form of sexuality and 'ordinary sexuality', already disciplined by the rules of *Lebensordnung*. As he says in *Life and Death in Psychoanalysis*: 'Sexuality is thus present on both sides of the conflict: "free" sexuality on one side, "bound" sexuality on the other (i.e., on the side of the ego)'.[46] Translated into our terminology, this indicates an *agon between Erros and Eros* – with no need for the separate hypothesis of the death drive.[47]

Freud's ambivalence comes to the fore most visibly in depicting the subsequent stages of this crucial agon. Although its goal seems to be settled – *Erros* must bow down to the procreative function of Eros – Freud does not sound very enthusiastic:

> The final outcome of sexual development lies in what is known as the normal sexual life of the adult, in which the pursuit of pleasure *comes under the sway* of the reproductive function and in which the component instincts under the primacy of a single erotogenic zone, form a firm organization directed towards a sexual aim attached to some extraneous sexual object.
>
> TETS, 75; my emphasis

Already the formulation – 'coming under the sway', *in den Dienst treten* – betrays a note of regret after the loss of freedom and its antinomian creativity, now disciplined and domesticated by the 'normal' and 'natural' aim of biological reproduction. The whole evolution of libido in Freud's account – from oral, through anal and latent, to the final genital stage – is marked by a fatalistic 'teleology of nature' and its tragic Schopenhauerian finale: first in the brief triumph of Eros and then in the lasting triumph of Thanatos, where the act of reproduction indicates acceptance of one's own death and continuation of life in progeny. But what if we gave up on Freud's tragic teleology and saw the agon between *Erros* and Eros as an ongoing – *lingering* – battle which does not have its pre-established finale?

The agon between sexuality [*Sexualtrieb*] with the vital order [*Lebensordnung*] is the crux of Freud's early drive theory: it is here where these two powers – the sublimatory work of the drive fighting to maintain its independence from objects, on the one hand, and the biomorphic-nomotropic tendency, attempting to capture and cathect this free energy, on the other – determine the inner-psychic conflict. Critical of his early theory of seduction, Freud says: 'the effects of seduction do not help to reveal the early history of the sexual instinct; they rather confuse our view of it by presenting children prematurely with a sexual object for which the infantile sexual instinct *at first* shows no need' (TETS, 69; my emphasis).

But, if the infantile sexuality does not need an object 'at first', at the beginning, why does this need appear later on? Freud does not answer this question directly, but it is supplied very convincingly by Laplanche. The reason why libido must 'almost immediately' subordinate to the vital order lies in the absolute nature of its primary autoaffective enjoyment which is *infinite* and uncompromising. As such it aims at a total satisfaction which, according to the Schopenhauerian–Fechnerian–Freudian entropic definition of pleasure as the reduction of tension [*Auslöschung*], inevitably leads to nirvana, nothingness, and, in consequence – death. The self-preservatory instincts must thus intervene already 'in the beginning' in order not to allow for the absolute explosion of *jouissance* and maintain a minimal level excitation that is necessary for keeping on the functions of life. *Zunächst*, in the beginning, therefore, libido becomes 'almost immediately' weakened and exposed to the priorities of *Lebensordnung* the main interest of which is *conservatio vitae*. But it also means, continues Laplanche, that the original autoerotic libido does not differ from what later on Freud will call the death drive. Since the highest pleasure equals absolute *Auslöschung*, the aim towards which original sexuality drives is nothing but (or) death: the ultimate reduction of tension to the inorganic level of existence. Hence, deep down, there is no antagonism between Freud's early and late theory of drives: the later dualism of Eros and Thanatos (where it is actually the later which is stronger as the primordial source of all energy) is already present in Freud's concept of 'expanded sexuality' *in nuce*.

But, is this a good definition of pleasure? Jonathan Lear would rather say that instead of falling for a bad physics, which awkwardly extrapolated the principle of entropy on psychic phenomena, we should pay attention to the specificity of human drive, which is *excess*. It is not Thanatos which annihilates the structures of psychic organization in its drive towards the entropic jouissance shattering the vessel of life– but *too-much-ness-of-life* which proves to be equally lethal. *Too much life will kill you*: not the 'internal death', which one supposedly carries in one's extimate inwardness, but sexuality so enlarged, expanded and boundless that no biological vessel can bear it. The main conflict in the psyche, therefore, occurs between *Erros* in its full 'magnificence' of 'more life', which no living creature can look face to face and survive – and 'mere life' which only wants to remain and preserve itself. The key difference between these two types of dualism – Thanatos versus Eros on the one hand, and *Erros* versus Eros, on the other – is that while the former makes death-wish the very essence of the original drive to nirvanic pleasure, the latter sees the lethal consequences of excessive sexuality as merely its secondary feature.[48]

Perhaps it is precisely this originary agon and the subtle interplay between the two beginnings – the first manifestation of the Young Libido and the first intervention of the vital order – that delivers a clue to the understanding of one of the darkest Freudian notions: the *primary repression*. Before there emerges the ego and the superego – the two instances capable of repressing the demands posed by the id – the drive energy becomes repressed already 'at first', *zunächst*, because it is too powerful to be contained in the fragile vessel of the psychic apparatus. If – to use again Lurianic idiom – the psyche defends itself against 'breaking of the vessels' (*shevirat ha-kelim*), it is only because it always already withstands the impact of this primal unbound energy.

It would, however, be wrong to assume that *in the beginning*, sexuality is weak, while the natural vital order is strong. Although sexuality arises in places borrowed from self-preservatory functions, it is actually more powerful than the remnants of biological instincts which, in turn, borrow energy from libido. Laplanche, therefore, locates Freud firmly within the Herderian anthropology of *Mangelwesen*:

> A deficiency or prematuration of the vital order in the human infant: these are terms with which we are familiar, and which are already in Freud. They allow us to understand that, in the entirety of its extension, that 'order' is infested by the sexual 'order'. *Infested*, but also *sustained*. Why does one so often have to force children to eat, to offer them 'one spoon for daddy, one spoon for mommy', – i.e., one spoon for daddy's love, one spoon for mommy's love – were it not that appetite is sustained, supplemented, and, to an extent, replaced in the human child by love?[49]

The term *infestation* used by Laplanche suggests that the contract between libido and vital order – energy in exchange for places and objects – is not without risks, and that for both parties, because their interests remain divergent. The infestation here is also an *incarnation*, thanks to which the 'invisible', unbound and purely energetic, drive becomes flesh due to its localization in places of the vital order (as mouth or anus) and interception of its objects (as food or faeces). But it can also lead to drive's self-estrangement: it can forget itself in the world of material objects. Despite the weakness of the biological system of self-preservation – or rather, precisely because of that – the first stages of psychic development are spent under the auspices of *conservatio vitae*, which marginalizes realization of sexual interests. The infant psyche is ruled not by biology, which remains weak and deficient, but by *biomorphism*: a tendency whose aim is to strengthen the feeble 'representation of life' (ibid.). The first task is not finding joy, it is – *survival*.

The vital order, therefore, must avail itself of ruse and cunning: its essential strategy of capturing and retaining the sexual energy is *seduction* which purports to fixate it on objects and thus persuade libido that it is only through objects that it can find enjoyment. Accordingly, libido, instead of exploding in autoerotic spasms of objectless bliss, orients itself towards the object which originally correlated with self-preservatory functions, as hunger or thirst. It takes lessons – or, is 'taught to live' in the first *torat hayim* – from the vital order as to how to handle the object so it does not lead to its immediate 'degradation', 'consummation' and 'destruction': the infant who wants to devour the breast, delivering both food and pleasure, risks that its object will simply disappear. *Lebensordnung*, therefore, not only lures and seduces the libido, but also teaches it how to be 'relational' and have some regard for the object on which it begins to depend. Theologically speaking, the *incarnation* of the original drive is not just a *Fall* (as the more Gnostically minded religious traditions would like to see it), but also a collateral gain: the pure drive energy meets matter for the first time – and does not destroy it. Although it constantly risks a too-deep seduction by material images of fulfilment, it nonetheless also learns a minimal respect for the material mode of being, which it now also assumes. The spirit, no longer blindly opposed to anything carnal and finite, begins to permeate the bodily realm of finitude. If this indeed is a Fall, then not fully unfortunate.

Yet, this initial subordination of libido to *conservatio vitae* does not last very long. In the first stage, vital order has advantage over sexuality which manifests itself as an *imitation* of the satisfaction achieved in connection with other physiological processes. While analysing the activity of sucking, Freud says:

> It is also easy to guess the occasions on which the child had his first experiences of the pleasure which he is now striving to renew. It was the child's first and most

vital activity, his sucking at his mother's breast, or at substitutes for it, that must have familiarized him with this pleasure. The child's lips, in our view behave like an erotogenic zone, and no doubt stimulation by the warm flow of milk is the cause of the pleasurable sensation. The satisfaction of the erotogenic zone is associated, in the first instance with the satisfaction of the need for nourishment. *To begin with, sexual activity attaches itself to functions serving the purpose of self-preservation and does not become independent of them until later* ... Our study of thumb-sucking or sensual sucking has already given us the three essential characteristics of an infantile sexual manifestation. *At its origin it attaches itself to one of the vital somatic functions; it has as yet no sexual object, and is thus auto-erotic; and its sexual aim is dominated by an erotogenic zone.*

TETS, 60–1; my emphasis

Soon, however, libido will try to detach itself from the object and return to its original autoerotic formula. Despite libido's *anaclisis* [*Anlehnung*] on the vital functions, it nonetheless regains autonomy, or at least, the upper hand. The first triumph of sexuality consists in transforming the places destined to fulfil alimentary needs into erotogenic spheres. Having no place of its own, 'no fixed abode', libido can colonize every space of the body and then use it for its own autoerotic pleasure, once again forgetting about the 'extraneous object':

Here sexual activity has not yet been separated from the ingestion of food; nor are opposite currents within the activity differentiated. The *object* of both activities is the same; the sexual *aim* consists in the incorporation of the object – the *prototype* of a process which, in the form of identification, is later to play such an important psychological part. A relic of this constructed phase or organization, which is forced upon our notice by pathology, may be seen in thumb-sucking, in which the sexual activity, detached from the nutritive activity, has substituted [gave up, *aufgegeben hat*] for the extraneous object one situated in the subject's own body.

TETS, 62

But again, this triumph does not last long. The next stages in the libido's development are marked by the same oscillation – Fichte would have said: *Schweben* – between autoerotic narcissism and borrowed object cathexes, both 'aberrant' [*abirrende*] and because of that targeted by social repression. In consequence, the Young Libido, having no channel to express itself, goes into hiding – into a latent stage out of which it will emerge only much later, fully subordinated to the mature genital organization, where only small remainders of its earlier 'polymorphous perversion' will have become incorporated into the rituals of erotic fore-play. The 'mature' form of libido, therefore, will be strictly object-orientated, according to the iron rule formulated by Freud: 'The finding of an object is in fact a re-finding of it' [*Die Objektfindung ist eigentlich eine Wiederfindung*] (TETS, 99).

This sad story of defeat, in which sexuality is allowed to return from exile only on the condition that it submits to the procreative goals of the vital order, would indeed sound tragic – if not for the one *peripetia* called sublimation. Before Freud described perversion in terms of a 'lingering' energetic remnant which cannot be fully exhausted by the functions of *Lebensordnung* – and exactly the same characteristic applies now to sublimation, which also wants to use sexuality to purposes different than coital. Perversion and sublimation – these two (but are they really two?) ways of resistance to which the unruly *Erros* resorts in his agon with his more normative brother Eros, turn out to be the only chance of survival of the objectless libido fallen/incarnated into the world of objects: '*The same pathways*, however, along which sexual disturbances encroach upon the other somatic functions must also perform another important function in normal health. They must serve as paths for the attraction of sexual instinctual forces to aims that are other than sexual, that is to say, for the *sublimation of sexuality*' (TETS, 84; my emphasis).

As if in the eternal psychotheological repetition of the agon between Jacob and Esau, the hubristic versus the natural brother (already suggested by Bloom), *Erros* can get out victorious from the wrestling with the vital order only through a subterfuge. By 'encroaching' [*übergreifen*] upon the somatic functions, it first steals the 'blessing of more life' – but then, afterwards, it can only regain itself as 'limping': living-on, yet damaged, altered and compromised. But this agonistic outcome is not the end of the story. As *Zohar* reminds us, 'Unless Esau's tears are not wiped out, the Messiah will not come'[^51] – which can only mean that Jacob must find a way to reconcile himself with his natural brother: the Kafkan 'man of the country' or the Derridean 'beast'.

The truce: from biomorphism to biophilia

If Freud himself admits that his drive theory remained in the 'inchoate stage' until the very end, then the concept of sublimation is definitely its least elaborated component; as Laplanche and Pontalis claim in their dictionary *The Language of Psychoanalysis*,[^51] there is no such thing as a 'theory of sublimation'. And although Freud used this concept as early as in his *Studies on Hysteria*, it remained nothing but an operative term or a an auxiliary lemma helping to fix the holes in the dogmatic architecture.

According to Freud's tentative description, sublimation is the process of the 'the attraction of sexual instinctual forces to aims that are other than sexual' (TETS, 84) and as such constitutes one of the four possible 'drive vicissitudes' – next to gratification, repression and reaction formation. In 'The Ego and the Id', Freud writes:

> We have reckoned as though there existed in the mind – whether in the ego or in the id – a *displaceable energy*, which, neutral in itself, can be added to qualitatively differentiated erotic or destructive impulse, and augments its total cathexis. *Without assuming the existence of a displaceable energy of this kind we can make no headway.* The only question is where it comes from, what it belongs to, and what it signifies.
>
> FR, 648; my emphasis

The first thing that strikes us in this quotation is Freud's surprising change of heart towards the drive 'without qualities'. Now, it is no longer disciplined and compulsorily fed with objects, but suddenly needed as a free-floating volatile energy that can jump places, objects and aims – and we cannot do without it, because it makes sublimation possible. The general definition of sublimation, as we know it from *Civilization and Its Discontents*, says that it is a way to achieve satisfaction thanks to the reorientation or displacement of libido from sexual to the culturally accepted aims. Yet, in fact, this is hardly a definition, because no word used here means exactly what it should in Freud's system. 'Satisfaction' is something else than pleasure; although more efficient and lasting than sexual enjoyment, it is also a lesser form since it is 'inhibited towards its goal' and, because of that, is often called *Ersatzbefriedigung*, a substitute enjoyment. 'Displacement of libido' sounds equally mysterious. How does it occur? What is the role of repression here? And to what extent is the drive damaged or lessened by this reorienting operation? What of it remains to enjoy itself in the end? Perhaps even, no repression is involved here at all, just a *change of object*, which does not require any special reorienting effort.[52]

The two most classical passages on sublimation, coming respectively from *Civilization and Its Discontents* and Freud's essay on Leonardo da Vinci, do not help much in solving these problems. In the first one, sublimation is mentioned next to the ascetic technics of 'mastering the life of instincts', which inevitably leads to 'the undeniable diminution in the potentialities of enjoyment' (FR, 731):

Another technique for fending off suffering is the employment of the displacement of libido which our mental apparatus permits of and through which its function gains so much in flexibility. *The task here is that of shifting the instinctual instincts in such a way that they cannot come up against frustration from the external world.* In this, sublimation of the instincts lends its assistance. One gains the most if one can sufficiently heighten the yield of pleasure from the sources of psychical and intellectual work. *When that is so, fate can do little against one.* A satisfaction of this kind, such as an artist's joy in creating, in giving his phantasies body, or a scientist's in solving problems or discovering truths, has a special quality which we shall certainly one day be able to characterize in metapsychological terms. At present we can only say figuratively that *such satisfactions seem 'finer and higher,' but their intensity is lessened in comparison with the more primitive and robust forms of instinctual fulfillment: they do not shake our carnal being.*

                                                                  ibid.; my emphasis

Thus, although Freud suggests that sublimation differs from ascesis, which aims only at the inhibition of the drives, the result is similar: 'the feeling of happiness derived from the satisfaction of a wild instinctual impulse untamed by the ego is *incomparably more intense* that than derived from sating an instinct that has been tamed' (FR, 731). I have already pointed to this dogmatic limitation of Freudian psychoanalysis in the section devoted to Lyotard and Lévinas in Chapter 2: the regressive-nostalgic ideal of happiness, which binds highest possible pleasure to the love-objects of family romance, turns every other later form of joy into pale, ultimately less satisfactory copies of the former. The assumption of the unsurpassable 'pattern [*Vorbild*] for our search of happiness' transforms every other later moment of joy into a mere substitute, an *ersatz*: 'What is more natural than that we should persist in looking for happiness along the path on which we first encountered it?' (FR, 733). Thus, even if, as in the case of sublimation, the drive is neither killed nor severely damaged and grows 'sufficiently' in order to reach its peculiar 'yield of pleasure,' Freud's metapsychology, bound by its regressive norm of happiness, can never do it full justice.

This deficiency becomes even clearer in the second passage, from 'Leonardo da Vinci and a Memory of His Childhood', where sublimation resulting in intellectual curiosity [*Wißbegierde*] arises directly from the early form of infantile curiosity concerning sexual matters. The 'third type of man', capable of the highest kind of sublimation, is considerably *happier* than those who, together with their sexual curiosity, relinquished all intellectual pursuits, as well as those for whom thinking is only a substitute activity deriving from compulsory neurosis:

> In virtue of a special disposition, the third type, which the rarest and most perfect, escapes both inhibition of thought and neurotic compulsive thinking. It is true that here too sexual repression comes about, but it does not succeed in relegating a component instinct of sexual desire to the unconscious. Instead, *the libido evades the fate of repression by being sublimated from the very beginning into curiosity* and by becoming attached to the powerful instinct for research as a reinforcement. Here, too, the research becomes to some extent compulsive and a substitute for sexual activity; but owing to the complete difference in the underlying psychical processes (sublimation instead of irruption from the unconscious) the quality of neurosis is absent; there is no attachment to the original complexes of infantile sexual research, and the instinct can operate freely in the service of intellectual interest. Sexual repression, which has made the instinct so strong through the addition to it of sublimated libido, is still taken into account by the instinct, in that it avoids any concern with sexual themes.
>
> FR, 453–4

Thus, although the repression occurs and inhibits a child's sexual curiosity, the drive itself, understood in quantitative terms of sheer force [*Drang*], avoids the repression, which means that it gets out of the whole operation 'unscathed' (to recall Hegel's *unverletzt* and Derrida's *indemne*), and from this time on freely and joyfully engages in all sorts of intellectual *plays*. The only cost of this 'displacement' consists in renouncing erotic pleasure, but Leonardo, characterized by 'the concurrence of his overpowerful instinct for research and the atrophy of his sexual life' (FR, 454), does not seem to be too bothered. On the contrary: his creative-explorative enjoyment is so highly 'sufficient' that, as Freud himself enviously remarks, we can only feel jealous when confronted with such unperturbed happiness. By sublimating *from the beginning* and *without loss implied by repression*, da Vinci towers above us all as almost superhuman: a truly wondrous monster who managed to escape the tragic fate of neurotic substitution. Just as Jesus for Blake and Hegel – the exception made flesh and example [*Vorbild*] – so is Leonardo for Freud: a Hölderlinian fateless creature which went against the natural verdict, by having achieved *defatalization*. For, 'when that is so, fate can do little against one' (FR, 731).

Here, however, the words – 'happiness', 'joy', 'pleasure' – no longer mean what they were designed to signify in Freud's system: they are clearly high and autonomous forms of satisfaction of a drive which has a distinctly and originally non-sexual nature. But, as Freud tries to persuade us, it can be non-sexual only because it once was sexual and now is desexualized or, to put it in even more confusing terms: *it is desexualized because sexual drive is especially prone towards becoming non-sexual* – 'The sexual instinct is particularly well fitted to make contributions of this kind since it is endowed with a capacity for sublimation: that is, it has the power to replace its immediate aim by other aims which may be valued more highly and which are not sexual' (FR, 452).[53]

But wouldn't it be easier – and theoretically more elegant – to drop the whole idea of 'displacement', which portrays sublimation as a laborious secondary process, and see it rather as a continuation of the primary process in which libido maintains its volatile and plastic form *von Anfang an*, 'from the beginning'? In such an approach, sublimation would no longer be a paler substitute of sexual enjoyment, but the originary type of enjoyment recovered after its 'fall/incarnation' into erotic object-fixations: a true *Paradise Regained*. It would no longer be a consolation prize sweetening the melancholy process of socialization – but a moment of rekindling the sparks of the original 'great joy', which later on became tarnished by false lures of sexual object-attachments.

If we, however, decide for *another sublimation*, which allows the original libido to manifest itself 'from the beginning' and 'without loss', we must also radically transform our view of the symbolic sphere. Now, it also emerges as something infinitely more significant than just a *substitute* which merely offers itself instead of 'real' things (and real pleasures). As I have already suggested in 'Another sublimation, or *Erros* in language', the symbolic figurations are not so much *losses* of literality as *restitutions* of the self-troping and self-transgressive nature of *Erros* which, being 'without qualities', is – in the beginning, *zunächst* – an objectless volatility and plasticity itself, 'going in all directions'.

Yet, *Erros* can have and has a *relation* with objects. Between absolute objectless freedom and equally fixed object attachment, there emerges room for a third possibility which is – precisely – *relation*. In this dialectical story which we are telling here, language, particularly in its poetic variant is – precisely as in Hölderlin – 'related to many of the living' regarded as 'countless singularities': not as objects, but as neighbours/strangers; not as means of gratification, but as the Rosenzweigian, autotelic and lovable whatevers, *loci tenentes*, which just happen to be there; not as fulfilments of our functional needs, but as remnants that transgress any functionality. Thus, even if the drive, in its incarnational vicissitudes, is bound to fall into object fixations, there always remains a halo of its non-cathected original form, which is the bearer of sublimatory energy. *Sublimation does not allow libido to regress to its primary process of pure objectless stage: it forces it to stay with the objects, yet in a different mode from fixation.* The sublimatory relation is much more *free* and *playful*: its object is simultaneously co-created by libido and respected as an autonomous remnant which remains 'there', outside the libidinal link. And its new medium is – *language*.

Winnicott delivers here important clues, by stressing the essentially non-erotic nature of play and its own indigenous type of enjoyment that cannot be reduced to a derivative or a mere substitute of sexual pleasure. On the contrary, this sublimatory type of joy feels threatened by the encroachment of sexual excitement:

> Bodily excitement in erotogenic zones constantly threatens playing, and therefore threatens the child's sense of existing as a person. *The instincts are the main threat to play as to the ego*; in seduction some external agency exploits the child's instincts and helps to annihilate the child's sense of existing as an autonomous unit, making playing impossible . . . *Playing is essentially satisfying.* This is true even if it leads to the high degree of anxiety. There is a degree of anxiety that is unbearable and this destroys playing.
>
> PR, 52; my emphasis

For Winnicott, therefore, the cultural sphere of language and symbolic communication is not just an *ersatz* compensation for the lost instinctual fulfilment. By commenting on Trilling's remark that 'Freud's relation to culture must be described as an ambivalent one' (PR, 106), Winnicott tries to show a more affirmative source of symbolic activity which is the *non-erotic play*, fully and essentially satisfying in its own way: 'playing leads on naturally to cultural experience and indeed forms its foundation' (PR, 106). The reason for this is the fluidity and variability of individual experiences as opposed to the 'fixity of instinctual endowment' (ibid.). In that sense, play may be seen as a recovery of the original in/de/finite drive, which bypasses the fixed behaviour of the *Lebensordnung*, including also the erotic object-cathexes that meekly followed the pattern of the 'vital order', but which nonetheless stays in contact with objects. Echoing Freud's statement on Leonardo as the 'third type of man', Winnicott defines play as 'the third way of living' (PR, 107), which liquidates the rigid fixity of both: the 'outer' way (well-determined self-preservatory behaviour) and the 'inner' way (equally determined 'personality organization', based on the introjection of the family romance).

Winnicott's favourite play is the variant of the Freudian game of *Fort-Da!*, in which 'two objects are being *both joined and separated* by the string':

> This is the paradox which I accept and do not attempt to resolve. The baby's separating-out of the world of objects from the self is achieved only through the absence of a space between, the *potential* space . . . Here where there is trust and reliability is a potential space, one that can become an *infinite area of separation*,

which the baby, child, adolescent, adult may creatively fill with playing, which in time becomes the enjoyment of the cultural heritage.

                                                                    PR, 108; my emphasis

Play recovers the in/de/finite character of the original drive and envelops it into infinite liminoid sphere of potential fluidity and variability, which is possible only thanks to the gradual process of separation: to the 'breathing space' penetrating into the dyadic union with the maternal body. The frequent motif of the 'string play', which represents the 'paradox of relation' – being simultaneously separated and joined – eases the pressure of anxiety that accompanies every act of playing. This anxiety, however, is not just a manifestation of the excess of unbound libido, as in Freud's original account. It is that – and something more: it is also, in more Rankian terms, a manifestation of fear of 'becoming distinct', of transgressing the biomorphic realm of the vital order into an experimental, unprincipled and uncharted territory of individuation. Anxiety, the site of which is the individuating ego, inevitably increases once the subject acquires the status of the inimitable *remnant* beyond any *Nachahmung*, i.e. any strategy of *mimesis* or nomotropism: the indivisible remainder of all normalizing principles and partitions. The symbolic activity of language, for which the 'paradox of relation' – being simultaneously separated and joined – is foundational, allows us to play down the anxiety of becoming distinct, by offering two things at once: the autonarrative vehicle for the narcissistic sense of one's unique self (which Derrida calls the *récit* of every auto-bio-graphical life), on the one hand, and the connection with other equally singularized entities: the Rosenzweigian *connection without attachment*, on the other. The more individuated the psyche – 'singled out' – the stronger the development of language as a symbolic means of maintaining the universal *nexus* without any firmly fixating object-cathexes.

Winnicott tackles the issue of becoming *one and unique* in one of his essays from *Home Is Where We Start From*: 'Sum, I Am'. He starts with the pun which plays on the English meaning of 'sum' as arithmetical addition: 'When I say that the central feature in human development is the arrival and secure maintenance of the stage of I AM, I know this is also a statement of the central fact of arithmetic, or (as one could say) of sums.'[54]

Yet he also immediately suggests that although the human psyche becomes a 'unit' by claiming certain parts of the world as 'I' and by rejecting other as 'Not-I', its sense of I AM cannot be exhausted by the sum of internalized or appropriated objects: the subject of this quasi-mathematical operation which 'does the sums' places itself beyond them. Winnicott never uses the concept of the *remnant*, but this is what he could be said to address: I AM stands for this part of the psyche that remains *behind all sums* in which the psychic 'unit' anxiously checks its sense of individuality as made and composed of internalized objects, taken in by the psyche as the model [*Vorbild*] for the mimetic identification. He thus also proposes a different understanding of the depressive position than the classical Kleinian one which, as he indicates, relies too much on the success of internalization, forming a steady and no longer questioned object-relation (ibid., 73). For Winnicott, depression is a withdrawal from the life with objects, in which the subject recollects the original state of objectlessness. The depressive position puts thus all that is 'mine' in brackets in a radical *epoché* of all subjective predicates, which *undoes* the 'arithmetic' operation of self-constitution: Is this really me? Is this truly my identity? Can I get rid of it, stop being it, and still remain I? 'To our surprise – continues Winnicott – a person may come out of a depression stronger, wiser and more stable than before he or she went into it' (ibid., 77). And this effect of strength emerges when the loss of object-attachments *turns*, precisely in the manner already announced by Santner, into a positive sense of separation which no sum of internalized objects can ever exhaust.

Winnicott's essay on 'Sum, I AM' does not limit its scope just to therapeutic reflections: it is also openly *psychotheological*. It makes a direct link between the deep self of I AM and the conception of monotheistic God:

> It is difficult for us to remember how modern is the concept of a human individual. The struggle to reach to this concept is reflected, perhaps, in the early Hebrew name for God. Monotheism seems to be closely linked to the name I AM. I am that I am ... *Does not this name (I AM) given to God reflect the danger that the individual feels he or she is in on reaching the state of individual being?* If I am, then I have gathered together this and that and have claimed it as me, and I have repudiated everything else; *in repudiating the not-me I have, so to speak, insulted the world, and I must expect to be attacked.* So when people first came to the concept of individuality, they quickly put it up in the sky and gave it a voice that only a Moses could hear. This accurately portrays *the anxiety that is inherent in the arrival of every human being who gets there at the I AM stage.*
>
> ibid., 56–7; my emphasis

God's name, *I am that I am*, expresses pure singularity or, in Rosenzweig's formulation, idiosyncrasy of a being which claims to be *echad*: one and unique. *I am that I am* names, therefore, a perfect remnant which can do *without any sums*, i.e. possesses a strong sense of the self without any need of interaction with external objects. God does not need to become depressed every now and then in order to 'rally what remains' – that is, make decisions whether he can do without this or that object and cast it out as 'not-I'. God, the pure ideal remnant, does not have to undergo the periodical reduction in which 'everything is slowed down and brought towards a state of deadness' (ibid., 75). But only God can *withdraw* so radically and clear himself of everything in order to become the eternal *I am that I am*. Human beings, on the other hand, can 'take breath' and stay in the remnant only for a short moment, but then it is bound to resume its sums and divisions, and thus begin anew its interactions with the world (which, to recall the conclusion of Chapter 2, is equivalent of the renewal of the act of birth). God can remain a pure objectless spirit – but Man must enter into negotiation with matter which, if he neglects it, will not let him survive.

Remnant is thus the outcome of the act of separation – from any pattern, any matrix of imitation, any object to follow, any mimetic function, any nomotropic tendency – arousing enormous anxiety in which the original drive comes to the first full self-recognition: 'I am that I am – and I cannot live or survive like that.' Separation, therefore, belongs to the primordial ambivalent concepts for it means simultaneously: deadness *and* aliveness. In Winnicott, this ambivalence is played out by the subject of 'I am (alive)' in a 'game of repetition' which toys with the trauma of separation in an attenuating manner, trying to convert it into a positive fact: the beginning/birth of my own 'psychic reality'. This play of regression, undertaken by the deep subject, is again a variant of the Freudian *Fort-Da!*; this time, however, its target is not the absence of the mother, but rather the *absence of the self*: not being-in-the-world, not being situated, not being a part of what is happening, withdrawal into the deadness of latency. Here, the separated remnant is being tried and exercised as a mode of being alternative to the blind attachment to objects. This regression, however, being merely a play, is not meant to be treated with full 'seriousness' as a permanent state of existence. It is rather a moment within the complex natalistic strategy of individuation, which repeats itself in the sequence of 'rebirths'. When Rosenzweig calls the Jewish soul a 'survivor', he means precisely such pulsating form of living which amplifies by reduction and 'rises forth out of the rites of degradation' in a Phoenix-like manner (Santner): out of nothingness back into the world of objects, again and again. If the subject wants to strike a free relation with the world, it is only after he undergoes the deep *epoché* thanks to which the subject begins to understand that he can love only what it no longer needs.

In Chapter 1, in the section called 'Love: A Perfect Affect for the Imperfect World (Contingency)', I have indicated that this pulsation is the foundational libidinal bedrock of language conceived, in the Rosenzweigian manner as a 'living speech', drawing on the deep movements of life. Language indeed is structured like the libido: it can withdraw all objectual cathexes and reduce itself to abstraction bordering on nothing, and then strike relation with 'anything and everything' – or, at least, 'many' – in a thrust of curiosity that has nothing to do with any fixed attachment. For language, just as the Pauline love, does not look for any 'satisfaction of its own'. Cured from too much hope in object attachments by the depressive position (the Kleinian equivalent of Rosenzweigian 'disappointment'), it sees things as they are: not as *objects* of a potential fulfilment, but as remnants – as separated and 'singled out' as the subject itself: just the Rilkean 'innumerable individuals' who are out there and wait for us to be named, affirmed in their singularity. In the end, therefore, after the 'depression' does it good job, the psyche is ready for the next *conversion*. Before it was the subject who needed the world as the container of objects for its gratification – now it is the world which is in the need of man's language, the living address of speech, which responds to the call of things or Rilke's *Auftrag* [task/calling]: 'Perhaps we are here in order to say: / house, bridge, fountain, gate, pitcher, fruit-tree, window... / but to say them, you must understand, / oh to say them more intensely than the things themselves / ever dreamed of existing ...'.[55]

I have been evoking Lear, Santner, Laplanche, Bloom and Winnicott in order to avoid one conclusion that late-modern thought practically assumed as self-evident – that in order to become a separate 'I', the subject must assume death and 'die to the world': detach himself from the 'gregarious conglomerations of Eros' (Lacan) and identify with his and his alone death drive. Could any other psychic power counteract the biomorphic tendency, in which the drive formats itself *kata phusein*, i.e. according to the 'vital order' of self-preservation, fixates rigidly on objects and thus loses its original suppleness and indeterminacy? Lacan, the true heir of the Kojèvian-Heideggerian school, understands this naturalizing tendency in terms of *Todesvergessenheit*, 'forgetfulness-of-death': once Thanatos is recalled with all its powerful traumatic force, the biological circle of smooth functionality gets irreversibly torn, while the psyche contracts its glorious 'sickness unto death' which only then turns it into a proper human subject. But the answer of Jean Laplanche, although he does not reject the death drive himself, can be phrased differently: *not in the thanatic register, which sees sublimation as rising above the clamour of life, but in the natalistic register, which sees sublimation as subsequent births and renewals of life*. Instead of employing the mythological arsenal of Eros versus Thanatos, to the biomorphic nostalgia Laplanche opposes a truly anthropogenic moment of *seduction* [*Verführen*], which differs from the seductive attraction of the objects put forward to sexuality by the vital order: the enigmatic influence of the first significant Other, constituting an exciting reverse to the material body fulfilling the biological needs of the infant. While the latter is pure functionalism of the mother–infant dyad, the former is the very antithesis of natural functionality, causing the immediate rift in the totality of primary narcissism. This rift is like a 'second birth' or a *neogenesis of sexuality*:

> *Verführen* means to make someone deviate from the straight path . . ., and in this case it means to make the infant deviate from the path of the biological and its 'attachments', and *create sexuality*, which will lead us towards something I have already mentioned a propos drive theory: we pass here by a contingent drive object and stop at the object that stimulates the child with a different kind of excitement, *Reiz*.[56]

The seduction inaugurates the *exodus out of biomorphic attachment* in which the desire deviates from the orthodoxy of *kata phusein* and begins to wander on the 'bent paths' of uncharted territories, in the pursuit of an enigmatic object which excites it with a new secret kind of attraction. *Reiz* does not refer here to anything concrete in the object capable of gratifying a need, but to the aura which determines its *otherness* and transcends any natural utility. In the moment of seduction, sexuality suddenly remembers what it was *zunächst* and *von Anfang an*: in this anamnetic 'neogenesis', it once again recovers its 'erring' quality.[57]

But this is also the moment in which sublimation takes a different route from perversion. While perversion seems so focused on the recovery of the autoerotic pleasure that it easily forgets about its object, which it either 'degrades' or turns into a dead fetish, a simple trigger of its own autonomous process – sublimation, availing itself of the symbolic realm of language, navigates between absolute objectless freedom of the drive and its equally absolute fixation on the object.[58] While perversion triumphs over Eros, by severing the link with the object, sublimation triumphs over Eros, by forming with the object a new type of relation which we may call with a term punning on the Pauline *agape*: 'strangerly love'.

This new object-choice is possible only due to a *truce* between sexuality and vital order: the 'messianic peace' between the fighting brothers, made possible only 'if the tears of Esau are wiped out' and Jacob reconciles himself with the 'man of nature'. It was actually Melanie Klein who formulated it that way. According to Klein, sublimation derives from the ceasefire between libido and self-preservatory drives, which constitutes the greatest achievement of the ego, always acting in the role of an inner-psychic peacemaker. Freud, whom she follows here very closely, says that 'sublimation takes place through the mediation of the ego', where libido subjugates to the ego's interests and becomes *ichgerecht*, ego-orientated.[59] But Klein's theory of the *ego* is richer than Freud's identification of the ego-drives with self-preservatory drives. The reason of the ego's intervention lies also in the fact that, of all psychic instances, only the ego can entertain relation with *total objects*: not the partial ones which cater to the needs and then become annexed by perversions, but the objects which truly transcend the realm of functionality.

Total object, despite what it might suggest, can never appear to the subject as such; it is *total* precisely because it cannot be grasped and appropriated in full; it never comes to absolute presence and thus resists internalization. It is total, because it is tolerated as partly absent and transcendent to any immanent system of needs, which it will always disturb, frustrate and invalidate. And the only instance which can bear it – similarly to the Pauline love which 'bears all' – is the ego, because only the ego can assume the 'depressive position'. Or, putting things more simply: ego *is* the depressive position itself.

For Klein – and we saw it already in Winnicott – the sublimatory process is parallel to the formation of the depressive position in which the psyche withdraws from immediate claims of objectual gratifications and, while retreating from the world, creates the outline of the 'I'. In the more primary schizoid-paranoid position, libido gets caught in a hopeless clinch of alternate attachment and destruction: first it claims objects of the vital order for its autoerotic purposes and then destroys them in the surplus enjoyment that does not want to know any limits. The genius of the depressive position allows us to get out of this idle cycle, by creating an *objectual partner for the remnant of the unbound libido*: an object which is also in the status of the remnant. Or, to put it in the rhetorical terms of Harold Bloom, it constitutes a total *figure* built on the canvas of the partial *sensus literalis* – where, for instance, the breast is no longer just the source of nourishment, but becomes a *synecdoche* or a *pars pro toto*, 'a part for a whole' of the enigmatic thing, simultaneously present and absent, called the mother. This *work of figuration* occurring in language, which Freud calls 'the work of idealization', is done precisely by the innovative play of the libidinal remnant which *creates the other in its own image*, i.e. partly hidden and in/de/finite, not to be exhausted by any attachment.

Pace Lacan, therefore, who perceives the sublimatory pursuit of desire as an endless metonymic succession of objects, in which none appears as *the* object able to embody the ideal[60] – I would say that the unreachability of the libidinal 'promised land' derives from the fact that the ultimate objectual correlate of human libido is and will always remain a *figure*. The Lacanian model based on the nostalgia after literalness does not give justice to the specificity of human drive which, following the Blakean Edenic Tigers, finds its proper element in the figurative constitution which lets its object *be*, by letting it be alien and absent, elusive and evasive – rather *fort*, than *da*.[61]

The truce between sexuality and vital order consists, thus, in establishing the common part between the two feuding parties: *survival*. Not just the drive unbound – and not simply quasi-instinctual self-preservation, but *sur-vie* in the precise Derridean understanding of the term, combining and reconciling both. Just as the Hegelian moment of reconciliation reveals the dialectical identity between the contraries, the depressive position works through the antithesis of 'life expanded' and 'life ordinary' – *more life* (*sur*) of Erros versus *mere life* (*vie*) of Eros – in order to find a liveable compromise. So far, it has been a battle to death, in which the victory of one party led to the destruction of the other. Now, thanks to the invention of the ego-forming depressivity, libido learns the lesson of ambivalence: even though life fights here against life, if the struggle is to continue, both antagonists must simply *live on*. The elementary maintenance in life, therefore, emerges – eventually and *at first* reluctantly – also as the interest of libido. The Ego 'desires to live and be loved', says Freud in 'The Ego and the Id' (FR, 657), which means that it wants simultaneously the continuation of life and the surplus of life in the form of love: the Derridean living/loving as the expression of self-preference. As a compromise formation, the ego is the mature form of the living subject which is finally capable of both.

But that also indicates a departure from Freud's too restrictive definition of the ego as the representative of the self-preservatory interests or, in Laplanche's words, a 'biomorphic formation'.[62] The ego would rather represent *more life* in which the two sides of the conflict, sexuality and vital order, finally come to reconciliation with respect to the issue of survival. For, when Freud writes that the Ego 'becomes filled with libido [and] it thus itself becomes the representative of Eros and thenceforward desires to live and to be loved' (FR, 657), and when Laplanche comments by stipulating that the ego not only becomes an 'image of life' but also an instance of '*love for life*; love for another, but also a love for oneself which makes our life more autonomous, less dependent on the changeable fate of our love for another'[63] – they both assign to the ego a role that clearly exceeds the self-preservatory function. If the ego supports here the *conservatio vitae*, it is not due to a quasi-instinctual impulse, but due to the libidinal investment in a *new* object called *life*: not just *my* life, but also the life of all those living creatures which now inspire its sympathy, curiosity, even fascination. The ego, therefore, constitutes something much more than just a biomorphic emanation of drives miming instincts of self-preservation; its 'will to live' is wider, *biophilic*. The ego engages in the process of sublimation in which it *converts* libido to the love of the living – and, thanks to this manoeuvre, becomes the Benjaminian *Fürschprech der Kreatur*, an advocate of the creaturely life which it now consciously shares with others, the *co-survivors*. The *converted libido* is thus still antagonistic to the simple *Lebensordnung* in its wish to transcend the latter's narrow demands; this wish, however, no longer realizes itself in a way which is destructive for the living psyche. Just as in Derrida's *torat hayim*, which combines the self-preservatory interest of 'myself' with the universal respect for the 'right to live', the exodus out of biomorphism occurs here not against life, but in the name of life: the biophilic *more life*, simultaneously rooted in 'my' life and transcending it towards universalization which, as Derrida emphasizes, can only occur in and thanks to language. We can now finally give full flesh to the enigmatic statement of Derrida that accompanied this book throughout as a harbinger of the 'awakening of the Judaic tradition': this is precisely what is means to dialectically oppose 'life against life, but always for life and in life'. It is the way of sur-vival of the mature living/loving ego, in love with its own and others' life 'alike', *kamokha*.[64]

To recapitulate the whole story: The first element of the original libido *ohne Bindung* is the amorphic night of *jouissance* whose only manifestation in the material world of objects is violent and destructive: by turning everything and anything into a vehicle of its pleromatic autoerotic joy, libido annihilates every single finite object it attaches itself to. The next stage is marked by self-oblivion and distortion; libido, by submitting to the vital order, lends it its energy and begins to serve the biological purposes of Eros, from self-preservation to self-reproduction. It is only due to the truce negotiated by the ego that the objectless drive 'without qualities' undergoes dialectical *conversion* which – synonymous with the psychoanalytic miracle of turning the vinegar of anxiety back into wine – fully deserves the messianic name of *geringes Zurechtstellen*, this slight and at the same time revolutionary reversal that occurs in the human psyche: libido for the first time enters the light of the day. The self-contained autotelic joy which knows nothing apart from itself, is not overcome and defeated; rather, it *converts* into a biophilic love ready to 'pace the orbit of the whole world'. It is only with this last conversion – of the original drive to life – that *finitum* becomes *capax infiniti*: before the excessive drive could have only destroyed the finite vessel of the psyche, now the drive's in/de/finity can be reconciled with its finite ways. *From objectlessness, through fixation, to relations.*

The sublimated love, therefore, is the libido which crossed the line and joined the side of *survie*. Or, in more Rosenzweigian idiom, love is the libido that began to believe in life, i.e. underwent a *conversion to life*, where *con-versio* maintains common root with *per-versio*, both suggesting a deviation from the straight path of anything 'natural'. It is thanks to this conversion that the original in/de/finite libido – this most problematic given of human life, its truly *damned part*, or a curse constantly threatening with self-annihilation – turns eventually into a blessing: the apocalyptic night of universal destruction, correlating only with *nothing*, turns into a wide open day which, via language, lets live 'anything and everything'. In the last lines of *Paradise Lost*, Milton depicts this conversion as a sudden change of heart of the first parents who wipe their 'natural tears' – 'the tears of Esau' indeed – and see *the whole world before them* ... This new vision, forbidden to their former autoerotic pleasures, entices in them *curiosity* – a new *Reiz* – which immediately makes them forget about the Paradise. The new pleroma is right before their eyes, Here Below, on earth: ready to be addressed by this great poem which performatively does on the level of form what it also describes on the level of content.

*   *   *

Nietzsche calls this new libidinal attitude a 'great love', *die grosse Liebe*: the arch-affirming Yes that conditions and precedes all later negations and which comes to the fore at the 'noon, moment of shortest shadow'.[65] Paraphrasing Nietzsche, we can now finally ask: 'Have all these Platonic shadows cease to darken our minds?'[66] Have we managed to rescue the finite life out of the influence of the acephalic Neoplatonic 'metaphysics of death' which still haunts us with its vision of the Fall, despite the long-gone loss of its divine head? Have we rehabilitated *survival* as a living/loving condition against its continuous denigration as unworthy of any symbolic investment? Have we reconstructed another finitude as a being-towards-birth, now properly instructed how to tarry with the negativity of dying? Have we proven, after *torat hayim*, that love is as strong as death? Have we succeeded in our series of *conversions*, reversing the Fall into falling-in-love, dying into birthing, ending into initiating, Thanatos into *Erros*?

As Derrida would have probably replied: *perhaps, perhaps...* The thanatic syndrome of the systematic overestimation of death, from Plato to Lacan, is not something that could go away at one blow: it must constantly be opposed and patiently deconstructed. Philosophy will always favour its thanatic games, so, in the end, the true appreciation of survival can only be found in those who see into the life of language and understand that it is precisely its symbolic play that allows us to fall in love with the finite condition of ourselves and others 'alike'. It would seem, therefore, that what truly remains, establish the poets:

> But because being here is a lot: because everything here
> Seems to need us, this fleeting world, which is in some strange way
> Concerns us. Us, the most fleeting of all. *Once*
> For each thing, just *once*. *Once* and no more. And we too,
> Just *once*. And never again. But to have been
> This *once*, even if only *once*:
> To have been earthly, seems irrevocable.[67]

Notes

Preface: *Finitum Capax Infiniti*

1   Hannah Arendt, *Between Past and Future: Eight Exercises in Political Thought*, London: Penguin, 2006, p. 75.

2   Søren Kierkegaard, *The Sickness Unto Death*, trans. Walter Lowrie, New York: Anchor, 1954, p. 163; my emphasis.

3   Ernest Becker, *The Denial of Death*, New York: The Free Press, 1973, p. 51.

4   Saint Augustine, *The City of God*, trans. John Healey, Edinburgh: John Grant, 1909, XIII, 10. On the relationship between Heidegger and Augustine, see most of all Judith Wolfe, *Heidegger's Eschatology: Theological Horizons in Martin Heidegger's Early Thought*, Oxford: Oxford University Press, 2013, Chapter 3.

5   Nietzsche describes the philosophical task of 'vanquishing God's shadow' as a 'new struggle': 'After Buddha was dead, his shadow was still shown for centuries in a cave – a tremendous, gruesome shadow. God is dead; but given the way of men, there may still be caves for thousands of years in which his shadow will be shown. – And we – we still have to vanquish his shadow, too': Friedrich Nietzsche, *The Gay Science*, trans. Walter Kaufman, New York: Vintage Books, 1974, aphorism no. 108, p. 167.

6   The quote reverses the statement of Jean-Luc Nancy: 'Finitude is not privation' (SOTW, 29).

7   In *Kant and the Problem of Metaphysics*, where Heidegger for the first time thinks finitude in strictly necessary metaphysical terms – as a new foundation of metaphysics, which allows a 'comprehension of Being as such' – the *Endlichkeit* is nonetheless traditionally conceived in privative terms, i.e. as *Nichtigkeit*, the mode of being lapsing into nothingness, the mark of which is anxiety:

> Anxiety is that fundamental feeling which places us before the Nothing. The Being of the essent is comprehensible . . . only if Dasein on the basis of its essence holds itself into Nothing. Holding oneself into Nothing is no arbitrary and casual attempt to 'think' about this Nothing but an event which underlies all feeling oneself [*Sichbefinden*] in the midst of essents already on hand. The intrinsic possibility of this event must be clarified: in this lies the innermost finitude of transcendence in a fundamental-ontological analytic of Dasein.
> Martin Heidegger, *Kant and the Problem of Metaphysics*, trans. James S. Churchill, Bloomington: Indiana University Press, 1962, p. 246

Compare also the comment of Emmanuel Lévinas: 'Since Kant, philosophy has been finitude without infinity' (GDT, 36).

8 Friedrich Nietzsche, *The Twilight of the Idols or How to Philosophize with a Hammer*, trans. Judith Norman, Cambridge: Cambridge University Press, 2005, p. 171.

9 Heidegger, *Kant*, p. 247.

10 For Benjamin, the secret of this reversal lies in the nature of allegory which denies the world experience its illusory richness and dries it up to the bone: 'In God's world allegorist awakens . . . Subjectivity, like an angel falling into the depths, is brought back by allegories, and is held fast in heaven, in God, by *ponderacion mysteriosa*': Walter Benjamin, *The Origin of German Tragic Drama*, trans. John Osborne, London: Verso, 1998, pp. 232, 235.

11 See most of all Scholem's essay, 'Nihilism as a Religious Phenomenon' ('*Der Nihilismus als religiöses Phänomen*'), as well as the detailed analysis of his position in my *Jewish Cryptotheologies of Late Modernity: Philosophical Marranos*, Abingdon: Routledge, 2014, especially the chapter: 'Another Nihilism: Disenchantment in Jewish Perspective', pp. 255–91.

12 The rule refers to the famous line from Hölderlin's *Patmos*: 'Wo aber ist Gefähr, wächst das Rettende auch' (in James Mitchell's translation: 'But where there is danger, a rescuing element grows as well': see Friedrich Hölderlin, *Poems of Friedrich Hölderlin*, trans. James Mitchell, San Francisco: Ithuriel's Spear, 2004, p. 39). Scholem articulated his own version of Hölderlin's rule in one of his poems: 'Nie könnte Gott dir näher sein, / Also wo Verzweiflung auch zerbirst: / In Zions selbstversunkenem Licht' ('Never is God closer to you / as in the deepest doubt: / in the selfwithdrawn light of Zion').

13 Becker, *The Denial of Death*, p. 201.

14 The best description of this ideal hypostasis of 'the unexhaustible infinity of Life: its tireless, unwearied, unfailing nature, as if boiling over with life' can be found in Pierre Hadot's *Plotinus or the Simplicity of Vision*, trans. Michael Chase, Chicago: University of Chicago Press, 1993, pp. 46–7 (my emphasis):

> With this experience of total presence, we touch upon the most profound point of the Plotinian experience of Life. Life is total presence, since it is a simple, infinite force which diffuses itself in dynamic continuity. Plotinus seizes Life from within as pure movement which is everywhere and unceasing. It is 'already there', prior to all articular forms it engenders, and it does not cease in them . . . it is *pure presence . . . Life is a presence which always precedes us.*

Life, therefore, is not an attribute of the living: it is a hypostatic 'well of infinity' in which all the living participate 'for a while.'

15 Augustine, *Confessions*, trans. Henry Chadwick, Oxford: Oxford University Press, 1991, X, xvii, 26. On the notion of the vicarious living 'by proxy', see also Jean-Luc Marion who confirms that Heidegger's *Sein-zum-Tode* is indeed of the Augustinian provenance:

For ... no living thing is its own life; every living thing lives through the life that
it is not and does not possess, not through itself ... What is proper to the living
consists in that it does not possess its own life but remains a tenant of it. 'To live'
means 'to live for the time being' because, more essentially, by a proxy – by virtue
of the proxy that life accords the living [...] *living gives only the certainty of dying.*
Only the Living par excellence lives from itself.

> Jean-Luc Marion, *In the Self's Place: The Approach of Saint Augustine*, trans.
> Jeffrey Kosky, Stanford: Stanford University Press, 2012, p. 60; my emphasis

16 The transformation of 'mere life' into 'more life', yet still within the condition of
finitude, is highly characteristic of the Jewish type of messianism, to which I will
very often return in this book. Unlike Christian messianism which contrasts finite
life with life infinite and immortal, Jewish messianism, operating within Judaism as
predominantly 'religion of the finite life', translates this opposition into the
immanentist tension between 'bare life' – minimal, vegetative and thus barely living
– and 'more life', augmented, asserted and intensified. On the application of this
messianic rule: see my *The Saving Lie: Harold Bloom and Deconstruction*, Evanston,
IL: Northwestern University Press, 2011, which explains the uses of the Bloomian
slogan of *more life!*, as well as *Jewish Cryptotheologies*, especially the chapter on Jacob
Taubes ('The Identity of the Spirit'), from whom the formula of the 'maximalization
of existence' derives.

17 Some could say, however, that this is precisely what Heidegger himself intended to
do, that is: to think human finitude beyond the 'list of imperfections' and as a new
ground of metaphysics, which would allow Dasein to enjoy a different type of
infinity, by being infinitely creative. And indeed, the last paragraph of *Kant and the
Problem of Metaphysics* attests to this tendency:

> Does it make sense and is it justifiable to think that man, because his finitude
> makes an ontology, i.e., a comprehension of Being necessary to him, is 'creative'
> and therefore 'infinite' when nothing is so radically opposed to ontology as the
> idea of an infinite being? But is it possible to develop the finitude in Dasein even
> as a problem without 'presupposing' an infinitude? What is the nature of this
> 'presupposition' in Dasein? What is the significance of the infinitude thus 'posed'?
>
> p. 254

My book attempts to answer these questions, yet by moving away from the shadow
of the Heideggerian analytics of Dasein.

18 The idea that human existence is a 'living contradiction' because it constitutes the
dynamic clash of the finite and the infinite, appears for the first time in Hegel's
philosophy, yet it has earlier theological roots. Hegel uses Martin Luther's notion of
finitum capax infiniti, 'the finite capable to grasp/carry the infinite', which separated
the Lutheran Reformation from that of Calvin and Zwingli who claimed otherwise:

finitum non capax infiniti, i.e. the finite is not able either to grasp or contain the infinite. On the use of Luther's seminal formula of *finitum capax infiniti* see the comprehensive commentary of Ulrich Asendorf, *Luther and Hegel: Untersuchung zur Grundlegung einer Neuen Systematischen Theologie*, Wiesbaden: Franz Steiner, 1982, most of all pp. 196, 358, 389.

19 G.W.F. Hegel, *Science of Logic*, trans. A.V. Miller, London: Allen and Unwin, 1969, p. 770; my emphasis.

20 In the Note to paragraph 81 of *The Encyclopaedia of Philosophical Sciences*, called 'Dialectic', Hegel makes a direct connection between dialectical thinking and the self-contradictory nature of the finite life:

> We say, for instance, that man is mortal, and seem to think that the ground of his death is in external circumstances only; so that if this way of looking were correct, man would have two special properties, vitality and – also – mortality. But the true view of the matter is that *life as life, involves the germ of death, and that the finite, being radically self-contradictory, involves its own self-suppression.*
> G.W.F. Hegel, *The Encyclopaedia of Philosophical Sciences*, trans. William Wallace, Oxford: Clarendon Press, 1971; my emphasis

21 Here I will just point to one important early modern source that seems precursory to the late-modern vitalist arguments of the so-called affirmative biopolitics: Fichte's lectures on 'the blessed life', to which Gilles Deleuze refers in his last cultic essay, 'Immanence: A Life'. These late public lectures, composed a few decades after the *Wissenschaftslehre*, which followed strictly the Kantian transcendental doctrine, announce a curious shift in regard to the problem of finitude as raised by Kant: a kind of a Neoplatonic backlash against the Kantian restrictions, yet, officially, still conducted within the post-Kantian frame of thinking. The beginning of the lecture sounds very promising (at least, from my perspective) and could indeed derive straight from late Derrida. Fichte says:

> Life is itself Blessedness. It cannot be otherwise; for Life is Love, and the whole form and power of Life consists in Love, and spring from love ... Love is satisfaction with itself, joy in itself, enjoyment of itself – and therefore Blessedness; and thus it is clear that Life, Love, and Blessedness, are absolutely one and the same ... What thou lovest, is that thou livest. This very Love is thy Life – the root, the seat, the central-point of thy being.
> Johann Gottlieb Fichte, *The Way Towards the Blessed Life, or the Doctrine of Religion*, trans. William Smith, London: John Chapman, 1849, pp. 2–3

Yet, it soon becomes absolutely clear that the life you love is not the life you actually have, which turns out to be an only 'apparent life': an 'incomplete existence which is an admixture of the dead with the living' (ibid., 3) or, as Hegel put it, a contradiction that '*involves its own self-suppression*'. The 'true life', on the other hand, cannot die, for 'there can be no real Death' (ibid., 3): the true being knows no mutability, transience, lack. Therefore, if you love your life, you love only *a* 'true life' which knows no death – the spark of the life eternal burning in your soul – and not the finite process of life, which is nothing but an 'appearance', a mere *Schein*, belonging to the lower realm of degradation and privation of real being. This vitalist ruse will be repeated, practically verbatim, by Deleuze: you might think that what you love is your life as it is, but no – after a careful philosophical analysis, it becomes, as Fichte used to say, *sonnenklar*, that one can only love the eternal and everlasting: the indefinite *A Life* as a pleroma of a not yet actualized virtuality. Just as for Fichte, for Deleuze too, life is a pure flow of unrestricted energy: it is 'the immanence of immanence, absolute immanence: it is complete power, complete bliss': Gilles Deleuze, *Pure Immanence: Essays on A Life*, trans. Anne Boyman, New York: Zone Books, 2001, p. 27. While *the* life bound by the subjective structure, which sets the limit on its original *flux*, is a 'neutralizing, mortifying life', *a* life unbound and free knows no limit apart from what it is itself: '*a* pure plane of immanence, univocality, composition, upon which everything is given, upon which unformed elements and materials dance that are distinguished from one another only by their speed and that enter into this or that individuated assemblage depending on their connections, their relations of movement. *A fixed plane of life upon which everything stirs, slows down or accelerates*': Gilles Deleuze and Félix Guattari, *A Thousand Plateaus*, trans. Robert Hurley, Mark Seem and Helen R. Lane, Minneapolis: University of Minnesota Press, 2000, p. 255; my emphasis. This is precisely the assumption which I will challenge in this book, by claiming – after Derrida – the very opposite: that just as one can only live *this* life, one can only love the finite and precarious.

22 The term 'sombre mythology' derives from Freud's letter to Albert Einstein from 1932, in which he states his pessimistic views on the innate violence of human drives. See Sigmund Freud, *Why War?* (SE 22, 211).

23 Nietzsche, *The Gay Science*, 'Preface for the Second Edition', p. 37.

24 In a sense, my project could also be seen as a continuation of the great work of Eric Santner (see PEL), but with a strong *clinamen* from the precursor: while Santner unites New Thinking with the predominantly Lacanian psychoanalysis and focuses mostly on the issue of death and Thanatos, I aim at the synthesis of Rosenzweig's vitalism with Freud's early theory of drives, which was discarded by Lacan.

Introduction: Life Before Death, an Outline

1 See Hegel again: 'Nature is for man only the starting-point which he has to transform. The theological doctrine of original sin is a profound truth; but modern

enlightenment prefers to believe that man is naturally good, and that he acts right so long as he continues *true to nature*': *Encyclopaedia of Philosophical Sciences*, par. 24.

2   In the classical formulation of Anaximander, to which Heidegger devoted his famous essay: 'Whence things have their origin, / Thence also their destruction happens, / According to necessity; / For they give to each other justice and recompense / For their injustice / In conformity with the ordinance of Time.' Martin Heidegger, 'Anaximander Fragment', in *Early Greek Thinking*, trans. David Farrell Krell, San Francisco: Harper and Row, 1975, p. 20.

3   Foucault defines 'biopolitics' as 'the attempt, starting from the eighteenth century, to rationalize the problems posed to governmental practice by phenomena characteristic of a set of living beings forming a population: health, hygiene, birthrate, life expectancy, race': Michel Foucault, *The Birth of Biopolitics: Lectures at the Collège de France 1978–79*, ed. Michel Senellart, trans. Graham Burchell, Houndmills and New York: Palgrave Macmillan, 2008, p. 317. In Foucault's description of the 'birth of biopolitics', this investment in 'naturalness' of the process of governing is already completely disenchanted: the physiocracy of the first modern biopoliticians does not extol any sacred and eternal laws of nature that would secure their legitimacy. They rather seek to attune their method of governing to the natural rhythm, based on the rule of all physicians (i.e. literally, the 'experts on nature') which is *primum non nocere*, 'first: do not interfere'. Naturalness has its own course, its own spontaneous manner of achieving 'success' and it is precisely this natural efficiency that becomes the guiding light of the liberal government:

> Political economy does not discover natural rights that exist prior to the exercise of governmentality; it discovers a certain naturalness specific to the practice of government itself . . . The notion of nature will thus be transformed with the appearance of political economy. For political economy, nature is not an original and reserved region on which the exercise of power should not impinge, on pain of being illegitimate. Nature is something that runs under, through, and in the exercise of governmentality. It is, if you like, its indispensable hypodermis . . . governmental practice can only do what it has to do by respecting this nature.
>
>   ibid., pp. 15–16

4   The best speculative account of the history of the concept of *phusis* is given by Pierre Hadot in his book *The Veil of Isis: An Essay on the History of the Idea of Nature*, trans. Michael Chase, Cambridge, MA: The Belknap Press of Harvard University Press, 2006, where he begins with Heraclitus, goes through Schiller and Nietzsche, and ends with Merleau-Ponty. The main subject of the essay is the 'secret of nature' which 'loves to hide' (p. 1), i.e. the mysterious bond of inner natural necessities which organize every individual 'growth' into a system of becoming and perishing. Hadot thus interprets the famous aphorism of Heraclitus – *phusis kruptesthai philei* – as 'what is born tends to disappear' or 'what is born wants to die' (p. 11).

5   The mistrust towards nature as the least inventive system of beings – just 'sitting there', hopelessly and aimlessly – constitutes a frequent motif in Jewish writings of all ages, from Mishna to Derrida. Even such a seemingly enthusiastic naturalist as Spinoza thought nature to be 'badly arranged' and as such wasting too much energy, which should be used in cooperation rather than squandered on futile antagonisms, the last of which is death: the ultimate 'bad encounter' of two blindly hostile *conatus*. We will find the same line of critique in Henri Bergson and Hans Jonas. In their 'philosophy of biology' they both build a clear opposition between the two forces of life: the conservative, self-repeating and inertial system of preservation (which tends towards necessities and laws) and the progressive, innovative force of ongoing creation (which is creation proper, i.e. capable of creating truly new forms, not just forms potentially pre-existing). But there is no lofty secret hidden in the former that only sustains the circulation of birth and decay; the mystery now travels on the other side, where the proper creative evolution takes place. On this understanding, 'nature', as a self-preserving system, is nothing but a tautology: a not-at-all mysterious self-evidence of being which, in order to be, must preserve itself in a form of repetition. Hans Jonas says:

> The foundation of all order in nature, of any nature at all, lies in the laws of conservation. But these have come to govern because it is only self-conserving reality that conserves itself. *This tautology explains the lawfulness of nature as it is given to us*: nature itself is already a result of selection, a universal result which then posits rules for further, more specific, and local selections.
>
> Hans Jonas, *Mortality and Morality: Search for God After Auschwitz*, trans. Lawrence Vogel, Chicago: Northwestern University Press, p. 168; my emphasis

6   Compare Erich Gutkind who, in his *Choose Life*, nicely summarizes the discursive atmosphere of the group of the German Jewry in between the wars (Landauer, Buber, Bloch, Benjamin) who decided to redefine 'philosophically' the Hebrew *torat hayim*: 'The Jewish revolution restores the growth, man's never ending transcendence of himself. Revolution and transcendence are very much akin. The equation: transcendence-revolution may restore both terms to their fullest efficacy; it is a mutual reevaluation'; Erich Gutkind, *Choose Life: The Biblical Call to Revolt*, New York: Henry Shuman, 1952, p. 74.

7   See Walter Benjamin, 'Der Erzähler. Betrachtungen zum Werk Nikolai Lesskows', *Gesammelte Schriften*, Bd II, 2, Frankfurt am Main: Suhrkamp, 1977, p. 463.

8   Gilbert Simondon, 'The Genesis of the Individual', in *Incorporations*, ed. J. Crary and S. Kwinter, New York: Zone Books, 1992, p. 305; my emphasis.

9   Simondon's idea of the subject bringing more and more preindividual reality into play via the linguistic medium will find an interesting reflection in D.W. Winnicott's psychoanalytic approach to play, most of all playing with language, which I am going to explore in Chapter 4.

10 In this context, compare the praise of vital curiosity as a 'feeler' going boldly 'in all directions' coming from Adorno's last sketch to *The Dialectic of Enlightenment*:

> The higher animals have themselves to thank for their greater freedom; their existence is evidence that feelers were once stretched out in new directions and not repulsed. Each of their species is a monument to countless others whose attempts to develop were blocked at the outset, which gave way to fright if only a single feeler stirred in the path of their evolution. The *suppression of possibilities* by the direct resistance of surrounding nature is extended inwardly by the wasting of organs through fright. *Each time an animal looks out with curiosity a new form of the living dawns, a form which might emerge from the clearly formed species to which the individual creature belongs.*
>
> DE, 213; my emphasis

11 'In some remote corner of the universe, poured out and glittering in innumerable solar systems, there once was a star on which clever animals invented knowledge. That was the highest and most mendacious minute of world history – *yet only a minute*. After nature had drawn a few breaths the star grew cold, and the clever animals had to die': Friedrich Nietzsche, 'On Truth and Lie in an Extra-Moral Sense', in *Friedrich Nietzsche on Rhetoric and Language*, ed. and trans. Sander L. Gilman, Carole Blair and David J. Parent, Oxford: Oxford University Press, 1989, p. 246.

12 Friedrich Nietzsche, *Beyond Good and Evil: Prelude to a Philosophy of the Future*, trans. Helen Zimmern, CreateSpace, 2016, p. 7.

13 Esposito, however, who is more eager to affirm a more ambitious aspect of biopolitics, claims that Foucault is wrong in attributing a disciplining strain to the modern biopolitical regime. For him, discipline belongs only to the sovereign form of power which is strictly external to life. He proposes instead to use the term 'regularization': 'It [biopower] is the power to make live. Sovereignty took life and let live. And now we have the emergence of a power that I would call the power of regularization, and it, in contrast, consists in making live and letting die' (B, 49). Yet, this is precisely the move anticipated by Foucault himself: the way late Foucault modifies and redefines his concept of disciplining practices within the Neostoic context of 'perfecting our nature', chimes well with the milder, merely regularizing, procedures affirmed by Esposito. When discipline becomes internalized and the law becomes life itself, there is no longer a gap of externality that would separate them – while this gap is the necessary condition of a sovereign power which must be perceived as coming 'from beyond'.

14 Marcus Aurelius, *Meditations*, trans. G.M.A. Grube, Indianapolis: Bobbs-Merrill, 1963, pp. 16, 14.

15 Michel Foucault, 'Le souci de la verité: Entretien avec F. Ewald', *Dits et écrits II, 1976–1988*, Paris: Gallimard, 2001, p. 1492.

16 Foucault makes this 'medicinal' connection very clear himself:

> In keeping with a tradition that goes back a very long way in Greek culture, the
> care of the self is in close correlation with medical thought and practice ... The
> practice of the self implies that one should form the image of oneself not simply
> as an imperfect, ignorant individual who requires correction, training, and
> instruction, but also one who suffers from certain ills and who needs to have
> them treated, either by oneself or by someone who has the necessary competence.
> Everyone one must discover that he is in a state of need, that he needs to receive
> medication and assistance.
>
> Michel Foucault, *Care of the Self: The History of Sexuality III*,
> trans. Robert Hurley, London: Penguin, 1986, pp. 54, 57

For Galen, irrational passions and logical mistakes belong to the same domain: 'both
are commonly called errors in a generic sense' (ibid., 56).

17 Michel Foucault, 'La vie: l'expérience et la science', *Dits et écrits II*, p. 1595.

18 The same motif appears also in Sloterdijk's concept of *Zähmung/Züchtung*
[domestication] as opposed to the dangers of *Enthemmung* [unchainment]. In his
essay, *Regeln für den Menschenpark* [*Rules of the Human Zoo*], Sloterdijk sketches the
biopolitical vision of postmodern humanity as the Nietzschean Last Men who
alternate between domestication and unchainment, i.e. between the necessary
submission to the laws regulating human behaviour and occasional outbursts of
instinctual anarchy. Similarly to Foucault, Sloterdijk accepts the 'natural' confinement
of human life as finite, mortal and reduced to the physiological cycle of birth and
death, but rejects liberal naiveté in regard to the seemingly natural human capability
of self-regulation. Sloterdijk follows Herder's definition of man as *Mangelwesen*
[deficient being] which, deprived naturally, has to compensate for this lack in
cultural self-formation. Culture may then indeed be seen as a process of cultivation:
of turning an anarchic, dangerous and destructive human animal into a tamed
creature, only then capable of survival. Following Herder, but also Heidegger,
Sloterdijk calls man an 'early birther' (*frühgeburtliches Wesen*), characterized by a
'growing excess of animal unpreparedness to survive in its surrounding world' (*der
wachsende Überschuss an animalischer Unfertigkeit in ihre Umwelten heraustreten*).
The human being is thus a creature determined by the concepts of neoteny and 'the
chronic animal immaturity': 'Man is the product of a hyper-birth which turns him
from a suckling into a worldling [*Weltling*]'. Because of his premature birth, the
human being is born unable to survive on its own and is far more helpless than any
other natural being – yet this natural lack is soon compensated by the richness of the
world experience that no animal, always limited to its niche, can attain: Peter
Sloterdijk, *Regeln für den Menschenpark: Ein Antwortschreiben zu Heideggers Brief
über Humanismus*, Frankfurt am Main: Suhrkamp, 1999, pp. 33–4. And while

Sloterdijk refers to Herder, Foucault finds an analogical support in Georges Canguilhem. Just as Herder saw the instinctual equipment of human beings deficient and regarded culture as a necessary compensation for this natural lack, Canguilhem perceived life – and particularly human life – as the 'process of error' to which cultures, with their religious, philosophical and finally scientific insistence on 'truth' offer indispensable 'correction': 'The opposition of true and false ... is probably nothing else but the secondary response to the possibility of error intrinsic to life ... For Canguilhem, the error is the permanent aleatory matrix around which the whole history of life and human development evolves': Foucault, 'La vie: l'expérience et la science', pp. 1593–4. In fact, Stoics already maintained a similar view of the anthropological difference. In *Care of the Self*, Foucault, while referring to Epictetus, summarizes it as follows:

> Man is defined in the *Discourses* as the being who was destined to care for himself. This is where the basic difference between him and other creatures resides. The animals find 'ready prepared' that which they need in order to live, for nature had so arranged things that animals are at our disposal without their having to look after themselves, and without our having to look after them. Man, on the other hand, must attend to himself.
>
>   p. 47

And although Epictetus immediately adds that this care is not a 'consequence of some defect that would put man in a situation of need and make him in this respect inferior to the animals' (ibid.), the 'medicinal' context in which he discusses *epimeleia heautou or cura sui* as indeed 'curation' leaves no doubt as to the final conclusion: that the human 'situation' is not blessing in itself, but it can turn for good – as the exercise of self-care unknown in the animal kingdom – only if properly 'treated'.

19 Santner defines nomotropism as the Jewish mode of legalistic discipline which 'exits' the pagan world of natural erotic enjoyment and submits the subject to a thorough reconstitution 'according to the law':

> By nomotropism, I mean the obsessive compulsive preoccupation with nomos, in the matters of law, justice, and ethics, which for Freud also comprised the compulsive dimension of the search for scientific truth, the *Zwang* internal to *Wissenschaft*. In the one case – cosmotheism – we find direct enjoyment of cosmic Eros, of *deum sive natura*, while in nomotropism 'enjoyment' is conceived as an ambiguous libidinal tension strictly correlative to the turn to the Law.
>
>   Eric L. Santner, 'Freud's "Moses" and the Ethics of Nomotropic Desire',
>   *October*, 88 (1999): 14

And while Santner, here following the Jewish tradition, identifies the natural element within the human psyche with the erotic anarchy of drives, I claim that the idea of nature already emerges as a canvas for existential legislation and that the Greek rule of *kata phusein* is the first nomotropic step beyond the original instinctual anarchy. In that sense, the biopolitical paradigm may indeed indicate a regression to the 'pagan' philosophy of life, yet not in terms of the return of repressed instincts, but rather in the Foucauldian Neostoic terms of the nomotropic 'living according to nature'.

20 Johann Gottfried Herder, *Essay on the Origin of Language*, trans. Alexander Gode, Chicago: University of Chicago Press 1966, p. 108.

21 Sigmund Freud, *Civilization and Its Discontents*, SE21, section 7: first paragraph.

22 See Jean Laplanche, *Nouveaux fondements pour la psychanalyse*, PUF: Paris 1987, p. 51: 'This false interiorized biology has its deep reasons: in the infantile psyche, the vital order, which represents the self-preservatory interests, cannot be just represented, it must also be helped and assisted (*vicarié et supplée*), because the excess of the libido could make the psyche accept immediate death.' And while commenting on Freud's *Three Essays in the Theory of Sexuality*, Laplanche says: 'Their main purpose is to demonstrate the fundamental orientation which governs the evolution of human psyche and which runs from the instinct lost to the instinct regained ... Yet, this instinct regained is merely an instinct mimed (*instinct mimé*), a substitute instinct, which only imitates the instinct proper' (ibid., 33–4). Thus, biomorphism merely compensates for the lost biologism, it cannot fully replace it. More on this in Chapter 4.

23 See note 25.

24 A quite separate attempt to restore the tradition of life has been recently undertaken by Luce Irigaray who in *To Be Born* (Cham, Switzerland: Palgrave Macmillan, 2017) claims that 'instead of recognizing that life itself involves transcendence, and of teaching children to transcend themselves, than to a cultivation and a sharing of life, teachers more often than not require them to *forget life*, to live life at home ... and to confine life as such at the level of needs' (p. 2; my emphasis). For Irigaray, the paradigmatic event of life, which needs to be cultivated by a symbolic tradition, is birth and the first breath in which the child for the first time seizes life as its own and thus effectuates a break that ruptures the dependent existence of the prenatal stage. Although referring mostly to Heidegger and not mentioning Arendt even once, Irigaray's little book is wholly on the latter's natalist side: we shall come back to this topic in Chapter 2, 'Being-Towards-Birth'.

25 The notion of the 'symbolic suicide' as the model for the modern revolutionary who boldly disdains the necessities of life and is ready to 'die for a Cause' is championed mostly by Slavoj Žižek who in this act of self-offering / submission to the Law of Death locates the very gist of humanity: 'The death drive is not merely a direct nihilistic opposition to any life-asserting attachment; rather, it is the very formal structure of the reference to Nothingness that enables us to overcome the *stupid self-contended life-rhythm*, in order to become "passionately attached" to some Cause – be it love, art,

knowledge or politics – for which we are ready to risk everything': Slavoj Žižek, *The Ticklish Subject: The Absent Centre of Political Ontology*, London: Verso, 2009, p. 127; my emphasis.

26 A polemical paraphrase of Žižek's statement: 'Serving the Law is the highest adventure': Slavoj Žižek, *The Puppet and the Dwarf: The Perverse Core of Christianity*, Cambridge, MA: MIT Press, 2003, p. 56.

27 Slavoj Žižek, *Less than Nothing: Hegel and the Shadow of Dialectical Materialism*, London: Verso, 2012, p. 905.

28 Gershom Scholem, *Über einige Grundbegriffe des Judentums*, Frankfurt am Main: Suhrkamp, 1970, p. 167. The idea of the life in postponement, however, appears in Scholem's work as early as 1919, where it serves to describe the structure of the Jewish messianic temporality, and it is quite tempting to assume that Adorno, who knew and read Scholem, could have used it in his analysis of the bourgeois mentality which always waits and defers the vital fulfilment – or happiness – indefinitely.

29 This diagnosis has been recently confirmed in a powerful way by Roberto Esposito who – in a similar manner, although with no reference to *The Dialectic of Enlightenment* – criticized the 'Hobbesian subject' as the one who overprotects himself against the dangers of nature (both biological and social) and because of that loses life:

> What is sacrificed is nothing other than the *cum*, the relation among men, and for that reason as well, in some way men themselves are sacrificed. They are paradoxically sacrificed to their own survival. They live in and of their refusal to live together [convivere]. It's impossible not to recognize here a remnant of irrationality that is subtly introduced into the folds of the most rational of systems: life is preserved through the presupposition of its sacrifice, the sum of refusals out of which sovereign authorization is made. *Life is sacrificed to the preservation of life*. In this convergence of the preservation of life and its capacity to be sacrificed, modern immunization reaches the height of its own destructive power [*potenza*].
>
> Roberto Esposito, *Communitas: The Origin and Destiny of Community*, trans. Timothy Campbell, Stanford: Stanford University Press, 2009, p. 14; my emphasis

In Chapter 3, devoted to Derrida, we will see the same logic unfolding under the heading of auto/immunity.

30 Theodor W. Adorno, *The Jargon of Authenticity*, trans. Knut Tarnowski and Frederic Will, Evanston, IL: Northwestern University Press, 1973, pp. 134–5.

31 Adorno, *Jargon*, p. 133.

32 Adorno never changed his mind about Heidegger, who remained for him a deeply non-metaphysical thinker. Despite all his lofty declarations, Heidegger can never truly transgress the subjective predicament of self-preservation, marked by fear and violence, and this lack of transcendence deprived him of any deeper reflection on death:

Curiously, Heidegger sought to use reflection on death to discourage, precisely, reflection on death … any reflections on death are [here] of such a necessarily general and formal kind that they amount to tautologies, like the definition of death as the possibility of the absolute non-being of existence … or another, less well-known formulation of Heidegger, in which he solemnly announces that, when we die, a corpse is left behind.

MCP, 130–1

According to Adorno, this tautological character of Heideggerian *Todesdenken* derives from the self-preservatory defence mechanisms that, in fact, block any serious thinking of death. Thus, even if 'humans are clearly the only ones which in general have a consciousness of the fact that they must die' – 'human consciousness is not capable of withstanding the experience of death' (MCP, 131). Heidegger, therefore, despite his praise of the unfallen authentic life at the heights of death-awareness, would still *fall* – the irony of ironies indeed! – into 'a too much thrall to the biological life' (MCP, 132), which is precisely the gist of his accusation against Judaism formulated in the Black Notebooks. More on this in Chapter 1.

33 Jacques Derrida, 'Canons and Metonymies: An Interview with Jacques Derrida', trans. Richard Rand and Amy Wygant, in *Logomachia: The Conflict of the Faculties*, ed. Richard Rand, Lincoln: University of Nebraska Press, 1992, pp. 211–12. Compare also an emotional statement of Elie Wiesel which could become an epigraph to Derrida's efforts: 'For the survivor death is not a problem. Death was an everyday occurrence. We learned to live with death. The problem is to adjust to life, to living. You must teach us about living!': Elie Wiesel, 'The Holocaust Patient', an address to Cedars-Sinai Medical Staff, Los Angeles, 1982, quot. in Robert Krell, 'Alternative Therapeutic Approaches to Holocaust Survivors', in *Healing Their Wounds: Psychotherapy with Holocaust Survivors and Their Families*, ed. Paul Marcus and Alan Rosenberg, Westport, CT: Praeger, 1989, p. 216. Also the phrase, 'I am at war with myself', which was used as the original French title of Derrida's last interview, curiously echoes a statement of Primo Levi: 'I am not at peace with myself because I bore witness': Primo Levi, *If This is A Man / The Truce*, trans. Stuart Woolf, London: Abacus, 1991, p. 232. Perhaps the *Je suis en guerre* should read implicitly as: 'I am not at peace with myself because I bore witness – to survival.'

34 'The principle of life (*torat hayim*) remains a great intangible Judaic principle' (ATTIA, 112).

35 Compare this quote from 'Faith and Knowledge': '*The religion of the living – is this not a tautology?* Absolute imperative, holy law, law of salvation: saving the living intact, the unscathed, the safe and sound (*heilig*) that has the right to absolute respect, restraint, modesty' (AR, 85; my emphasis).

36 Jacques Derrida, 'Final Words', trans. Gila Walker, in *The Late Derrida*, eds. W.J.T. Mitchell and Arnold I. Davidson, Chicago: University of Chicago Press, 2007, p. 244.

37 Jacques Derrida, 'Living On: Borderlines', *Deconstruction and Criticism*, ed. Harold
    Bloom, New York: Continuum, 1979, p. 104; my emphasis.
38 Sigmund Freud, *Totem and Taboo*, SE 13, p. 93. In my book on Harold Bloom, *The
    Saving Lie*, I show how this 'Satanic' logic of the phantasy of omnipotence works for
    the life of the poets: if they are to survive the overwhelming powers of the tradition,
    they must *imagine* themselves as invulnerable and then narcissistically invest in this
    belief. The narcissistic phantasy, therefore, not only should not be corrected too soon,
    as Freud postulates, but rather reinforced as the necessary ruse of survival, which
    helps to achieve what otherwise would be impossible: the new living subjectivity
    claiming 'more life' to itself (see most of all the section 'Notes Towards the Supreme
    Fiction of the Self: The Romantic Fantasy', pp. 67–73).
39 PS, 19: 'This tarrying with the negative is the magical power that converts it into
    being.' See also Bergson: 'We are seeking only the precise meaning that our
    consciousness gives to this word "exist," and we find that, for a conscious living being,
    to exist is to change, to change is to mature, *to mature is to go on creating oneself
    endlessly*.': Henri Bergson, *Creative Evolution*, trans. Arthur Mitchell, London:
    Macmillan, p. 8; my emphasis.
40 Gilles Deleuze, *Negotiations, 1972–1990*, trans. Martin Joughin, New York: Columbia
    University Press, 1995, p. 143.
41 Žižek, *Less than Nothing*, p. 945.
42 See most of all Michel Henry, *Incarnation: A Philosophy of Flesh*, trans. Karl Hefty,
    Evanston, IL: Northwestern University Press, 2015, where the living flesh is
    characterized in auto-affective terms of the immanent and pathetic self-impression
    of life or life's 'trial of oneself' (p. 19). Derrida's interest in life can indeed be seen as
    joining Henry, but also deviating from his insights in all those places where Judaism
    could be seen as differing from Christianity. Thus, while Derrida is eager to take on
    Henry's notion of life's auto-affectivity – 'Affectivity is the essence of life': Michel
    Henry, *The Essence of Manifestation*, transl. by G. Etzkor, The Hague: Martin Nijhoff,
    1973, p. 519 – he immediately modifies it in such a way that it becomes originally
    heterogenous, open to its other and self-transcending, and for that reason
    ungraspable in Henry's terms of pure immanence or 'the pure trial of oneself'. While
    Henry emphasizes the self-revelatory nature of life – 'Life is . . . the very fact of
    self-revealing as such. Everywhere that something like a self-revelation is produced
    there is Life. Everywhere there is Life, this self-revelation is produced': Michel Henry,
    I Am the Truth: Toward a Philosophy of Christianity, transl. by S. Emanuel, Stanford:
    Stanford University Press, 2003, p. 27 – Derrida counteracts it with an equally
    original self-concealing of life which centres around its unmanifestable 'secret'.
    While Henry claims that life is by nature tautological – 'Life is nothing other than
    that which reveals itself – not something that might have an added property of
    self-revealing, but the very fact of self-revealing as such' (ibid.) – Derrida accepts this

diagnosis, but, again, pointing not to the ecstatic self-incarnatory manifestation of life, but to its more intimate self-preference. So, while Henry will claim that Christianity is the tautologico-performative truth of life itself based on its self-revelatory nature –

> It is the first decisive characteristic of Truth of Christianity that it no way differs from what it makes true . . . The phenomenalization of phenomenality itself is a pure phenomenological matter, a substance whose whole essence is to appear – phenomenality in its actualization and in its pure phenomenological effectivity. What manifests itself is itself. What reveals itself is revelation itself; it is a revelation of revelation, a self-revelation in its original and immediate effulgence . . . God is that pure Revelation that reveals nothing other than itself.
>
> ibid., pp. 24–5

– Derrida transforms the nature of this tautology which determines 'the religion of the living': it is not the auto-phenomenalization but the auto-preference of life that makes God mostly and primarily the 'living/loving God', the God who lives and wills life. And finally, while Henry stakes on the 'absolute Life, which generates itself, and is nothing other than the way in which the process of self-generation takes place' (Henry, *Incarnation*, p. 19) – Derrida believes only in what Henry describes as 'the terrestrial body, a [Judaic] notion of man as destitute and destined for death' (ibid., p. 7), or, in less derogatory terms, a finite life destined for survival. The leading role of incarnation in Henry's phenomenology of life, missing in Derrida, was well summed up by Carla Canullo: 'The link between Life and every living being exists namely through the flesh that Christ takes on first and that every single living being takes on': Carla Canullo, 'Michel Henry: From the Essence of Manifestation to the Essence of Religion', *Open Theology* 3 (2017): 182. See also the discussion on the difference between Henry and Derrida concerning the trope of incarnation, which explores the latter's reluctance towards the idea of a 'spiritual flesh' in Michael O'Sullivan, *Michel Henry: Incarnation, Barbarism, and Belief: An Introduction to the Work of Michel Henry*, Bern: Peter Lang, 2006, pp. 87–96.

43 See Michel Henry, *Marx: A Philosophy of Human Reality*, transl. by K. McLaughlin, Bloomington: Indiana University Press, 1993.

44 This may seem like a blatant contradiction of Derrida's praise of Cixous's 'mighty life', but only apparently so: it is a totally different thing to know death and not believe in it (Cixous) and not to know death and not to want to hear about it (Henry).

45 If Henry's apology of pure absolute life represents one contrasting pole to Derrida's phenomenology of survival, Leonard Lawlor's *life-ism*, with its emphasis on *Verendlichung*/finitization of life, occupies the other extreme. Lawlor, following Heidegger (combined with Merleau-Ponty, Foucault and Deleuze) postulates overcoming of metaphysics as a thought bound to confuse the ontological difference

by turning to *life-ism*. While life-ism is a view that allows a 'completion of immanence' in the Deleuzian sense, it also makes room for the ontological difference properly understood: what now determines the distinction between life and the living is a 'minuscule *hiatus*, which is death itself, *la place du mort*': Leonard Lawlor, *Implications of Immanence: Toward a New Concept of Life*, New York: Fordham University Press, 2006, p. 3. In the article that contains this argument *in nuce*, Lawlor identifies Heidegger's *Verendlichung* (finitization but also de-finition) comprised in his famous sentence – 'As soon as a human being is born, he is old enough to die' (BT, 228) – with Foucault's reflections on Xavier Bichat, from which follows that 'death is coextensive with life'; 'As abyssal, life always contains disease as a potentiality, or better, as a virtuality based on life itself', which is responsible for the process of simultaneously finitization and singularization: Leonard Lawlor, 'Verendlichung (Finitization): The Overcoming of Metaphysics with Life', *Philosophy Today* 48, no. 4 (2004): 406. Contrary to both Henry and Lawlor, Derrida's concept of *survival* is neither 'pure life' nor 'death co-extensive with life': although contaminated with life, it is nonetheless a process which – perhaps more faithfully to Bichat's conception of life as the sum of functions *resisting* death – focuses on the dialectics of resistance: the constant 'war', conflict, the very opposite of 'resting in peace', either fully on the side of life or on the side of death. And although in his later book, *This Is Not Sufficient: An Essay on Animality and Human Nature in Derrida*, New York: Columbia University Press, 2007, Lawlor claims that, in his phenomenological approach to autoaffection, he is 'following the thought of Derrida, but also, the thought of Deleuze and Foucault' (p. 5), it is definitely the latter who take the upper hand: Deleuze's immanentist 'a life' combined with Foucault's 'mortalism': 'Autoaffection has always defined life. Immanence, then, is equivalent to life, to a life or to one life, as Deleuze would say ... the indefinite and yet singular article in the phrase "a life" will be important ... Understood through this loss or privation of singularity, life therefore must be conceived in terms of powerlessness. There is a kind of *mortalism* within life' (ibid., pp. 4–5). I will explain this difference in detail in Chapter 3; here however, it suffices to say that, for Derrida, the singular can never coincide with the indefinite; life is always *this* life, grappling with survival, and death does not reveal the place of creative virtualities, as in Deleuze. Neither simply *vitalist* nor simply *mortalist*, Derrida's thinking of *sur-vie* approaches death in life dialectically, in terms of a *pharmakon*: an ingredient that can turn out deadly, but also enlivening if in the right measure.

46 To name just few most significant titles: Francoise Dastur, *Death: An Essay on Finitude*, trans. John Llewelyn, London: Bloomsbury, 2000; Merold Westphal, *God, Guilt, and Death: Existential Phenomenology of Religion*, Bloomington: Indiana University Press, 1987; Antony Flew, *The Logic of Mortality*, Oxford: Blackwell, 1987; Jay F. Rosenberg, *Thinking Clearly About Death*, Indianapolis: Hackett, 1999; Todd

May, *Death (The Art of Living)*, Abingdon: Routledge, 2009; Sami Pihlström, *Death and Finitude: Toward a Pragmatic Transcendental Anthropology of Human Limits and Mortality*, Lanham, MD: Lexington Books, 2016. The latter, being a good contemporary guide to philosophical thanatology, offers 'a kind of dialectics of control and surrender' (p. 180) and focuses on the concept of death as the 'transcendental limit': 'the limit is genuine – our mortality does set limits to our humanity – yet it is no "failure" or "inability" on our part, a matter of our inevitably failing to do something that we in some sense should do, that is, not a contingent or factual limitation at all' (p. 182). Yet, its approach can be characterized as mildly Heideggerian, with death squarely in the centre of the experience of finitude: '*Mortality thus defines our lives themselves*, whether or not these lives are structured by a humble acceptance of mortality or by a revolt against it, by metaphysical or religious search for immortality' (p. 187; my emphasis). There is, however, an important exception to this 'Heideggerian' rule: the essay of Thomas Nagel, written in 1970 and called simply 'Death', advises us precisely not to overestimate death and not to treat it as an *invalidation* of the given time spent in the life's middle:

> When looked at in terms of our own experience, subjectively, our life experience seems open ended. We can see no reason why our normal experiences cannot continue indefinitely. On this view death, no matter how inevitable, is the cancellation of an indefinitely extendible good. *The fact that death is inevitable does not affect how it feels in our experience to look forward to the end of our experience.*
>
> Thomas Nagel, 'Death', in Metaphysics of Death, ed. John Martin Fisher, Stanford: Stanford University Press, 1993, p. 68; my emphasis

What I am trying to do here is precisely an exercise in 'not being affected' by death and approaching finite life as 'an indefinitely extendible good' without any promise of immortality: *my experiment consists in thinking about finitude without the automatic and seemingly self-evident overestimation of death.* Thus, while I will not indulge in any 'denial of death', I will also avoid putting death in the very centre of the experience of finitude. My alternative marker of the finite life will be love – love-strong-as-death – playing itself in the conscious and self-asserted *middle of life*. Hence my contribution could also bear the title paraphrasing the one of Francoise Dastur: *Love: An Essay on Finitude.*

47 My project, however, should not be mistaken with the new vogue of the 'sacralization of life' of which the best example is offered by Don Cupitt's *New Religion of Life in Everyday Speech*:

> We have supposed that what is happening has been the secularization of religion, and we have failed to see the much greater event of the sacralization of life ... Life as a concept quite effortlessly passes between the poles of reductionism and

mysticism – life can be defined down to the molecular level, at the same time that
the notion of the irreducibility and mystery of life raises the concept up to
existential and spiritual levels.

Don Cupitt, *The New Religion of Life in Everyday Speech*,
London: SCM Press, 1999, pp. 2, 250

Ironically enough, I rather agree here with Heidegger whose dissatisfaction with
Lebensphilosophie eventually led him to drop the concept of life altogether. In his
early lectures on Aristotle, Heidegger says: 'Life is a *how*, a category of being, and not
something wild, profound, and mystical. It is characteristic of the "philosophy of life"
that it never goes so far as to inquire into what is genuinely meant by the concept
"life" as a category of being': Martin Heidegger, *Basic Concepts of Aristotelian
Philosophy*, trans. Robert D. Metcalf and Mark B. Tanzer, Bloomington: Indiana
University Press, 2009, p. 16. In my enlightened 'religion of the finite life', I will stick
to the concept of life, which he wished to elaborate in an equidistance from both, the
naturalistic reduction and the mystical quasi-profundity.

Chapter 1: Falling – in Love: Rosenzweig Versus Heidegger

1   See most of all Donatella di Cesare, *Heidegger, die Juden, die Shoah*, Frankfurt am
    Main: Vittorio Klostermann, 2016, p. 9.
2   Compare Heidegger's remark from 1942 – 'Die Judenschaft ist im Zeitraum des
    christlichen Abendlandes, d. h. der Metaphysik, das Prinzip der Zerstörung' (In the
    timeframe of the Christian West, that is, of metaphysics, Judaism is the principle of
    destruction). He also refers to the Holocaust as *Selbstvernichtung der Juden*, a
    'self-destruction of the Jews', implying that the Shoah is self-inflicted: it is the
    principle of metaphysical violence that, inevitably, must turn against itself and end in
    the 'ontological massacre': GA 97, p. 20. The reason why Judaism destroys
    metaphysics is because it is a *torat hayim*, i.e. a 'principle of life' that Heidegger
    associates firmly and reductively only with 'the biological': 'What is destructive is the
    reversal of the completion of metaphysics – i.e. of Hegel's metaphysics by Marx.
    Spirit and culture become the superstructure of "life" – i.e. of economics, i.e. of
    organization – i.e. of the biological – i.e. of the "people"' (GA 97, 20; in Richard Polt's
    translation). This detrimental reversal, in which Being gets lost in forgetfulness and
    everything *falls* into biopolitical pragmatism, culminates in the self-annihilation,
    where the 'Jewish' principle turns against the Jews themselves: 'When what is "Jewish"
    in the metaphysical sense combats what is Jewish, the high point of self-annihilation
    in history has been attained – supposing that the "Jewish" has everywhere completely
    seized mastery, so that even the fight against "the Jewish," and it above all, becomes
    subject to it' (ibid.). To fight against the Jews, therefore, as the vulgar Nazis do, would

thus amount to being 'Jewish' already. So, Heidegger advocates a more radical – and, at the same time, more contemplative – move of returning to the Greek origin of thinking, as the Greeks truly remained outside any Judaic influence: 'On this basis one must assess what it means, for thinking that enters the concealed, inceptive essence of the history of the Occident, to meditate on the first inception among the Greeks, which remained outside Judaism and thus outside Christianity' (ibid.).

3   'In Heidegger, the ethical relation, the *Miteinandersein*, the being-with-another-person, is only one moment of our presence in the world. It does not have the central place. *Mit* is always being next to . . . it is not in the first instance the Face, it is *zusammensein* [being-together], perhaps *zusammenmarschieren* [marching-together]': Emmanuel Lévinas, 'Philosophy, Justice, and Love', in *Entre Nous, Thinking of The Other*, trans. Michael B. Smith and Barbara Harshav, New York: Columbia University Press, 1998, p. 116.

4   G.W.F. Hegel, *On Christianity: Early Theological Writings by Friedrich Hegel*, trans. T.M. Knox; with an introduction, and fragments translated by Richard Kroner, Gloucester, MA: Peter Smith, 1970, p. 185.

5   'Is not death – though it is the strongest – necessary to the time whose course it seems to halt? The love that is stronger than death – a privileged formulation' (GDT, 104).

6   Compare Richard Wolin, *Heidegger's Children: Hannah Arendt, Hans Jonas, and Herbert Marcuse*, Princeton: Princeton University Press, 2015. *Pace* Wolin, I do not see this progeny as being so unproblematic.

7   On Rosenzweig's reflections on the death-driven German culture after the First World War and his attempts to turn life into a philosophical argument again, see my: 'The Thanatic Strain: Kojève and Rosenzweig as Two Readers of Hegel', *Journal for Cultural Research* 19, no. 3 (2015): 274–90.

8   The classical locus of this overestimation is the fragment from Heidegger's lectures from 1929 to 1930, where he first states that death 'belongs to the innermost essence of life' and then defines death as the touchstone of any serious philosophical inquiry: 'The touchstone [*Prüfstein*] for determining the suitability and originality of every inquiry into the essence of life and vice-versa is whether the inquiry has sufficiently grasped the problem of death, and whether it is able to bring that problem in the correct way into the question concerning the essence of life' Martin Heidegger, *The Fundamental Concepts of Metaphysics: World – Finitude – Solitude*, trans. William McNeill and Nicholas Walker, Bloomington: Indiana University Press, 1995, p. 387. See also David Farrell Krell's commentary:

> Meanwhile recall a parallel passage in Heidegger's Nietzsche lectures in which the problem of 'the nothing' is declared the testing-stone [*Probierstein*] that determines whether we gain entry into the realm of philosophy or remain barred from it. What might seem to be a merely regional issue, the question of death in

'theoretical biology,' in fact embraces both the existential-ontological project and Heidegger's incipient 'other' thinking, for both of which death, as 'the shrine of the nothing,' is the touchstone – for all philosophy.

David Farrell Krell, *Derrida and Our Animal Others: Derrida's Final Seminar, The Beast and the Sovereign*, Bloomington: Indiana University Press, 2013, p. 104

9   Jean-Luc Nancy, *Being Singular Plural*, trans. Robert D. Richardson and Anne E. O'Byrne, Stanford: Stanford University Press, 2000, p. 15; my emphasis.

10 An intuition very nicely summed up by Lionel Trilling: 'How wise that the truest, surest, most reliable things are dead, dead-shot, dead-right, dead-centre, dead-certain, dead-ahead': Lionel Trilling, *The Middle of the Journey*, London: Penguin, 1963, p. 284. The doubt whether the death-certain death can indeed function as the factor of heroic mobilization was also expressed by another French commentator of Heidegger, Michel Haar: 'Is death really what is at issue in being-towards-death? If death is a present possibility, why then situate it away in some more or less remote future? Why should it disclose the future, since it definitely closes it off?': Michel Haar, *Heidegger and the Essence of Man*, trans. William McNeill, Albany, NY: SUNY Press, 1993, p. 12.

11 Maurice Blanchot, *The Space of Literature*, trans. Ann Smock, Lincoln, NE and London: Nebraska University Press, 1982, pp. 106, 154–5, my emphasis. Yet another version of the deconstructive interpretation of Heidegger's formula is offered by Giorgio Agamben in his reading of Melville's Bartleby, where it is the latter's 'formula' (*I'd prefer not to*) that helps to explain how death may indeed be a possibility of impossibility – in the form of a 'potentiality to not-be'. Only when possibility becomes separated from the urge towards actualization, can 'dying' become the model of the right way to be faithful to a pure potentiality. See Giorgio Agamben, 'Bartleby, or on Contingency', in *Potentialities*, trans. Daniel Heller-Roazen, Stanford: Stanford University Press, 1999, pp. 243–74.

12 In *Aporias*, a book explicitly devoted to the rise of *thanatology* as a properly philosophical discipline, Derrida comments on the significance of the 'turn' conducted by Blanchot:

When Blanchot constantly repeats – and it is a long complaint and not a triumph of life – the impossible dying, the impossibility, alas, of dying, he says at once the same thing and something completely different from Heidegger. It is just a question of knowing in which sense (in the sense of direction and trajectory) one reads the expression of the possibility of impossibility. If death, the most proper possibility of Dasein, is the possibility of its impossibility, *death becomes the most improper possibility and the most ex-propriating, the most inauthenticating one.*

Jacques Derrida, *Aporias*, trans. Thomas Dutoit, Stanford: Stanford University Press, 1994, p. 77; my emphasis

13 See most of all: Georges Bataille, 'Hegel, Death and Sacrifice', trans. Jonathan Strauss, *Yale French Studies (On Bataille)* 78 (1990): 9–28.

14 Blanchot's intuition that, in Heidegger, death could do the trick of defining and activating Dasein only if Dasein secretly *resisted* death, which would then ruin the official idea of *Sein-zum-Tode*, finds its confirmation in one of the essays of Georg Simmel whose *Lebensphilosophie* exerted a strong influence on Heidegger's existential analytics. In 'Death and Immortality', Simmel describes death as internal to the process of life, yet he also makes room for the 'aversion to death', which only in the dialectical tension with the former allows death to function as a 'shaper' (*Gestalter*) of human existence:

> Every step of life appears not only as a temporal approach toward death, but as positively and a priori formed by death, which is a real element of life. Furthermore, this forming is thus codetermined precisely by the *aversion* to death, by the fact that striving and enjoyment, toil and rest, and all our other ways of behaviour considered natural – and an instinctive or conscious flight from death. *Life, which we consume in order to bring us closer to death, we consume in order to flee it.*
>
> Georg Simmel, *The View of Life: Four Metaphysical Essays with Journal Aphorisms*, trans. John A.Y. Andrews and Donald N. Levine, Chicago: Chicago University Press, 2010, p. 70; my emphasis

This double movement – towards and away – is indeed a 'living contradiction', but only as such it can turn death into a limit: a defining boundary whose pressure can be felt only if there is a countermovement pressing from within. Also – strangely enough – Blanchot's suspicious deconstruction of Heidegger chimes very closely with Adorno's opinion on Heidegger's *Todesdenken* as full of platitudes: the line of critique stubbornly maintained by Adorno from his pamphletic *Jargon of Authenticity*, through the *Lectures on Metaphysics*, up to *Negative Dialectics*. Regardless of all the differences of idioms, Blanchot's conclusions are not very far from Adorno's. In Blanchot's analysis, Dasein can either forget the real 'dying' and then pretend to use 'death' as a factor mobilizing life – or truly remember 'dying' and then consent to die already, by letting it in as an entropic force shattering all life's projects.

15 This would obviously be the extreme version of the nominalistic theology – from the Asharite kalam, via William Ockham, through Kierkegaard, *Lebensphilosophie*, up to Heidegger and Carl Schmitt – in which God, the highest possibility, is always an enemy of the actual world, even if it was him who created this actuality in the first place. In Blanchot's reading, Heidegger's death functions precisely as the nominalistic 'divine enemy' of all finite actualizations, who can never 'yield to our freedom', as attested by Heidegger himself who, in 'What Is Metaphysics?', says: 'We are so finite that we cannot even bring ourselves originally before the nothing through our own

determination and will. So abysmally [*abgründig*] does finitization [*Verendlichung*] entrench itself that our most proper and deepest limitation [*Endlichkeit*] refuses to yield to freedom' Martin Heidegger, *Pathmarks*, trans. William McNeill, Cambridge: Cambridge University Press, 1998, p. 93. This 'divine' association has been confirmed by Leo Strauss who remarked on the margin of his copy of *Sein und Zeit* that in Heidegger, unlike in Nietzsche, it is not that God is dead, but Death itself becomes God. We know about this thanks to Heinrich Meier and his instructive essay on Strauss's reading of *Sein und Zeit*, 'Death as God: A Note on Martin Heidegger', which is devoted to the elucidation of this single, highly esoteric sentence left by Strauss in pencil: 'Heidegger: God is death' (*Heidegger: Gott ist Tod*). The play on Nietzsche's verdict *God is dead* (*Gott ist tot*) suggests that, *pace* Nietzsche, the divine shadow not only did not leave us in late modernity, inaugurated by Heidegger's thought, but only strengthened its dark presence in the form of Death itself, now divinized according to the rules of premodern theological absolutism. See Heinrich Meier, *Leo Strauss and the Theologico-Political Problem*, trans. Marcus Brainard, Cambridge: Cambridge University Press, 2006, p. 45. A similar objection towards late Heidegger, although without explicit reference to the nominalist theology (but to 'extreme paranoia' instead), was also made by David Farrell Krell in his recent *Ecstasy, Catastrophe: Heidegger from* Being and Time *to the* Black Notebooks, Albany, NY: SUNY Press, 2016, pp. 6–7.

16 Which reads like an unconscious parody of Kierkegaard's *Repetition* where Job irrationally expects his life to be given back to him after it had been taken away: a parody, because there is no God here other than Death, who would be capable of offering such reward.

17 Derrida, *Aporias*, p. 77. Compare also: 'The aporia is what stops or arrests, often in the form of a judgment or verdict. The aporia is what paralyzes, what blocks the exit, closes the doors and seems to doom us to an impasse – to death, a dead end, a deadlock' (DP2, 30).

18 This alternative form of 'resoluteness', playing itself out in Rosenzweig, was well spotted by Lévinas:

> What interests Rosenzweig himself is the discovery of *being as life*, of *being as life-in-relation*: the discovery of a thought which is the very life of this being. The person no longer goes back into the system he conceives, as in Hegel, in order to become fixed and renounce his singularity. Singularity is necessary to the exercise of this thought and this life precisely as an irreplaceable singularity, the only one capable of love, the only one that can be loved, that knows how to love, that can form a religious community.
>
> Emmanuel Lévinas, '*Between Two Worlds* (The Way of Franz Rosenzweig)', in *Difficult Freedom*, trans. Seán Hand, Baltimore, MD: Johns Hopkins University Press, 1990, p. 192

19 To the possible objection that I tend to conflate here two completely different visions of death – before and after the 'turn' – I can only answer that, to me, they are simply not that different. In both cases, the issue of death is dominant because it allows access to the highest truth of Being, which is not to be found *Diesseits*, Here Below, but always Beyond as 'the side of life averted from us' where 'death and the realm of the dead belong to the whole of beings as its other side': Martin Heidegger, 'What Are Poets For?', in *Poetry, Language, Thought*, trans. A. Hofstadter, New York: Harper and Row, 1971, p. 125. Still systematically overestimated, death merely changes the function: before, it individuated Dasein – after, it negates all separation, by reconciling us with the hidden holistic aspect of Being. The evolutionary continuity between *Sein-zum-Tode* and *Gelassenheit*, based precisely on the concept of *Verendlichung* – the constant finitization occurring in Dasein, of which Heidegger speaks in 'What Is Metaphysics?' – was also spotted by Leonard Lawlor who also seems to follow Blanchot's reading of Heidegger:

> Unlike what we see in *Being and Time*, here in 'What is Metaphysics?' death is no longer a possibility in relation to which one can be an 'anxious freedom towards' and thereby grasp one's ownmost existential possibilities. *Our deepest limitation refuses to yield to our freedom.* Heidegger indeed seems to have developed an idea inspired by this saying: 'As soon as a human being is born, he is old enough to die' (BT, 228) ... Death is not an absolute limit; rather, as becoming-finite, death is a relative limit. *The limit has been distributed throughout existence* ... Death is not a possibility of no longer existing, but rather, as becoming-finite, *death is actually life itself.*
>
> Lawlor, 'Verendlichung', pp. 403–4; my emphasis

20 The Hellenist most responsible for this *Verjudung* of Odysseus was Victor Bérard who, in the chapter on 'Les Phéniciens et l'Odyssée' in his *La Résurrection d'Homère*, Paris: Bernard Gresset, 1930, claimed that the prototype of Odyssey was a Phoenician myth dealing with sailors and merchants – a topic rather unusual for Greek mythology. Heidegger is not the only one who used the topos of the Jewish Ulysses; in the same time James Joyce, having read Bérard, composes his *Ulysses* with Leopold Bloom in the leading role, and a decade later Adorno and Horkheimer, explicitly referring to Bérard, will present Odysseus as the Semitic prototype of the modern bourgeois in their *Dialectic of Enlightenment* (DE, 61). On the complex context of the Judaization of Odysseus, as well as his affinity to Jacob, see my 'Jewish Ulysses: Post-Secular Meditation on the Loss of Hope', in *Jewish Cryptotheologies*.

21 Walter Benjamin, 'The Storyteller: Observations on the Works of Nikolai Leskov': SW3, 154.

22 One can also read Freud's conclusion of *Beyond the Pleasure Principle* in such life-affirming manner: 'What we are left with is the fact that the organism wishes to die only in its own fashion' (FR, 613); more on this in Chapter 4.

23 See Hans Ehrenberg, 'New Philosophy', in *Franz Rosenzweig's 'New Thinking'*, eds. Alan Udoff and Barbara E. Galli, New York: Syracuse University Press, 1999, p. 119: 'The only thing I regret about the book . . . is the unnecessary last word with which the author, who surely does not need to speak in this way, concludes, paying tribute to our times by suddenly joining in the call: *from philosophy to life*.' On the other hand, however, see Zachary Braiterman, ' "Into Life"??! Franz Rosenzweig and the Figure of Death', *AJS Review* 23, no. 2 (1998): 203–21, where Rosenzweig is criticized by for being – not unlike Heidegger – morbidly fascinated with 'death, light, silence' (p. 212), which, according to the author, constitute the true goal of *The Star*, despite its final injunction to go back 'into life'.

24 What Derrida writes about Cixous also perfectly applies to Rosenzweig's deliberate attempt not to overestimate death: '[Life] remains a unique side without another side, and this would be life itself . . . this unique side, this unilaterality is *of life for life*, life itself, life promised to life, sworn life, whereas death, which she knows and understands as well as anyone, is not denied, certainly, but it is not a side, it is a nonside' (HCL, 52).

25 See Karl Löwith, 'M. Heidegger and F. Rosenzweig: Or Temporality and Eternity', *Philosophy and Phenomenological Research* 3, no. 1 (1942): 53–77.

26 György Lukacs, 'Metaphysics of Tragedy', in *Soul and Form*, trans. Anna Bostock, Merlin Press: London, 1974, pp. 152–3, my emphasis. Heidegger's insistence on *Ver-endlichung* as the factor of de-finition which, simultaneously, kills Dasein and gives it a form, is indeed the old motif of *Lebensphilosophie*, from which his thought emerged. For Wilhelm Dilthey, the founder of the movement, life as such is beyond any conceptual grasp, because life is a constant becoming which does not allow anything to be 'lived to the end'. According to Dilthey, 'philosophy is an activity which raises life to consciousness and *thinks it to the end*': Wilhelm Dilthey, *Briefwechsel zwischen Wilhelm Dilthey und dem Grafen Paul Yorck von Wartenburg 1877–1897*, ed. Sigrid von der Schulenburg, Halle an der Saale: Max Niemeyer, 1923, p. 247; my emphasis. Georg Simmel commented on Dilthey's sentence by specifying what this 'thinking to the end' must be: 'The life of all organic beings receives its form from the act of dying': *A View of Life*, p. 65. It is precisely this line of thought insisting on the 'form-giving activity of death' (ibid.) that leads straight to György Lukacs. On Rosenzweig's view, however, life does not need a defining 'sculpting' touch – just as it does not need death. When submerged in its proper/improper element of the middle – *in der Mitte des Lebens* – life resorts to the ruse of *deproximation* which is the very opposite of the de-fining *Verendlichung*, i.e. the approximation of the end (more on the strategy of deproximation as applied by Derrida in Chapter 3).

27 See Maurice Blanchot, *The Step Not Beyond*, trans. Lycette Nelson, Albany, NY: SUNY Press, 1992, as well as *L'arrêt de mort*, Paris: Gallimard, 1948.

28 As Catherine Malabou shows in *The Future of Hegel: Plasticity, Temporality and the Dialectic*, trans. Lisabeth During, Abingdon: Routledge, 2005, this is a Hegelian argument through and through, and no wonder that Rosenzweig, himself a great Hegelian scholar, retained many of his master's notions even after the official break with philosophy. After all, Hegel's concept of life as a dynamic and plastic unity-in-transience, which falls ill the very moment it stops flowing, constitutes the very bedrock of his dialectics as the speculative movement of constant transition that keeps passing through differences, yet without losing integrity. In the *Encyclopaedia*, Hegel defines illness in exactly the same terms in which Rosenzweig describes the pathological paralysis brought in by the obsessive thought of death: 'The organism finds itself ill, when one of its systems or one of its organs . . . retreats into itself and continues to aim its own actions antagonistically against the interests of the whole, and the fluidity of the whole . . . is thereby disturbed and brought to a halt': G.W.F. Hegel, *Philosophy of Nature: Part 2 of the Encyclopaedia of Philosophical Sciences*, trans. M.J. Petry, London: Allen and Unwin, 1970, par. 371. Malabou comments: 'For this reason, the treatment of madness, like that of organic illness, will consist in putting back into circulation that vital mobile energy': Catherine Malabou, *The Future of Hegel*, p. 36.

29 Not only Goethe but the whole of German Romanticism reverberates in Rosenzweig's concept of love as dynamic and plastic, all-reaching and all-binding connection. See, for instance, this aphorism of Novalis: 'Die Basis aller ewiger Verbindung ist eine absolute Tendenz nach allen Richtungen' [The ground of all eternal connection is an absolute tendency in all directions]: Novalis, *Werke, Tagebücher und Briefe Friedrich von Hardenbergs: Werke in drei Bänden,* ed. Hans-Joachim Mähl, Richard Samuel and Hans Jürgen Balmes, Munich: Carl Hanser Verlag, 1987, vol. 2, p. 445. Which, by the way, nicely chimes with Canguilhem's description of the adventurous life: 'Life is experience, that is to say, improvisation, the utilization of occurrences; *it is an attempt in all directions*' (KL, 90).

30 Jean-Luc Nancy appears aware of this alternative, which comes most visibly to the fore in his essay 'Shattered Love', where, otherwise Heideggerian through-and-through, he allows himself a respite from the influence of the deadly 'master from Germany' and reaches for another source of inspiration: Lévinas, whose philosophy he calls a new 'metaphysics of love' (FT, 269). He thus reproaches Heidegger for not making room for love as an existential category of Dasein's analytics where it is poorly represented only by a *Fürsorge*, that is, a highly idealized version of Christian *agape* (ibid.). Lévinas, with his insistence on the traumatic shattering as constitutive for human subjectivity, is precisely what Nancy needs in his description of the finite condition as exposed, precarious, fragile; he even quotes Nachman of Bratslav who famously said that 'no heart is as whole as a broken heart'. For Nancy, love is a possibility of maintaining oneself in the state of desire as *incompletion*; as a broken

part of a broken whole – or we could say, continuing Rabbi Nachman's and Rosenzweig's Lurianic vein – as a dispersed fragment of the cosmic breaking of the vessels, which created the finite world and the finite way of being. The common denominator of *all* manifestations of love is that it *lets the finite being be*, be fully as it is and present itself in a dazzling, blinding self-manifestation:

> It is the question of presence: the joy is an extremity of presence, *self* exposed, presence *of self* joying outside itself, in a presence that no present absorbs and that does not (re)present, but that offers itself endlessly ... *self* that joys joys of its presence in *the presence of the other* ... The presence that cuts across is a burst. To joy, joy itself, is to receive the burst of a singular being: it is more than manifest presence, its seeming beyond all appearance – *ekphanestaton*, Plato said.
>
> FT, 272–3

The presence of the joying – loving and loved – self in face of the other is not a simple pleromatic manifestation of a self-contained being. Its coming to the fore is almost unbearable – bursting, shattering, traumatic – both for the self and the witnessing other, yet when accepted by love which, in the Pauline manner, 'bears and endures all', this *Unruhe* turns into *jouissance*, anxiety transforms into joy: 'But there is this brilliant, shattering constitution of being. "Love" does not define it, but it names it, and obliges us to think it' (FT, 273). What would otherwise cause fear and anxiety, *Angst und Sorge* – this incessant slipping of being out of itself, pulsating like a supernova, alternately bursting and collapsing – love takes and enjoys. Love does not put being in harmony with itself: it lets it be in its aporetic 'living contradiction'.

31 This association of love and falling, although Shakespearian in origin, has been beautifully confirmed by Margaret Atwood in her *Handmaid's Tale*, where the heroine, enslaved by the right-wing regime of the Gilead republic, reminisces about the good old liberal times and, by punning on the Gileadian description of herself and all other previously divorced women as 'fallen', says that, indeed, they were all fallen women – constantly falling – falling in love: '*Falling in love*, we said, *I fell for him*. We were falling women. We believed in it, this downward motion': Margaret Atwood, *The Handmaid's Tale*, London: Vintage, 1996, p. 236.

32 This motif – of love connecting all – both in Goethe and in Rosenzweig, derives originally from Giovanni Pico della Mirandola and the renaissance affirmation of humanity's indefinite non-essence, which offers a more optimistic counterpart to the Herderian anthropology, where this promising opening soon transforms into life-threatening deficiency. In Pico della Mirandola's commentary on Genesis, Man is portrayed as a creature deprived of essence, so it can be nothing and everything at the same time according to his will:

> At last, the Supreme Maker decreed that this creature, to whom He could give nothing wholly his own, should have a share in the particular endowment of

every other creature. Taking man, therefore, this *creature of indeterminate image*, He set him in the middle of the world and thus spoke to him: 'We have given you, Oh Adam; no visage proper to yourself, nor any endowment properly your own, in order that whatever place, whatever form, whatever gifts you may, with premeditation, select, these same you may have and possess through your own judgment and decision. The nature of all other creatures is defined and restricted within laws which We have laid down; you, by contrast, impeded by no such restrictions, may, by your own free will, to whose custody We have assigned you, trace for yourself the lineaments of your own nature. I have placed you at the very center of the world, so that from that vantage point you may with greater ease glance round about you on all that the world contains. We have made you a creature neither of heaven nor of earth, neither mortal nor immortal, in order that you may, as the free and proud shaper of your own being, fashion yourself in the form you may prefer. It will be in your power to descend to the lower, brutish forms of life; you will be able, through your own decision, to rise again to the superior orders whose life is divine'.

> Giovanni Pico della Mirandola, *Oration on the Dignity of Man*,
> trans. Robert A. Caponigri, Chicago: A Gateway Edition,
> Henry Regnery Company, 1956, pp. 6–8; my emphasis

Thus, while Heidegger attempts to reduce human non-essence to the more essential nothing – Rosenzweig, staying on the bright side of the anthropological difference, perceives man as a Mirandolian microcosm capable of striking relation with potentially everything: a Protean 'image' of all beings linked by one cosmoerotic bond.

33 In his studies on *dementia praecox*, Carl Gustav Jung analyses anxiety as the libido which withdrew from the world and did not choose any object instead; in all the cases of the depressive withdrawal, *Angst* comes forward as the affective sign of isolation and the lack of relation, which often expresses itself in the loss of speech. Unable to connect libidinally with any object, himself included, the 'dement' falls into a mute stupor which makes him dead while alive: Carl Gustav Jung, *Symbols of Transformation: An Analysis of the Prelude to a Case of Schizophrenia*, London: Routledge, 1967.

34 G.W.F. Hegel, *The Philosophical Propaedeutic*, trans. A.V. Miller, Oxford: Blackwell, 1986, p. 11.

35 Compare Catherine Malabou, *Ontologie de l'accident: Essai sur la plasticité destructrice*, Paris: Éditions Léo Scheer, 2009.

36 This term, coined by Walter Benjamin, appears in his essay on Kafka: Walter Benjamin, 'Franz Kafka', in *Illuminations: Essays and Reflections*, trans. Harry Zohn, New York: Schocken Books, 1968, p. 134.

37 In *Negative Dialectics*, in the all-telling chapter 'Suffering Physical', Adorno insists on maintaining the non-theoretical and non-conceptual moment of compassion as 'the

moving forces of dialectical thinking': 'The smallest trace of senseless suffering in the empirical world belies all the identitarian philosophy that would talk us out of that suffering . . . The physical moment tells our knowledge that suffering ought not to be, that things should be different. *Woe speaks: "Go"'* (ND, 202–3).

38 Alexandre Kojève, 'The Idea of Death in the Philosophy of Hegel: Complete Text of the Last Two Lectures of the Academic Year 1933–1934', trans. Joseph J. Carpino, in *Interpretation: A Journal of Political Philosophy* 3 no. 2/3 (1973): 133; my emphasis.

39 Compare Søren Kierkegaard, *Works of Love*, trans. Howard V. Hong and Edna H. Hong, Princeton, NL Princeton University Press, 1995.

40 Emil Fackenheim, *The Religious Dimension of Hegel's Thought*, Chicago: University of Chicago Press, 1982, p. 115.

41 Quot. in Emmanuel Falque, *Crossing the Rubicon: The Borderlands of Philosophy and Theology*, trans. Reuben Shank, New York: Fordham University Press, 2016, p. 127. Falque comments:

> As the subtle Doctor opens a new horizon for modernity, the importance of his assertion lies not in the negation of infinity or even the possibility that God would assume and transform the mode of contingency given here. *In reality, all that counts is thickness of our being-here-below* – the pilgrim human or the homo viator who ceases finally attempting to escape into another world (as it is the case with the Platonic leap) and recognizes pure and simple humanity as the starting point.
>
> ibid., 127–8; my emphasis

Scotus's thesis is also an obvious precursor of Nancy's statement that 'finitude is not privation'.

42   Through this we already see *what life adds to existence*. It withstands the inherent weakness of existence as creature, existence that is in itself so rich and so all-inclusive due to firm, immovable, structured essences in itself; with regard to the 'phenomena' of existence, the living essences are really 'essences.' Whereas knowledge of existence is knowledge of its changes, *knowledge of life would be knowledge of its preservation* . . . Life and existence do not overlap – yet. The profusion of the phenomenon that had begun to sparkle in the cosmos, the ineffable richness of individuality, is that which assumes duration, figure and solidity in the living. *It wants to persist in its figure.*

SR-G, 239–40; my emphasis

43 Which is a manoeuvre precursory to the *Dialectic of Enlightenment*, discussed in the Introduction: just as Hölderlin struggles to get out of myth by using the mythic form, so is the story of Odysseus a myth about exiting the realm of myth.

44 Friedrich Hölderlin, *Odes and Elegies*, trans. Nick Hoff, Middletown, CT: Wesleyan University Press, 2008, p. 113.

45 Ibid., p. 177. Sind denn dir nicht bekannt viele Lebendigen? / Geht auf Wahrem dein Fuß nicht, wie auf Teppichen? / Drum, mein Genius! tritt nur / Bar ins Leben, und sorge nicht!

46 Indeed, in the section 72 of *Sein und Zeit*, where Heidegger discusses briefly both 'ends' of human existence, birth and death, he uses the concept of *Sich-erstreckung*: the 'self-stretching' in the element of the middle, which occurs only thanks to the neutralization or occlusion of the polar opposites.

47 In *Benjamin's -abilities*, Cambridge, MA: Harvard University Press, 2008, Samuel Weber also emphasizes Benjamin's use of the Hölderlinian word *Erstreckung*, 'stretching' (or 'extension'), as a characteristic feature of the happy living creature, spreading in the space of the world and connecting with everything it encounters in a 'carpet-like pattern' of mutual intertwinement – which he then opposes to *Erstrickung*, 'narrowing', or the Egyptian condition that isolates every living as a death-bound monad.

48 A beautiful interpretation of Benjamin's essay, very much paralleling mine, has been given by Eli Friedlander who read it in the light of the Lurianic notion of *tsimtsum*: Eli Friedlander, 'The Retreat of the Poet in Walter Benjamin's "Two Poems of Friedrich Hölderlin"', in *Tsimtsum in Modernity: Lurianic Heritage in Modern Philosophy and Theology*, ed. Agata Bielik-Robson and Daniel H. Weiss, Bloomington: Indiana University Press, forthcoming.

Chapter 2: Being-Towards-Birth: Arendt and the Finitude of Origins

1   If death comes to punctuate all of philosophy (from Plato to Hegel and Heidegger) as the truth itself, as the phenomenon of truth, this is . . . because it is the only presentation of essence as essence. For this reason, philosophy is marked as deadly – and the end of philosophy, in the exhaustion of its sense as sense, is a suicide programmed in to the Socratic tragedy.

Jean-Luc Nancy, Corpus, trans. Richard Rand, New York: Fordham University Press, 2008, p. 32

2   Nancy, *Being Singular Plural*, p. 194.

3   Some commentators, however, claim that Arendt simply follows Heidegger's *Being and Time*, particularly the passage: 'Factical Dasein exists natively [*gebürtig*] and natively it dies also already in the sense of being-towards-death. In the unity of thrownness and fleeting, that is, anticipatory being-towards-death, birth and death existentially "hang together"' (BT, 374). But already this fragment demonstrates that Arendt might have been inspired by it only negatively, i.e. spurned towards the

opposite conception of natality in which birth and death do *not* 'hang together' in
the obvious manner. On the significance of this quote for Arendt, see most of all:
Richard Wolin, *Heidegger's Children*, especially the section, '*Caritas* and *Existenz*'
(pp. 41–4) in the chapter on Arendt; Hauke Brunkhorst, *Hannah Arendt*, Munich:
Beck, 1999, p. 28, as well as Patricia Bowen-Moore, *Hannah Arendt's Philosophy of
Natality*, New York: St. Martin's Press, 1989, p. 2. A good discussion on the possible
indebtedness of Arendt to Heidegger is offered by Miguel Vatter in his essay, 'Natality
and Biopolitics in Hannah Arendt', *Revista de Ciencia Politica* 26, no. 2 (2006): 138–9,
in which he emphasizes Arendt's agonistic intentions towards her teacher. And
recently, David Farrell Krell devoted the large part of his *Ecstasy, Catastrophe* to the
issue of natality, even by taking the Heidegger's sentence – *Das faktische Dasein
existiert gebürtig* – as the book's motto. Krell wonders why Heidegger, later on so
obsessed with *ersterer Anfang*, the 'firster beginning' of all things, ignores the fact of
birth, which he mentions as 'the other end' of human existence, but does not dwell
upon: 'Among commencements, scarcely one is more firster than our birth': David
Farrell Krell, *Ecstasy, Catastrophe*, p. 61. And then he launches 'a far-flung fantasy' in
which 'the focus of our newly fashioned *Sein und Zeit* would be birth – birth and the
extended period of latency, of a puberty and an adolescence that do not figure as
themes for existential analysis – rather than death' and whose main heroes would be
not so much the world-weary adult Dasein destined to die as the *da-da-da-da!
Da-Sein*: the Bebe Dasein and Childe Heidegger (ibid., 67–8). Yet, despite the
promising change of characters, Krell's version of *Being and Time* is still a 'tragic play'
in which 'Childe Dasein either gradually or quite suddenly encounters the fogbank
of death and the grim necessity of mourning' (ibid., 72), which only confirms
Heidegger's dismissal of 'the other end' as indeed merely a beginning of dying. The
primacy of death remains thus unchallenged.

4   Possibly (but not only) having Heidegger in mind, Arendt criticizes the thanatic
thrust of her contemporary philosophical thought in her review of Hermann Broch's
The Death of Virgil, where she praises the Austrian writer for not falling into 'the trap
of modern death-philosophy, for which life has in itself the germ of death and for
which, consequently, the moment of death appears as the "goal of life"': Hannah
Arendt, *Essays in Understanding, 1930–1954*, ed. Jerome Kohn, New York: Harcourt,
1994, p. 161. In the next chapter we shall see that this opposition – between death-
driven philosophy and life-loving literature – holds for Derrida as well. Compare
also the diagnosis of Hans Jonas, at that time Arendt's close friend: 'Our thinking
today is under the ontological dominance of death': Hans Jonas, *The Phenomenon of
Life: Toward a Philosophical Biology*, Evanston, IL, Chicago: Northwestern University
Press, 1966, p. 12.

5   Arendt anticipates here Denis de Rougemont who, in his *Love in the Western World*,
written a decade later, criticizes Plato from the Christian/Pauline position just as

Arendt objects to the Neoplatonic framework of the Augustinian Christianity. They also both evoke the alternative, Hebrew, version of love, which cannot be accommodated into the Ero-Thanatic mode of Plato's theory of sublimation, and share the opinion that the (Neo)Platonic love is, in fact, merely a thinly masked death drive which invalidates the finite dimension of our worldly existence, making no room for the love of the other as the concrete living singularity:

> Eros . . . requires union – that is, the complete absorption of the essence of individuals into the god. The existence of distinct individuals is considered to be due to a grievous error, and their part is to rise progressively till they are dissolved in the divine perfection. Let not a man attach himself to his fellow-creatures, for they are devoid of all excellence, and in so far as they are particular individuals they merely represent so many deficiencies of being. *There is no such thing as our neighbour.* And the intensification of love must be at the same time a lover's *askesis*, whereby he will eventually escape out of life.
>
> Denis de Rougemont, *Love in the Western World*, trans. Montgomery Belgion, New York: Harcourt & Brace, 1940, pp. 65–6; my emphasis

6 Compare Lévinas: 'Creation is by no means the limitation of being, but its basis. This is the very opposite of Heideggerian *Geworfenheit*': Emmanuel Lévinas, *Difficult Freedom*, p. 190.

7 Hannah Arendt, *The Life of the Mind: Thinking and Willing*, New York: Harcourt, 1977, p. 109. See also Nancy's comment:

> Singularity consists in the 'just once, this time,' whose mere enunciation – similar to the infant's cry at birth, and it is necessarily *each time* a question of birth – establishes a relation at the same time that it *infinitely* hollows out the time and space that are supposed to be 'common' around the point of enunciation. At this point, it is each time freedom that is singularly *born*. (And it is birth that *frees*.)
>
> Jean-Luc Nancy, *Experience of Freedom*, p. 66; Nancy's emphasis

8 John Milton, *Paradise Lost*, London: Penguin Popular Classics, 1996, Book V.

9 As in T.S. Eliot's poem, 'East Coker', then used by Winnicott as the title of one of his books: *Home Is Where We Start From*.

10 Compare Emmanuel Lévinas, 'God and Philosophy', in *Of God Who Comes to Mind*, trans. Bettina Bergo, Stanford: Stanford University Press 1998, p. 55: 'The history of Western thought is the history of the destruction of transcendence.'

11 This is why I cannot agree with Esposito when he says that 'Heidegger's thought emerges in the first half of the twentieth century as the only one able to support the philosophical confrontation with biopolitics' (B, 152). However, it must also be said that Arendt never properly developed her theme of natality, though it remained one of her most frequent 'thought trains'; see Scott and Stark, the editors of the Augustine

thesis, in their essay 'Rediscovering Hannah Arendt', LA, p. 147. Scott and Stark enumerate all the instances of Arendt's return to the theme of natality. First, in 'What Is Freedom?' from 1960 (reprinted in *Between Past and Future* 1977, p. 167): 'Because he is a beginning, man can begin; to be human and to be free are one and the same. God created man in order to introduce into the world the faculty of beginning: freedom.' The same line is repeated almost verbatim in *The Origins of Totalitarianism*, New York: Harcourt & Brace, 1966, p. 479, where she persistently uses theological terminology and calls such outbursts of freedom 'miracles'. And finally in *The Life of the Mind*, vol. 2, *Willing*: 'This very capacity for beginning is rooted in natality, and by no means in creativity, not in a gift but in a fact that human begins, new men, again and again appear in the world by virtue of birth' (p. 217). In what follows, I will try to develop Arendt's intuitions into coherent standpoint that will form the strongest antidote possible to the biopolitical renaturalization of humankind.

12 The importance of Rosenzweig for Arendt was nicely summed up in the essay of Rafael Zawisza, 'Thank God We're Creatures: Arendt Reads Rosenzweig', still in manuscript; I am grateful to Rafael for making me aware that it is the Rosenzweigian *Kreatürlichkeit* that lies at the bottom of Arendt's 'createdness'.

13 Emmanuel Lévinas, *Totality and Infinity: An Essay on Exteriority*, trans. Alphonso Lingis, Dordrecht: Kluwer Academic 1991, p. 56; my emphasis.

14 The natalistic structure of reversal or metalepsis allows for the fruitful 'revenge against time', that is, precisely for what Nietzsche deemed absolutely impossible and, precisely as such, characteristic of the Semitic resentment towards being: 'This, and this alone, is what *revenge* itself is: the will's ill-will toward time and its "It was"': Friedrich Nietzsche, *Thus Spoke Zarathustra: A Book for Everyone and Nobody*, trans. Graham Parkes, Oxford: Oxford University Press, 2005, p. 121; my emphasis. But for Bloom, who bases his whole system on his polemic with Nietzsche and Heidegger, the resignation of will in face of time's transience would never do. In *The Anxiety of Influence*, he defines creativity as a combination of repetition and memory, where the latter is always a remembrance of one's origins, pulling against the temporal flow: 'Creativity is thus always the mode of repetition *and* of memory and also of what Nietzsche called the will's revenge against time and against time's statement of "It was."' (AI, 98).

15 This most radical understanding of birth as resurrection capable of conquering death has been recently defended by Emmanuel Falque's *Metamorphosis of Finitude*, which stubbornly sticks to the Christian dogma of life eternal and insists on 'cracking and opening up of immanence and temporality (the crust of our finitude), even though finitude may be impassable simply at the level of our existence as part of mankind': Emmanuel Falque, *The Metamorphosis of Finitude: An Essay on Birth and Resurrection*, New York: Fordham University Press, 2012, p. xiv. Christianity's role here is indeed highly ambivalent: torn between the Pauline *agape* and the

Neoplatonic Eros, the Christian doctrine oscillates between the recognition of the creaturely mode of being and its violent rejection. For ages the Christian thinkers have had a natural tendency to misread the main line of *Shir ha-Shirim* as 'Love *stronger* than death', for instance, Werner Jeanrond, in his recent monograph on the Christian theology of love: 'All we need is love. God is love. Love is all that matters. *Love is stronger than death*': Werner Jeanrond, *A Theology of Love*, New York: T&T Clark, 2010, p. 1 (actually, the very first paragraph!).

16 To paraphrase the most dialectical formula of Rabbi Tarphon in *Pirke Aboth*: 'You are not required to complete the work, but neither you are free to desist from it': 1945. *Pirke Aboth: The Sayings of the Fathers*, trans. Joseph Hertz, London: Behrman House Publishers, 1945, 2:21.

17 J.-B. Pontalis, *Frontiers in Psychoanalysis: Between the Dream and the Psychic Pain*, trans. C. Cullen and P. Cullen, London: The Hogarth Press and the Institute of Psychoanalysis, 1981, p. 145; my emphasis. Pontalis also says of the *ego*, the psychoanalytic heir of the philosophical Cartesian subjectivity, that while 'it claims to represent the interests of personality as a whole and to act as an autonomous subject by denying its dependent relationships . . . there is no question of an autonomy of the ego, even a relative one – but only of its dependence' (ibid., p. 137). The others are inherently and necessarily inscribed in the life of the subject, seen precisely from the perspective of *life*.

18 Hannah Arendt, *Denktagebuch 1950–1973*, eds. Ursula Ludz and Ingeborg Nordmann, Munich: Piper Verlag, 2016, pp. 280–1; my emphasis.

19 Phrases such as this one – 'the overall gigantic circle of nature herself, where no beginning and no end exists and where all natural things swing into changeless, deathless repetition' (HC, 96) – is not a neutral diagnosis: it is metaphysical horror itself. In this Arendt does not differ much from Adorno, who describes his version of *horror metaphysicus* as the myth of total enclosure: 'the mythus is nothing else than the closed system of immanence, of that which is' (ND, 402).

20 This aporia comes to the fore most visibly in Miguel Vatter's recent reading of Hannah Arendt, which tries to present her as belonging to the sphere of 'affirmative biopolitics', despite all her criticism of the biological cycle of life conceived as a mere *zoe*. While I agree with his rejection of Arendt's alleged 'Greek humanism', I cannot nevertheless accept the traditional vitalist solution which forces her to adopt 'the natural fertility of biological life, as well as the natural surplus of labor' as the blessing and miracle in itself. Vatter is right when he says: 'What Arendt needs, *instead*, is a counter-natural yet living condition of human freedom' (Vatter, 'Natality and Biopolitics in Hannah Arendt', p. 154). But his vision of the *instead* does not seem alternative enough, it is still caught in the Aristotelian distinction between *bios* and *zoe*, only this time on the latter's side. But if Arendt truly subverts the Aristotelian dualism, then natality cannot be brought back to the level of *zoe*; if it is

truly beyond the alternative of either 'biological life' or the 'political life' based on the contemptuous rejection of the former, it must be something else – a 'creaturely life'. A similar aporia concerning the 'affirmative-biopolitical' readings of Arendt can be found in Vatter's important precursor, Roberto Esposito. According to Esposito's *Bios*, Arendt chooses birth as the 'threshold concept' that covers the zone of indeterminateness between biology and non-biological life, just like the concept of 'non-biological death' in Heidegger: 'Birth is precisely this threshold. It is the unlocalizable place in space or the unassimilable moment in the linear flowing of time in which *bios* is placed at the maximum distance from *zoe* or in which life is given form in a modality that is drastically distant from its own biological bareness' (B, 178). More than that, on Esposito's reading birth is the moment in which *bios* becomes 'frontally opposed to *zoe*' (B, 179), thus generating the most productive denaturalizing tension – which blatantly contradicts his later comment that Arendt, just like Heidegger, still remains trapped 'on this side of the biopolitical paradigm' (B, 179). It would thus seem that only if we give up on the *bios–zoe* distinction altogether, Arendt's conception of natality can be given full justice. Of all Arendt's commentators, it is Kristeva who is most sensitive to the non-biological – even more: non-natural – character of birth, which constitutes the crux of the human paradox of *finitum capax infiniti*. Although the context of the birth is the *physei*, i.e. 'the indisputable factual data', it also constitutes the opening in which this given will be constantly and infinitely reworked: 'And yet, following Arendt's work on Saint Augustine, the term "birth" . . . is incapable of being limited to a piece of biological data, even one that is recognized and that deserves such recognition . . . Nor is birth a pure given of Being; rather, it exposes newness at the heart of a plurality to be forever rediscovered and reconsidered': Julia Kristeva, *Hannah Arendt*, trans. Ross Guberman, New York: Columbia University Press, p. 67.

21 In her book, *Regions of Sorrow: Anxiety and Messianism in Hannah Arendt and W.H. Auden*, Stanford: Stanford University Press, 2003, Susannah Gottlieb makes a very perceptive point about the last sentence of this truly Marrano fragment, in which Christianity becomes secretly tinged with Jewish messianism: it does not appear in the Gospels, but in the Isaiah, here given in King's James version. And then she most rightly comments: 'Her argument proceeds in accordance with the worldliness of Isaiah as opposed to the otherworldly spirit of *The New Testament* . . . The "glad tidings" Arendt announces express *faith in the world* – not in God': p. 135, 137; my emphasis. Yet, it is still a *faith*, although directed towards the finite condition, and as such very much in harmony with the basic idea of *torat hayim*.

22 In German, the word *Wurf*, stemming from *werfen*, 'to throw', means 'litter': literally 'the thrown one'.

23 As, for instance, in Lacan, who describes the anthropogenic initiation in reference to 'What the Thunder Said', the fifth part of T.S. Eliot's *Waste Land*: 'That is what

the divine voice caused to be heard in the thunder: Submission, gift, grace. *Da da da'* (E, 107).

24 See this beautiful apology of the middle of life formulated by Geoffrey Hartman:

> Human life, like a poetical figure, is an indeterminate middle between overspecified poles always threatening to collapse it. The poles may be birth and death, father and mother, mother and wife, love and judgment, heaven and earth, first things and last things. Art narrates that middle region and charts it like a purgatory, for only if it exists can life exist; only if the imagination presses against the poles are *error and life . . .* possible.
>
> Geoffrey Hartman, 'The Voice of the Shuttle: Language from the Point of View of Literature', in Geoffrey Hartman and Daniel T. O'Hara, ed. *The Geoffrey Hartman Reader*, New York: Fordham University Press, 2004, p. 231; my emphasis

Even Heidegger, although himself a paradigmatic 'life-collapser', has to attest that 'as care Dasein is this "in-between" [*Als Sorge ist das Dasein das 'Zwischen'*]' (BT, 374).

25 Melanie Klein, 'Some Theoretical Conclusions Regarding the Emotional Life of the Infant', in *Envy and Gratitude and Other Works 1946–1963: The Writings of Melanie Klein*, vol. 3, New York: Free Press, 1975, pp. 61–2.

26 The term, 'metaphysics of death', derives from Hermann Cohen's 'Jewish Writings': *Reason and Hope: Selections from the Jewish Writings of Hermann Cohen*, trans. Eva Jospe, New York: W.W. Norton, 1971, p. 73, and defines the fatalistic type of religiosity built around the tragic sense of life, which imbues the whole Greek mode of 'finite thinking'. Adorno, who borrowed Cohen's term, originally referring to ancient pagan religions, applied it to Heidegger in order to demonstrate its recurring danger (MCP, 131).

27 John Milton, *Paradise Lost*, Book XII.

28 Sandor Ferenczi, *Thalassa: A Theory of Genitality*, London: Karnack Books, 1994, p. 40; my emphasis.

29 See Harold Bloom, *The Book of J*, trans. David Rosenberg, New York: Harper, 1990. On my interpretation of this motif see also my *The Saving Lie*, especially the chapter 'Jacob's Way'.

30 Erich Fromm has a very similar opinion on the primary attachments: 'they keep us in the prison of the motherly racial-national-religious fixation': Erich Fromm, *The Heart of Man: Its Genius for Good and Evil*, New York: Harper and Row, 1964, p. 107.

31 Jean-Francois Lyotard, 'Figure Foreclosed', in *Lyotard Reader*, trans. Andrew Benjamin, Oxford: Blackwell, 1989.

32 This is also how Lyotard develops the main Christian accusation against the Jews, which Freud so vigilantly diagnosed in *Moses and Monotheism*. Unlike the mediating and positively neurotic Christians, Jews will never be able to remember that they had killed their Founding Father: 'Parricide is disavowed because castration has been

foreclosed; why would one have to kill the father if it were as though the threat of castration had never existed?' (ibid., 103).

33 Despite some superficial affinities – the common dislike for traumatic solutions and belief in the powers of sublimation – Winnicott, who will figure quite large in the last chapter, is actually as anti-Lyotardian as possible. For: while for Lyotard, language is a symbolic system of a codified womb-nostalgia, in which every word attempts to undo the trauma of separation – for Winnicott, language is a symbolic system that allows us to play with the law of finitude and ease the effects of separation, by simultaneously confirming them. Language – based on the Freudian play of *Fort-Da!*, this Play of Plays – throws a net of interconnection between absent and separate units of existence; *it does not undo the trauma of birth*, but merely secures the sense of community with things that no longer participate in the unity of primary narcissism. The anti-nostalgic thrust of Winnicott's reflections on the potential sphere comes to the fore most distinctly in his analysis of the decathection of the first transitional object, which narrates what Lyotard refers to as the 'foreclosure' in a completely different manner:

> Its fate is to be gradually allowed to be decathected, so that in the course of years it becomes not so much forgotten as *relegated to limbo*. By this I mean that in health the transitional object does not 'go inside' nor does the feeling about it necessarily undergo repression. *It is not forgotten and it is not mourned.* It loses meaning, and this is because the transitional phenomena have become diffused, have become spread out over the whole intermediate territory between 'inner psychic reality' and 'the external world as perceived by two persons in common,' that is to say, over the whole cultural field.
>
> PR, 5; my emphasis

34 Emmanuel Lévinas, *Difficult Freedom*, p. 233.

35 The apology of the permanent birthing as a radical discontinuity based on *nothing* that should not be compensated by any fake semi-essence appears also very strongly in Irigaray:

> We become existent by cutting ourselves off – by ec-sisting – from our origin . . . Human being cannot develop from roots as a tree, or from an environment as an animal. Human being must take responsibility for existence beyond any continuity with regards to the roots and background. And it is understandable that Heidegger wants Being to compensate for this lack of origin, when others resort to god, a mere natural immanence or a world built by man in various modes. However, human being only exists by taking on the not-being of a continuum – a break, a void, a nothing – with regard to its provenance and its environment. A human must give itself a being with faithfulness to the living that it is.
>
> Irigaray, *To Be Born*, p. vi

36 Wallace Stevens, *A Discovery of Thought*, in *Opus Posthumous: Poems, Plays, Prose*, London: Vintage, 1990, p. 123.

Chapter 3: Derrida's *Torat Hayim*, or the Religion of the Finite Life

1 Here I am obviously making an allusion to Derrida's reading of Kafka's parable from *The Trial*, called *Vor dem Gesetz*, 'Before the Law': Jacques Derrida, 'Before the Law', in *Acts of Literature*, ed. Derek Attridge, trans. Avital Ronnel, New York: Routledge, 1992. The clue of Derrida's interpretation is the play of both spatial and temporal meaning of the phrase: *devant et avant la loi* – with a special emphasis on the latter as indicating a liminoid 'lingering on the threshold'. As it will soon become clear, this lesson of *lingering* will deliver the clue to Derrida's subtle version of messianic vitalism.

2 Martin Heidegger, *Einführung in die Metaphysik*, Hague: de Gruyter, 1987, p. 139: 'For the stubborn, life is just life. For them, death is death and only that. But the Being of life is also death. Everything that comes to life thereby already begins to die as well, to go towards its death and death is also life' (IM, 100; translation slightly modified). On the same page earlier, Heidegger defines *der Eigensinn* as a ' "caprice", *idia phronesis*, for which *logos* remains closed off, [and which] always takes hold only of this side or the other' (ibid.): this 'one-sidedness' or 'this-sidedness' is, as we remember, an essential moment in Derrida's appreciation of Cixous's dismissal of death.

3 Derrida's deliberate contrariety comes to the fore in his playful confrontation with Avital Ronell's take on the inherent connection between stupidity and life. In her book, while mentioning Nietzsche, Ronell writes: 'In fact, stupidity, purveyor of self-assured assertiveness, mutes just about everything that would seek to disturb its impervious hierarchies ... Typically for a genealogist, stupidity, in the end, is extolled for promoting life and growth: ... "and thus in a certain sense stupidity is a condition of life and growth." ': Avital Ronell, *Stupidity*, Urbana. IL and Chicago: University of Illinois Press, 2002, p. 3. Derrida is also well aware of a similar association of life with stupidity, coming from Adorno. In his sketches to the *Dialectic of Enlightenment*, Adorno links 'the genesis of stupidity' to life's self-preservatory routines which kill disinterested curiosity. 'Stupidity is a scar', because it grows in place of an amputated 'filler', which ventured out into the world, in order to connect with it, but got burnt:

> Every partial stupidity in a human being marks a spot where the awakening play of muscles has been inhibited instead of fostered ... Like the genera within the series of fauna, the intellectual gradations within the human species, indeed, the

blind spots within the same individual, *mark the points where hope has come to a halt and in their ossification bear witness to what holds all living things in thrall.*

DE, 214; my emphasis

As we have seen in my Introduction, Derrida's polemic with Adorno consists in the revindication of the concept of survival, not so 'stupid' as it may seem in the beginning.

4   Derrida does not refer to Georg Simmel explicitly, but he uses his term – *mehr-als-Leben*, 'more-than-life'. I am taking liberty here to add to Derrida's vocabulary Simmel's symmetrical term – *mehr-Leben* – to complete the dialectical formula that governs Derrida's thinking of life.

5   On the idea of transcendence as the antithetical *Gegenprinzip der Welt*, see most of all Jacob Taubes, *Occidental Eschatology*, trans. David Ratmoko, Stanford: Stanford University Press, 2009, p. 11, as well as my essay on Taubes, 'The Identity of the Spirit: Taubes between Apocalyptics and Historiosophy', in *Jewish Cryptotheologies of Late Modernity*, where I discuss the problem of the 'operative antinomianism': the advantages and disadvantages of transcendence for the immanent life.

6   This is perhaps a good opportunity to signal a major difference between Derrida and Agamben on the issue of the finite life. *Pace* the Derridean conviction that human life is dialectical and aporetic, even in its most ordinary mundane version, Agamben advocates the idea of a 'simply human life': *haplos*, undivided and unproblematic, which could have been lived without care if humankind did not choose (wrongly) the cruel process of civilization and the torture of 'anthropological machines'. The famous report from limbo – the middle realm between salvation and damnation, populated by the souls of unbaptized children – with which Agamben opens his messianic anticipations of the 'coming community', gives us a taste of what this quiet and quietistic life would look like:

> The greatest punishment, the lack of the vision of God, thus turns into a *natural joy*; irremediably lost, they persist without pain in *divine abandon*. God has not forgotten them, but rather *they have always already forgotten God* ... Their nullity ... is principally a *neutrality with respect to salvation* – the most radical objection that has ever been levied against the very idea of redemption. The truly unsaveable life is the one in which there is nothing to save ... *these beings have left the world of guilt and justice behind them*: The light that rains down on them is that irreparable light of the dawn following the *novissima dies* of judgment. But the life that begins on earth after the last day is *simply human life.*
>
> Giorgio Agamben, *The Coming Community*, trans. Michael Hardt, Minneapolis and London: Minnesota University Press, 1993, 5–6; emphasis mine

The 'simply human life' – 'beyond every idea of law': Giorgio Agamben, *Homo Sacer: Sovereign Power and Bare Life*, trans. Daniel Heller-Roazen, Stanford, CA: Stanford

University Press, 1998, p. 59 – is the greatest messianic achievement: beyond 'the world of guilt and justice', as well as beyond God, spirit or basically everything that the human subject used to assume in order to give its life a *form*; beyond any *task* whose maximum fulfilment was symbolized by the idea of redemption, or 'mission accomplished'. It just is what it is, like an *unbaptized child* abandoned from the moment of its inception, with no task or work, counting for nothing in great eschatological schemes, and because of that 'naturally joyful'. Thus the Christian imperative – 'be like children' – comes here with a non-Christian twist: 'be like *unbaptized* children'. I only signal this crucial difference here and leave the more elaborate polemic with Agamben for the next book which will come as a sequel to this one: *The Paradox of the Pious Atheism: Towards the Modern Metaphysics of Finitude* (in progress).

7 Martin Heidegger, *Ontology: Hermeneutics of Facticity*, trans. John van Buren, Bloomington: Indiana University Press, 2008, p. 5. I am grateful to King-Ho Leung for pointing out this fragment to me during the discussion on his doctoral thesis, 'Being, Living, Thinking: Metaphysics and Philosophy as a Way of Life', written under the supervision of John Milbank, University of Nottingham, and devoted to the scholastic category of life as a 'middle term' and its uneasy survival in modernity.

8 The question of being becoming transitive in factical life appears also in Heidegger's lectures on Aristotle: 'Our approach springs from the phenomenological interpretation of the phenomenon, "life," and is articulated through the intransitive and transitive senses of being in, out of, for, with, and against a world': Martin Heidegger, *Phenomenological Interpretations of Aristotle: Initiation into Phenomenological Research*, trans. Richard Rojcewicz, Bloomington: Indiana University Press, 2008, p. 65. Being becomes transitive in being simultaneously lived and interpreted by the living 'being-in-the-world': 'interpreting is itself a possible and distinctive *how* of the character of being of facticity. Interpreting is a being which belongs to the being of factical life itself [*Die Auslegung is Seiendes vom Sein des faktischen Lebens selbst*]': Heidegger, *Ontology*, p. 12.

9 On Heidegger's often unacknowledged debt to *Lebensphilosophie*, see most of all David Farrell Krell, *Daimon Life: Heidegger and Life-Philosophy*, Bloomington: Indiana University Press, 1992, p. xi: 'However much Heidegger inveighs against life-philosophy his own fundamental ontology and poetics of being thrust him back onto *Lebensphilosophie* again and again.'

10 In stressing the importance of Heidegger's notion of 'factical life' for Derrida, I am partly following John D. Caputo who, in the chapter 'A Number of Messianisms', tries to elucidate Derrida's messianic thrust by referring to the 'existential structures', extracted by Heidegger from the 'experience of the factical life in the early Christian communities': John D. Caputo, *The Prayers and Tears of Jacques Derrida: Religion Without Religion*, Bloomington: Indiana University Press, 1997, p. 139. The factical

life is thus called because its experience is singular and preconceptual: it is not a life captured by philosophy or biological sciences and it does not belong to the totality of nature. I therefore agree with Caputo that 'factical life' is important for Derrida's messianic effort to see *what human life is capable of before it is structured – and tamed down – by the pre-established set of concepts.* The *transitivity* of being, therefore, can reveal itself *only* in the factical life – precisely because it is an open existential module in which Dasein boldly experiments with the life it lives. But if I say that I follow Caputo only partly, it is also because I want to avoid interpreting Derrida's messianicity in reference to Blanchot.

11 See the classical locus of this elimination of life in Heidegger's 'Letter on Humanism':

> Above and beyond everything else, however, it finally remains to ask whether the essence of man [*das Wesen des Menschen*] primordially and most decisively lies in the dimension of *animalitas* at all. Are we really on the right track toward the essence of man as long as we set him off *as one living creature among others* in contrast to plants, beasts, and God? . . . Metaphysics thinks of man on the basis of *animalitas* and does not think in the direction of his *humanitas*.
>
> Martin Heidegger, 'Letter on Humanism', in *Basic Writings*, trans. David Farrell Krell, London: Routledge, 1993, pp. 153, 157; my emphasis

12 In his *Encyclopaedia*, Hegel distinguishes three kinds of soul: vegetative, sensuous and real, of which the middle one is the living soul, as long as life, in Hegel's definition, is a contradiction manifesting itself mostly in the affect of pain:

> The [sensuous] subject is immersed in particularity of its affections, yet, at the same time, through the ideal aspect of their particularity, it builds itself into a subjective whole. In this way it becomes a *Selbstgefühl*, a self-affection – but always a particular one . . . [It is, therefore,] still prone to pathology [*Krankheit*], which consists in its stubbornly sticking to the particularity of its own self-affection, which it cannot (or, will not) work through and raise to the level of ideality.
>
> G.W.F. Hegel, *Enzyclopädie der philosophischen Wissenschaften im Grundrisse*, ed. Georg Lasson, Leipzig: Verlag der Dürr'schen Buchhandlung, 1905, p. 360; §§407–8

Stuck in the middle between non-reflective vegetative life process and the pure rationality of the 'real soul', *die fühlende Seele* is *krank*, 'sick' and in pain: it *stubbornly* sticks to its living particularity, at the same time knowing that it inevitably ends in the generality of death.

13 On this secret identity, see the powerful reading of Descartes's *Meditations* offered by Hans Blumenberg in *The Legitimacy of the Modern Age*, trans. Robert M. Wallace, Cambridge, MA: MIT Press, 1985, in the chapter '*Cogito* and Theological Absolutism', where *cogito* emerges out of an apotropaic defence against the omnipotence of the nominalist deity, called by Ockham *Deus Fallax*, or the *Devious God*: pp. 196–7.

14 Maurice Blanchot, *The Instant of My Death*, trans. Elizabeth Rottenberg, Stanford: Stanford University Press, 2000, p. 10: 'He was perhaps suddenly invincible. Dead – immortal . . . Henceforth, he was bound to death by a surreptitious friendship.' Derrida comments:

> The syntax of this *sentence without sentence*, of this *death without sentence* of which Blanchot also speaks elsewhere, sums up everything in a single stroke. *No verb.* A hyphen, a line of union and separation, a disjunctive link wordlessly marks the place of all logical modalities: *dead and yet immortal, dead because immortal, dead insofar as immortal* (an immortal does not live), immortal from the moment that and in so far as dead, although and for as long as dead; for once dead no longer dies and, according to all possible modes, one has become immortal, thus accustoming oneself to – nothing. He is already dead, since there has been a verdict, but *an immortal is someone who is dead.*
>
> > Jacques Derrida, *Demeure: Fiction and Testimony* (postscript to Maurice Blanchot, *The Instant of My Death*), trans. Elizabeth Rottenberg, Stanford: Stanford University Press, 2000, p. 67; my emphasis

15 See the epigraph to Jacques Derrida, *Voice and Phenomenon: Introduction to the Problem of the Sign in Husserl's Phenomenology*, trans. Leonard Lawlor, Evanston, IL: Northwestern University Press, 2010.

16 While commenting on Derrida's critique of Heidegger in his last seminar, David Farrell Krell agrees that, in Heidegger, life ultimately remains unthought:

> in one of the very first remarks about 'life' in *Being and Time*, Heidegger says, 'Life is neither pure being-at-hand nor Dasein.' That means that neither 'categories' nor 'existentials' apply to life, and this leaves ontology very little to say about life. Ontology gapes at the mystery of life, even of human life, which like all life, you will remember, comes to an end. At the same time, such a collapse of the distinction between Dasein and its others might open a space in which other life-forms, precisely in their exposure to a shattering, could join Dasein as *commourans*.
>
> > David Farrell Krell, *Derrida and Our Animal Others*, p. 107

Krell, however, always loyal to Heidegger, remains ultimately on the side of his *memento mori* – while Derrida would like to change the emphasis and present his sense of solidarity with other living beings in terms of the universal task of *survival*: the 'animal others', therefore, would be not so much *commourans* as *co-survivors*. See also Krell's comment deriving from his later book, slightly more critical towards Heidegger:

> The other end is birth, and a fundamental ontology of Dasein cannot ignore it. If one were to focus on this other 'end', the end that is the beginning of Dasein, one would perhaps make the discovery that Dasein is *alive*. Does Heidegger deny this? Does he ever doubt that Dasein, which dies, is alive? No, not really. Yet he is

not comfortable admitting it. There is something about the *viviparity* of Dasein
that offends.

David Farrell Krell, *Ecstasy, Catastrophe*, p. 62

This life-negating tendency has been also spotted by Michel Haar: 'The potentiality
for dying can be identified only with the pure potentiality for being at the expense of
a *forgetting of life* ... In Heidegger we find a recoil in the face of life ... Life is
alienation, the temptation of existence to *fall below itself*': Haar, *Heidegger*, p. 13; my
emphasis. This 'fallenness', however, constituting a vital dimension of 'following' and
'falling *for life*', is precisely what Derrida hears in his own translation of Dasein as
'Here Below' (HCL, 88).

17 And although Derrida puts Lévinas in the same line of 'aggressively' anthropological
thinkers, his own critique of the Heideggerian elimination of life for the sake of pure
thinking / pure being – 'mortality without life' – very much resembles a similar
objection which was posed against Heidegger by Lévinas in the series of lectures
from 1975, *God, Death, and Time*. In the opening lecture, Lévinas claims that the
Heideggerian reduction of Dasein only to *Angst und Sorge* about being, which is
always its being, immerses Dasein in the 'ontological affair' without any remainder
and defines it through its 'undeniable attachment to the task of being' (GDT, 35):
'The *conatus* measures his obedience to being, the wholeness of this to-be-in-
service-to-being, which is in man's charge. The affair of being is to such a degree his
own that the meaning of being is *his affair*' (GDT, 25). Dasein, obsessed with being
and *just* being, must, however, face the paradox. By binding the anticipation of death
with anxiety as the basic emotive mode of self-preservation – a motif also spotted by
Adorno – Heidegger forces Dasein to submit to the inexorable law of the cycle,
which, in the end, becomes the law of identity: 'to have to be *is* to have to die' (GDT,
41). This absolute subordination to ontology, says Lévinas, must then result in
Dasein assuming death as its mode of living, according to Heidegger's own dictum:
'Death is a form of being that Dasein assumes from the moment that it is' (BT, 289).
Desperately labouring on living up to the task of being, therefore, Dasein becomes
ready to die as soon as it is born.

18 One correction: since Hegel knew Herder, the anthropology of initial deficiency and
immaturity was also known to him, although obviously not in modern terms of
'neoteny'.

19 Jacques Lacan, *Écrits*, Paris: Editions de Seuil, 1966, pp. 819–20; my emphasis; in a
different English translation: E, 316.

20 The Derridean Kingdom of *khora* could thus be compared to the Garden of Eden as
Paradise Regained: 'The key to such a regeneration of paradise, of the Golden Age to
come, in Derrida's view, is to recognize the Earth's surface as a garden of infinite
differences and differentiations, a garden not spoiled by any single sovereign
division, which always amounts to an 'us' versus 'them'. Especially where other

animals are concerned': David Farrell Krell, *Derrida and the Animal Others*, p. 101. What unites all creatures is the garden is the *shared task of survival*, which may be achieved by different means, but always governed by the same goal: to linger awhile, to stay, to remain.

21 Michael Naas, 'The Philosophy and Literature of the Death Penalty: Two Sides of the Same Sovereign', *The Southern Journal of Philosophy* 50, Spindel Supplement (2012): 53.

22 The demonstration of the possibility of the religion of the finite life can also be read as a direct polemic with Martin Hägglund's 'radically atheist' interpretation of Derrida, for whom there is only one, fully exhaustive, alternative: either religion of the infinite life or complete irreligiosity. According to Hägglund, Derrida, who defends the 'time of life' against any eternalizing hypostasis, is the most radical type of atheist, and fundamentally so in the phenomenological sense of the word. His investment in the ever-disseminating temporality, which can only leave a transient trace of its presence, makes Derrida a staunch enemy of any form of the Absolute conceived as a timeless *nunc stans*. By insisting on the inherent connection between transience and life, Derrida dismisses all religious attempts to think in terms of life infinite and immortal as leading out of the domain of life and into the realm of death: the unchanging and untouchable Absolute can never be alive, it is death pure and simple. As long as there is life, there is exposure to time, scathedness and vulnerability: the idea of Absolute Life, essential to *all* religions, is thus a *contradictio in adjecto*. Life can only affirm itself as a constant effort of survival, which, according to Hägglund, is the defining feature of radical atheism. It is the desire for survival that dissimulates itself as the desire for immortality; but while it precedes the latter, it also contradicts it from within: 'There is thus an internal contradiction in the so-called desire for immortality. If one were not attached to mortal life, there would be no fear of death and no desire to live on': Martin Hägglund, *Radical Atheism: Derrida and the Time of Life*, Stanford: Stanford University Press, 2008, p. 2. Hägglund's interpretation aims to re-read the whole of Derrida's work (from his earliest deconstruction of Husserl up to his latest seminars on death penalty and sovereignty) as the stubborn attempt to reformulate our attitude to survival as ultimately positive: 'The radical finitude of survival – he says – is not a lack of being that is desirable to overcome. Rather, the finitude of survival opens the chance for everything that is desired and the threat of everything that is feared' (ibid.). Because of that the very concept of God who is 'beyond everything that can be predicated by a finite being' (ibid., 7) and who, by definition given by Jean-Luc Marion, cannot die ('If God were not immortal, he would not be God', ibid., 8) – must be abandoned. To say, therefore, that 'God is dead' is not yet enough. According to Hägglund, Derrida radicalizes the atheist thesis by implying that *God is death* – as the direct opposite of everything finite and alive: 'If to be alive is to be mortal, it follows that to *not* be

mortal – to be immortal – is to be dead. If one cannot die, one is dead. Hence, Derrida does not limit himself to the atheist claim that God is dead; he repeatedly makes the radically atheist claim that *God is death*' (ibid., 8). I have no quarrel whatsoever with this beautifully clear analysis. If indeed, God were to be defined in Jean-Luc Marion's way, it would be advisable to become a 'radical atheist'. Fortunately, however, there is a *third* option – the religion of the finite life – and there is a plenty of evidence in Derrida himself to demonstrate it.

23 Compare the commentary of Matthias Fritsch:

> And that is why the death penalty is for Derrida the 'keystone' of a theologico-political matrix welded together out of, first, a philosophical onto-theology that is seen, by Heidegger and Derrida, to dominate the history of Western metaphysics; second, out of a thinking of the political along the lines of the sovereign state; and third, out of a certain concept of what is 'proper to man' as that which transcends his mere life, his dignity residing precisely in something above mere or bare life, in the ability to risk his life, a dignity to which justice relates and on which rational law (both moral and juridical) is founded.
>
> Matthias Fritsch, 'Derrida on the Death Penalty', *The Southern Journal of Philosophy* 50, Spindel Supplement (2012): 61

24 Derrida juxtaposes Shakespeare's '*Mercy seasons justice*', falling on it with a gentle rain of Christ's blood, with a similar line in Hugo: 'the gentle [*douce*] law of Christ will finally permeate the legal code and radiate out from there' (quot. in DP1, 201). And comments:

> It is going to irrigate the law, the written legislation. Little by little, Christ, the spirit, the soul, the gentle law, the gentleness of Christ, charity, the blood of Christ, is going to *irrigate the legal code and transform legislative writing*. So he is playing here natural law against written law while hoping, while even being sure that natural law – the heart, finally, Jesus is the heart, the blood is the heart – the heart is going to transform the written and positive, historical law. *Little by little, the legal code, written law, historical law, will be irrigated, inspired, vivified, spiritualized, by gentleness, the gentle law of Christ.*
>
> DP1, 201; my emphasis

25 This rule, as for so many others in the domain of the philosophy of life, has also been formulated first by Schopenhauer who said: 'no one has a really lively conviction of the certainty of his death, as otherwise there could not be a very great difference between his frame of mind and that of the condemned criminal': Arthur Schopenhauer, *The World as Will and Representation*, trans. E.F.J. Payne, New York: Dover, 1969, p. 281.

26 Or, simply: Thanatos and Eros. See Jacques Derrida, *Given Time: I. Counterfeit Money*, trans. Peggy Kamuf, Chicago: Chicago University Press, 1994.

27 It is also this aspect of extension, as opposed to intensity, that Benjamin sees not just in Scheherazade, Leskov and Kafka, but also, as we have seen, in Hölderlin, especially in *Die Blödigkeit*: 'walking on the carpet of the living' is preferable here to the vertical ascension to the divine heights populated by the immortals. In case of Cixous, however, Derrida spots a different strategy, the one of 'acceleration', the result of which, however, seems similar: to outplay time, deprive the middle of life of all sharp sides and edges, give it its own span: 'that life may live for life and in order to see, at full speed, briskly [*vivement*]: at all times but at speed that, playing with time, outplays time' (HCL, 61–2).

28 This allusion to John Donne's *Holy Sonnets*, where the True Church (and also the True Israel) is being compared to a *fallen woman* who offers her services to everybody, with no discrimination or distinction, is far from accidental on my part. Also in *Rogues*, the theme of *khora* emerges messianically contaminated with the figure of Shekhinah: the last and most kenotic of the Kabbalistic divine hypostases, which signifies God's presence on earth.

29 Hegel, *On Christianity*, p. 229; my emphasis. On the theme of criminality, here also associated with the 'Jewish principle of destruction', compare again Heidegger's *Black Notes* from 1941:

> The authentic experience that has been allotted to today's generation, but which it was not able to take over, see through, and lay back into its essential inception, is the unrestricted outbreak of the unconditioned criminality of the modern human essence, in accordance with its role in the empowerment of power into machination. Criminality [*Verbrechen*]: that is no mere breaking up [*Zerbrechen*], but the devastation of everything into what is broken. *What is broken is broken off from the inception and dispersed into the realm of the fragmentary.* Here, there remains only one possibility of being – in the mode of order. Ordering is only the reverse of criminality, understood in terms of the history of being (not, say, in a juridical-moral way).
>
> GA 96, p. 266; my emphasis

30 Theodor Reik, *The Compulsion to Confess: On the Psychoanalysis of Crime and Punishment*, New York: Grove Press, 1961.

31 'When one loves intimately, if one loves life (but can one love in general without loving life?) for whoever loves life, life is worth the *peine* [trouble, pain] of being lived . . . Is there a price of life that would not be above life itself – and that therefore would not be other than life itself, of another order?' (DP2, 111; my emphasis)

32 'Du bist der Natur einen Tod schuldig': this sentence from *Traumdeutung* is translated by James Strachey as 'Thou owest Nature a death', for which he finds the sources in Shakespeare's *Henry IV*, where Falstaff says: *Thou owest God a death* and calls it Freud's 'favourite misquotation'. In the text written right after the outbreak of the First World War, *Thoughts for the Time of War and Death*, Freud repeats this message, by scolding modern people for having forgotten the correct attitude towards death:

To anyone who listened to us we were of course prepared to maintain that death was the necessary outcome of life, that everyone owes nature a death (*dass jeder von uns der Natur einen Tod schuldet*) and must expect to pay the debt (*die Schuld zu bezahlen*) – in short, that death was natural, undeniable and unavoidable. In reality, however, we were accustomed to behave as if it were otherwise. We showed an unmistakable tendency to put death on one side, to eliminate it from life. We tried to hush it up.

SE 14, 289

But, Freud continues, speaking here as a true thanatic believer, converted to the faith in death by the event of war: 'death will no longer be denied; we are forced to *believe in it*' (ibid., 291; my emphasis).

33 This juxtaposition of 'machine' and 'miracle', where the latter emerges as an almost impossible rarity, alludes to the title of Michael Naas's commentary on Derrida's 'Faith and Knowledge', which presents it as the main messianic target of deconstruction: Michael Naas, *Miracle and Machine*, New York: Fordham University Press, 2012.

34 This is the reason why Derrida postulates the existence of the *talionic drive* which would represent the unconsciousness's take on justice:

> A law that is pure, one that is allegedly purely rational, is just translating the unconscious drive. Like a refined and intellectualized descendent, it proceeds, descends, and stems from its archaic ancestor, the *talionic drive*, all of whose family features it preserves. Reik describes the allegedly rational law, the juridical discourse on the law of the talion, as the intellectualized 'outgrowth' of the archaic unconscious drive.
>
> DP2, 178–9; my emphasis

35 Reik, *The Compulsion to Confess*, p. 425; DP2, 170.

36 This deep unconscious complex which turns every death into a 'death penalty' has been confirmed by Otto Rank. On Rank's account, a neurotic is someone who feels that he

> must bribe life itself, for which, according to Schopenhauer's deep insight, we all *pay with death* ... He does this through a constant restriction of life (restraint through fear), that is, *he refuses the loan (life) in order thus to escape the payment of the debt (death)* ... his own instigation transforms the death punishment that is placed upon life into lifelong punishment he imposes upon himself.
>
> MBH, 271; my emphasis

A neurotic, therefore, would refuse to make *use* of life because of a deep anxiety which tells him that life does not belong to him.

37 See again the ambivalent fragment from Freud's reflections on war and death: 'To sum up: our unconscious is just as inaccessible to the idea of our own death, just as

murderously inclined towards strangers, just as divided (that is, ambivalent) towards those we love, as was primaeval man. But how far we have moved from the primal state in our conventional and cultural attitude towards death!' (SE14, 299).

38 Jacques Derrida, *The Postcard: From Socrates to Freud and Beyond*, trans. Alan Bass, Chicago: University of Chicago Press, 1987.

39 This is also the moment in which Derrida diverts from Lévinas and his equally 'disinterested' view of ethics, even if inspired by the radically non-Kantian heteronomy of the Other. In her *Precarious Life*, Judith Butler, who also claims to pursue 'the possible Jewish ethic of non-violence': Judith Butler, *Precarious Life: The Power of Mourning and Violence*, London: Verso, 2004, p. 131, sums up Lévinas's position very aptly, pointing precisely to the foundational moment of the ethical 'awakening' that has nothing to do with the extrapolation of *my* own self-preservatory interest on the condition of the Other:

> To respond to face, to understand its meaning, means to be awake to what is precarious in another life or, rather, the precariousness of life itself. This cannot be an awakeness, to use his word, to my own life, and then an extrapolation from an understanding of my own precariousness to an understanding of another's precarious life. It has to be an understanding of the precariousness of the Other. This is what makes the face belong to the sphere of ethics.
>
> ibid., 134

For Derrida, however, this sudden suspension of the self-preservatory interest seems suspect – precisely as the sign of the thanatic cruelty of the unconscious taken to the superegoic level, where it fulfils its 'wish to kill' by turning it against the ego itself. Similarly, Butler also does not believe that it is possible – or even desirable – 'to sidestep self-preservation in the way that Lévinas implies', because 'as a super-egoic state, ethics threatens to become a pure culture of the death-drive' (ibid., 140). What she, however, finds valuable in Lévinas is the constant tension between self-preservation and the biophilic respect for another life, which Lévinas depicts succinctly in one phrase referring to Jacob awaiting Esau in the desert: *frightened for his own life, but anxious he might have to kill.* In Derrida's account this tension moves into a single subject divided between her conscious and unconscious life: while the latter wants to kill, the former feels anxious for its existence and devises a defence mechanism in the form of discourse/narrative/*récit*. As Butler nicely puts it: 'the inability to kill is the situation of discourse' in which 'language communicates the precariousness of life that establishes the ongoing tension of the non-violent ethics' (ibid., 139). And although Butler does not recognize much affinity between her and Derrida, they both seem to be driving at a similar revision of Lévinas with Spinoza/ Rosenzweig in the background (however unlikely it might sound from the perspective of the Lévinasian orthodoxy): they both look for a *limit* to the egoism of self-preservation that would *not* come from the thanatic angle, i.e. not from the contempt-for-life, but from the love-of-life, which – when generalized thanks to the discourse – keeps the particular *conatus* and its self-preservatory interest in check.

40 Naas, as usual, comments very aptly: 'In other words, the generalization and reinscription of autoimmunity allows him to pose questions of nature and life *otherwise*': Michael Naas, *Derrida From Now On*, New York: Fordham University Press, 2008, p. 140; my emphasis. This Lévinasian *otherwise* is essential here, because it allows us to differentiate Derrida's approach from other contemporary – mostly biopolitical – philosophies of auto/immunology (e.g. Esposito). Yet, although Derrida insists on the more-than-biological understanding of his definition of life as 'self-preference', he himself also commented on biology in the context of deconstruction. For instance, in the still unpublished seminar from 1975–6, *La vie le mort* [Life/Death], Derrida refers to the work of Francois Jacob on DNA and examines it in terms of his theory of textuality as developed in *On the Grammatology*. On Derrida's engagement with biology, see most of all: Francesco Vitale, *Biodeconstruction: Jacques Derrida and Life Sciences*, trans. Mauro Senatore, Albany, NY: SUNY Press, 2018.

41 Henri Bergson, *Two Sources of Morality and Religion*, trans. R Ashley Audra and Cloudesley Brereton, Notre Dame, IN: Notre Dame University Press, 1977.

42 Compare the fragment in *The Star of Redemption*, in which Rosenzweig defines life as a phenomenon transcending the realm of biology, characterized by the resistance to the 'ephemerality' of mere existence:

> It is only the visible sign of a *concept of life that extends its domain of intervention well beyond the limits of organic nature*. Not only living essences exist, but also institutions, societies, feelings, things, works – *everything, really everything can be alive*. But what does this being-alive mean, then, as opposed to mere existence? Really only what we have just now already said: the figure that is its very own, forming itself and coming out from within and hence necessarily lasting.
>
> SR-G, 239–40; my emphasis

43 Perhaps the Jewish dimension of this living-loving can be best visible in Derrida's secret/Marrano pun on the name of his father Hayim Aime: 'Aime being merely the French or Christian transliteration of Haim, that is to say, as you know, life. My father was therefore called Life – he was called "Life" all his life, for life. Life: *aimé*, loved' (HCL, 57).

44 Johann Gottlieb Fichte, *The Way Towards the Blessed Life*, p. 2.

45 Which made Rosenzweig criticize Hegel in turn and reinstall the concept of love – precisely as loving-living, i.e. the generally biophilic affect of the Slave, in whom *love* arises to challenge the Lordly thanaticism. See again my 'The Thanatic Strain: Kojève and Rosenzweig as Two Readers of Hegel'.

46 'I am a kind of Marrano of French Catholic Culture, and I also have my Christian
body, inherited from St. Augustine . . . I am one of those Marranos who, even in the
intimacy of their own hearts, do not admit to being Jewish': Jacques Derrida,
Circumfession, in Jacques Derrida and Geoffrey Bennington, *Jacques Derrida*,
Chicago: University of Chicago Press, 1993, p. 160.

47 Another religion would thus be announced with the concept of the unconditional
once and for all dissociated from the concept of sovereignty. In the live exchange
with Yvonne Sherwood, Kevin Hart and John D. Caputo, called 'Epoché and Faith',
Derrida says:

> I have tried again and again to dissociate two concepts that are usually
> indissociable: unconditionality and sovereignty. I would like to think about
> something unconditional in forgiving, in grace, in forgiveness, in the gift, in
> hospitality – an unconditionality that wouldn't be a sign of power, a sign of
> sovereignty . . . One has to dissociate God's sovereignty from God, from the very
> idea of God. We would have God without sovereignty, without omnipotence.
>
> Jacques Derrida, 'Epoché and Faith', in *Derrida and Religion: Other Testaments*,
> ed. Yvonne Sherwood and Kevin Hart, New York: Routledge, 2005, p. 42

48 Derrida's insistence on the redemptive aspect of *hora incerta*, which gives life its
time, can also be read as yet another polemical vista towards Heidegger. It is, after all,
in *Being and Time*, where Heidegger says: 'Along with the certainty of death goes the
indefiniteness of its "when"' (BT, 302). Yet, while Heidegger criticizes the fallen mode
of 'everyday existence' for 'covering up' the indefiniteness of 'when', by 'interposing
before it those urgencies and possibilities which can be taken in at a glance, and
which belong to the everyday matters that are closest to us' (ibid.) – Derrida
endorses the 'everyday' strategy of Dasein / Here Below as the one of active
postponement. And while Heidegger needs the indefiniteness of 'when' only to make
death imminent, i.e. 'possible at any moment' (ibid.) – Derrida uses it as the means of
deproximation, i.e. keeping death at bay.

49 The writers indeed seem to have good feel of the blessings deriving from the
indeterminate 'lingering', e.g. Paul Bowles in *The Sheltering Sky*, where he makes his
hero, Port Moresby, a *moriturus* who is to die soon, but does not yet know about it,
say: 'Death is always on the way, but the fact that you don't know when it will arrive
seems to take away from the finiteness of life. It's that terrible precision that we hate
so much. But because we don't know, we get to think of life as an inexhaustible well':
Paul Bowles, *The Sheltering Sky*, London: Penguin Classics, 2004, p. 253.

50 Again, the Derridean argument that what gives life its proper sense of temporality is
the blessed ignorance of the exact date of our expiration also comes from Simmel
who, in 'Death and Immortality', says: 'In the form in which we live, life is only
possible precisely on this basis of knowledge of the fact and non-knowledge of its
time-point': Georg Simmel, *The View of Life*, p. 68.

Chapter 4: Another Infinity: Towards Messianic Psychoanalysis

1   Compare also:

> What psychoanalysts call more or less complacently the unconscious remains, it
> seems to me, one of the privileged sources, one of the vitally mortal and mortally
> vital reserves or resources, for this implacable law of the self-destructive
> conservation of the 'subject' or of egological ipseity … Without autoimmunity
> there would be neither psychoanalysis nor what psychoanalysis calls the
> 'unconscious.' Not to mention, therefore, the 'death drive,' the cruelty of 'primary
> sadism and masochism' – or even what we just as complacently call 'consciousness.'
>
> R, 55

But Derrida seems to be dissatisfied with the death drive hypothesis from very early
on. The doubt whether Thanatos is the best way to represent the presence of death in
life appears already in Derrida's reading of Freud's *Beyond the Pleasure Principle* in
his seminar *La vie le mort* from the 1970s. Clearly unhappy with the definition of the
death drive as a strict 'beyond' to all functions of life – or, perhaps, unhappy with the
hypothesis of the death drive as such – Derrida exposes in Freud a different kind of
pleasure which eventually overrules the reductive and unimaginative understanding
of *Lust* as determined by Eros's self-preservatory and self-reproductory goals. To
speculate on the death drive brings Freud enormous pleasure, which once again
locates death 'within the pleasure principle' and not, as an oppositional force, outside
life. The *speculative pleasure*, therefore, overrules the death drive towards the *beyond*
of life and thus retains the death drive as its object *within* life: precisely the way
Heinz, Freud's grandson, pulls back into his cot the string in the famous play of
Fort-Da! On Derrida's reading, pleasure – particularly the speculative one – would
thus be as strong as death, bound together in the insoluble unity of *sur-vie*: I will
develop this intuition further on, in the section devoted to Another Sublimation (I
would like to thank here Elisabeth Rottenberg for her analysis of this seminal
fragment of Derrida's yet unpublished seminar, which she gave in her keynote lecture
during the Derrida Today conference in Montreal, in May 2018).

2   See Gershom Scholem, 'Reflections on Jewish Theology', in *On Jews and Judaism in
    Crisis: Selected Essays*, New York: Schocken Books, 1976, p. 278; Jacob Taubes,
    'Religion and the Future of Psychoanalysis', in *From Cult to Culture: Fragments
    Towards a Critique of Historical Reason*, trans. Aleida Assmann, Stanford: Stanford
    University Press, 2009; Yosef Hayim Yerushalmi, *Freud's Moses: Judaism Terminable
    and Interminable*, New Haven, CT: Yale University Press, 1991; MM, p. 64. Also
    Walter Benjamin, in 'Capitalism as Religion', claims that the tragic economy of guilt
    and self-sacrifice are at the basis of psychoanalysis: 'Freudian theory also belongs to

the priestly domination of this cult. It is conceived in a thoroughly capitalist manner. The repressed, the sinful representation is, – by virtue of a profound analogy, yet to be thought through – capital, which pays interest on the hell of the unconscious' (SW 1, 289). It does so, by generating always more guilt, which infinitely and actively delays the recovery of the 'innocence of becoming', which, for Benjamin, is the necessary feature of the messianic redemption. If psychoanalysis is on the side of guilt *only*, then it belongs to the tragic paradigm.

3 Walter Benjamin, *Illuminations*, p. 133.

4 See Ernst Bloch, *Traces*, trans. Anthony Nassar, Stanford: Stanford University Press, 2006, the fragment 'Invisible Hand', p. 158. Having told the story of a miraculous, yet at the same time quite ordinary, candle that saved life of a certain Jewish travelling businessman, Bloch concludes:

> So there is in this horror story a remarkable twist that undoes it, or rather a moment that is still alive today, already familiar to every businessman: the invisible hand. The practical intuition that does not massively shift things but only twists them the right way a little, and puts them in place, with this organ's quiet sense of touch. It lets itself be guided by fortune, by the same fortune that is buried, yet is the believer's obscure foundation in his world . . . Another rabbi, a true Kabbalist, once said: To bring about the kingdom of freedom, it is not necessary that everything be destroyed, and a new world begin; rather, this cup, or that bush, or that stone, and so all things must only be shifted a little. Because this 'a little' is a hard thing to do, and its measure so hard to find, humanity cannot do it in this world; instead this is why the Messiah comes.

5 Also Adorno commented on the possibility of the miraculous 'slight adjustment' apropos his critique of Heidegger's 'unimaginative' approach to death:

> In a *life that is no longer disfigured*, that no longer prohibits, in a life that would no longer cheat men out of their dues – in such a life men would probably no longer have to hope, in vain, that this life would after all give them what it had so far refused. For the same reason they would not have to fear so greatly that they would lose this life, no matter how deeply this fear had been ingrained in them.
>
> Theodor W. Adorno, *Jargon*, p. 155; my emphasis

And in another place from a similar period:

> *The less people really live* – or, perhaps, more correctly, the more they become aware that *they have not really lived* – the more abrupt and frightening death becomes for them, and the more it appears as a misfortune. It is as if, in death, they experienced their own reification: that they were corpses from the first . . . And it might therefore be said that if life were lived rightly, the experience of death would also be changed radically, in its innermost composition.
>
> MCP, 136

The idea of life lived to the full, not just mere living, figures also very strongly in Peter Sloterdijk's *Critique of Cynical Reason*, deeply indebted to late Adorno's messianic variation on the vitalist themes:

> Our being in society comprises almost a priori the threat that we will not be allowed to realize the vitality with which we were born. Every socialized life lives with the premonition that its energies, time, willing, and wishing will not be at an end when the death knell rings, *Life builds residues – an immense, burning Not Yet that needs more time and future than is granted to the individual. Life dreams beyond itself and dies full of defiance.* For this reason, the history of higher civilizations vibrates with countless and boundless Not Yet screams-with a million-voiced No to a death that is not the expiration of the dying embers of life but a violent suffocation of a flame that in any case did not burn as brightly as it could have done in a vital freedom ... Religion is not primarily the opiate of the people but the reminder that there is more life in us than this life lives. The function of faith is an achievement of devitalized bodies that cannot be completely robbed of the memory that in them much deeper sources of vitality, strength, pleasure, and of the enigma and intoxication of being-there must lie hidden than can be seen in everyday life. This gives religions their ambiguous role in societies: they can be used to legitimate and double oppression. They can, however, also liberate individuals to a greater power of resistance and creativity by helping them to overcome fear. Thus, depending on circumstances, religion can be both an instrument of domination *and* the core of resistance against domination; a medium of repression *and* a medium of emancipation; an instrument of devitalization and a precept of revitalization.
>
> Peter Sloterdijk, *Critique of Cynical Reason*, trans. Michael Eldred, Minneapolis: University of Minnesota Press, 1988, pp. 277–8; my emphasis

6   See Sigmund Freud and Josef Breuer, *Studies on Hysteria*, trans. James Strachey, Basic Books: New York, 2000, s. 350.

7   The transcendental nature of anxiety as a free-floating energy has been confirmed by Freud himself who described it as able to 'attach itself to any suitable representation at any time' (SE, 3, 93). The Kantian allusion would thus promote anxiety to the status of the originary 'intuition' of self-consciousness, which constitutes the ultimate centre of the psychic life, called for this reason by Kant 'transcendental apperception':

> The 'I think' must be able to accompany all my representations; for otherwise something would be represented in me that could not be thought at all, which is as much as to say that the representation would either be impossible or else at least *would be nothing for me.* That representation that can be given prior to all thinking is called intuition. Thus all manifold of intuition has a necessary relation to the I think in the same subject in which this manifold is to be encountered ... I call it

the pure apperception, in order to distinguish it from the empirical one, or also the *original apperception*, since it is that self-consciousness which, because it produces the representation I think, which must be able to accompany all others and which in all consciousness is one and the same, cannot be accompanied by any further representation. I also call its unity the transcendental unity of self-consciousness in order to designate the possibility of a priori cognition from it.

> Immanuel Kant, 'On the Original-Synthetic Unity of Apperception',
> in *Critique of Pure Reason*, B 132, trans. Paul Guyer and Allen W. Wood,
> Cambridge: Cambridge University Press, 1999, p. 246; my emphasis

In 'Beyond Anxiety', Samuel Weber deepens the Kantian association by ascribing to anxiety an arch-original status, prior to any distinction between the external and the internal, the objective and the subjective: 'The reality of anxiety and of the danger to which it reacts, emerges as neither simply external nor internal, neither straightforwardly functional, nor dysfunctional; the functioning of the psyche is, intrinsically, as it were, bound up with an irreducible exteriority, with an alterity that it simultaneously denies and affirms': Samuel Weber, *Return to Freud: Jacques Lacan's Dislocation of Psychoanalysis*, trans. Michael Levine, Cambridge: Cambridge University Press, 1991, p. 156. This alterity, very aptly called by Lacan 'extimate', constitutes the core of any psychic life, for better and for worse – and this is why Lacan, having taken his lesson from Kierkegaard, instructs that 'one should not come to terms too quickly with anxiety' (quot. in Weber, 162). Heidegger, too, makes a similar move when he, in the section of *Being and Time* devoted to the discussion of Kant's transcendental apperception, substitutes Kant's abstract thinking for caring, *die Sorge*, which also has capability to accompany all interactions with the world (BT, 318–22, pp. 366–8). The difference with Heidegger, however, will be that while Freud leaves open a possibility of anxiety evolving into another form of accompanying self-intuition, for Heidegger *Angst und Sorge* are fixed *existentialia* belonging to the very ontology of Dasein.

8 Freud maintained the view that anxiety is the direct product of the libido transformation for a very long time but eventually gave it up in 1926 with the publication *Inhibitions, Symptoms, and Anxiety*, where the ego becomes the privileged 'seat of anxiety' and anxiety is seen by Freud mostly as a reaction to trauma or danger. Yet, even at this level, Freud still uses the term of 'instinctual anxiety' (or 'id-anxiety'), marking the surplus of libido, as opposed to the 'ego-anxiety' which, according to Freud, employs 'desexualized energy' and because of that 'weakens the close connection between anxiety and libido'; Sigmund Freud, *Inhibitions, Symptoms, and Anxiety*, trans. Alix Strachey, ed. James Strachey, New York: W.W. Norton, 1959, p. 87. Without getting into the complex details of Freud's ever-changing metapsychology, we should only keep in mind that there *is* a correlation between a surplus of unused energy (no matter sexual or desexualized,

since Freud himself could never properly define the specificity of human libido) and the phenomenon of anxiety. As Freud himself asserts: 'what finds discharge in the generating of anxiety is precisely the surplus of unutilized libido' (ibid., p. 141).

9　Note that Strachey uses the word 'instinct', whereas the Freudian *Trieb* should rather be translated as 'drive'.

10　Freud then adds hesitantly: 'A further discussion of this problem will be found in my *Introductory Lectures on Psycho-Analysis*, chapter 25, though even there, it must be confessed, the question is not finally cleared up' (ibid.)

11　See Eric L. Santner, 'Miracles Happen: Benjamin, Rosenzweig, Freud, and the Matter of the Neighbor', in Slavoj Žižek, Eric L. Santner and Kenneth Reinhard, *The Neighbor: Three Inquiries into Political Theology*, Chicago: University of Chicago Press, 2005.

12　It is always a tricky question to ask how much Freud really knew his Bible, but perhaps he was not unfamiliar with Isaiah 5:20 which talks about the shifts from bitterness to sweetness and *vice versa*: 'Woe unto them that call evil good, and good evil; that put darkness for light, and light for darkness; that put bitter for sweet, and sweet for bitter!' And although Isaiah frames his remark as a severe ethical warning, this fragment became an inspiration for the antinomian strain of Jewish messianism, which has always staked on radical reversals: what now appears bitter may, in fact, harbour an intimation of a future, yet untasted, sweetness. The 'from vinegar to wine' reversal (where wine, in its ancient taste, stands for sweetness) could thus be regarded as a typically Jewish, antinomian-messianic, type of operation. Indeed, Jewish mysticism often alludes to this transformation while playing on two words – *'onig* and *nega*, meaning 'bliss' and 'suffering' – which derive from the same root, *n-g*, and mirror one another in inversion. The bliss/wine is thus an inverted form of suffering/vinegar: it is the same root, the same libidinal energy taking two different forms. See, for instance, the messianic inversion as depicted by Jacob Frank (the Polish follower of the Sabbatians) in reference to the inhabitants of Edom or the modern form of Egypt: 'Their delight called *Ovnig* will invert and turn into *Nevga*, a plague – while our *Nevga* will turn into *Ovnig*': Jakub Frank, *Słowa Pańskie: Nauki Jakuba Franka z Brna i Offenbachu* (*The Words of the Lord: The Teachings of Jacob Frank from Brno and Offenbach*), ed. Jan Doktór, Warszawa: Żydowski Instytut Historyczny, 2017, p. 81.

13　Eric L. Santner, *On Creaturely Life: Rilke, Benjamin, Sebald*, Chicago: University of Chicago Press 2006, pp. 105–6; p. 144; my emphasis.

14　The definition of life as 'toomuchness' derives from Jonathan Lear's HDRL, p. 109: 'Life is too much.' More on this soon.

15　And this is precisely what Freud calls 'the ego-anxiety', as issuing from the pressures of the excessive 'id-anxiety'.

16　As we remember from the previous chapter, it is precisely this lingering refusal to attach to the natural reality, which Lyotard sees as the essentially 'psychotic' characteristic of Judaism. In that sense, the stage of capacitor can also be compared to what Nicolas Abraham and Maria Torok designate as the 'interpsychic crypt': a secret place inside the psyche, that preserves the withdrawn libido in the state of an 'exquisite corpse', deposited and stored for the sake of a possible future use, but not now. The energy is not wasted: it lies there, as if buried and deactivated, but still capable of introjection. The association with the 'crypt' is also pertinent because of its importance for Derrida who, in 'Faith and Knowledge', sees it as a burial place of the divine transcendence. In his preface to Abraham's and Torok's *The Wolf Man's Magic Word*, called 'Fors', Derrida writes:

> What is a crypt? No crypt presents itself. The grounds *[lieux]* are so disposed as to disguise and to hide: something, always a body in some way. But also to disguise the act of hiding and to hide the disguise: the crypt hides as it holds . . . The inner forum is (a) safe, an outcast outside inside the inside. That is the condition, and the stratagem, of the cryptic enclave's ability *to isolate, to protect, to shelter from any penetration*, from anything that can filter in from outside.
>
> Nicolas Abraham and Maria Torok, *The Wolf Man's Magic Word:*
> *A Cryptonymy*, trans. Nicholas Rand, Minneapolis:
> University of Minnesota Press, 1986, p. xiv; my emphasis

17 Friedrich Nietzsche, *The Birth of Tragedy*, trans. Roland Speirs, Cambridge: Cambridge University Press, 1999, p. 98. Speirs' translation is particularly apt, for it shows the ambivalence hidden in the German word *erlöst*, which can mean both redemption and releasement.

18 Jean Laplanche, *La sublimation: Problématiques III*, Paris: PUF 1980, p. 173.

19 Saul Bellow, *More Die of Heartbreak*, London: Penguin, 2007, p. 180.

20 See William Blake: 'Energy is the only life and is from the Body and Reason is the bound or outward circumference of Energy. Energy is Eternal Delight': William Blake, 'The Voice of the Devil', *The Marriage of Heaven and Hell*, in *Blake's Poetry and Designs*, ed. Mary Lynn Johnson and John E. Grant, New York: W.W. Norton, 1979, p. 87.

21 Paul Ricoeur's analysis of Freud, giving a primacy to hermeneutic structures over energetic flow, offers here the best example: Paul Ricoeur, *Freud and Philosophy: An Essay on Interpretation*, trans. Denis Savage, New Haven, CT: Yale University Press, 1977.

22 Compare Žižek:

> For Lacan, creative sublimation and the death drive are strictly correlative: the death drive empties the (sacred) Place, creates the Clearing, the Void, the Frame, which is then filled by the object 'elevated to the dignity of the Thing.' Here, the subject finds itself totally deprived of its symbolic identity, thrown into the 'night of the world' in which its only correlative is the minimum of an excremental leftover, a piece of trash, a mote of dust in the eye, an almost-nothing that

sustains the pure Place-Frame-Void, so that here, finally, 'nothing but the place takes place.'

Slavoj Žižek, *The Fragile Absolute Or, Why Is the Christian Legacy Worth Fighting For?* London: Verso, 2000, p. 30

23 We can find a similar apology of positive disappointment in the earlier book of Jonathan Lear, *Love and its Place in Nature*, which offers an interesting counterpart to Santner's dramatic theory of seduction, based on Jean Laplanche, namely a theory of a 'good-enough world', this time based on D.W. Winnicott. Instead of a transmission of enigmatic lack, which excites every new generation with the mystery of *che voi?*, Lear proposes an exchange based on relations of love, where the inevitable loss of love-object becomes compensated by its loving internalization. Lear is here on the side of what we might call, after Winnicott, a *benign separation*:

> Psychic structure, Freud realizes, is created by a dialectic of love and loss. The structure of the mind is an inner recreation of the structure of the loved world … *Because my love affair is with a distinctly existing world, I must be disappointed by it*. A distinctly existing world cannot possibly satisfy all my wishes. *Out of the ensuing frustration and disappointment, I am born*. Melancholia, or some archaic precursor, must lie at the heart of every I.
>
> L, 160; my emphasis

Out of disillusionment I am born – but also the world is born as such, being there, i.e. *both disappointing and still lovable*. Thus, though melancholy (and anxiety) lies at the heart of every I and every other real object-neighbour, it can develop into more energetic relation, provided that we understand the positive aspect of disillusionment.

24 Compare the seminal fragment from *Écrits*:

> The subject says 'No!' to this intersubjective game of hunt-the-slipper in which desire makes itself recognized for a moment, only to become lost in a will that is will of the other. Patiently, the subject withdraws his precarious life from the sheeplike conglomerations of the Eros of the symbol in order to affirm it at the last in an unspoken curse. So when we wish to attain in the subject what was before the serial articulations of speech, and what is primordial to the birth of symbols, we find it in *death, from which his existence takes all the meaning it has*.
>
> E, 104–5; my emphasis

Note the Lacanian close association between the primacy of meaningful signification and the primacy of Thanatos which delivers the subject from the hopeless pursuits of erotic life.

25 Santner, *Neighbor*, pp. 132–3; my emphasis. This line of argument is in full harmony with Levinas for whom transcendence can have only one meaning: of the relation

with the other which realizes itself in the realm of *otherwise than being*, i.e. 'beyond essence': outside the pragmatic, object-oriented, and 'interested' rule of 'ontologism'. When it congeals into a 'world behind the scenes', not only does it not break with the ontological hegemony, but only strengthens it, by becoming its metaphysical *arche*:

> To be or not to be is not the question where transcendence is concerned. The statement of being's *other*, of the otherwise than being, claims to state a difference over and beyond that which separates being from nothingness – the very difference of the *beyond*, the difference of transcendence. But one immediately wonders if the formula 'otherwise than being' the adverb 'otherwise' does not inevitably refer to the verb to be . . . Our languages woven about the verb to be would not only reflect this undethronable royalty, stronger than that of the gods; they would be the very purple of this royalty. But then no transcendence other than the facticious transcendence of worlds behind the scenes, of the Heavenly City gravitating in the skies over the terrestrial city, would have meaning.
>
> Emmanuel Lévinas, *Otherwise than Being or Beyond Essence*,
> trans. Alphonso Lingis, The Hague: Martinus Nijhoff, 1981, pp. 3–4

What Lévinas proposes is the alternative meaning of transcendence located in the very alterity of every other.

26 Santner – following both anarchistic Benjamin and thanatic Lacan – has a worrying tendency to perceive the submission to the Jewish God of Law in exactly the same terms as *any other seduction by an enigmatic signifier*, which, according to him, constitutes the 'undead' and 'anxious' condition of 'our private Egyptomania' (the position which he takes directly from Benjamin's 'Critique of Violence' (SW1), where indeed *every* type of law – 'Tora, *nomos, ius*' – becomes negatively stigmatized as a mythic force). He thus seems to be missing the possibility that it is only thanks to the prohibition issued by the Law that libido retreats from the erotic pursuit of natural objects and undergoes what Santner himself endorses, i.e. denaturalization and infinitization. For it is only due to the intervention of this law-giving authority (and not *just* love-giving revelation) that 'Jews, as Rosenzweig asserts, do lack the passionate attachment to the things that constitute the primary libidinal "objects" of other historical peoples and nations' (PEL, 110). The status of the Law, therefore, is one thing – but there is also another, more fundamental, problem. Santner constantly hesitates which 'path' to choose: the *disenchantment backward* or the *disenchantment forward*, i.e. the disenchantment, which he interprets as a retrogressive *release* of all tension – or the positive disenchantment, which he, after Rosenzweig, locates in the sobering presence of a neighbour. The first impulse he realizes by backing himself up with Lacan, for whom there is only one escape from the cycle of 'metaphysical seduction' – into dying as a practice of the inner lack of existence, which allows us to traverse the phantasm of the pleromatic Big Other. This 'disenchantment means,

then, a *deanimation of creaturely life* or, better, of the 'undeadness' proper to this
dimension': Santner, *Creaturely Life*, p. 27; my emphasis. The 'deanimating' flattening
of the hunch means thus a 'releasement' in terms of the Heideggerian *Gelassenheit*
and the Lacanian *destitution*. But the other line, which would like to see the tension
not so much dissolved as liberated into free energy, is also constantly present in
Santner's work, as, for instance, in his contribution to *The Neighbor*. Against
Reinhardt, who in the same volume follows closely Schmitt's political theology,
Santner argues that 'imperative to love' is *not* an expression of a sovereign power,
stating the law which cannot become a law proper – but a *step beyond* the
relationship of sovereignty where God is no longer perceived as a law-making
Creator, but as a Redeemer, who himself wants to lift creation from the mythic
condition of 'proto-cosmos', and thus urges his believers to tear the veil of the false
mythic enchantments. The 'disenchantment forward', therefore, does not release the
tension of surplus animation but, quite to the contrary, intensifies it, by liberating it
of its transfixing mysteries. Far from annulling the surplus as an error, it invests in its
derailed exceptionality and thus remains faithful to the initial denaturalizing
tendency of human libido.

27 Which chimes very well with Derrida's claim, uttered apropos Cixous, that death is
not a *side* that can be opposed to the side of life and that one simply cannot take the
side of death (HCL, 2).

28 The phrase 'magnificence of our drives' is Bloom's coinage from his essay on Freud:
'Freud: Frontier Concepts, Jewishness, and Interpretation', in *Trauma: Explorations in
Memory*, ed. Cathy Caruth, Baltimore, MD: Johns Hopkins University Press, 1995,
p. 127, where Bloom insists on reading the Freudian concept of the drive in terms of
the absolute – unbound and infinite – excess. As Bloom himself admits, the
'magnificence of our drives', a notion pointing to the pulsional overflowing fullness
rather than deficiency and lack, could only be conceived on the basis of the Hebrew
concept of *yetser*: desire, but also a formative power thanks to which God, according
to the oldest Book of J, fashions Adam out of clay. In the Graeco-Christian,
predominantly Platonic conceptual universe, desire is firmly associated with lack,
penia: from Augustine through Hegel to Koiève and Lacan, desire marks the 'gaping
hole' in the psyche, which can be filled only with phantasms. Whereas *yetser*
constitutes an originary excess: the 'too-muchness' of the pulsional pressure which
threatens to break the psychic vessel; an indefinite surplus which cannot find its
object in the existing reality and thus must *create* something new instead. This is
precisely what Bloom ascribes to Blake's state of Eden where the Edenic Tigers,
living in perpetual energetic delight, love only what they themselves create.

29 Harold Bloom, *The Breaking of the Vessels: The Wellek Library Lectures at the
University of California*, ed. F. Lentricchia, Chicago: University of Chicago Press,
1982, p. 49.

30 Jean Laplanche, *Life and Death in Psychoanalysis*, trans. Jeffrey Melham, Baltimore, MD: Johns Hopkins University Press 1976, p. 16, 20, 22, 23.

31 On the language-generating passage from literal function to figurative meaning see also the classic work of Abraham and Torok, where the medium of this passage is described as the mechanism of introjection. Introjection not only deals with the loss of the object, but also *converts* it into a new libidinal possibility; for instance, the loss of the oral object leaves the child's mouth empty, but thanks to the process of introjection the object's absence is figuratively replaced by the words of language which, in Abraham's and Torok's beautiful formulation is a 'community of empty mouths':

> The transition from a mouth filled with the breast to a mouth filled with words occurs by virtue of the intervening experiences of the empty mouth. Learning to fill the emptiness of the mouth with words is the initial model for introjection . . . *The absence of objects and the empty mouth are transformed into words*; at last, even experiences related to words are converted into other words. *So the wants of the original oral vacancy are remedied by being turned into verbal relationships with the speaking community at large.* Introjecting a desire, a pain, a situation means channelling them through language into a *communion of empty mouths*. This is how the literal ingestion of foods becomes introjection when viewed figuratively. The passage from food to language presupposes the successful replacement of the object's presence with the self's cognizance of its absence.
>
> Nicolas Abraham and Maria Torok, 'Mourning *or* Melancholia: Introjection versus Incorporation', in *The Shell and the Kernel*, vol. 1, ed. and trans. Nicholas T. Rand, Chicago: University of Chicago Press, 1994, pp. 127–8; my emphasis

32 Writing on the Jewish priest, whom he originally defines as a 'denier of life', Nietzsche cannot help but change his tune and discover *another vitality*:

> One already understands me: this ascetic priest, this apparent enemy of life, this denier – precisely he belongs to the altogether great conserving and Yes-creating forces of life . . . The No he says to life, his No, brings to light, as if by magic, an *abundance of tender Yeses*; yes indeed, even when he wounds himself, this master of destruction, of self-destruction – *it is henceforth the wound itself that compels him to live.*
>
> *On the Genealogy of Morality*, pp. 120–1; my emphasis

33 Which can also be formulated in Arendt's natalist terms: 'To think and to be fully alive are the same, and this implies that thinking must always begin afresh': Hannah Arendt, *The Life of the Mind*, vol. 1, *Thinking*, p. 171.

34 Kafka's short story featuring Odradek bears the title: *Die Sorge des Hausvaters* (*The Cares of the Family Man*).

35 For Freud, the phenomenon of life is a result of an accident which created the first
   act of *survival*:

> For a long time, perhaps, living substance was thus being constantly created
> afresh and easily dying, till *decisive external influences* altered it in such a way as
> to oblige the still surviving substance to diverge ever more widely from its
> original course of life and to make *ever more complicated détours* before reaching
> its aim of death. These *circuitous paths to death*, faithfully kept to by conservative
> instincts, would thus present us today with the picture of the phenomena of life.
>
>   FR, 613; my emphasis

In 'The Ego and the Id', Freud explains the meandering nature of life by pointing to
the conflict of the two essentially conservative drives that compete by forcing two
types of regression, either towards 'nothingness' or towards the first 'survival':

> On the basis of theoretical considerations, supported by biology, we put forward
> the hypothesis of a death instinct, the task of which is to lead organic life back
> into the inanimate state; on the other hand, we supposed that Eros, by bringing
> about a more and more far-reaching combination of the particles into which
> living substance is dispersed, aims at complicating life and at the same time, of
> course, at preserving it. Acting in this way, both the instincts would be
> conservative in the strictest sense of the word, since both would be endeavouring
> to re-establish a state of things that was *disturbed* by the emergence of life. *The*
> *emergence of life would thus be the cause of the continuance of life and also at the*
> *same time of the striving towards death; and life itself would be a conflict and*
> *compromise between these two trends.*
>
>   FR, 646; my emphasis

36 Compare also Derrida's quote with which we have finished Chapter 3, on 'an
   appellation of life that knows equally neither death nor immortality, namely eternity
   outside time. *Everything takes place in the instant*' (HCL, 81).

37 The issue of 'lingering' and 'taking time' is indeed one of the oldest themes of Greek
   tragedy or, in Heidegger's words, 'early Greek thinking'. In the 1946 piece called *Der*
   Spruch des Anaximander, published as the last essay of *Holzwege*, Heidegger gives his
   own translation of the famous aphorism of Anaximander on justice 'dike' whose
   aim is precisely to eliminate the 'lingering': 'But that from which things arise [genesis]
   also gives rise to the passing away [*phthora*], according to what is necessary; for
   things render justice and pay penalty to one another for their injustice 'adikia',
   according to the ordinance of time': Martin Heidegger, 'Anaximander Fragment', in
   Early Greek Thinking, trans. David Farrell Krell, San Francisco: Harper and Row,
   1975, p. 20. It is, therefore, just for the things to pass away, so that they can give place
   to other things not yet in existence. If any of them 'lingers' too long – or simply:
   lingers – and resists the just ordinance of time, it becomes an agent of *adikia*: by

showing all signs of hubris, manifesting itself precisely in the prolonged 'will-to-be' (or, as Rosenzweig will call it, 'will to remain'), it brings on itself an even harsher form of penalty [*tisin*]. The will is thus accused of an excessive 'craving to persist' and 'clinging to itself', which Derrida would call a self-preference: '*Lingering as persisting* ... is an *insurrection* on behalf of sheer endurance' (ibid., 43; my emphasis), i.e. a rebellion against the *dike* of all things, which causes human beings, those bearers of the will, to step out of the world of *phusis* and enter history as the 'realm of errancy': the time of *Un-Fug*, 'out-of-jointness', and arbitrary violence done to Being. The more Dasein wishes to 'linger' in the world, the more it sins against the just ordinance of time; it is thus only when it immediately admits that it is 'present only insofar as it lets itself belong to the non-present' (ibid.) – that is, if it sees itself as always already dying and in this manner repaying the debt of existence – it is in the right: 'In the jointure whatever lingers awhile keeps to its while. *It does not incline toward the disjunction of sheer persistence.* The jointure belongs to whatever lingers awhile, which in turn belongs in the jointure. *The jointure is order*' (ibid., my emphasis).

38 See Becker's full Schopenhauerian comment on Freud's later dualism of drives and its 'sombre mythology':

> As in Greek mythology too, Eros and Thanatos are inseparable; death is the natural twin brother of sex ... Nature conquers death not by creating eternal organisms but my making it possible for ephemeral ones to procreate ... sex represents, then, species consciousness and, as such, the defeat of individuality, of personality ... Resistance to sex is a resistance to fatality.
>
> Becker, *The Denial of Death*, pp. 163–4

39 See again his quote on the haggadic meandering against the halachic Law (SW 2, 496–7) in Chapter 3.

40 In his interpretation of contingency as the Aristotelian *tuche*, Lacan follows Freud's ambivalent remark on nature (strangely echoing Herder's reflections on nature as our negligent 'step-mother'), which should secure the purposefulness of sexual fulfilment in principle, yet we cannot truly rely on her teleological wisdom: 'and we may expect that Nature will have made safe provisions so that this experience of satisfaction shall not be left to chance' (TETS, 62). Then, in the 1920 edition, he adds: 'In biological discussions it is scarcely possible to avoid a teleological way of thinking, even though one is aware that in any particular instance one is not secure against error' (TETS, 62f). Lacan thus merely liberates Freud's intuition from the nineteenth-century belief in the purposeful arrangement of nature, which allows him to reveal the normality of human inevitably perverse sexuality as always founded on blind chance. See Jacques Lacan, 'Tuche and Automaton', in *The Four Fundamental Concepts of Psycho-analysis*, ed. Jacques-Alain Miller, trans. Alan Sheridan, London: Penguin Books, 1979.

41 Compare, for instance, Scholem's comment on the eighteenth-century Polish
   follower of Sabbatai Zevi, who also thought about himself as a New Jacob and the
   true Messiah, Jacob Frank, and who indeed advocated a polymorphously perverse
   awakening of life:

> Frank will always repeat the double ground motif of his teaching: abolishment of all
> values, positive laws and religions *in the name of life*. The road to this goal leads
> through the abyss of destruction. The concept of life serves Frank as the key to the
> expression of his anarchistic pathos. For him, life is not a harmonic order of nature
> and its mild ruling; he is not an advocate of Rousseau's return to nature ... *Life is*
> *freedom from all binding and law. This anarchic life is the sole object and content of*
> *his utopia, driven by a simple desire of a lawless freedom and promiscuity of all things.*
> Gershom Scholem, 'Der Nihilismus als religiöses Phänomen',
> in *Judaica 4*, Frankfurt: Suhrkamp, 1995, p. 178; my emphasis

42 Strachey's translation consistently underplays the greatness of those 'achievements'
   – *Leistungen* – which Freud attributes to the works of sublimation/perversion which,
   at this stage, is yet undifferentiated.

43 Or, as Derrida would have said: *auto-intimation* – see again the analogy with Fichte
   in Chapter 3.

44 Also Laplanche is *almost* ready to jump in into the Jungian monism; well, almost...
   In *Sublimation*, Laplanche writes: 'But Freud himself admits that drive energy
   constitutes certain X, i.e. the unknown which carries from one equation to another.
   So, why not become Jungian? Why not assume the theory of one energy called
   'libido' which will be the same everywhere, without any distinctly sexual features,
   just serving as a substrate of all these operations Jung names "symbolic equations"?':
   Jean Laplanche, *La sublimation*, p. 204.

45 ibid., p. 207.

46 Laplanche, *Life and Death*, p. 83.

47 This is also where I part with Laplanche, on the two closely related fronts. First, while
   I would like to see the objectless freedom of the original libido based on the Fichtean
   model of 'intellectual intuition', Laplanche follows faithfully Freud and binds the
   'expanded sexuality' with its specific object: 'What defines the originality of the drive,
   its autoeroticism, can mean only one thing: that the energy circulates not so much
   among objects as among representations of objects, which makes it *bound by the*
   phantasms': Jean Laplanche, *La sublimation*, p. 207; my emphasis. The so called 'free
   energy', therefore, is not free absolutely: cut off from the external objects, it is
   nonetheless cathected by their phantasmatic representations. And indeed, the
   discovery of the phantasmatic object, which Laplanche sees as one of the greatest
   achievements of psychoanalysis, is the final blow to the idea of *Objektlosigkeit*.
   Methodologically speaking, however, it is completely irrefutable and dogmatic: since

libido allegedly *must* have its object, it will have it even if it does not have it. The second disagreement concerns the hypothesis of the death drive, which Laplanche upholds and identifies it with 'expanded sexuality' – precisely the move I am trying to avoid here.

48 According to Laplanche, the opposition between the destructive sexuality and self-preservatory vital order is one of the most fundamental discoveries of psychoanalysis. In the 'Report from the Meeting of Viennese Psychoanalytic Society', that took place in April 1910, Freud announced his theory of suicide according to which 'suicide is an act in which life drive is attacked and overcome by libido'. Following this remark, Laplanche sketches the history of Freudian drive concepts and their vicissitudes. While the self-preservatory *Lebensordnung* transforms into life-drive (first as *Lebensnot*, then as *Lebenstrieb*), then the life-drive eventually passes into the ego-drive (*Trieb des Ichs*), and finally, after 1920, evolves into Eros which strives towards propagation of Life – the parallel line sees first sexuality (*Sexualtrieb*) slowly but surely metamorphosing into death drive (*Todestrieb*), which represents the most primordial and powerful tendency of the self-destructive regression towards nirvanic *jouissance*. Laplanche writes apropos Freud's remark on suicide:

> Life-drive situates itself on the side of the ego-drive; even if it is not fully co-extensive with the latter, it nonetheless fosters self-preservation; the 'renunciation of the ego-drive' results in the automatic weakening of the life-drive. The latter, not to be confused with sexuality, is, in the moment of suicide, most adversarial to it. *From which it follows that it is sexuality which, in this early classification of drives, becomes the prototype of the later death drive.*
>
> Jean Laplanche, *Le primat de l'autre en psychanalyse*,
> Paris: Flammarion, 1992, p. 136; my emphasis

This conclusion indeed is infallible, but only on the one proviso that strongly identifies life and life-drive with self-preservatory functions of the vital order. However, if we reject this premise and insist on the Derridean dialectics of *life against life*, the conflict may just as well be explained without recourse to the notion of Thanatos: it will then be the agon between 'life expanded', represented by sexuality, and 'life natural', represented by the biomorphic *conservatio vitae*.

49 Laplanche, *Love and Death*, p. 48.

50 Zohar II, *Shemot* 12b.

51 Jean Laplanche and J.-B. Pontalis, *The Language of Psychoanalysis*, trans. Donald Nicholson-Smith, London: Karnac Books, 1988, p. 433.

52 This latter possibility, which we are going to pursue here, was very aptly spotted by Lacan who, in his seminar on sublimation, says: 'The other formulation consists of informing us that sublimation is the satisfaction of the drive with a change of object,

that is, *without repression*. This definition is a profounder one, but it would also open up an even knottier problematic, if it weren't for the fact that my teaching allows you to spot where the rabbit is hidden': Jacques Lacan, *The Ethics of Psychoanalysis: The Seminar of Jacques Lacan 1959–1960, Book 7*, ed. Jacques-Alain Miller, trans. Dennis Porter, London: Routledge, 1992, p. 293; my emphasis. It is precisely this 'profounder' approach which I am going to develop here.

53 Or, in an even less persuasive passage from 'The Ego and the Id', where the non-sexual still retains the sexual by keeping the erotic tendency towards unity and harmony: 'If this displaceable energy is desexualized libido, it may also be described as sublimated energy: for it would still retain the main purpose of Eros – that of uniting and binding – in so far as it helps towards establishing the unity, or tendency to unity, which is particularly characteristic of the ego' (FR, 649).

54 Donald Woods Winnicott, *Home Is Where We Start From: Essays by a Psychoanalyst*, London: Penguin Books, 1986, p. 56.

55 Rainer Maria Rilke, *The Ninth Duino Elegy*, in *Duino Elegies and The Sonnets to Orpheus*, trans. Steven Mitchell, New York: Vintage International, 2009, p. 56. On Rilke's concept of *der Auftrag* in the context of the psychoanalytical 'depressive conversion', see my: 'Bad Timing: The Subject as a Work of Time', *Angelaki: Journal of the Theoretical Humanities* 5, no. 3 (2000): 71–91.

56 Laplanche, *La sublimation*, pp. 112, 87; my emphasis.

57 The great advantage of Laplanche's solution is that it gives up on the dubious gender distinction, still to be found in Lacan, in which the Mother represents the bodily-natural-material small other, while the Father, the true *Atrui*, intervenes with the non-material and anti-natural Word. In Laplanche's theory of seduction, it is actually the Mother who bifurcates into a biomorphic caterer and an enigmatic signifier – and as such becomes the prototype of every 'metaphysical seduction' in which the concept of God is equally doubled (this doubling is the explicit theme of Kierkegaard's *Fear and Trembling*, trans. Alastair Hannay, London: Penguin, 2005, where Abraham and Isaac – passing through the stage of the 'blackened breast' – are on their way to discover a much more exciting and seductive version of God than the provider and caterer). Laplanche's advantage lies also in the way he insists on the necessity of the seduction phase in the 'neogenetic' development of human sexuality. *Pace* Santner who, as we have just seen, rebels against *any* form of 'metaphysical seduction', Laplanche shows that without *Verführung* human libido would never be able to leave the Egypt of biomorphic mimesis. Hence the image of the Hebrew God as a distant and enigmatic figure who leads his people out of the Egyptian fatland into a desert, where nature disappears, lends a psychotheological 'great code' for Laplanche's theory of seduction.

58 The view, according to which perversion is deprived of relation with the other, is confirmed by Gilles Deleuze, who says, even more strongly, that perversion kills all

alterity by definition: 'The world of the pervert is a world without other, and thereby a world without possibility. The other is what possibilizes . . . All perversion is *autruicide*, altricide, a murder of possibilities. But altricide is not committed by perverse behavior, it is presupposed in the perverse structure': Gilles Deleuze, *Logic of Sense*, trans. Mark Lester and Charles Stivale, London: Athlone Books, 1990, p. 320.

59   The transformation of object-libido into narcissistic libido . . . obviously implies an abandonment of sexual aims, a desexualization – a kind of sublimation, therefore. Indeed, the question arises, and deserves careful consideration, whether this is not the universal road to sublimation, whether all sublimation does not take place through the mediation of the ego, which begins by changing sexual object-libido into narcissistic libido and then, perhaps, goes on to give it another aim.

'The Ego and the Id' (FR, 639)

60 Compare again the fragment from Lacan's *Ethics of Psychoanalysis*. . .

In the definition of sublimation as satisfaction without repression, whether implicitly or explicitly, there is a passage from not-knowing to knowing, a recognition of the fact that *desire is nothing more than the metonymy of the discourse of demand* . . . desire is formed as something supporting this metonymy, namely, as something the demand means beyond whatever it is able to formulate. And that is why the question of the realization of desire is necessarily formulated from the point of view of a Last Judgment.

Jacques Lacan, *The Ethics of Psychoanalysis*, p. 294

. . . when it will have become clear to the subject that the desire is 'the desire of nothing, the relationship of man to his lack of being' (ibid., 298). This is also the reason why Lacan will eventually discard sublimation as not yet sufficiently 'knowledgeable' about the desire, and choose perversion instead. In the 23rd seminar from 1975–6, *Le sinthome*, Lacan redefines perversion as that what ultimately remains after the destitution of desire: an isolated and self-enclosed drive which gave up on any objectual fulfilment and celebrates now its inner 'nothing'. The drive loses any interest in an object and becomes an autotelic, self-circulatory *monos pros monon*, wallowing in the aura of autoerotic jouissance which, in contrast to its primary lethal form, is a diffused and thus liveable kind of joy. Perversion thus understood is also a compromise with the self-preservatory functions but it differs from the sublimation precisely in the fact that it does not seek any post-phantasmatic relation with objects. The only thing it cultivates is 'the death of the somatic subject [which] has its place in drives', i.e. the thanatic moment of arresting the biological life and entering the separate 'life of language', which Lacan analyses on the basis of James Joyce's novels. This perverse life also loves itself, but this love

– very different from the biophilic living/loving – consists in a compassionate acceptance of one's *sinthome*: lack, error, hole or the 'deficiency in being': Jacques Lacan, *Le sinthome*, ed. J-A Miller, *Ornicar?* 6–11 (1976–7): 59–60.

61 This figurative approach to the object corresponds well with the Adornian description of the highest form of life he calls *ephemeral*. Adorno's ephemerality perfectly reflects the moment in which the volatile nature of the Young Libido *ohne Bindung* becomes recovered at the higher level of a playful 'happy reflection' engaged in a free pursuit of metaphysical curiosity, which is object-oriented but not object-determined. In his lectures on metaphysics, while discussing the nature of a happy metaphysical experience as found in Proust, Adorno says: 'happiness – and there is an extremely deep constellation between metaphysical experience and happiness – is something within objects and, at the same time, remote from them' (MCP, 140).

62 Laplanche, *Nouveaux fondements*, p. 51.

63 *Ibid*.

64 On the universal biophilic aspect of the mature narcissistic self, see also Julia Kristeva's *Tales of Love*: a story of the amatory relationships starting with the formation of the ego whose only desire is 'to live and to be loved'. Kristeva indeed confirms the Derridean thesis that 'the love of Self is the prototype of any other love, to the extent that theologians have wondered which of the two is primary': Julia Kristeva, *Tales of Love*, trans. Leon S. Roudiez, New York: Columbia University Press, 1987, p. 147. The Hebrew *kamokha* – 'like yourself' – stating the right measure for neighbourly love [*ahavah l'reakha*], implies that every other form of love is Narcissus' palimpsest: an act of loving that can only spring from the ego and which overwrites the original text of the narcissistic self-investment. Love is thus narcissistic in its essence, but it is also the other way round: the Narcissus-ego can only exist through the act of perpetual self-love. For it is love that has a unique power to create being and identity out of nothingness, by throwing a screen over the abyss constituted by the subject's primordial *emptiness*: while all other forms of love are 'screens' overwriting the original model of narcissistic self-loving, the latter is a 'screen' thrown directly over nothing. Without love, therefore, the structure of subjectivity would immediately collapse revealing 'dizzy ravines' of psychotic non-being; with love, however, the subject slowly constructs itself or, simply, *loves itself into existence*, creating its own sphere of interiority and sublimation, in which it slowly differentiates from the biological body. It not only 'veils' its emptiness, but also protects it as a separate mode of existence. Polemical against Lacan's scathing rejection of the imaginary, Kristeva affirms the need of narcissistic self-images which paint the 'screens' projected over the nothing:

> the *emptiness* that is intrinsic to the beginnings of the symbolic function appears as the first separation between what is not yet an *Ego* and what is not yet an object. Might narcissism be a means for protecting that emptiness? But against

what? – a protection of emptiness (of 'arbitrariness' of the 'gaping hole') through the display of a decidedly narcissistic parry, so that emptiness can be maintained, lest chaos prevail and borders dissolve. *Narcissism protects emptiness, causes it to exist, and thus, as lining of that emptiness, insures an elementary separation.* Without that solidarity between emptiness and narcissism, chaos would sweep away any possibility of distinction, trace, and symbolization, which would in turn confuse the limits of the body, words, the real, and the symbolic. The child, with all due respect to Lacan, not only *needs* the real and the symbolic – it signifies itself as child, in other words as the subject that it is, and neither as a psychotic nor as an adult, precisely in that zone where *emptiness and narcissism*, the one upholding the other, constitute the zero degree of imagination.

ibid., 24; my emphasis

65 Nietzsche, *The Twilight of the Idols*, p. 171. On the motif of the 'shortest shadow' as not reducible to 'full sun' in which all differentiations disappear, but, on the contrary, as that unique kind of light which puts alterities in the strongest possible relief, see also: Alenka Zupančič, *The Shortest Shadow: Nietzsche's Philosophy of the Two*, Cambridge, MA: MIT Press, 2003. Compare also Bergson's notion of the 'third love': 'Joy indeed would be that simplicity of life diffused throughout the world by an ever-spreading mystic intuition': Henri Bergson, *Two Sources of Morality and Religion*, p. 317.

66 Nietzsche, *The Gay Science*, p. 168.

67 Rilke, *Ninth Duino Elegy*, p. 59.

References

Abraham, Nicolas, and Maria Torok, *The Wolf Man's Magic Word: A Cryptonymy*, trans. Nicholas Rand, Minneapolis: University of Minnesota Press, 1986.

Abraham, Nicolas, and Maria Torok, *The Shell and the Kernel*, vol. 1, ed. and trans. Nicholas T. Rand, Chicago: University of Chicago Press, 1994.

Adorno, Theodor W., *The Jargon of Authenticity*, trans. Knut Tarnowski and Frederic Will, Evanston, IL: Northwestern University Press, 1973.

Agamben, Giorgio, *The Coming Community*, trans. Michael Hardt, Minneapolis: Minnesota University Press, 1993.

Agamben, Giorgio, *Homo Sacer: Sovereign Power and Bare Life*, trans. Daniel Heller-Roazen, Stanford, CA: Stanford University Press, 1998.

Agamben, Giorgio, *Potentialities*, ed. and trans. Daniel Heller-Roazen, Stanford, CA: Stanford University Press, 1999.

Arendt, Hannah, *The Origins of Totalitarianism*, New York: Harcourt & Brace, 1966.

Arendt, Hannah, *The Life of the Mind: Thinking and Willing (One-Volume Edition)*, New York: Harcourt, 1977.

Arendt, Hannah, *Essays in Understanding, 1930–1954*, ed. Jerome Kohn, New York: Harcourt, 1994.

Arendt, Hannah, *Between Past and Future: Eight Exercises in Political Thought*, London: Penguin, 2006.

Arendt, Hannah, *Denktagebuch 1950–1973*, ed. Ursula Ludz and Ingeborg Nordmann, München: Piper, 2016.

Asendorf, Ulrich, *Luther und Hegel: Untersuchung zur Grundlegung einer Neuen Systematischen Theologie*, Wiesbaden: Franz Steiner, 1982.

Atwood, Margaret, *The Handmaid's Tale*, London: Vintage, 1996.

Augustine, *The City of God*, trans. John Healey, Edinburgh: John Grant, 1909.

Augustine, *Confessions*, trans. Henry Chadwick, Oxford: Oxford University Press, 1991.

Aurelius, Marcus, *Meditations*, trans. G.M.A. Grube, Indianapolis, IN: Bobbs-Merrill, 1963.

Bataille, Georges, 'Hegel, Death and Sacrifice', trans. Jonathan Strauss, *Yale French Studies (On Bataille)* 78 (1990): 9–28.

Becker, Ernest, *The Denial of Death*, New York: The Free Press, 1973.

Bellow, Saul, *More Die of Heartbreak*, London: Penguin, 2007.

Benjamin, Walter, 'Der Erzähler: Betrachtungen zum Werk Nikolai Lesskows'. In *Gesammelte Schriften*, Bd II.2, Frankfurt am Main: Suhrkamp, 1977.

Benjamin, Walter, *Illuminations: Essays and Reflections*, trans. Harry Zohn, New York: Schocken Books, 1968.

Benjamin, Walter, *The Origin of German Tragic Drama*, trans. John Osborne, London: Verso, 1998.

Bérard, Victor, 'Les Phéniciens et l'Odyssée'. In *La Résurrection d'Homère*, Paris: Bernard Grasset, 1930.

Bergson, Henri, *Creative Evolution*, trans. Arthur Mitchell, London: Macmillan, 1922.

Bergson, Henri, *Two Sources of Morality and Religion*, trans. R. Ashley Audra and Cloudesley Brereton, Notre Dame, IN: Notre Dame University Press, 1977.

Bielik-Robson, Agata, 'Bad Timing: The Subject as a Work of Time', *Angelaki: Journal of the Theoretical Humanities* 5, no. 3 (2000): 71–91.

Bielik-Robson, Agata, *The Saving Lie: Harold Bloom and Deconstruction*, Evanston, IL: Northwestern University Press, 2011.

Bielik-Robson, Agata, *Jewish Cryptotheologies of Late Modernity: Philosophical Marranos*, Abingdon: Routledge, 2014.

Bielik-Robson, Agata, 'The Thanatic Strain: Kojève and Rosenzweig as Two Readers of Hegel', *Journal for Cultural Research* 19, no. 3 (2015): 274–90.

Blake, William, *Blake's Poetry and Designs*, ed. Mary Lynn Johnson and John E. Grant, New York: W.W. Norton, 1979.

Blanchot, Maurice, *L'arrêt de mort*, Paris: Gallimard, 1948.

Blanchot, Maurice, *The Space of Literature*, trans. Ann Smock, Lincoln: Nebraska University Press, 1982.

Blanchot, Maurice, *The Step Not Beyond*, trans. Lycette Nelson, Albany, NY: SUNY Press, 1992.

Blanchot, Maurice, *The Instant of My Death*, trans. Elizabeth Rottenberg, Stanford, CA: Stanford University Press, 2000.

Bloch, Ernst, *Traces*, trans. Anthony Nassar, Stanford: Stanford University Press, 2006.

Bloom, Harold, *The Breaking of the Vessels: The Wellek Library Lectures at the University of California*, ed. F. Lentricchia, Chicago: University of Chicago Press, 1982.

Bloom, Harold, *The Book of J*, trans. David Rosenberg, New York: Harper, 1990.

Bloom, Harold, 'Freud: Frontier Concepts, Jewishness, and Interpretation', in *Trauma: Explorations in Memory*, ed. Cathy Caruth, 113–27, Baltimore, MD: Johns Hopkins University Press, 1995.

Blumenberg, Hans, *The Legitimacy of the Modern Age*, trans. Robert M. Wallace, Cambridge, MA: MIT Press, 1985.

Bowen-Moore, Patricia, *Hannah Arendt's Philosophy of Natality*, New York: St. Martin's Press, 1989.

Bowles, Paul, *The Sheltering Sky*, London: Penguin Classics, 2004.

Braiterman, Zachary, ' "Into Life"??! Franz Rosenzweig and the Figure of Death', *AJS Review* 23, no. 2 (1998): 203–21.

Brunkhorst, Hauke, *Hannah Arendt*, Munich: Beck, 1999.

Butler, Judith, *Precarious Life: The Power of Mourning and Violence*, London: Verso, 2004.

Canullo, Carla, 'Michel Henry: From the Essence of Manifestation to the Essence of Religion', *Open Theology* 3, no. 1 (2017): 174–83.

Caputo, John D., *The Prayers and Tears of Jacques Derrida: Religion Without Religion*, Bloomington: Indiana University Press, 1997.

Cohen, Hermann, *Reason and Hope: Selections from the Jewish Writings of Hermann Cohen*, trans. Eva Jospe, New York: W.W. Norton, 1971.

Cupitt, Don, *The New Religion of Life in Everyday Speech*, London: SCM Press, 1999.

Dastur, Francoise, *Death: An Essay on Finitude*, trans. John Llewelyn, London: Bloomsbury, 2000.

de Rougemont, Denis, *Love in the Western World*, trans. Montgomery Belgion, New York: Harcourt & Brace, 1940.

Deleuze, Gilles, *Logic of Sense*, trans. Mark Lester and Charles Stivale, London: Athlone Books, 1990.

Deleuze, Gilles, *Negotiations, 1972–1990*, trans. Martin Joughin, New York: Columbia University Press, 1995.

Deleuze, Gilles, *Pure Immanence: Essays on a Life*, trans. Anne Boyman, New York: Zone Books, 2001.

Deleuze, Gilles and Félix Guattari, *A Thousand Plateaus*, trans. Robert Hurley, Mark Seem and Helen R. Lane, Minneapolis: University of Minnesota Press, 2000.

Derrida, Jacques, *Acts of Literature*, ed. Derek Attridge, trans. Avital Ronnel, New York: Routledge, 1992.

Derrida, Jacques, *Aporias*, trans. Thomas Dutoit, Stanford, CA: Stanford University Press, 1994.

Derrida, Jacques, 'Canons and Metonymies: An Interview with Jacques Derrida', trans. Richard Rand and Amy Wygant, in *Logomachia: The Conflict of the Faculties*, ed. Richard Rand, Lincoln: University of Nebraska Press, 1992.

Derrida, Jacques, 'Circumfession', in Jacques Derrida and Geoffrey Bennington, *Jacques Derrida*, Chicago: University of Chicago Press, 1993.

Derrida, Jacques, *Demeure: Fiction and Testimony* (postscript to Maurice Blanchot, *The Instant of My Death*), trans. Elizabeth Rottenberg, Stanford, CA: Stanford University Press, 2000.

Derrida, Jacques, 'Epoché and Faith', in *Derrida and Religion: Other Testaments*, ed. Yvonne Sherwood and Kevin Hart, New York: Routledge, 2005.

Derrida, Jacques, 'Final Words', trans. Gila Walker, in *The Late Derrida*, ed. W.J.T. Mitchell and Arnold I. Davidson, Chicago: University of Chicago Press, 2007.

Derrida, Jacques, *Given Time: I. Counterfeit Money*, trans. Peggy Kamuf, Chicago: University of Chicago Press, 1994.

Derrida, Jacques, 'Living On: Borderlines', in *Deconstruction and Criticism*, ed. Harold Bloom, New York: Continuum, 1979.

Derrida, Jacques, *The Postcard: From Socrates to Freud and Beyond*, trans. Alan Bass, Chicago: University of Chicago Press, 1987.

Derrida, Jacques, *Voice and Phenomenon: Introduction to the Problem of the Sign in Husserl's Phenomenology*, trans. Leonard Lawlor, Evanston, IL: Northwestern University Press, 2010.

di Cesare, Donatella, *Heidegger, die Juden, die Shoah*, Frankfurt am Main: Vittorio Klostermann, 2016.

Dilthey, Wilhelm, *Briefwechsel zwischen Wilhelm Dilthey und dem Grafen Paul Yorck von Wartenburg 1877–1897*, ed. Sigrid von der Schulenburg, Halle an der Saale: Max Niemeyer, 1923.

Ehrenberg, Hans, 'New Philosophy', in *Franz Rosenzweig's 'New Thinking'*, eds. Alan Udoff and Barbara E. Galli, New York: Syracuse University Press, 1999.

Esposito, Roberto, *Communitas: The Origin and Destiny of Community*, trans. Timothy Campbell, Stanford, CA: Stanford University Press, 2009.

Fackenheim, Emil, *The Religious Dimension of Hegel's Thought*, Chicago: University of Chicago Press, 1982.

Falque, Emmanuel, *The Metamorphosis of Finitude: An Essay on Birth and Resurrection*, New York: Fordham University Press, 2012.

Falque, Emmanuel, *Crossing the Rubicon: The Borderlands of Philosophy and Theology*, trans. Reuben Shank, New York: Fordham University Press, 2016.

Ferenczi, Sandor, *Thalassa: A Theory of Genitality*, London: Karnack Books, 1994.

Fichte, Johann Gottlieb, *The Way Towards the Blessed Life, or the Doctrine of Religion*, trans. William Smith, London: John Chapman, 1849.

Flew, Antony, *The Logic of Mortality*, Oxford: Blackwell, 1987.

Foucault, Michel, *Care of the Self: The History of Sexuality III*, trans. Robert Hurley, London: Penguin, 1986.

Foucault, Michel, *Dits et écrits II, 1976–1988*, Paris: Gallimard, 2001.

Foucault, Michel, *The Birth of Biopolitics: Lectures at the College de France 1978–79*, ed. Michel Senellart, trans. Graham Burchell, Basingstoke: Palgrave Macmillan, 2008.

Frank, Jakub, *Słowa Pańskie: Nauki Jakuba Franka z Brna i Offenbachu (The Words of the Lord: The Teachings of Jacob Frank from Brno and Offenbach)*, ed. Jan Doktor, Warszawa: Żydowski Instytut Historyczny, 2017.

Freud, Sigmund, *Inhibitions, Symptoms, and Anxiety*, trans. Alix Strachey, ed. James Strachey, New York: W.W. Norton, 1959.

Freud, Sigmund and Josef Breuer, *Studies on Hysteria*, trans. James Strachey, Basic Books: New York, 2000.

Friedlander, Eli, 'The Retreat of the Poet in Walter Benjamin's "Two Poems of Friedrich Hölderlin"', in *Tsimtsum in Modernity: Lurianic Heritage in Modern Philosophy and Theology*, ed. Agata Bielik-Robson and Daniel H. Weiss, Bloomington: Indiana University Press, forthcoming.

Fritsch, Matthias, 'Derrida on the Death Penalty', *The Southern Journal of Philosophy* 50, Spindel Supplement (2012): 56–73.

Fromm, Erich, *The Heart of Man: Its Genius for Good and Evil*, New York: Harper and Row, 1964.

Gottlieb, Susannah, *Regions of Sorrow: Anxiety and Messianism in Hannah Arendt and W.H. Auden*, Stanford, CA: Stanford University Press, 2003.

Gutkind, Erich, *Choose Life: The Biblical Call to Revolt*, New York: Henry Schuman, 1952.

Haar, Michel, *Heidegger and the Essence of Man*, trans. William McNeill, Albany, NY: SUNY Press, 1993.

Hadot, Pierre, *Plotinus or the Simplicity of Vision*, trans. Michael Chase, Chicago: University of Chicago Press, 1993.

Hadot, Pierre, *The Veil of Isis: An Essay on the History of the Idea of Nature*, trans. Michael Chase, Cambridge, MA: The Belknap Press of Harvard University Press, 2006.

Hägglund, Martin, *Radical Atheism: Derrida and the Time of Life*, Stanford, CA: Stanford University Press, 2008.

Hartman, Geoffrey, 'The Voice of the Shuttle: Language from the Point of View of Literature', in *The Geoffrey Hartman Reader*, ed. Geoffrey Hartman and Daniel T. O'Hara, New York: Fordham University Press, 2004.

Hegel, G.W.F., *The Encyclopaedia of Philosophical Sciences*, trans. William Wallace, Oxford: Clarendon Press, 1971.

Hegel, G.W.F., *Enzyclopädie der philosophischen Wissenschaften im Grundrisse*, ed. Georg Lasson, Leipzig: Verlag der Dürr'schen Buchhandlung, 1905.

Hegel, G.W.F., *On Christianity: Early Theological Writings by Friedrich Hegel*, trans. T.M. Knox; with an introduction, and fragments translated by Richard Kroner, Gloucester, MA: Peter Smith, 1970.

Hegel, G.W.F., *The Philosophical Propaedeutic*, trans. A.V. Miller, Oxford: Blackwell, 1986.

Hegel, G.W.F., *Philosophy of Nature: Part 2 of the Encyclopaedia of Philosophical Sciences*, trans. M.J. Petry, London: Allen and Unwin, 1970.

Hegel, G.W.F., *Science of Logic*, trans. A.V. Miller, London: Allen and Unwin, 1969.

Heidegger, Martin, 'Anaximander Fragment', in *Early Greek Thinking*, trans. David Farrell Krell, San Francisco: Harper and Row, 1975.

Heidegger, Martin, *Basic Concepts of Aristotelian Philosophy*, trans. Robert D. Metcalf and Mark B. Tanzer, Bloomington: Indiana University Press, 2009.

Heidegger, Martin, *Basic Writings*, trans. David Farrell Krell, London: Routledge, 1993.

Heidegger, Martin, *Einführung in die Metaphysik*, Hague: de Gruyter, 1987.

Heidegger, Martin, *The Fundamental Concepts of Metaphysics: World – Finitude – Solitude*, trans. William McNeill and Nicholas Walker, Bloomington: Indiana University Press, 1995.

Heidegger, Martin, *Kant and the Problem of Metaphysics*, trans. James S. Churchill, Bloomington: Indiana University Press, 1962.

Heidegger, Martin, *Ontology: Hermeneutics of Facticity*, trans. John van Buren, Bloomington: Indiana University Press, 2008.

Heidegger, Martin, *Phenomenological Interpretations of Aristotle: Initiation into Phenomenological Research*, trans. Richard Rojcewicz, Bloomington: Indiana University Press, 2008.

Heidegger, Martin, 'What Are Poets For?', in *Poetry, Language, Thought*, trans.
    A. Hofstadter, New York: Harper and Row, 1971.

Heidegger, Martin, 'What Is Metaphysics?', in *Pathmarks*, trans. William McNeill,
    Cambridge: Cambridge University Press, 1998.

Henry, Michel, *The Essence of Manifestation*, trans. G. Etzkorn, The Hague:
    Martin Nijhoff, 1973.

Henry, Michel, *I Am the Truth: Toward a Philosophy of Christianity*, trans. S. Emanuel,
    Stanford, CA: Stanford University Press, 2003.

Henry, Michel, *Incarnation: A Philosophy of Flesh*, trans. Karl Hefty, Evanston, IL:
    Northwestern University Press, 2015.

Henry, Michel, *Marx: A Philosophy of Human Reality*, trans. K. McLaughlin,
    Bloomington: Indiana University Press, 1993.

Herder, Johann Gottfried, *Essay on the Origin of Language*, trans. Alexander Gode,
    Chicago: University of Chicago Press 1966.

Hölderlin, Friedrich, *Odes and Elegies*, trans. Nick Hoff, Middletown, CT: Wesleyan
    University Press, 2008.

Hölderlin, Friedrich, *Poems of Friedrich Hölderlin*, trans. James Mitchell, San Francisco:
    Ithuriel's Spear, 2004.

Irigaray, Luce, *To Be Born*, Cham: Palgrave Macmillan, 2017.

Jeanrond, Werner G., *A Theology of Love*, New York: T&T Clark, 2010.

Jonas, Hans, *Mortality and Morality: A Search for the Good after Auschwitz*, trans.
    Lawrence Vogel, Chicago: Northwestern University Press, 1996.

Jonas, Hans, *The Phenomenon of Life: Toward a Philosophical Biology*, Evanston, IL:
    Northwestern University Press, 1966.

Jung, Carl Gustav, *Symbols of Transformation: An Analysis of the Prelude to a Case of
    Schizophrenia*, London: Routledge, 1967.

Kant, Immanuel, *Critique of Pure Reason*, trans. Paul Guyer and Allen W. Wood,
    Cambridge: Cambridge University Press, 1999.

Kierkegaard, Soren, *Fear and Trembling*, trans. Alastair Hannay, London: Penguin,
    2005.

Kierkegaard, Soren, *The Sickness Unto Death*, trans. Walter Lowrie, New York: Anchor,
    1954.

Kierkegaard, Soren, *Works of Love*, trans. Howard V. Hong and Edna H. Hong, Princeton
    NJ: Princeton University Press, 1995.

Klein, Melanie, 'Some Theoretical Conclusions Regarding the Emotional Life of the
    Infant', in *Envy and Gratitude, and Other Works 1946–1963: The Writings of Melanie
    Klein*, vol. 3, New York: Free Press, 1975.

Kojève, Alexandre, 'The Idea of Death in the Philosophy of Hegel: Complete Text of the
    Last Two Lectures of the Academic Year 1933–1934', trans. Joseph J. Carpino,
    Interpretation: A Journal of Political Philosophy 3, no. 2/3 (1973): 114–56.

Krell, David Farrell, *Daimon Life: Heidegger and Life-Philosophy*, Bloomington: Indiana
    University Press, 1992.

Krell, David Farrell, *Derrida and Our Animal Others: Derrida's Final Seminar, The Beast and the Sovereign*, Bloomington: Indiana University Press, 2013.

Krell, David Farrell, *Ecstasy, Catastrophe: Heidegger from* Being and Time *to the* Black Notebooks, Albany, NY: SUNY University Press, 2015.

Krell, Robert, 'Alternative Therapeutic Approaches to Holocaust Survivors', in *Healing Their Wounds: Psychotherapy with Holocaust Survivors and Their Families*, ed. Paul Marcus and Alan Rosenberg, Westport, CT: Praeger, 1989.

Kristeva, Julia, *Hannah Arendt*, trans. Ross Guberman, New York: Columbia University Press, 2001.

Kristeva, Julia, *Tales of Love*, trans. Leon S. Roudiez, New York: Columbia University Press, 1987.

Lacan, Jacques, *Écrits*, Paris: Editions de Seuil, 1966.

Lacan, Jacques, *The Ethics of Psychoanalysis: The Seminar of Jacques Lacan 1959–1960, Book 7*, ed. Jacques-Alain Miller, trans. Dennis Porter, London: Routledge, 1992.

Lacan, Jacques, *The Four Fundamental Concepts of Psycho-analysis*, ed. Jacques-Alain Miller, trans. Alan Sheridan, London: Penguin Books, 1979.

Lacan, Jacques, *Le sinthome*, ed. J.-A. Miller, *Ornicar?* 6–11, 1976–7.

Laplanche, Jean, *Life and Death in Psychoanalysis*, trans. Jeffrey Melham, Baltimore, MD: Johns Hopkins University Press, 1976.

Laplanche, Jean, *La sublimation: Problématiques III*, Paris: PUF, 1980.

Laplanche, Jean, *Nouveaux fondements pour la psychanalyse*, Paris: PUF, 1987.

Laplanche, Jean, *Le primat de l'autre en psychanalyse*, Paris: Flammarion, 1992.

Laplanche, Jean and J.-B. Pontalis, *The Language of Psychoanalysis*, trans. D. Nicholson-Smith, London: Karnac Books, 1988.

Lawlor, Leonard, *Implications of Immanence: Toward a New Concept of Life*, New York: Fordham University Press, 2006.

Lawlor, Leonard, *This Is Not Sufficient: An Essay on Animality and Human Nature in Derrida*, New York: Columbia University Press, 2007.

Lawlor, Leonard, 'Verendlichung (Finitization): The Overcoming of Metaphysics with Life', *Philosophy Today* 48, no. 4 (2004): 399–412.

Levi, Primo, *If This is A Man / The Truce*, trans. Stuart Woolf, London: Abacus, 1991.

Lévinas, Emmanuel, *Difficult Freedom: Essays of Judaism*, trans. Seán Hand, Baltimore, MD: Johns Hopkins University Press, 1990.

Lévinas, Emmanuel, *Entre Nous, Thinking-of-the-Other*, trans. Michael B. Smith and Barbara Harshav, New York: Columbia University Press, 1998.

Lévinas, Emmanuel, *Of God Who Comes to Mind*, trans. Bettina Bergo, Stanford: Stanford University Press 1998.

Lévinas, Emmanuel, *Otherwise than Being or Beyond Essence*, trans. Alphonso Lingis, The Hague: Martinus Nijhoff, 1981.

Lévinas, Emmanuel, *Totality and Infinity: An Essay on Exteriority*, trans. Alphonso Lingis, Dordrecht: Kluwer Academic, 1991.

Löwith, Karl, 'M. Heidegger and F. Rosenzweig, or Temporality and Eternity', *Philosophy and Phenomenological Research* 3, no. 1 (1942): 53–77.

Lukacs, György, 'Metaphysics of Tragedy', in *Soul and Form*, trans. Anna Bostock, London: Merlin Press, 1974.

Lyotard, Jean-Francois, 'Figure Foreclosed', in *Lyotard Reader*, trans. Andrew Benjamin, Oxford: Blackwell, 1989.

Lyotard, Jean-Francois, 'Jewish Oedipus', trans. Susan Hanson, *Genre* 10 no. 3 (1977): 395–411.

Malabou, Catherine, *The Future of Hegel: Plasticity, Temporality and Dialectic*, trans. Lisabeth During, Abingdon: Routledge, 2005.

Malabou, Catherine, *Ontologie de l'accident: Essai sur la plasticité destructrice*, Paris: Éditions Léo Scheer, 2009.

Marion, Jean-Luc, *In the Self's Place: The Approach of Saint Augustine*, trans. Jeffrey L. Kosky, Stanford, CA: Stanford University Press, 2012.

May, Todd, *Death*, Abingdon: Routledge, 2009.

Meier, Heinrich, *Leo Strauss and the Theologico-Political Problem*, trans. Marcus Brainard, Cambridge: Cambridge University Press, 2006.

Milton, John, *Paradise Lost*, London: Penguin Popular Classics, 1996.

Naas, Michael, *Derrida From Now On*, New York: Fordham University Press, 2008.

Naas, Michael, *Miracle and Machine*, New York: Fordham University Press, 2012.

Naas, Michael, 'The Philosophy and Literature of the Death Penalty: Two Sides of the Same Sovereign, *The Southern Journal of Philosophy* 50, Spindel Supplement (2012): 39–55.

Nagel, Thomas, 'Death', in *Metaphysics of Death*, ed. John Martin Fisher, Stanford, CA: Stanford University Press, 1993.

Nancy, Jean-Luc, *Being Singular Plural*, trans. Robert D. Richardson and Anne E. O'Byrne, Stanford, CA: Stanford University Press, 2000.

Nancy, Jean-Luc, *Corpus*, trans. Richard Rand, New York: Fordham University Press, 2008.

Nietzsche, Friedrich, *Beyond Good and Evil: Prelude to a Philosophy of the Future*, trans. Helen Zimmern, CreateSpace, 2016.

Nietzsche, Friedrich, *The Birth of Tragedy*, trans. Roland Speirs, Cambridge: Cambridge University Press, 1999.

Nietzsche, Friedrich, *The Gay Science*, trans. Walter Kaufman, New York: Vintage Books, 1974.

Nietzsche, Friedrich, *On the Genealogy of Morality*, trans. Carol Diethe, Cambridge: Cambridge University Press, 2006.

Nietzsche, Friedrich, 'On Truth and Lie in an Extra-Moral Sense', in *Friedrich Nietzsche on Rhetoric and Language*, ed. and trans. Sander L. Gilman, Carole Blair and David J. Parent, Oxford: Oxford University Press, 1989.

Nietzsche, Friedrich, *Thus Spoke Zarathustra: A Book for Everyone and Nobody*, trans. Graham Parkes, Oxford: Oxford University Press, 2005.

Nietzsche, Friedrich, *The Twilight of the Idols or How to Philosophize with a Hammer*, trans. Judith Norman, Cambridge: Cambridge University Press, 2005.

Novalis, *Werke, Tagebücher und Briefe Friedrich von Hardenbergs: Werke in drei Bänden*, ed. Hans-Joachim Mähl, Richard Samuel and Hans Jürgen Bahmes, Munich: Carl Hanser Verlag, 1987.

O'Sullivan, Michael, *Michel Henry: Incarnation, Barbarism, and Belief – An Introduction to the Work of Michel Henry*, Bern: Peter Lang, 2006.

Pico della Mirandola, Giovanni, *Oration on the Dignity of Man*, trans. Robert A. Caponigri, Chicago: A Gateway Edition, Henry Regnery Company, 1956.

Pihlström, Sami, *Death and Finitude: Toward a Pragmatic Transcendental Anthropology of Human Limits and Mortality*, Lanham, MD: Lexington Books, 2016.

Pirke Aboth: The Sayings of the Fathers, trans. Joseph Hertz, London: Behrman House, 1945.

Pontalis, J.-B., *Frontiers in Psychoanalysis: Between the Dream and the Psychic Pain*, trans. C. Cullen and P. Cullen, London: The Hogarth Press and the Institute of Psychoanalysis, 1981.

Reik, Theodor, *The Compulsion to Confess: On the Psychoanalysis of Crime and Punishment*, New York: Grove Press, 1961.

Ricoeur, Paul, *Freud and Philosophy: An Essay on Interpretation*, trans. Denis Savage, New Haven, CT: Yale University Press, 1977.

Rilke, Rainer Maria, *Duino Elegies and The Sonnets to Orpheus*, trans. Steven Mitchell, New York: Vintage International, 2009.

Ronell, Avital, *Stupidity*, Urbana: University of Illinois Press, 2002.

Rosenberg, Jay F., *Thinking Clearly About Death*, Indianapolis, IN: Hackett, 1999.

Santner, Eric L., 'Freud's "Moses" and the Ethics of Nomotropic Desire', *October* 88 (1999): 3–41.

Santner, Eric L., 'Miracles Happen: Benjamin, Rosenzweig, Freud, and the Matter of the Neighbor', in Slavoj Žižek, Eric L. Santner and Kenneth Reinhard, *The Neighbor: Three Inquiries into Political Theology*, Chicago: University of Chicago Press, 2005.

Santner, Eric L., *On Creaturely Life: Rilke, Benjamin, Sebald*, Chicago: University of Chicago Press, 2006.

Scholem, Gershom, *Über einige Grundbegriffe des Judentums*, Frankfurt am Main: Suhrkamp, 1970.

Scholem, Gershom, 'Reflections on Jewish Theology', in *On Jews and Judaism in Crisis: Selected Essays*, New York: Schocken Books, 1976.

Scholem, Gershom, 'Der Nihilismus als religiöses Phänomen', in *Judaica 4*, Frankfurt: Suhrkamp, 1995.

Schopenhauer, Arthur, *The World as Will and Representation*, trans. E.F.J. Payne, New York: Dover, 1969.

Simmel, Georg, *The View of Life: Four Metaphysical Essays with Journal Aphorisms*, trans. John A.Y. Andrews and Donald N. Levine, Chicago: Chicago University Press, 2010.

Simondon, Gilbert, 'The Genesis of the Individual', in *Incorporations*, ed. J. Crary and
S. Kwinter, New York: Zone Books, 1992.

Sloterdijk, Peter, *Critique of Cynical Reason*, Minneapolis: University of Minnesota
Press, 1988.

Sloterdijk, Peter, *Regeln für den Menschenpark: Ein Antwortschreiben zu Heideggers
Brief über Humanismus*, Frankfurt am Main: Suhrkamp, 1999.

Stevens, Wallace, *Opus Posthumous: Poems, Plays, Prose*, London: Vintage, 1990.

Taubes, Jacob, *From Cult to Culture: Fragments Towards a Critique of Historical Reason*,
trans. Aleida Assmann, Stanford, CA: Stanford University Press, 2009.

Taubes, Jacob, *Occidental Eschatology*, trans. David Ratmoko, Stanford, CA: Stanford
University Press, 2009.

Trilling, Lionel, *The Middle of the Journey*, London: Penguin, 1963.

Vatter, Miguel, 'Natality and Biopolitics in Hannah Arendt', *Revista de Ciencia Politica*
26, no. 2 (2006): 137–59.

Vitale, Francesco, *Biodeconstruction: Jacques Derrida and Life Sciences*, trans. Mauro
Senatore, Albany, NY: SUNY Press, 2018.

Weber, Samuel, *Benjamin's -abilities*, Cambridge, MA: Harvard University Press, 2008.

Weber, Samuel, *Return to Freud: Jacques Lacan's Dislocation of Psychoanalysis*, trans.
Michael Levine, Cambridge: Cambridge University Press, 1991.

Westphal, Merold, *God, Guilt, and Death: Existential Phenomenology of Religion*,
Bloomington: Indiana University Press, 1987.

Winnicott, Donald Woods, *Home Is Where We Start From: Essays by a Psychoanalyst*,
London: Penguin Books, 1986.

Wolfe, Judith, *Heidegger's Eschatology: Theological Horizons in Martin Heidegger's Early
Thought*, Oxford: Oxford University Press, 2013.

Wolin, Richard, *Heidegger's Children: Hannah Arendt, Hans Jonas, and Herbert Marcuse*,
Princeton, NJ: Princeton University Press, 2015.

Yerushalmi, Yosef Hayim, *Freud's Moses: Judaism Terminable and Interminable*, New
Haven, CT: Yale University Press, 1991.

Zawisza, Rafael, 'Thank God We're Creatures: Arendt Reads Rosenzweig', a manuscript
being a part of the doctoral dissertation.

Žižek, Slavoj, *The Fragile Absolute Or, Why Is the Christian Legacy Worth Fighting For?*,
London: Verso, 2000.

Žižek, Slavoj, *The Puppet and the Dwarf: The Perverse Core of Christianity*, Cambridge,
MA: MIT Press, 2003.

Žižek, Slavoj, *The Ticklish Subject: The Absent Centre of Political Ontology*, London:
Verso, 2009.

Žižek, Slavoj, *Less than Nothing: Hegel and the Shadow of Dialectical Materialism*,
London: Verso, 2012.

Zupančič, Alenka, *The Shortest Shadow: Nietzsche's Philosophy of the Two*, Cambridge,
MA: MIT Press, 2003.

Index of Names

Index of Terms

Made in the USA
Middletown, DE
28 September 2023

39479327R00175